VIDEO GAMES AND CREATIVITY

Explorations in Creativity Research

Series Editor

JAMES C. KAUFMAN

VIDEO GAMES AND CREATIVITY

Edited by

GARO P. GREEN

California State University,
San Bernardino, CA, USA

AND

JAMES C. KAUFMAN

Neag School of Education,
University of Connecticut,
Storrs, CT, USA

ELSEVIER

AMSTERDAM • BOSTON • HEIDELBERG • LONDON
NEW YORK • OXFORD • PARIS • SAN DIEGO
SAN FRANCISCO • SINGAPORE • SYDNEY • TOKYO
Academic Press is an imprint of Elsevier

Academic Press is an imprint of Elsevier
125 London Wall, London, EC2Y 5AS, UK
525 B Street, Suite 1800, San Diego, CA 92101–4495, USA
225 Wyman Street, Waltham, MA 02451, USA
The Boulevard, Langford Lane, Kidlington, Oxford OX5 1GB, UK

Notices
Knowledge and best practice in this field are constantly changing. As new research and experience broaden our understanding, changes in research methods, professional practices, or medical treatment may become necessary.

Practitioners and researchers must always rely on their own experience and knowledge in evaluating and using any information, methods, compounds, or experiments described herein. In using such information or methods they should be mindful of their own safety and the safety of others, including parties for whom they have a professional responsibility.

To the fullest extent of the law, neither the Publisher nor the authors, contributors, or editors, assume any liability for any injury and/or damage to persons or property as a matter of products liability, negligence or otherwise, or from any use or operation of any methods, products, instructions, or ideas contained in the material herein.

Library of Congress Cataloging-in-Publication Data
A catalog record for this book is available from the Library of Congress

British Library Cataloguing in Publication Data
A catalogue record for this book is available from the British Library

ISBN: 978-0-12-801462-2

For information on all Academic Press publications
visit our website at http://store.elsevier.com/

Publisher: Nikki Levy
Acquisition Editor: Nikki Levy
Editorial Project Manager: Barbara Makinster
Production Project Manager: Caroline Johnson
Designer: Matthew Limbert

Working together
to grow libraries in
developing countries

www.elsevier.com • www.bookaid.org

Dedication

In dedication and memory of Linda A. Jackson, PhD (1939–2014)

To Lynda Weinman, my dear friend, for showing me that true success and happiness come from sharing what you know with others with authenticity and generosity—GPG

For my niece, Kate Singleton, whose poetry, resiliency, humor, and passion inspire me, with love—JCK

Contents

I

CREATIVITY AND VIDEO GAME PLAY

1. Video Games and Creativity
LINDA A. JACKSON AND ALEXANDER I. GAMES

2. The Impact of Video Game Play on Human (and Orc) Creativity
NICHOLAS D. BOWMAN, RACHEL KOWERT AND CHRISTOPHER J. FERGUSON

II
CREATIVITY AND VIDEO GAMES IN EDUCATION

III

CREATIVITY AND VIDEO GAME DEVELOPMENT

11. Creating Code Creatively: Automated Discovery of Game Mechanics Through Code Generation

MICHAEL COOK

12. Patented Creativity: Reflecting on Video Game Patents

CASEY O'DONNELL

13. Tension and Opportunity: Creativity in the Video Gaming Medium

GRANT TAVINOR

14. Creative Interactivity: Customizing and Creating Game Content

KATHARINA-MARIE BEHR, RICHARD HUSKEY AND RENÉ WEBER

Contributors

Mario Barajas Department of Didactics and Educational Organization, University of Barcelona, Barcelona, Spain

Erin L. Beatty Defence Research and Development Canada, Toronto Research Centre, Toronto, ON, Canada

Katharina-Marie Behr Department of Communication, University of California Santa Barbara, Santa Barbara, CA, USA

Jorge A. Blanco-Herrera Department of Psychology, Iowa State University, Ames, IA, USA

Fran C. Blumberg Division of Psychological & Educational Services, Fordham University, New York, NY, USA

Nicholas D. Bowman Communication Studies, West Virginia University, Morgantown, WV, USA

Beomkyu Choi Educational Psychology, University of Connecticut, Storrs, CT, USA

Michael Cook Department of Computing, Imperial College, London, UK

David H. Cropley Defence and Systems Institute (DASI), University of South Australia, Adelaide, SA, Australia

Christopher J. Ferguson Department Chair Psychology, Stetson University, DeLand, FL, USA

Frédérique Frossard Department of Didactics and Educational Organization, University of Barcelona, Barcelona, Spain

Alexander I. Games Microsoft Corporation, Inc., Redmond, WA, USA

Douglas A. Gentile Department of Psychology, Iowa State University, Ames, IA, USA

Garo P. Green California State University, San Bernardino, CA, USA

Christopher L. Groves Department of Psychology, Iowa State University, Ames, IA, USA

Karla R. Hamlen Department of Curriculum and Foundations, Cleveland State University, Cleveland, OH, USA

Richard Huskey Department of Communication, University of California Santa Barbara, Santa Barbara, CA, USA

Linda A. Jackson Michigan State University, East Lansing, MI, USA

James C. Kaufman Neag School of Education, University of Connecticut, Storrs, CT, USA

Yoon J. Kim Instructional Systems and Learning Technologies, Florida State University, Tallahassee, FL, USA

Rachel Kowert University of Münster, Münster, Germany

Ann M. Lewis Department of Psychology, Iowa State University, Ames, IA, USA

Casey O'Donnell Department of Media and Information, Michigan State University, East Lansing, MI, USA

Valerie J. Shute Instructional Systems and Learning Technologies, Florida State University, Tallahassee, FL, USA

Stephen T. Slota Educational Psychology, University of Connecticut, Storrs, CT, USA

Grant Tavinor Faculty of Environment, Society and Design, Lincoln University, Lincoln, New Zealand

Roger Travis Educational Psychology, University of Connecticut, Storrs, CT, USA

Anna Trifonova Department of Didactics and Educational Organization, University of Barcelona, Barcelona, Spain

Oshin Vartanian Department of Psychology, University of Toronto Scarborough, Toronto, ON, Canada

Thomas B. Ward Department of Psychology, University of Alabama, Tuscaloosa, AL, USA

René Weber Department of Communication, University of California Santa Barbara, Santa Barbara, CA, USA

Michael F. Young Educational Psychology, University of Connecticut, Storrs, CT, USA

Acknowledgments

A book like this is only possible through the hard work and expertise of many passionate expert contributors, and we were fortunate enough to work with some of the very best and brightest. We were humbled by their expertise and knowledge on video games and creativity, their willingness to consider our feedback, and their endless passion for sharing what they know with others. We learned a lot and enjoyed the process immensely. We would also like to thank Nikki Levy at Academic Press for her support for this book and the Explorations in Creativity Research series. We would also like to thank Barbara Makinster and Caroline Johnson for their attention to detail, keeping us on schedule, and the many gentle reminders when we were late! Garo would like to thank his partner, Mark, for his endless support and putting up with the constant mess of papers on the dining room table. James would like to thank his friends and colleagues at the University of Connecticut and his family for their continued support.

Video Games and Creativity: An Introduction

Garo P. Green, James C. Kaufman

WHY VIDEO GAMES AND CREATIVITY?

During the last few decades, and especially in the last 10 years, video games have increasingly become a ubiquitous part of society across the globe. Much of this increase has been due to the global proliferation of mobile devices, which has put thousands of engaging and visually stimulating video games within our grasp 24/7. At the surface, it's clear that video games are a form of creative expression and entertainment, but we wanted to know more about the underlying relationships between video games and creativity. For example, can video games be used to develop or enhance creativity? Is there a place for video games in the classroom? What types of creativity are needed to develop video games? More specifically, while video games can be sources of entertainment, the role of video games in the classroom has emerged as an important component of improving our education system. The research and development of game-based learning has revealed the power of using games to teach and promote learning. In parallel, and not surprisingly, the role and importance of creativity in everyday life has also been identified as a requisite skill for success. From personal expression, to innovative problem solving, to successful product development, and economic prosperity, creativity is a vital skill needed for individuals to flourish and solve many of society's biggest challenges.

Both video games and creativity are topics so complex, deep, and nuanced that hundreds of books and thousands of scholarly research articles have been published on each topic. While there are several scholarly "handbooks" that focus on these two topics separately, we couldn't find one that focused exclusively on the many intersections between video games and creativity. Given the importance of these two topics in contemporary society we believed the relationships that exist between video games and creativity were so important and numerous that it warranted a book with this focus.

WHAT'S COVERED IN THIS BOOK?

The biggest challenge in writing a book about a topic so complex and deep is including enough content to be interesting while covering it deeply enough to be informative to a wide range of readers. A book like this is never complete, and this one is certainly no exception. We have to constantly make tradeoffs between focus and page count/cost. While we would have liked to include many more sections and chapters, we decided to focus on three key areas: Creativity and Video Game Play, Creativity and Video Games in Education, and Creativity and Video Game Development. These sections will provide enough foundational knowledge for readers new to this topic, while allowing us to go deep enough in a few core areas to make it informative to a broad range of readers.

This book is divided into three sections:

- *Part 1—Creativity and Video Game Play* focuses on creativity while playing video games. This section begins with *Video Games and Creativity*, by Linda A. Jackson and Alex I. Games, and provides a great introduction to the topics and will help new readers get up to speed quickly. *The Impact of Video Game Play on Human (and Orc) Creativity*, by Nicholas D. Bowman, Rachel Kowert, and Christopher J. Ferguson, provides a detailed history of video games and illustrates how video game play is more than a form of entertainment, including how video game play is associated with creativity. *Video Games and Malevolent Creativity: Does One Thing Lead to Another?*, by David H. Cropley, is a fascinating look at the relationship (or lack thereof) between video games and malevolent creativity. This chapter examines what is known about video game play and the influence on learning, including creativity and antisocial behavior. *Problem Solving through "Cheating" in Video Games*, by Karla R. Hamlen and Fran C. Blumberg, examines how cheating in video games is a form of problem solving (functional creativity). This chapter provides a detailed explanation of the types of cheating, including the moral implications within video game play. *Opportunities and Challenges in Assessing and Supporting Creativity in Video Games*, by Yoon Jeon Kim and Valerie J. Shute, illustrates the many opportunities for creativity within video game play, while articulating the challenges with assessing these creative activities, and provides a real-world solution with Physics Playground. *Content, Collaboration, and Creativity in Virtual Worlds*, by Thomas B. Ward, examines the various creativity opportunities available in Social Virtual Worlds (SVWs), including video games such as *Second Life* and others. This chapter provides a unique perspective into the online and interactive communities that have developed around SVWs and creative opportunities that exist within these virtual environments, such as content creation.
- *Part 2—Creativity and Video Games in Education* is focused on how video games can be used to teach and enhance creativity within education. This section begins with *Teaching Creativity: Theoretical*

Models and Applications, by Jorge A. Blanco-Herrera, Chris Groves, Annie M. Lewis, and Douglas A. Gentile. This chapter is a great introduction to this section and illustrates how video games can teach, including a model of learning and how video games follow learning principles. *Teachers Designing Learning Games: Impact on Creativity*, by F. Frossard, A. Trifonova, and M. Barajas, is a comprehensive examination of how teacher-designed video games can enhance creative pedagogies, including real-world examples from their own experiences. *Cognitive Brain Training, Video Games, and Creativity*, by Oshin Vartanian and Erin L. Beatty, provides a summary of research on video games and how they enhance motor skills, auditory processing, spatial imagery, and visual processing. This chapter concludes by illustrating how these enhancements are related to creativity and can be a mechanism for improving creativity. *Game Narrative, Interactive Fiction, and Storytelling: Creating a "Time for Telling" in the Classroom*, by Michael F. Young, Stephen T. Slota, Roger Travis, and Beomykyu Choi, examines the role of narrative in video games and game-based learning solutions, including how video game narratives can be used as a tool to nurture teacher and student creativity.

- *Part 3—Creativity and Video Game Development* is focused on the creative opportunities that exist during the video game development process. This section begins with *Creating Code Creatively: Automated Discovery of Game Mechanics Through Code Generation*, by Michael Cook, a fascinating examination of video game rules and system design, along with the "mechanics," including many real-world creative solutions implemented by video games developers. This chapter illustrates one of the lesser known, but equally important, relationships between video games and creativity. *Patented Creativity: Reflecting on Video Game Patents*, by Casey O'Donnell, provides another unique perspective into the relationship between video games and creativity by examining how video game developers have used functional creativity (problem solving) to differentiate and patent their products, including several real-world examples. *Tension and Opportunity: Creativity in the Video Gaming Medium*, by Grant Tavinor, is a fascinating examination of the natural and structural tensions that exist in the video game development process and how creativity is needed to develop appropriate solutions. *Creative Interactivity: Customizing and Creating Game Content*, by Katharina-Maria Behr, Richard Husky, and Rene Weber, illustrates how customization and creation of video game content can occur after a video game has been released and why these processes represent a creative dimension of video game interactivity.

IS THIS BOOK FOR YOU?

At the most general level, this book is for anyone interested in the many associations between video games and creativity, and there are many. That said, this book has been written and developed by scholars and academic researchers with expertise in video games and creativity. As such, it will be most appealing to other scholars and researchers with similar interests, including educators searching for ways to incorporate video games into their curriculum. Both undergraduate and graduate student researchers will find this book helpful in learning about contemporary video game and creativity research and future research opportunities. It is our hope that anyone that reads this book will find it both informative and enjoyable to read.

COMPANION WEBSITE

We've created a companion website for this book at www.videogamesandcreativity.com, where you can connect with the contributing authors, share feedback, find book updates and errata, and find more information about video games and creativity research. Please check this site for updates or if you'd like to connect with the editors or any of the contributors.

ABOUT THE EXPLORATION IN CREATIVITY RESEARCH SERIES

This book is part of a series of written and edited books that highlight exciting and topical areas within creativity research. Other books in this series either published or forthcoming include *Creativity in Engineering* by David Cropley, *Domain Specificity in Creativity* by John Baer, and *Animal Creativity and Innovation*, edited by Allison B. Kaufman and James C. Kaufman.

CREATIVITY AND VIDEO GAME PLAY

Video Games and Creativity

Linda A. Jackson[1] and Alexander I. Games[2]
[1]Michigan State University, East Lansing, MI, USA
[2]Microsoft Corporation, Inc., Redmond, WA, USA

OUTLINE

WHAT IS CREATIVITY?

There is no doubt that creativity is the most important human resource of all.
Without creativity, there would be no progress, and we would be forever repeating
the same patterns. *Edward de Bono (Lucas, 2003)*

Before any discussion of the effects of video game playing on creativity it is important to define what we mean by creativity. From a historical perspective, Wallis (1926) is credited with the first formal theory of creativity. In Wallas's stage model, creative insights and illuminations are explained by a process consisting of five stages: (1) *preparation*—preparatory work on a problem that focuses the individual's mind on the problem and explores the problem's dimensions; (2) *incubation*—where the problem is internalized into the unconscious mind and nothing appears externally to be happening; (3) *intimation*—the creative person gets a "feeling" that a solution is on its way; (4) *illumination* or insight—where the creative idea bursts forth from its preconscious processing into conscious awareness; and (5) *verification*—where the idea is consciously verified, elaborated, and then applied. Wallas considered creativity to be a legacy of the evolutionary process which allowed humans to quickly adapt to rapidly changing environments. Simonton (1999) provides an updated perspective on this view in his book, *Origins of genius: Darwinian perspectives on creativity*.

In 1927, Alfred North Whitehead wrote the first scholarly book on creativity, *Process and reality*, reprinted in 1978. He is credited with having coined the term "creativity," still the preferred currency of exchange in literature, science, and the arts. In a later article titled "Creativity syndrome: Integration, application, and innovation," Mumford and Gustafon (1988) argued that, in many ways, the ultimate concern in studies of creativity is the production of novel, socially valued products. They suggested that an integration and reorganization of cognitive structures is likely to underlie major creative contributions and that the application of existing cognitive structures is likely to underlie minor contributions. Extending this interpretation to the processes traditionally held to underlie individual differences in creativity, they noted that both major and minor forms of creativity require a number of different knowledges, skills, and abilities. Furthermore, effective translation of ideas into action will depend on a variety of individual (Person) and situational (Environmental) factors.

Two important issues raised in Mumford and Gustafon's (1988) article concern the roles of intelligence and divergent thinking in creativity. They concluded, as have many researchers since then, that intelligence is important to creativity "up to a point," beyond which greater intelligence does not lead to greater creativity (Habibollah, Rohani, Aizan, Sharir, & Kumar, 2010; O'Hara & Sternberg, 1999; Silvia, 2008). Divergent thinking, on the other hand, is critical to creativity. It was Guilford (1950, 1967a) who first drew the distinction between convergent and divergent thinking. Convergent thinking is the ability to apply rules to arrive at a single "correct" solution to a problem, such as the answer to an achievement test question. This process is systematic and linear. Divergent thinking, on the other hand, involves the creative generation of multiple answers to a set of problems. It occurs in a spontaneous, free-flowing, "nonlinear" manner. It is sometimes used as a synonym for creativity in the psychological literature but, as Mumford and Gustafon (1988) and other researchers later pointed out, there is far more to creativity than divergent thinking (Csikszentmihalyi, 1999; Kozbelt, Beghetto, & Runco, 2010; Meusburger, Funke, & Wunder, 2009; Mumford, 2003; Runco & Albert, 2010; Sternberg, Kaufman, & Pretz, 2002).

In a later summary of the scientific research, Mumford suggested that "Over the course of the last decade we seem to have reached a general agreement that creativity involves the production of novel, useful products." Creativity can also be defined "as the process of producing something that is both original and worthwhile characterized by expressiveness and imagination" (Mumford, 2003, p. 110; see also Csikszentmihalyi, 1999, 2009; Lubart & Mouchiroud, 2003; Meusburger et al., 2009; Runco & Albert, 2010; Sternberg, 2006; Torrance, 1995). The product of creativity may take many forms and is not limited to a particular subject or area. Beyond these general commonalities, authors vary in how they conceptualize creativity and, consequently, in how they measure it.

Another popular perspective on creativity is that it involves four qualities: (1) *Person*—characteristics; (2) *Process*—preferences associated with aspects of the creative process; (3) *Products*—qualities of creative products; and (4) *Press (Environment)*—factors in the environment that facilitate creative performance (Puccio & Murdock, 1999). Amabile (1996), on the other hand, argues for a model of creativity where the interaction between personal and social influences leads to three factors whose presence or absence can enable or hinder creative performance: (1) The presence or absence of individual domain-relevant skills in the activity that requires creativity; (2) The individual's engagement in creativity-relevant processes such as abandoning well-rehearsed performance scripts and exploring new angles for extended periods; and (3) The degree to which the activity would be intrinsically motivating to the individual versus compelled by extrinsic factors. All of these qualities should be considered in the measurement of creativity.

THEORIES OF CREATIVITY

Ten Theoretical Approaches to Creativity

Kozbelt et al. (2010) provided a comprehensive review of 10 popular theoretical approaches to creativity. They are Developmental theories, Psychodynamic theories, Economic theories, Stage and Componential theories, Cognitive theories, Theories Based on Problem Solving and Expertise, Problem-Finding theories, Evolutionary theories, Typological theories, and Systems theories.

Developmental theories maintain that creativity develops over time, mediated by an interaction among the four "Ps": Person, Process, Products, and Press (Environment) (Helson, 1999; Subotnik & Arnold, 1996; Weisberg, 2006a, 2006b).

Psychodynamic theories argue that creativity can be measured reliably, differentiating it from related constructs (e.g., IQ) and highlighting its domain-specific nature (Guilford, 1968; Wallach & Kogan, 1965).

Economic theories state that creative ideation and behavior are influenced by market forces and cost–benefit analysis (Rubenson & Runco, 1992; Sternberg & Lubart, 1992).

Stage and componential process theories maintain that creativity proceeds through a series of stages and that this process has linear and recursive elements (Amabile, 1999; Runco & Chand, 1995).

Cognitive theories focus on ideational thought processes as fundamental to creative persons and accomplishments (Fink, Ward, & Smith, 1992; Mednick, 1962).

Problem-solving and expertise theories argue that creative solutions to ill-defined problems result from a rational process which relies on general cognitive processes and domain expertise (Ericsson, 1999; Simon, 1966, 1972; Weisberg, 1999, 2006a, 2006b).

Problem-finding theories maintain that creative people proactively engage in a subjective and exploratory process of identifying problems to be solved (Getzels & Csikszentmihalyi, 1976; Runco, 1994).

Evolutionary theories hold that creativity results from the evolutionary processes of blind generation and selective retention (i.e., natural selection; Campbell, 1960; Simonton, 1988, 1999).

Typological theories maintain that creators vary in key individual differences which are related to both macro- and micro-level factors and can be classified via typologies (Galenson, 2001, 2006; Kozbelt, 2008a−c).

Systems theories hold that creativity results from a complex system of interacting and interrelated factors (Csikszentmihalyi, 1988; Gruber, 1981; Sawyer, 2006).

Honing Theory

Honing theory, developed by Gabora (Gabora, 1995, 1997, Gabora & Aerts, 2002), posits that creativity arises due to the self-organizing, self-mending nature of a worldview, and that it is by way of the creative process that an individual hones an integrated worldview. Honing theory places equal emphasis on the externally visible creative outcome and the internal cognitive restructuring brought about by the creative process. Indeed, one factor that distinguishes honing theory from other theories is that it focuses not just on restructuring as it pertains to the conception of the task, but also on the individual's worldview. When faced with a creatively demanding task, there is an interaction between the conception of the task and the worldview. The conception of the task changes through interaction with the worldview, and the worldview changes through interaction with the task. This interaction is reiterated until the task is complete, at which point not only is the task conceived of differently, but the worldview is subtly or dramatically changed.

Explicit−Implicit Interaction Theory

He'lie and Sun (2010) proposed this theory as a unified framework for understanding creativity in problem solving. It represents an attempt to provide a more unified explanation of phenomena relevant to creativity by reinterpreting and integrating various fragmentary existing theories of incubation and insight. The explicit−implicit interaction (EII) theory relies mainly on five basic principles: (1) the coexistence of and difference between explicit and implicit knowledge; (2) the simultaneous involvement of implicit and explicit processes in creative tasks; (3) the redundant representation of explicit and implicit knowledge; (4) the integration of the results of explicit and implicit processing; and (5) the iterative and possibly bidirectional nature of processing.

Computational Theory

Jurgen Schmidhuber's formal theory of creativity is based on a computational perspective. It postulates that creativity, curiosity, and interestingness are by-products of a simple computational principle for measuring and optimizing learning progress (Schmidhuber, 2006, 2010, 2012). Consider an agent able to manipulate its environment and thus its own sensory inputs. The agent can use a black box optimization method such as reinforcement learning to learn (through informed trial and error) sequences of actions that maximize the expected sum of its future reward signals. There are extrinsic reward signals for achieving externally given goals, such as finding food when hungry. But Schmidhuber's objective function to be maximized also includes an additional, intrinsic term to model what he calls "wow-effects." They motivate purely creative behavior even in the absence of external goals.

MEASUREMENT OF CREATIVITY

Since the 1950s, researchers have developed an array of methods for measuring creativity (Batey, 2012; Puccio, Argona, Daley, & Fonseza, 2010). In general, creativity can be measured by Self-Assessments, Ratings Scales, Interviews, Checklists, Peer, Parent, Teacher Ratings/ Nominations, Observations, Products, Personality Tests, Biographical Sketches, Aptitude and Ability Tests, Awards, Acceleration, Mentorship, Enrichment Programs, and Problem Finding/Solving. There are several widely used approaches to the measurement of creativity, each with its strengths and weaknesses (Batey & Furnham, 2006; Boden, 2004; Cooper, 1991; Cropley, 2000; Hocevar & Bachelor, 1989; Michael & Wright, 1989; Simonton, 2012; Zeng, Proctor, & Salvendy, 2011).

APPROACHES TO THE MEASUREMENT OF CREATIVITY

The Psychometric Approach

Guilford's (1950) pioneering work on creativity launched what is referred to as the psychometric approach to its measurement. In 1967, he developed the Guilford Test of Divergent Thinking, remnants of which can be found in the most popular psychometric measures used today, the Torrance Tests of Creative Thinking (TTCT) (Torrance, 1974), which we used in our research (Jackson et al., 2012). Briefly, Guilford proposed the following measures to capture the concept: (1) Plot Titles—participants are given the plot of a story and asked to write original titles; (2) Quick Response—a word-association test scored for uncommonness; (3) Figure Concepts—participants were given simple drawings of objects and individuals and asked to find qualities or features that are common to two or more drawings, scored for uncommonness; (4) Unusual Uses—finding unusual uses for common everyday objects; (5) Remote Associations—participants are asked to find a word between two given words (e.g., Hand__Call); and (6) Remote Consequences—participants are asked to generate a list of consequences of unexpected events. Additional psychometric measures of creativity are discussed later.

Social-Personality Approach

This approach uses personality traits, such as independence of judgment, self-confidence, attraction to complexity, esthetic orientation, and risk-taking as measures of an individual's creativity. A meta-analysis by Feist (1998) showed that creative people tend to be "more open to new experiences, less conventional and less conscientious, more self-confident, self-accepting, driven, ambitious, dominant, hostile and impulsive." Of these characteristics, openness to new experiences, conscientiousness, self-acceptance, hostility, and impulsivity make the strongest contribution to the creative personality (Batey & Furnham, 2006). Consistent with these findings, within the framework of the Big Five Personality Factors (Costa & McCrae, 1992) openness to experience has been most consistently related to a variety of assessments of creativity (Batey, Furnham, & Safiullina, 2010).

Affective Approach

Some theories suggest that creativity is particularly susceptible to affective influences. "Affect" in this context refers to liking or disliking key aspects of the topic in question. This work largely follows from findings in psychology regarding the ways in which affective states are involved in human judgment and decision making (Winkielman & Knutson, 2007).

According to psychologist Alice Isen (Isen, Daubman, & Nowicki, 1987), positive affect has three primary effects on cognitive activity: (1) it makes additional cognitive material available for processing, increasing the number of cognitive elements available for association; (2) it leads to defocused attention and a more complex cognitive context, increasing the breadth of those elements that are treated as relevant to the problem; and (3) it increases cognitive flexibility, thereby increasing the probability that diverse cognitive elements will become associated. Taken together these processes lead positive affect to have a positive influence on creativity (Baas, De Dreu, & Nijstad, 2008; Davis, 2009).

On the other hand, there is also evidence that negative affect, as manifested in affective mental disorders such as depression, bipolar disorder, and addiction, is also associated with extreme forms of creativity (Ludwig, 1995). In a study of 1005 prominent twentieth century individuals from over 45 different professions, Ludwig found a slight but significant correlation between depression and level of creative achievement. In addition, several systematic studies of highly creative individuals and their relatives revealed a higher incidence of affective disorders (primarily bipolar disorder and depression) than found in the general population (Andreasen & Glick, 1988; Jamison, 1989; Lapp, Collins, & Izzo, 1994; Poldinger, 1986; Post, 1994, 1996).

Neurobiological Approach

Cognitive neuroscientists have become increasingly interested in the phenomenon of creativity. The neurobiology of creativity is addressed in an article titled "Creative Innovation: Possible Brain Mechanisms" (Heilman, Nadeau, & Beversdorf, 2003). The authors suggest that creative innovation requires coactivation and communication between regions of the brain that ordinarily are not strongly connected. Highly creative people tend to differ from others in three ways: (1) they have a high level of specialized knowledge; (2) they are capable of divergent thinking mediated by the frontal lobe; and (3) they are able to modulate neurotransmitters such as norepinephrine in the frontal lobe. Thus, the frontal lobe appears to be that part of the cortex most important in creativity.

In 2005, Flaherty (2005) presented a three-factor model of the neurobiology of the creative drive. Drawing from evidence in brain imaging, drug studies, and lesion analysis, she described the creative drive as resulting from an interaction of the frontal lobes, the temporal lobes, and dopamine from the limbic system. The frontal lobes are responsible for idea generation and the temporal lobes for idea editing and evaluation. Abnormalities in the frontal lobe (such as occur with depression or anxiety) generally decrease creativity, while abnormalities in the temporal lobe often increase creativity. High activity in the temporal lobe typically inhibits activity in the frontal lobe, and vice versa. High dopamine levels increase general arousal and goal-directed behaviors and reduce latent inhibition. All three effects increase the drive to generate ideas. There is growing support for the neurobiological approach to creativity (Baas et al., 2008; Bogen & Bogen, 1988; Burch, Hemsley, Pavelis, & Corr, 2006; Carlsson, Wendt, & Risberg, 2000; Carson, Peterson, & Higgins, 2003; Coryell, Endicott, Keller, & Andreasen, 1989; Hoppe, 1988; Molle, Marshall, Wolf, Fehm, & Born, 1999).

MEASURES OF CREATIVITY

Person-Focused Measures

Because most measures of creativity in scientific research focus on the Person, and because there are so many measures, this discussion is limited to only the most widely used measures.

(1) *Torrance tests of creative thinking. Building on Guilford's work.* Torrance (1972) developed the TTCT. They are the most widely used tests in part because testing requires only the ability to reflect on one's own life experiences. These tests invite examinees to draw and give a title to drawings (pictures) or to write questions, reasons, consequences, and/or different uses for objects (words). These correspond to two test formats: Figural and Verbal.

The Figural TTCT involves thinking creatively with pictures. It is appropriate for all age groups, from kindergarten through adulthood. Picture-based exercises are used to assess five mental characteristics: (1) fluency; (2) resistance to premature closure; (3) elaboration; (4) abstractness of titles; and (5) originality.

The Verbal TTCT requires thinking creatively with words and is appropriate for first graders through adulthood. It uses six word-based exercises to assess three mental characteristics: (1) fluency; (2) flexibility; and (3) originality. These exercises provide opportunities to ask questions, improve products, and "just suppose." Torrance and his associates have administered these tests to thousands of schoolchildren. Several longitudinal studies have been conducted to follow up the elementary school-aged students who were first administered the tests in 1958 (Torrance, 1972, 1974, 1981, 1988, 1995). There was a 22-year follow-up (Torrance, 1980), a 40-year follow-up (Cramond, Matthews Morgan, Bandalos, & Zuo, 2005), and a 50-year follow-up (Runco, Millar, Acar, & Cramond, 2010). All demonstrated good reliability and validity of the TTCT.

(2) *Creativity Achievement Questionnaire.* The Creativity Achievement Questionnaire (CAQ) is a self-report test that measures creative achievement across 10 domains. It has proven to be a reliable and valid measure when compared to many other measures of creativity and to independent evaluations of creative output (Carson et al., 2005).

(3) *Creativity Assessment Packet.* The Creativity Assessment Packet (CAP), developed by Pro-Ed (http://www.proedinc.com/customer/productView.aspx?ID=777), measures the cognitive thought factors of fluency, flexibility, elaboration, originality, vocabulary, and comprehension. CAP consist of two group-administered instruments for children and youth ages 6 through 18: a Test of Divergent Thinking and a Test of Divergent Feeling. A third instrument, the Williams Scale, is a rating instrument for teachers.

(4) *Personality Measures.* A Creative Personality Scale for the Adjective Check List was developed by Gough (1979). As noted earlier, other personality measures have focused on openness to experience, one of the Big Five Personality Factors (Costa & McCrae, 1992). However, the ability of personality measures to predict creativity appears to depend on other personal characteristics, such as divergent thinking, intelligence, and achievement (Eysenck, 1994; Harris, 2004; McCrae, 1987).

Process-Focused Measures

(1) *Buffalo Creative Process Inventory.* This Inventory, developed by Puccio and colleagues (Puccio, Treffinger, & Talbot, 1995), is used to identify creativity styles in adolescents and adults. The objective of the inventory is to determine how the individual's creativity style relates to characteristics of work products and processes.
(2) *Kirton Adaption Innovation Survey (KAI).* This survey measures styles of problem solving and creativity in adolescents and adults. The objective is to improve managers' ability to enhance creativity in their employees by using a multidomain, integrationist creativity model of employee characteristics, leader characteristics, and leader-member exchange (Tierney, Farmer, & Graen, 1999).

Product-Focused Measures

(1) *Consensual Assessment Technique.* Developed by Amabile (1982), this method of judging creativity derives from a simple operational definition of creativity. Products or responses are considered creative to the extent that the appropriate observers (experts in the field) consider them creative.
(2) *Creative Product Semantic Scale.* Developed by O'Quin and Besemer (1989), the Creative Product Semantic Scale (CPSS) is based on a theoretical model which conceptualizes three dimensions of product attributes: Novelty, Resolution, and Elaboration/Synthesis. It has been used in research to evaluate the creativity of products rather than persons or processes. Whether the three scales that comprise this instrument measure different dimensions of product and process creativity remains an open question (O'Quin & Besemer, 1989).

Press/Environment-Focused Measures

(1) *KEYS: Assessing the Climate for Creativity.* Developed by Amabile and colleagues (Amabile, Conti, Coon, Lazenby, & Herron, 1996), KEYS is designed to assess perceived stimulants and obstacles to creativity in organizational work environments. A construct validity study showed that perceived work environments, as assessed by the KEYS, discriminate between high-creativity projects and

low-creativity projects, although some scales of the instrument are better discriminators than others.

(2) *Learning Style Inventory.* The Learning Style Inventory, developed by Kolb (1971, 2014), is a widely used instrument to assess children's learning style. Learning Style is, at best, a distant "cousin" of creativity. It focuses on two dimensions: Perceiving—Concrete Experience versus Abstract Conceptualization; and Processing—Active Experimentation versus Reflective Observation. Together these dimensions form four quadrants representing four learning styles: Accommodators, Convergers, Assimilators, and Divergers. These styles have proven effective in predicting a variety of learning outcomes and are often used to tailor individual instruction to the individual's learning style (Lowy & Hood, 2004). Learning style is considered a Press/Environment-focused measure because of its emphasis on how the person perceives and processes environmental events. However, it may also be considered a Person-focused measure because of its emphasis on individual differences.

Neurobiological Measures

Neurobiologists interested in the brain mechanisms underlying creativity have typically used one of the psychometric measures mentioned earlier and then correlated it with various aspects of brain activity (Arden, Chavez, Grazioplene, & Jung, 2010). In 2013, a new measure of creativity was introduced, one that is more amenable to neurobiological assessment than other measures. Prabhakaran and colleagues (Prabhakaran, Green, & Gray, 2013) demonstrated that individual differences in creative cognition can be measured by brief responses—single word utterances—and that this measure is reliable and correlates well with hypothesized measures of brain activity. Participants are instructed to say a verb upon seeing a noun displayed on a computer screen, and then cued to respond creatively to half of the nouns. For every noun–verb pair (72 pairs per subject), the semantic distance between the noun and the verb is assessed using Latent Semantic Analysis (LSA; Landauer, Foltz, & Laham, 1998).

Researchers found that the semantic distance was higher in the cued (creative) condition than the uncued condition, within subjects. Critically, between subjects, semantic distance in the cued condition had a strong relationship to a creativity factor derived from a battery of verbal, nonverbal, and achievement-based measures, a relationship that remained after controlling for intelligence and personality. Thus, the findings indicate that cognition can be assessed reliably and validly from "thin slices of behavior" (Ambady & Rosenthal, 1992; Arden et al., 2010; Chen, Himsel, Kasof, Greenberger, & Dmitrieva, 2006; Chen et al., 2005; Fink, Benedek,

Grabner, Staudt, & Neubauer, 2007; Howard-Jones, Blakemore, Samuel, Summers, & Claxton, 2005; Plucker & Beghetto, 2004; Silvia, Kaufman, & Pretz, 2009).

WHAT ARE VIDEO GAMES?

A video game is "an electronic game that involves human interaction with a user interface to generate visual feedback on a video device … which is any type of display device that can produce two- or three-dimensional images. The electronic systems used to play video games are known as platforms. The term 'platform' refers to the specific combination of electronic components or computer hardware which, in conjunction with software, allows a video game to operate" (http://en.wikipedia.org/wiki/Video_game).

The most commonly used platforms today are game consoles—devices specially designed to play games and consume digital media (e.g., Xbox, Playstation, and Nintendo 3Ds) on the living room TV or on handheld screens, personal computers and laptops; as well as mobile devices such as smartphones and tablets. Arcade games, the original game platform which has seen a steep numeric decline in recent decades, are a specialized type of electronic device that is typically designed to play only one game and is encased in a special cabinet.

In addition to a visual display, video games typically have additional means of providing interactivity and information to players. Audio is almost universal, using sound reproduction devices such as speakers and headphones. Other feedback may come from haptic peripherals, such as vibration or force feedback, with vibration sometimes used to simulate force feedback.

As others have discovered (Granic, Lober, & Engels, 2013), efforts to count the number of video games currently in existence are pointless. There are literally hundreds of games within platforms developed by an increasing number of game manufacturers as well as independent developers. Fortunately, video games share some commonalities which allow them to be categorized. The most common way of categorizing video games is by "genre." A video game genre is defined by a set of game play challenges rather than visual or narrative differences (Apperley, 2006). Genres are classified independent of the setting or game-world content, unlike other works of fiction such as films or books. Among game researchers there is still a lack of consensus about classifying games into genres, given that like other forms of creative expression, such as novels, games are a "live" form in a process of constant evolution (Bakhtin, 1981; Wittgenstein, 2010), with some games often presenting features of two or more genres at a time. Nevertheless genres remain the most popular video game taxonomy.

A common way of categorizing games into genres is by their *core mechanic*, a concept which game design scholars such as Eric Zimmerman and Katie Salen describe as the central activity players must do over and over in order to progress through the game (Salen & Zimmerman, 2004). The following is a list of commonly used video game genres by mechanic, with brief descriptions and examples of games in each. This list is by no means exhaustive since computer and video game design is continually evolving. But it does provide a basis for understanding video game effects if we know which genres have been used to produce which effects.

Video Game Genres

Action. An action video game requires players to use quick reflexes, accuracy, and timing to overcome obstacles. It is perhaps the most basic of gaming genres and certainly one of the most inclusive. Action game mechanics tend to emphasize combat. There are many subgenres of action games, such as fighting games and first-person shooter games. Examples are (a) Beat'em up and hack and slash; (b) Brawler games (e.g., *Street Smart, Fighter, Mortal Combat*); and (c) Shooter games (e.g., First-person shooter, Light Gun shooter).

Adventure. Adventure games were some of the earliest games created, beginning with *Colossal Cave Adventure* and *Zork* in the 1970s. Adventure games are not defined by story or content but rather by the manner of game play. They emphasize exploration of expansive areas and normally require the player to solve various puzzles by interacting with people or the environment in order to access new places, most often in a nonconfrontational way. It is considered a "purist" genre and tends to exclude anything which includes action elements, thus appealing to people who do not normally play video games. The genre peaked in popularity in the early 1990s and has since experienced a significant decline. Examples are (a) Real-time 3D adventures; (b) Text adventures; and (c) Graphic adventures.

Action-Adventure. Action-adventure games combine elements of the two component genres above, typically framing exploration and combat in a narrative that contextualizes long-term obstacles that must be overcome using a tool or item found through exploration as leverage (which is collected earlier in the game), as well as many smaller obstacles almost constantly in the way of goal achievement. Action-adventure games tend to combine exploration involving item gathering, simple puzzle solving, and combat. "Action-adventure" has become a label which is sometimes attached to games that do not fit neatly into other genres. Examples are (a) stealth games; (b) survivor horror games; (c) tactical combat games; (d) platformer games; and (e) third-person shooters.

Role playing. Role-playing games (RPGs) commonly extend the action–adventure genre by putting the player in control of a "party" of characters during exploration, puzzles, combat, and other encounters. Unlike other genres, however, RPGs tend to emphasize the use of statistics that describe character attributes (e.g., speed, agility, strength, intelligence) matched against probabilistic events (e.g., a chance to hit an enemy, pick a lock, convince another in conversation), to advance through the game storyline. Obtaining new items or successfully dealing with encounters yields modifiers to the party's statistics that in turn positively or negatively affect the probability of success in subsequent encounters. Since the emergence of an affordable home PC coincided with the development of this genre it is one of the first computer games and continues to be popular today. Early RPGs were strongly associated with medieval fantasy settings, but today many new settings are available. In addition, the advent of low-cost, high-speed internet connections and advanced multiplayer game architectures has led to the creation of Massive Multiplayer Online Role-Playing Games (MMORPGs), where millions of players can interact immersed in large online worlds and campaigns simultaneously, as in the immensely popular *World of Warcraft*.

Simulation and resource management. As their name implies, simulation games often require the player to manipulate and manage the components of a simulated real or fictional system to accomplish a stated goal. They have a very diverse set of characteristics. Typical examples are (a) vehicle simulation (e.g., flight simulators, train simulators); (b) city construction and management simulation; (c) business simulation; and (d) life simulation.

Sports. Sports games are a subgenre within simulations focused on the practice of traditional sports, including team sports, athletics, and extreme sports. Some games emphasize playing the sport (e.g., car racing games), while others emphasize strategy and organization (e.g., team management), and still others satirize the sport for comic effect. This genre has been popular throughout the history of video games and has the potential to be just as competitive as real-world sports. A number of game series feature the names and characteristics of real teams and players, and are updated annually to reflect real-world changes. Examples are (a) *Madden NFL*; (2b) *Out of the Park Baseball*; (c) *Need for Speed*; (d) *Arch Rivals*; and (e) *FIFA 2014*.

Strategy. Strategy video games often share mechanics with simulations, but require players to focus their attention on careful and skillful thinking and planning in order to compete for resources against others and achieve success. In most strategy video games the player is given a god-like view of the game world (the system), indirectly controlling the units under his command. Strategy video games generally take one of four forms, depending on whether the game is turn-based or real-time and whether the game's focus is on strategy or military tactics. Real-time strategy games are often a multiple-unit selection game in which multiple game characters can be selected at once to perform different tasks with a sky view (view looking down from above). More recent games in this genre are single-unit selection and provide a third-person view. Like many RPG games, many strategy games are moving away from turn-based systems to real-time systems. Examples are (a) 4X game; (b) Artillery games; (c) Real-time strategy; (d) Tower defense; (e) Turn-based strategy; and (f) Wargame.

Social games. This genre has grown as a result of social media platforms such as Facebook, and usually combines one of the above genres with the extra mechanic of recruiting "friends" to the player's team in order to accrue bonuses and advantages. Popular titles such as *Farmville* and *Mafia Wars* fall in this genre.

Sandbox games. This genre of video games has gained tremendous popularity over the last 10 years as social media technologies have integrated with game play. In this genre of games the core play mechanic is for players to use collections of materials to create their own game worlds to share with others in an online community, and to explore and play game worlds created by others. Creation can involve world building, character creation, and programming mechanics. Success is measured by the number of times a shared creation is played or remixed, and players advance by growing their reputations as creators. Examples of this genre are (a) *Minecraft*; (b) *Little Big Planet*; (c) *Disney Infinity*; (d) *Project Spark*; and (e) *ROBLOX*.

Other notable genres: The nature of video games in this genre vary considerably, as is apparent from their titles: (a) Music games; (b) Party games; (c) Programming games; (d) Trivia games; (e) Puzzle games; and (f) Board/Card games.

Genres by purpose. While most video games are designed for entertainment, many are designed for particular purposes. These purposes include to inform, to persuade or to stimulate, among others. Game play in this diverse genre varies from puzzles to action to adventure games. Examples are (a) Art games; (b) Casual games; (c) Exergames; and (d) Serious and Educational games—simulations of real-world events or processes designed for the purpose of educating, training, marketing, or other real-world purposes.

In a recent article titled "The benefits of playing video games," published in the *American Psychologist*, Granic et al. (2013) noted that the huge number and diversity of video games in terms of the dimensions along which they may vary makes developing a taxonomy of games a challenging task. They accepted this challenge by developing a taxonomy based on two dimensions: Level of complexity and the Extent of social interaction. Their taxonomy is presented in Figure 1.

Why is it important to have a taxonomy of video games that captures their essential dimensions? It is important because when researchers report that playing video games has a specific effect we need to know what *type* of video game has this effect. Will all video games produce the effect or only games of a certain genre/type? Too often research findings are

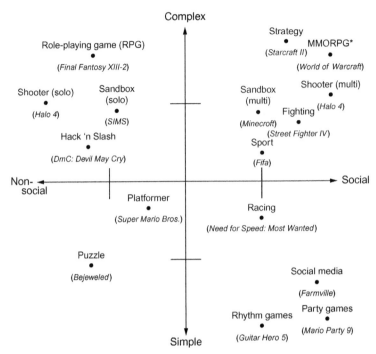

FIGURE 1   Conceptual map of the main game genre based on two dimensions: level of complexity and social interaction. Note: Names within quadrants are examples of video games in that quadrant. Not all genres are included in this taxonomy. Moreover, a game may belong to more than one quadrant. "MMORPG" = Massive Multiplayer Online Role-Playing Game.

generalized, often by the media, to *all* video games. Generalization to all video games is unjustified given that often only one or a small number of genre/types were used in the research. A workable taxonomy allows researchers to qualify statements about video game effects by indicating the genre/type of video game that produces (or is related to) the effect.

Granic et al.'s (2013) taxonomy facilitates the qualification of research findings by indicating two dimensions characteristic of all video games that may be important in predicting their effects. As we will suggest later in our review of video game effects, most research has used Action or Action-Adventure games, with a smaller number using Role-Playing, Strategy, and Simulation games. Using Granic et al.'s taxonomy, games used in most of the research fall into two quadrants: Complex-Social and Complex-Nonsocial. Thus, a tentative conclusion at this juncture is that video game effects demonstrated in the research are limited to games that involve action and complex cognition, games that are highly engaging, and games that are likely to be played by highly motivated players.

Before reviewing the effects of video games on cognitive, social, emotional, and motivational outcomes it is important to gain an appreciation of the scope of video game playing in the USA and why findings regarding their effects are likely to have a substantial impact on players, parents, educators, policymakers, and the general public. The following summary of facts about the video game industry provides an appreciation of the importance of research findings about video game effects.

VIDEO GAME INDUSTRY STATISTICS

How pervasive is video game playing? What are the characteristics of the average video game player? How involved are parents in their children's video game playing?

The video game industry is a large and growing industry. In 2012, it boasted $20.77 billion in sales in the US alone, and sales have been consistently increasing since the Entertainment Software Association (ESA; http://www.theesa.com/) began issuing its annual reports in 2008. Here are some of the essential facts from the 2013 Annual Report (http://www.theesa.com/facts/pdfs/esa_ef_2013.pdf) that are relevant, directly or indirectly, to understanding the effects of video games (Table 1).

THE EFFECTS OF VIDEO GAME PLAYING

What follows is a brief review of the effects of video game playing that have been demonstrated in the scientific research. Because a number of recent reviews already exist (Barlett, Anderson, & Swing, 2009; Ferguson, 2007; Gentile, 2011; Granic et al., 2013), this review will be brief. The interested reader is referred to existing reviews for more details. As mentioned earlier, the majority of studies of video game effects covered in the review used Action and Action–Adventure video games, or what Granic et al.'s (2013) taxonomy classifies as Complex-Social and Complex-Nonsocial games. And most of the studies used adults as subjects.

Cognitive Effects

Playing video games promotes a wide range of cognitive skills. This is particularly true for Action games (e.g., "shooter"games), many of which involve violence. The most convincing evidence comes from numerous training studies that recruit naive video gamers (those who have hardly or never played *shooter* video games) and randomly assign them to play either a shooter game or another type of game for the same period of time. Compared to control participants, those in the shooter game condition

TABLE 1   Facts About the US Computer and Video Game Industry

More than half (58%) of Americans play video games. There is an average of two gamers per household. The average household owns at least one dedicated game console, PC or smart phone

The average age of game players is 30 years old; 32% are under 18 years old, 32% are 18-35 years old and 36% are 36 years old or older

45% of game players are female. Females 18 and older represent a significantly greater portion of the game-playing population (31%) than boys aged 17 or younger (19%)

The average age of the most frequent game purchaser is 35 years old. More than half (54%) are male

43% of game players believe that computer and video games give them the most value for their money, compared to DVDs, music or going to the movies

Among the reasons gamers give for purchasing a particular game are quality of graphics, an interesting story line, a sequel to a favorite game or word of mouth

Types of Online video games most often played are Puzzle, Board Games, Game Show, Trivia, Card Games (34%); Action, Sports, Strategy, Role-Playing (26%), Casual, Social Games (19%); Persistent Multiplayer Universe (14%); Other (8%)

Types of Mobile games played most often are Puzzle, Board Games, Game Show, Trivia, Card Games (35%); Casual, Social Games (35%); Action, Sports, Strategy, Role Playing (13%); Other (13%); Persistent Multiplayer Universe (4%)

Gamers who play more video games than they did 3 years ago are also spending less time watching TV (49%), going to movies (47%), playing board games (58%), and watching movies at home (44%)

62% of game players play with others, either in person or online

32% of game players play Social Games

The majority of gamers play with friends and family: 16% with parents, 32% with other family members, 42% with friends, 16% with spouse or significant other

The average number of years gamers have been playing is 13; 15 years for adult males and 13 years for adult females

86% of parents feel that parental controls placed on all new video games are useful

79% of parents place limits on their children's video game playing

89% of the time parents are present when games are purchased or rented

93% of parents pay attention to the content of video games their children play

35% of parents play video games with their children at least weekly and 58% at least monthly

52% of parents say that video games are a positive part of their child's life

The best-selling video game genres in 2012 were Action (22%), Shooter (21%), and Sports (14%). All other genres accounted for less that 8% of sales

The best-selling computer game genres in 2012 were Role Playing (28%), Casual (28%), and Strategy (25%). All other genres accounted for less than 7% of sales

Entertainment Software Association: 2013 Annual Report.

1. CREATIVITY AND VIDEO GAME PLAY

show faster and more accurate attention allocation, higher spatial reso-lution in visual processing, and enhanced mental rotation abilities (see review by Green & Bavelier, 2012). A recently published meta-analysis concluded that the spatial skills improvements derived from playing com-mercially available shooter games are comparable to the effects of formal high school and university-level courses aimed at enhancing these skills (Uttal et al., 2013). Further, this meta-analysis showed that spatial skills can be trained with video games in a relatively brief period of time, that these training benefits last over an extended period of time and, crucially, that these skills transfer to other spatial tasks beyond the gaming context.

The importance of spatial skills cannot be overstated. A 25-year longi-tudinal study using a US representative sample established the power of spatial skills in predicting achievements in science, technology, engineer-ing, and mathematics (STEM). STEM areas of expertise have been linked to long-term career success and are predicted to be especially critical to positive life outcomes in the new millennium (Wai, Lubinski, Benbow, & Steiger, 2010).

Previous research has also demonstrated that the cognitive advantages of video game playing are also evident in measurable changes in neural processing and efficiency. For example, a recent functional magnetic res-onance imaging (fMRI) study found that the mechanisms that control at-tention allocation (i.e., the fronto-parietal network) were less active during a challenging pattern-detection task in regular gamers than in nongamers. This led researchers to suggest that shooter game players allocate their at-tentional resources more efficiently and filter out irrelevant information more effectively than nongamers (Bavelier, Achtman, Mani, & Föcker, 2012).

Nature Reviews Neuroscience summarized the preceding findings and other evidence implicating video game playing with brain changes as fol-lows: "Video games are controlled training regimens delivered in highly motivating behavioral contexts … because behavioral changes arise from brain changes, it is also no surprise that performance improvements are paralleled by enduring physical and functional neurological remodeling" (Bavelier et al., 2011, p. 763).

In addition to spatial skills, researchers have speculated that playing video games, regardless of the game genre, may facilitate the develop-ment of problem-solving skills because these skills are central to all genres. Problems range from simple to complex and game designers provide little instruction for solving them as a way to increase interest and challenge for the game player. Prensky (2012) has argued that exposure to games with open-ended problems has influenced the problem-solving skills of the millennial generation. Instead of learning through explicit linear in-struction, as did generations before (e.g., reading a manual), the millennial generation solves problems through trial and error, recursively collecting evidence and testing it through experimentation.

Only two studies have explicitly tested the relationship between playing video games and problem-solving skills. In both, problem solving was defined in the reflective sense (e.g., taking time to gather information, evaluate various options, formulate a plan, and consider changing strategies and/or goals before proceeding with an alternative plan). One study using *World of Warcraft*, a popular video game among youth, was a correlational study making it difficult to determine whether better problem solvers had better game performance or game playing improved problem-solving skills (Steinkuehler & Duncan, 2008). The second study was a longitudinal study which showed that the more adolescents reported playing Strategic video games, the greater the improvement in their self-reported problem-solving skills during the following year (Adachi & Willoughby, 2013). This relationship was not found for Sports games (e.g., racing) or Action games (e.g., fighting games), which is somewhat surprising given their fast-paced nature and the need to make quick decisions characteristic of these games. Also found in this research was an indirect positive relationship between playing strategic video games and academic grades, a relationship mediated by problem-solving skills.

As discussed earlier, in our own research we observed a relationship between video game playing and creativity (Jackson et al., 2012; Jackson & Games, 2012). Over a two-year period, among the nearly 500 12-year-olds who participated in the study, those who played video games more were more creative at the end of the study, as measured by an adaption of the Torrance Tests of Creativity (Torrance, 1966), than those who played less. This effect was independent of game genre, although the majority of our participants played Action, Action–Adventure, or Strategic games. Small sample sizes for other genres suggest caution in interpreting comparisons with these three most popular genres.

In summary, specific genres/types of video games seem to enhance a variety of cognitive skills, some of which generalize to real-world contexts. Research is needed to determine the extent to which these cognitive benefits are obtained using other video game genres/types, whether they generalize to other age and cultural groups, and whether they transfer to a variety of real-world contexts. Another challenge for future research is to determine whether there are additional cognitive benefits and possibly liabilities to video game playing and how/if they are dependent on a variety of characteristics, including those of the game player and game genre/type.

Social Effects

Unlike video games of the twentieth century, many of today's video games, including the most popular games, are social in nature. No longer does the typical video gamer fit the "nerdy social isolate" stereotype of the 1990s (Lenhart et al., 2008). As mentioned earlier in the discussion of industry statistics, 62% of today's game players play with others, either in person or online, and 77% play social games (ESA, 2013). The social nature of today's video games suggests that gamers may be learning social skills, including prosocial skills, to the extent that the game requires cooperation and mutual support to achieve desired goals (Ewoldsen et al., 2012). These social skills may extend beyond the video game context to benefit family, peer, work, and other interpersonal relationships (Gentile & Gentile, 2008; Gentile et al., 2009).

In support of this view, Gentile et al. (2009), summarizing international evidence from correlational, longitudinal, and experimental studies, found that playing prosocial video games was related to, or predicted, prosocial behaviors. Specifically, playing prosocial games led to causal, short-term effects on helping others. Long-term effects were also observed. Children who played more prosocial games at the beginning of the school year were more likely to exhibit helpful behaviors later that year. Surprisingly, violent video games were just as likely to promote prosocial behavior as games that emphasize prosocial behavior.

Why should playing violent video games increase prosocial behavior? Researchers have determined that the critical dimension is the extent to which playing is cooperative rather than competitive (Ferguson & Garza, 2011; Velez, Mahood, Ewoldsen, & Moyer-Gusé, 2012). Such results are contrary to highly popularized research findings that playing violent video games increases aggressive cognition and behavior, both immediately after playing and potentially for years to come (Anderson & Bushman, 2001; Anderson, Gentile, & Buckley, 2007; Carnagey, Anderson, & Bushman, 2007). Moreover, playing violent video games socially (in groups) reduces feelings of hostility compared to playing alone (Eastin, 2007). Likewise, violent video games played cooperatively versus competitively decreases players' access to aggressive cognitions and increases prosocial behavior beyond the game context (Ewoldsen et al., 2012). Cooperative play can even overcome the effects of out-group membership on behavior, making players more cooperative with out-group members than if they were playing competively (Velez et al., 2012). Recently published experimental studies suggest that even the most violent video games on the market (*Grand Theft Auto IV, Call of Duty*) fail to diminish this subsequent prosocial behavior when played coorperatively (Tear & Nielsen, 2013).

Another rather surprising finding was recently reported by Gino and Wiltermuth (2014). They found that dishonesty actually increased creativity. Their explanation for this finding was that both involve breaking the rules—the social principle that people should tell the truth, and that the heightened feeling of being unconstrained by rules both mediates and moderates the relationship between dishonesty and creativity. Similar findings have been observed in organizational contexts where breaking the rules, or thinking "outside of the box" (Guilford, 1967b; Runco, 2010; Simonton, 1999), contributes to corporate innovation and success (Baucus, Norton, Baucus, & Human, 2008; Brenkert, 2009; Kelley & Littman, 2001; Langley & Jones, 1988; Sternberg, 1988; Winslow & Solomon, 1993).

Social skills are advantageous not only to family, peer, work, and other interpersonal relationships but also have positive implications for civic engagement. In one large-scale, representative US sample, adolescents who played video games involving civic experiences (e.g., *Guild Wars 2*, an MMORPG) were more likely to be engaged in social and civic movements in their everyday lives (e.g., raising money for charity, volunteering, persuading others to vote) than did those who did not (Lenhart et al., 2008). Unfortunately, as is the case with most survey studies, this study could not establish the causal direction of effects. Moreover, most of the studies reviewed here examined immediate or short-term effects of cooperative play, although a handful found correlations with long-term effects. Again longitudinal research is needed to establish the social benefits of video game playing over time and across contexts.

Emotional Effects

People play video games because it makes them feel good. Uses and gratifications theory, one of the oldest and most well-validated theories in communications research (Ruggiero, 2000), specifies mood and emotional enhancement as one of the top reasons why people engage in media activities. Research has demonstrated a causal relationship between playing preferred video games, improved mood, and an increase in positive emotions (Russoniello, O'Brien, & Parks, 2009; Ryan, Rigby, & Przybylski, 2006). For example, studies suggest that playing *puzzle* video games, which are, according to Granic et al. (2013) taxonomy, simple, and nonsocial games, can nevertheless improve players' moods, promote relaxation, and ward off anxiety (Russoniello et al., 2009). McGonigal (2011) went so far as to suggest that playing video games has the potential to trigger intense positive emotional experiences, such as *flow* (Csikszentmihalyi, 2009). Flow is an experience described by gamers when they are fully engaged in an intrinsically rewarding activity that elicits a high sense of control while simultaneously evoking a loss of self-consciousness (Sherry, 2004). In psychology, flow experiences have been repeatedly linked to a host of positive outcomes for adolescents, including commitment and achievement in high school (e.g., Nakamura & Csikszentmihalyi, 2002), higher self-esteem, and less anxiety (Csikszentmihalyi, Rathunde, & Whalen, 1993). Experiencing flow during game play may lead to similar positive outcomes. However, this hypothesis, as well as hypotheses about the duration and generalizability of the flow experience and other positive emotions resulting from video game playing, have yet to be tested.

Experiencing positive emotions on a daily basis has been linked to a variety of positive outcomes. Fredrickson's (2001, 2008, 2013) "broaden-and-build theory" of positive emotions maintains that these experiences *broaden* the number of behaviors one perceives as both possible and motivating and *builds* social relationships that provide support for goal pursuit and coping with failure. Further, Fredrickson and colleagues have proposed that positive emotions help undo the detrimental and demotivating effects of negative emotions (e.g., Fredrickson, Cohn, Coffey, Pek, & Finkel, 2008; Kok et al., 2013). From this perspective positive emotions are seen as the foundation of well-being, crucial not only as end states but also as sources of inspiration and connectivity.

Evaluating the emotional benefits of playing video games leads to the study of emotion regulation in these contexts. Simple "up-regulation" of positive emotions is one emotion-regulation strategy that has been linked to beneficial outcomes (e.g., Fredrickson, 2001), but there may be additional emotion-regulation benefits to game play. It may also trigger a range of negative emotions, including frustration, anger, anxiety, and sadness. But similar to what research has shown about the function of traditional play, the pretend context of video games may be real enough to make the accomplishment of goals matter, yet safe enough to practice controlling or modulating negative emotions in the service of these goals. Adaptive regulation strategies such as acceptance, problem solving, and reappraisal have repeatedly been linked to less negative affect, more social support, and lower levels of depressive symptoms (Aldao, Nolen-Hoeksema, & Schweizer, 2010).

These same adaptive regulation strategies seem to be rewarded in gaming contexts because they are concretely and clearly linked to goal achievement. For example, reappraisal, a cognitive "habit" involving reevaluations of a situation or one's ability to cope with it, is a well-established emotion-regulation strategy (Gross & John, 2003) that appears to be fundamental to many video games. Games continuously provide novel challenges, demanding players to shift from already established appraisals to new ones in order to most efficiently achieve their goals. Thus, game playing may promote the ability to flexibly and efficiently reappraise emotional experiences, teaching players the benefits of dealing with frustration and anxiety in adaptive ways because less adaptive strategies, such as anger and rumination (Aldao et al., 2010), are less likely to be rewarded because they impede players from reacting quickly and flexibly to constantly changing and often frustrating challenges. However, the extent to which adaptive emotion-regulation strategies are learned through video game playing remains speculative, encouraging future research to establish this important connection.

Motivational Effects

The success or failure of a video game is intimately tied to its ability to engage the players for whom it is designed. Engagement requires attracting players into the virtual environment, providing goals that are meaningful to them, providing incentives for players to persevere after multiple failures and experience triumph when they achieve success—an outcome less frequent than failure in all video games in order to make them sufficiently challenging. What characteristics are associated with this persistent motivational style? Are they prerequisite to interest in video game playing or does video game playing facilitate the development of these characteristics? If the latter is true, does this motivational style extend beyond the video game context to influence how challenging tasks are approached in everyday life?

Decades of research in developmental and educational psychology suggest that motivational styles characterized by persistence and continuous effortful engagement are key contributors to success and achievement (for a review, see Dweck & Molden, 2005). According to Dweck and colleagues, children develop beliefs about their intelligence and abilities, beliefs that underlie specific motivational styles and directly affect their achievement (Blackwell, Trzesniewski, & Dweck, 2007). Children who are praised for their traits rather than their efforts develop an *entity* theory of intelligence, which maintains that intelligence is an innate trait, something that is fixed and cannot be changed. In contrast, children who are praised for their effort develop an *incremental* theory of intelligence. They come to believe that intelligence is malleable, something that can be developed through effort and time. In their review of the benefits of playing video games, Granic et al. (2013) proposed that video games facilitate the acquisition of an incremental theory of intelligence because they provide players with concrete, immediate feedback regarding their specific *efforts*, not their traits or abilities.

The immediate and concrete feedback provided by video games (e.g., points, coins, dead ends in puzzles) serves to reward continual effort and keep players within what Vygotsky referred to as their "zone of proximal development" (Vygotsky, 1978, p. 86). This zone is characterized by a balance between optimal levels of challenge and frustration and sufficient experiences of success and accomplishment (Sweetser & Wyeth, 2005). Granic et al. (2013) argued that the best video games on the market are popular because they fall into many players' zone of proximal development by dynamically adjusting the difficulty level, depending on the player's performance. Thus, game play becomes more challenging, demanding more dexterity, quicker reaction times, and more innovative and complex solutions as the player succeeds at lower levels and moves to higher levels of difficulty.

An individual's theory about the basis for his/her intelligence—entity or incremental—is extremely important to how the individual approaches learning and challenging tasks in many life situations. Individuals who endorse an incremental theory are more likely to persist in the face of failure and a challenging task, whereas those who endorse an entity theory are more likely to give up (Dweck & Molden, 2005). Believing that intelligence or ability is fixed prompts feelings of worthlessness in the face of failure. But believing that intelligence or ability is based on effortful engagement prompts persistence and the motivation to remain engaged and bolster one's efforts. This positive response in the face of failure has been shown to predict better academic performance (Blackwell et al., 2007).

Granic et al. (2013) maintain that video games use failure as a motivational tool by providing only intermittent chances for success. As behaviorists have documented for decades (e.g., Kendall, 1974), intermittent reinforcement schedules are the most effective for learning new behaviors. Ventura and colleagues proposed that persistence in the face of failure reaps valued rewards (Ventura, Shute, & Zhao, 2013). Moreover, contrary to what seems like a commonsense prediction, experiences of failure during video game play do not lead to anger, frustration, or sadness, although these negative emotions may be experienced intermittently. Instead, players often respond to game failures with excitement, interest, and even joy (Salminen & Ravaja, 2008). They become highly motivated to return to the task of winning and are "relentlessly optimistic" about reaching their goals (McGonigal, 2011). Previous research indicates that a persistent motivational style charged with positive affect is related to long-term academic success (Ventura et al., 2013).

Although Granic et al.'s (2013) analysis of the motivational implications of video games is compelling and optimistic, research has yet to test the relationship between playing video games, a persistent motivational style and long-term academic success or success in other life contexts. One study is suggestive of such a relationship. Ventura et al. (2013) demonstrated that the extent of video game playing predicted how long participants would persist at solving difficult anagrams. While these results are encouraging they are a far cry from demonstrating a causal relationship between video game playing and task persistence in the face of failure. Once again longitudinal research is needed to determine whether video game playing results in a persistent motivational style, an incremental theory of intelligence, and more successful life outcomes.

WHY VIDEO GAME PLAYING SHOULD INCREASE CREATIVITY

The purpose of this chapter was to lend support to our research finding that video game playing increases creativity (Jackson et al., 2012; Jackson & Games, 2012). We began by defining creativity—its conceptualization, theories and approaches, and describing how it has been measured. We then took a closer look at the meaning of video games—how they are characterized (genre/type) and industry statistics indicating the prevalence of video game playing and parents involvement in their children's game playing. Next, we briefly reviewed the research demonstrating the benefits of video game playing—cognitive, social, emotional, and motivational, most of which has been demonstrated only in the past decades. Taken as a whole, we believe we have provided compelling evidence for the conclusion that video games increase creativity and that the findings of our research are robust, replicable using different measures of creativity, and have implications for parents, educators, policymakers, and the general public for decisions about video game play, especially by children.

First, consider the evidence for the cognitive effects of video game playing. Playing video games, but especially Action games or, using Granic et al.'s (2013) taxonomy, Complex games, has the following effects: (1) faster and more accurate attention allocation; (2) higher spatial resolution in visual processing—spatial skills; (3) enhanced mental rotation abilities; (4) increased neural processing and processing efficiency; (5) enduring physical and functional neurological remodeling—brain changes that lead to behavioral changes; (6) performance improvements that result from physical and functional neurological remodeling; and (7) increased problem-solving skills, defined in a reflective sense—taking time to gather information, evaluate options, formulate plans, and consider changing strategies and/or goals before proceeding with an alternative plan.

Second, consider the evidence for the social effects of video game playing. These are likely to generalize across numerous genres and all games included in Granic et al.'s two quadrants of social games (Complex and Simple). Video game playing (1) increases social skills, an effect that extends beyond game play, at least in the short run; (2) increases prosocial behavior in games played cooperatively rather than competitively, regardless of whether the game is violent or nonviolent; (3) reduces feelings of hostility when played with others compared to when played alone; (4) decreases players' access to aggressive cognitions when playing violent video games cooperatively versus competitively; (5) overcomes the effects of out-group membership status, making players more cooperative when playing with out-group members than they otherwise would be; and (6) increases the likelihood of civic engagement.

Third, research on the emotional effects of video game playing indicates: (1) improved mood and an increase in positive emotions; (2) promotion of relaxation and a reduction in anxiety, regardless of the game genre/type; (3) potential for the experience of *flow*, which occurs when a gamer is fully engaged in an intrinsically rewarding activity that also elicits a high sense of control and a loss of self-consciousness; (4) an increase in the positive outcomes linked to flow for adolescents, including commitment and academic achievement, higher self-esteem, inspiration and lower anxiety; (5) positive emotions evoked by game play may broaden the number of behaviors that players perceive as both possible and motivating; (6) facilitation of the development of social relationships and connectivity that provide support for goal pursuit and coping with failure; (7) positive emotions evoked by game play that may help to undo the detrimental and demotivating effects of negative emotions; (8) potential development of adaptive regulation strategies such as acceptance, problem solving, and reappraisal—strategies that have been consistently linked to less negative affect, greater social support, and lower levels of depressive symptoms; and (9) game playing may promote the ability to flexibly and efficiently reappraise emotional experiences, teaching players the benefits of dealing with frustration and anxiety in adaptive ways, often by switching strategies, as required by the dynamic nature of problem solving required for success in video games.

Fourth, research on the motivational effects of video game playing indicates that: (1) players engaged in video games that provide meaningful goals and sufficient incentives to persevere after multiple failures and also experience triumph when successful may develop a motivational style characterized by persistence and continuous effortful engagement, key contributors to success and achievement in many real-world contexts; (2) video games provide immediate and concrete feedback, rewarding continual effort and keeping players within their "zone of proximal development" where optimal learning occurs; (3) video games use failure as a motivational tool, providing only intermittent reinforcement, the most effective reinforcement strategy for learning new behaviors; (4) video games players are "relentlessly optimistic," persisting in the face of failure because games are designed so that persistence has the potential to reap valued rewards; (5) video game playing may encourage an "incremental" theory of intelligence rather than an "entity" theory—in an incremental theory, failure signals the need to remain engaged and bolster one's efforts, whereas in an entity theory failure is a reason to give up; and (6) positive attitudes toward failure, characteristic of an incremental theory of intelligence, predict better academic performance and life outcomes.

From the perspective of a self-determination theory of motivation, research into video game play shows that games that motivate players to continue engaging in play tend to present mechanisms that give them a sense of autonomy (a player can choose her/his own destiny), competence (a player has skills necessary to succeed), and relatedness (connections to a community in the case of social games) necessary to sustain intrinsic motivation (Ryan et al., 2006) characteristic of Amabile's (1996) model of creative behavior enablement.

Our brief review of the cognitive, social, emotional, and motivational benefits of video game playing support findings obtained in our research

(Jackson et al., 2012; Jackson & Games, 2012). Video game playing should increase creativity, directly or indirectly, mediated by its beneficial cognitive, social, emotional, and motivational effects. Consider the play-by-play action in a video game. Decisions have to be made not only quickly but *creatively*. The games are designed to assure that the obvious move is the incorrect one. It's the ability to anticipate the unanticipated that leads to success in video games. Simply put, video games encourage creativity.

It remains for future research to examine the direct and indirect effects of video game playing on creativity, the processes involved in this relationship, the generalizability of the video game play-creativity link to a variety of game genre/types and beyond video games, and the long-term effects on important life outcomes such as academic performance and professional success. We have the tools and paradigms to accomplish these goals. Many will require longitudinal research that considers other personal characteristics such as gender and age, parental characteristics such as attitudes towards their child's video game playing, and cultural characteristics such as approval or disapproval for an activity that *seemingly* contributes nothing to the child's education or benefits to society.

References

Adachi, P. J., & Willoughby, T. (2013). More than just fun and games: The longitudinal relationships between strategic video games, self-reported problem solving skills, and academic grades. *Journal of Youth and Adolescence, 42*, 1041–1052.

Aldao, A., Nolen-Hoeksema, S., & Schweizer, S. (2010). Emotion-regulation strategies across psychopathology: A meta-analytic review. *Clinical Psychology Review, 30*, 217–237.

Amabile, T. T. (1982). Social psychology of creativity: A consensual assessment technique. *Journal of Personality and Social Psychology, 43*, 997–1013.

Amabile, T. M. (1996). *Creativity in context.* New York: Westview.

Amabile, T. M. (1999). Consensual assessment. In M. A. Runco & S. Pritzker (Eds.), *Encyclopedia of creativity* (pp. 346–349). San Diego, CA: Academic Press.

Amabile, T. M., Conti, R., Coon, H., Lazenby, J., & Herron, M. (1996). Assessing the work environment for creativity. *Academy of Management Journal, 39*, 1154–1184.

Ambady, N., & Rosenthal, R. J. (1992). Thin slices of expressive behavior as predictors of interpersonal consequences: A meta-analysis. *Psychological Bulletin, 111*, 256–274.

Anderson, C. A., & Bushman, B. J. (2001). Effects of violent video games on aggressive behavior, aggressive cognition, aggressive affect, physiological arousal, and prosocial behavior: A meta-analytic review of the scientific literature. *Psychological Science, 12*, 353–359.

Anderson, C. A., Gentile, D. A., & Buckley, K. E. (2007). *Violent computer game effects on children and adolescents: Theory, research, and public policy.* New York: Oxford University Press.

Andreasen, N. C., & Glick, I. D. (1988). Bipolar affective disorder and creativity: Implications and clinical management. *Comprehensive Psychiatry, 29*, 207–217.

Apperley, T. H. (2006). Genre and game studies. *Simulation & Gaming, 37*, 6–23.

Arden, R., Chavez, R. S., Grazioplene, R., & Jung, R. E. (2010). Neuroimaging creativity: A psychometric view. *Behavioural Brain Research, 214*, 143–156.

Baas, M., De Dreu, C. K. W., & Nijstad, B. A. (2008). A meta-analysis of 25 years of mood-creativity research: Hedonic tone, activation or regulatory focus? *Psychological Bulletin, 134*, 779–806.

Bakhtin, M. M. (1981). The dialogic imagination: Four essays. (ed.). Michael Holquist. Trans. *Caryl Emerson and Michael Holquist*. Austin and London: University of Texas Press.

Barlett, C. P., Anderson, C. A., & Swing, E. L. (2009). Video game effects—Confirmed, suspected, and speculative: A review of the evidence. *Simulation & Gaming, 40,* 377–403.

Batey, M. (2012). The measurement of creativity: From definitional consensus to the introduction of a new heuristic framework. *Creativity Research Journal, 24,* 55–65.

Batey, M., & Furnham, A. (2006). Creativity, intelligence and personality: A critical review of the scattered literature. *Genetic, Social, and General Psychology Monographs, 132,* 355–429.

Batey, M., Furnham, A. F., & Safiullina, X. (2010). Intelligence, general knowledge and personality as predictors of creativity. *Learning and Individual Differences, 20,* 532–535.

Baucus, M. S., Norton, W. I., Baucus, D. A., & Human, S. A. (2008). Fostering creativity and innovation without encouraging unethical behavior. *Journal of Business Ethics, 81,* 97–115.

Bavelier, D., Achtman, R. L., Mani, M., & Föcker, J. (2012). Neural bases of selective attention in action video game players. *Vision Research, 61,* 132–143.

Bavelier, D., Green, C. S., Han, D. H., Renshaw, P. F., Merzenich, M. M., & Gentile, D. A. (2011). Brains on video games. *Nature Reviews Neuroscience, 12,* 763–768.

Blackwell, L. S., Trzesniewski, K. H., & Dweck, C. S. (2007). Implicit theories of intelligence predict achievement across an adolescent transition: A longitudinal study and an intervention. *Child Development, 78,* 246–263.

Boden, M. A. (2004). *The creative mind: Myths & mechanisms* (2nd ed.). New York: Routledge.

Bogen, J. E., & Bogen, G. M. (1988). Creativity and the corpus callosum. *Psychiatric Clinics of North America, 11,* 293–301.

Brenkert, G. G. (2009). Innovation, rule breaking and the ethics of entrepreneurship. *Journal of Business Venturing, 24,* 448–464.

Burch, G.St.J., Hemsley, D., Pavelis, C., & Corr, P. J. (2006). Personality, creativity, and latent inhibition. *European Journal of Personality, 20,* 107–122.

Campbell, D. T. (1960). Blind generation and selective retention in creative thought as in other thought processes. *Psychological Review, 67,* 380–400.

Carlsson, I., Wendt, P. E., & Risberg, J. (2000). On the neurobiology of creativity. Differences in frontal activity between high and low creative subjects. *Neuropsychologia, 38,* 873–885.

Carnagey, N. L., Anderson, C. A., & Bushman, B. J. (2007). The effect of computer game violence on physiological desensitization to real-life violence. *Journal of Experimental Social Psychology, 43,* 489–501.

Carson, S. H., Peterson, J. B., & Higgins, D. M. (2003). Decreased latent inhibition is associated with increased creative achievement in high-functioning individuals. *Journal of Personality & Social Psychology, 85,* 499–506.

Carson, S., Peterson, J. B., & Higgins, D. M. (2005). Reliability, validity and factor structure of the creative achievement questionnaire. *Creativity Research Journal, 17,* 37–50.

Chen, C., Himsel, A., Kasof, J., Greenberger, E., & Dmitrieva, J. (2006). Boundless creativity: Evidence for the domain generality of individual differences in creativity. *Journal of Creative Behavior, 40,* 179–199.

Chen, C., Kasof, J., Himsel, A., Dmitrieva, J., Dong, Q., & Xue, G. (2005). Effects of explicit instruction to "Be Creative" across domains and cultures. *Journal of Creative Behavior, 39,* 89–110.

Cooper, E. (1991). A critique of six measures for assessing creativity. *Journal of Creative Behavior, 25,* 194–204.

Coryell, W., Endicott, J., Keller, M., & Andreasen, N. (1989). Bipolar affective disorder and high achievement: A familial association. *American Journal of Psychiatry, 146,* 983–988.

Costa, P. T., Jr., & McCrae, R. R. (1992). *Revised NEO personality inventory (NEO-PI-R) and NEO five-factor inventory (NEO-FFI) manual*. Odessa, FL: Psychological Assessment Resources.

Cramond, B., Matthews Morgan, J., Bandalos, D., & Zuo, L. (2005). A report on the 40 year follow-up of the Torrance tests of creative thinking: Alive and well in the new millennium. *Gifted Child Quarterly, 49,* 283–291.

Cropley, A. J. (2000). Defining and measuring creativity: Are creativity tests worth using? *Roper Review, 23*, 72–79.

Csikszentmihalyi, M. (1988). Society, culture, and person: A systems view of creativity. In R. J. Sternberg (Ed.), *The nature of creativity: Contemporary psychological perspectives* (pp. 324–338). New York: Cambridge University Press.

Csikszentmihalyi, M. (1999). Implications of a systems perspective for the study of creativity. In R. J. Sternberg (Ed.), *Creativity research handbook* (pp. 313–325). Cambridge, MA: Cambridge University Press.

Csikszentmihalyi, M. (2009). *Creativity: Flow and the psychology of discovery and invention.* New York: Harper Collins.

Csikszentmihalyi, M., Rathunde, K., & Whalen, S. (1993). *Talented teenagers.* Cambridge, MA: Cambridge University Press.

Davis, M. A. (2009). Understanding the relationship between mood and creativity: A meta-analysis. *Organizational Behavior and Human Decision Processes, 100*, 25–38.

Dweck, C. S., & Molden, D. C. (2005). Self-theories: Their impact on competence motivation and acquisition. In A. J. Elliot & C. S. Dweck (Eds.), *Handbook of competence and motivation* (pp. 122–140). New York: Guilford Press.

Eastin, M. S. (2007). The influence of competitive and cooperative group game play on state hostility. *Human Communication Research, 33*, 450–466.

Entertainment Software Association (ESA) (2013). Essential facts about the computer and video game industry. http://www.theesa.com/facts/pdfs/esa_ef_2013.pdf.

Ericsson, K. A. (1999). Creative expertise as superior reproducible performance: Innovative and flexible aspects of expert performance. *Psychological Inquiry, 10*, 329–333.

Ewoldsen, D. R., Eno, C. A., Okdie, B. M., Velez, J. A., Guadagno, R. E., & DeCoster, J. (2012). Effect of playing violent video games cooperatively or competitively on subsequent cooperative behavior. *Cyberpsychology, Behavior and Social Networking, 15*, 277–280.

Eysenck, H. J. (1994). Creativity and personality: Word association, origence, and psychoticism. *Great Research Journal, 7*, 209–216.

Flaherty, A. W. (2005). Frontotemporal and dopaminergic control of idea generation and creative drive. *Journal of Comparative Neurology, 493*, 147–153.

Feist, G. J. (1998). A meta-analysis of the impact of personality on scientific and artistic creativity. *Personality and Social Psychological Review, 2*, 290–309.

Ferguson, C. J. (2007). The good, the bad and the ugly: A meta-analytic review of positive and negative effects of violent video games. *Psychiatric Quarterly, 78*, 309–316.

Ferguson, C. J., & Garza, A. (2011). Call of (civic) duty: Action games and civic behavior in a large sample of youth. *Computers in Human Behavior, 27*, 770–775.

Fink, A., Benedek, M., Grabner, R. H., Staudt, B., & Neubauer, A. C. (2007). Creativity meets neuroscience: Experimental tasks for the neuroscientific study of creative thinking. *Methods, 42*, 68–76.

Fink, A., Ward, T. B., & Smith, S. M. (1992). *Creative cognition: Theory, research, and applications.* Cambridge, MA: MIT Press.

Fredrickson, B. L. (2001). The role of positive emotions in positive psychology: The broaden-and-build theory of positive emotions. *American Psychologist, 56*, 218–226.

Fredrickson, B. L. (2008). Promoting positive affect. In M. Eid & R. J. Larsen (Eds.), *The science of subjective well-being* (pp. 449–468). New York: Guilford Press.

Fredrickson, B. L. (2013). Positive emotions broaden and build. In E. Ashby Plant & P. G. Devine (Eds.), *Advances in experimental social psychology: 47* (pp. 1–53). Burlington, VT: Academic Press.

Fredrickson, B. L., Cohn, M. A., Coffey, K. A., Pek, J., & Finkel, S. M. (2008). Open hearts build lives: Positive emotions, induced through loving-kindness meditation, build consequential personal resources. *Journal of Personality and Social Psychology, 95*, 1045–1062.

Gabora, L. (1995). Meme and variations: A computer model of cultural evolution. In L. Nade & D. Stein (Eds.), *1993 lectures in complex systems.* New York: Addison-Wesley.

Gabora, L., & Aerts, D. (2002). *Contextualizing concepts*. In *Proceedings of the 15th International FLAIRS Conference, May 14–17*. Pensacola Beach, FL: American Association for Artificial Intelligence (Special Track 'Categorization and Concept Representation: Models and Implications').

Galenson, D. W. (2001). *Painting outside the lines: Patterns of creativity in modern art*. Cambridge, MA: Harvard University Press.

Galenson, D. W. (2006). *Old masters and young geniuses: The two life cycles of artistic creativity*. Princeton, NJ: Princeton University Press.

Gentile, D. A. (2011). The multiple dimensions of video game effects. *Child Development Perspectives, 5*, 75–81.

Gentile, D. A., Anderson, C. A., Yukawa, S., Ihori, N., Saleem, M., Ming, L. K., & Sakamoto, A. (2009). The effects of prosocial video games on prosocial behaviors: International evidence from correlational, longitudinal, and experimental studies. *Personality and Social Psychology Bulletin, 35*, 752–763.

Gentile, D. A., & Gentile, J. R. (2008). Violent video games as exemplary teachers: A conceptual analysis. *Journal of Youth and Adolescence, 9*, 127–141.

Getzels, J. W., & Csikszentmihalyi, M. (1976). *The creative vision: A longitudinal study of problem finding in art*. New York: Wiley.

Gino, F., & Wiltermuth, S. S. (2014). Evil genius? How dishonesty can lead to greater creativity. *Psychological Science, 25*, 973–981. http://dx.doi.org/10.1177/0956797614520714. First published February 18, 2014, http://pss.sagepub.com/content/early/2014/02/18/0956797614520714.

Gough, H. G. (1979). A creative personality scale for the adjective check list. *Journal of Personality and Social Psychology, 37*, 1398–1405.

Granic, I., Lober, A., & Engels, R.C.M.E. (2013). The benefits of playing video games. *American Psychologist, 69*, 1–13.

Green, C. S., & Bavelier, D. (2012). Learning, attentional control, and action video games. *Current Biology, 22*, 197–206.

Gross, J. J., & John, O. P. (2003). Individual differences in two emotion regulation processes: Implications for affect, relationships, and well-being. *Journal of Personality and Social Psychology, 85*, 348–362.

Gruber, H. E. (1981). *Darwin on man: A psychological study of scientific creativity* (Rev. ed.). Chicago: University of Chicago Press (Original work published 1974).

Guilford, J. P. (1950). Creativity. *American Psychologist, 5*, 444–454.

Guilford, J. P. (1967a). *The nature of human intelligence*. New York: McGraw-Hill.

Guilford, J. P. (1967b). Creativity: Yesterday, today and tomorrow. *Journal of Creative Research, 1*, 3–14.

Guilford, J. P. (1968). *Creativity, intelligence and their educational implications*. San Diego, CA: Knapp.

Habibollah, N., Rohani, A. H., Aizan, T., Sharir, J., & Kumar, V. (2010). Relationship between creativity and academic achievement: A study of gender differences. *Journal of American Science, 6*, 181–190.

Harris, J. A. (2004). Measured intelligence, achievement, openness to experience, and creativity. *Personality and Individual Differences, 36*, 913–929.

He'lie, S., & Sun, R. (2010). Incubation, insight, and creative problem solving: A unified theory and a connectionist model. *Psychological Review, 117*, 994–1024.

Heilman, K. M., Nadeau, S. E., & Beversdorf, D. Q. (2003). Creative innovation: Possible brain mechanism. *Neurocase, 9*, 369–379.

Helson, R. (1999). A longitudinal study of creative personality in women. *Creativity Research Journal, 12*, 89–101.

Hocevar, D., & Bachelor, P. (1989). A taxonomy and critique of measurements used in the study of creativity. In J. A. Glover, R. R. Ronning, & C. R. Reynolds (Eds.), *Perspectives on individual differences: Handbook of creativity* (pp. 53–75). New York: Plenum Press.

Hoppe, K. D. (1988). Hemispheric specialization and creativity. *Psychiatric Clinics of North America*, *11*, 303–315.

Howard-Jones, P. A., Blakemore, S. J., Samuel, E. A., Summers, I. R., & Claxton, G. (2005). Semantic divergence and creative story generation: An fMRI investigation. *Cognitive Brain Research*, *25*, 240–250.

Isen, A. M., Daubman, K. A., & Nowicki, G. P. (1987). Positive affect facilitates creative problem solving. *Journal of Personality and Social Psychology*, *52*, 1122–1131.

Jackson, L. A., & Games, A. I. (2012). The upside of video game playing. Invited paper. Special Issue *Games for Health Journal*, *1*, 452–455.

Jackson, L. A., Witt, E. A., Games, A. I., Fitzgerald, H. E., von Eye, A., & Zhao, Y. (2012). Information technology use and creativity: Findings from the Children and Technology Project. *Computers in Human Behavior*, *28*, 370–376.

Jamison, K. R. (1989). Mood disorders and patterns of creativity in British writers and artists. *Psychiatry*, *52*, 125–134.

Kelley, T., & Littman, J. (2001). *The art of innovation: Lessons in creativity from IDEO, America's leading design firm*. New York: Currency.

Kendall, S. B. (1974). Preference for intermittent reinforcement. *Journal of the Experimental Analysis of Behavior*, *21*, 463–473.

Kok, B. E., Coffey, K. A., Cohn, M. A., Catalino, L. I., Vacharkulksemsuk, T., Algoe, S. B., Brantley, M., & Fredrickson, B. L. (2013). How positive emotions build physical health: Perceived positive social connections account for the upward spiral between positive emotions and vagal tone. *Psychological Science*, *24*, 1123–1132.

Kolb, D. A. (1971). *Individual learning styles and the learning process*. Working paper #535-571, Cambridge, MA: Sloan School of Business, MIT.

Kolb, D. A., (2014). Kolb Learning Style Inventory (KLSI), version 4 online. Haye Group. http://www.haygroup.com/leadershipandtalentondemand/ourproducts/item_details.aspx?itemid=118&-type=2; http://learningfromexperience.com/tools/Kolb-learning-style-inventory-lsi/.

Kozbelt, A. 2008a. Gombrich, Galenson, and beyond: Integrating case study and typological frameworks in the study of creative individuals. *Empirical Studies of the Arts*, *26*, 51–68.

Kozbelt, A. 2008b. Hierarchical linear modeling of creative artists' problem solving behaviors. *Journal of Creative Behavior*, *42*, 181–200.

Kozbelt, A. 2008c. Longitudinal hit ratios of classical composers: Reconciling "Darwinian" and expertise acquisition perspectives on life-span creativity. *Psychology of Aesthetics: Creativity and the Arts*, *2*, 221–235.

Kozbelt, A., Beghetto, R. A., & Runco, M. A. (2010). Theories of creativity. In J. C. Kaufman & R. J. Sternberg (Eds.), *The Cambridge handbook of creativity*. New York: Cambridge University Press.

Landauer, T. K., Foltz, P. W., & Laham, D. (1998). An introduction to Latent Semantic Analysis. *Discourse Processes*, *25*, 259–284.

Langley, P., & Jones, R. (1988). A computational model of scientific insight. In R. J. Sternberg (Ed.), *The nature of creativity: Contemporary psychological perspectives* (pp. 171–201). New York: Cambridge University Press.

Lapp, W. M., Collins, R. L., & Izzo, C. V. (1994). On the enhancement of creativity by alcohol: Pharmacology or expectation? *American Journal of Psychology*, *107*, 173–206.

Lenhart, A., Kahne, J., Middaugh, E., Macgill, A. R., Evans, C., & Vitak, J. (2008). *Teens, video games, and civics: Teens' gaming experiences are diverse and include significant social interaction and civic engagement*. Washington, DC: Pew Internet & American Life Project. Retrieved from http://www.pewinternet.org/.

Lowy, A., & Hood, P. (2004). *The power of the 2×2 matrix: Using the 2×2 thinking to solve business problems and make better decisions*. San Francisco, CA: Wiley.

Lubart, T. I., & Mouchiroud, C. (2003). Creativity: A source of difficulty in problem solving. In J. E. Davidson & R. J. Sternberg (Eds.), *The Psychology of Problem Solving* (pp. 127–148). New York: Cambridge University Press.

Lucas, R. (2003). *The creative training idea book: Inspired tips and techniques for engaging and effective learning*. New York: AMACO, American Management Association. Retrieved from http://www.american.edu/training/Profdev/upload/April-6-Quotes-on-Creativity-SCB-2.pdf.

Ludwig, A. M. (1995). *The price of greatness: Resolving the creativity and madness controversy*. New York: Guilford Press.

McCrae, R. R. (1987). Creativity, divergent thinking, and openness to experience. *Journal of Personality and Social Psychology, 52*, 1258–1265.

McGonigal, J. (2011). *Reality is broken: Why games make us better and how they can change the world*. New York: Penguin Press.

Mednick, S. A. (1962). The associative basis of the creative process. *Psychological Review, 69*, 220–232.

Meusburger, P., Funke, J., & Wunder, E. (2009). *Milieus of creativity: The role of places, environments and spatial contexts: An interdisciplinary approach to spatiality of creativity*. New York: Springer.

Michael, W. B., & Wright, C. R. (1989). Psychometric issues in the assessment of creativity. In J. A. Glover, R. R. Ronning, & C. R. Reynolds (Eds.), *Perspectives on individual differences: Handbook of creativity* (pp. 33–50). New York: Plenum Press.

Molle, M., Marshall, L., Wolf, B., Fehm, H. L., & Born, J. (1999). EEG complexity and performance measures of creative thinking. *Psychophysiology, 36*, 95–104.

Mumford, M. D. (2003). Where have we been, where are we going? Taking stock in creativity research. *Creativity Research Journal, 15*, 107–120.

Mumford, M. D., & Gustafon, S. B. (1988). Creativity syndrome: Integration, application, and innovation. *Psychological Bulletin, 103*, 27–43.

Nakamura, J., & Csikszentmihalyi, M. (2002). The concept of flow. In C. R. Synder & S. J. Lopez (Eds.), *Handbook of positive psychology* (pp. 89–105). New York: Oxford University Press.

O'Hara, L. A., & Sternberg, R. J. (1999). Creativity and intelligence. In R. J. Sternberg (Ed.), *Handbook of creativity*. New York: Cambridge University Press.

O'Quin, K., & Besemer, S. P. (1989). The development, reliability and validity of the revised creative product semantic scale. *Creativity Research Journal, 2*, 267–278.

Plucker, J. A., & Beghetto, R. A. (2004). Why creativity is domain general, why it looks domain specific, and why the distinction does not matter. In R. J. Sternberg, E. L. Grigorenko, & J. L. Singer (Eds.), *Creativity: From potential to realization* (pp. 153–167). Washington, DC: American Psychological Association.

Poldinger, W. (1986). The relation between depression and art. *Psychopathology, 19*, 263–268.

Post, F. (1994). Creativity and psychopathology. A study of 291 world-famous men. *British Journal of Psychiatry, 165*, 22–34.

Post, F. (1996). Verbal creativity, depression and alcoholism. An investigation of 100 American and British writers. *British Journal of Psychiatry, 169*, 379.

Prabhakaran, R., Green, A. E., & Gray, J. R. (2013). Thin slices of creativity: Using single-word utterances to assess creative cognition. *Behavior Research Methods, 46*(3), 641–659. http://dx.doi.org/10.3758/s13428-013-0401-7.

Prensky, M. (2012). *From digital natives to digital wisdom: Hopeful essays for 21st century learning*. Thousand Oaks, CA: Corwin Press.

Puccio, G. J., Argona, C., Daley, K., & Fonseza, J. (2010). *The guidebook for creativity assessment measures and methods*. Buffalo, NY: SUNY Buffalo State College. Retrieved October 20, 2010 from http://www.buffalostate.edu/creativity/.

Puccio, G. J. & Murdock, M. C. (Eds.), (1999). *Creativity assessment: Readings and resources*. New York: Creative Education Foundation.

Puccio, G. J., Treffinger, D. J., & Talbot, R. J. (1995). Exploratory examination of relationships between creativity styles and creative products. *Creativity Research Journal, 8*, 157–172.

Rubenson, D. L., & Runco, M. A. (1992). The psychoeconomic approach to creativity. *New Ideas in Psychology, 10*, 131–147.

Ruggiero, T. E. (2000). Uses and gratifications in the 21st century. *Mass Communication & Society, 3*, 3–37.

Runco, M. A. (Ed.), (1994). *Problem finding, problem solving, and creativity*. Norwood, NJ: Ablex.

Runco, M. A. (2010). Divergent thinking, creativity and ideation. In J. C. Kaufman & R. J. Sternberg (Eds.), *Cambridge handbook of creativity* (pp. 413–446). New York: Cambridge University Press.

Runco, M. A., & Albert, R. S. (2010). Creativity research. In J. C. Kaufman & R. J. Sternberg (Eds.), *Cambridge handbook of creativity* (pp. 447–486). New York: Cambridge University Press.

Runco, M. A., & Chand, I. (1995). Cognition and creativity. *Educational Psychology Review, 7*, 243–267.

Runco, M. A., Millar, G., Acar, S., & Cramond, B. (2010). Torrance Tests of Creative Thinking as predictors of personal and public achievement: A fifty-year follow-up. *Creativity Research Journal, 22*, 361–368.

Russoniello, C. V., O'Brien, K., & Parks, J. M. (2009). EEG, HRV and psychological correlates while playing Bejeweled II: A randomized controlled study. In B. K. Wiederhold & G. Riva (Eds.), *Annual review of cybertherapy and telemedicine 2009: Advance technologies in the behavioral, social and neurosciences 7*. (pp. 189–192). Amsterdam, Netherlands: Interactive Media Institute and IOS Press.

Ryan, R. M., Rigby, C. S., & Przybylski, A. (2006). The motivational pull of video games: A self-determination theory approach. *Motivation and Emotion, 30*, 347–363.

Salminen, M., & Ravaja, N. (2008). Increased oscillatory theta activation evoked by violent digital game events. *Neuroscience Letters, 435*, 69–72.

Sawyer, R. K. (2006). *Explaining creativity: The science of human innovation*. New York: Oxford University Press.

Schmidhuber, J. (2006). Developmental robotics: Optimal artificial curiosity, creativity, music, and the fine arts. *Connection Science, 18*, 173–187.

Schmidhuber, J. (2010). Formal theory of creativity, fun, and intrinsic motivation (1990–2010). *IEEE Transactions on Autonomous Mental Development, 2*, 230–247.

Schmidhuber, J. (2012). A formal theory of creativity to model the creation of art. In J. McCormack & M. d'Inverno (Eds.), *Computers and creativity*. New York: Springer.

Sherry, J. L. (2004). Flow and media enjoyment. *Communication Theory, 14*, 328–347.

Silvia, P. J. (2008). Another look at creativity and intelligence: Exploring higher-order models and probably confounds. *Personality and Individual Differences, 44*, 1012–1021.

Silvia, P. J., Kaufman, J. C., & Pretz, J. E. (2009). Is creativity domain-specific? Latent class models of creative accomplishments and creative self-descriptions. *Psychology of Aesthetics, Creativity, and the Arts, 3*, 139–148.

Simon, H. A. (1966). Scientific discovery and the psychology of problem solving. In R. G. Colodny (Ed.), *Mind and cosmos: Essays in contemporary science and philosophy* (pp. 22–40). Pittsburgh, PA: University of Pittsburgh Press.

Simon, H. A. (1972). Theories of bounded rationality. In C. B. McGuire & R. Radner (Eds.), *Decision and organization: A volume in honor of Jacob Marschak* (pp. 161–176). Amsterdam, Netherlands: North-Holland.

Simonton, D. K. (1988). *Scientific genius*. New York: Cambridge University Press.

Simonton, D. K. (1999). *Origins of genius: Darwinian perspectives on creativity*. New York: Oxford University Press.

Simonton, D. K. (2012). Quantifying creativity: Can measures span the spectrum? *Dialogues in Clinical Neuroscience, 14*, 100–104.

Steinkuehler, C., & Duncan, S. (2008). Scientific habits of mind in virtual worlds. *Journal of Science Education and Technology, 17*, 530–543.

Sternberg, R. J. (1988). A three-facet model of creativity. In R. J. Sternberg (Ed.), *The nature of creativity: Contemporary psychological perspectives* (pp. 125–147). New York: Cambridge University Press.

Sternberg, R. J. (2006). The nature of creativity. *Creativity Research Journal, 18,* 87–98.

Sternberg, R. J., Kaufman, J. C., & Pretz, J. E. (2002). *The creativity conundrum: A propulsion model of kinds of creative contributions.* New York: Psychology Press.

Sternberg, R. J., & Lubart, T. I. (1992). Buy low and sell high: An investment approach to creativity. *Current Directions in Psychological Science, 1,* 1–5.

Subotnik, R. F., & Arnold, K. D. (1996). Success and sacrifice: The costs of talent fulfillment for women in science. In K. D. Nobel Arnold & R. F. Subotnik (Eds.), *Remarkable women: Perspectives on female talent development* (pp. 260–280). Cresskill, NJ: Hampton Press.

Sweetser, P., & Wyeth, P. (2005). GameFlow: A model for evaluating player enjoyment in games. *Computers in Entertainment, 3*(3A), 1–24.

Tear, M. J., & Nielsen, M. (2013). Failure to demonstrate that playing violent video games diminishes prosocial behavior. *PloS One, 8,* e68382.

Tierney, P., Farmer, S. M., & Graen, G. B. (1999). An examination of leadership and employee creativity: The relevance of traits and relationships. *Personnel Psychology, 52,* 591–620.

Torrance, E. P. (1966). *Torrance tests of creative thinking: Directions manual and scoring guide.* Bensenville, IL: Scholastic Testing Service.

Torrance, E. P. (1974). *Torrance Tests of Creative Thinking.* Scholastic Testing Service.

Torrance, E. P. (1980). Growing up creatively gifted: The 22-year longitudinal study. *Creative Child and Adult Quarterly, 3,* 148–158.

Torrance, E. P. (1995). Insights about creativity: Questioned, rejected, ridiculed, ignored. *Educational Psychology Review, 7,* 313–322.

Torrance, E. P. (1972). Predictive validity of Torrance Tests of Creative Thinking. *Journal of Creative Behavior, 6,* 236–262.

Uttal, D. H., Meadow, N. G., Tipton, E., Hand, L. L., Alden, A. R., Warren, C., et al. (2013). The malleability of spatial skills: A meta-analysis of training studies. *Psychological Bulletin, 139,* 352–402.

Velez, J. A., Mahood, C., Ewoldsen, D. R., & Moyer-Gusé, E. (2012). Ingroup versus outgroup conflict in the context of violent video game play: The effect of cooperation on increased helping and decreased aggression. *Communication Research, 41,* 607–626. http://dx.doi.org/10.1177/0093650212456202, Advance online publication.

Ventura, M., Shute, V., & Zhao, W. (2013). The relationship between video game use and a performance-based measure of persistence. *Computers & Education, 60,* 52–58.

Vygotsky, L. (1978). *Mind in society: The development of higher psychological functions.* Cambridge, MA: Harvard University Press.

Wai, J., Lubinski, D., Benbow, C. P., & Steiger, J. H. (2010). Accomplishment in science, technology, engineering, and mathematics (STEM) and its relation to STEM educational dose: A 25-year longitudinal study. *Journal of Educational Psychology, 102,* 860–871.

Wallach, M. A., & Kogan, N. (1965). *Modes of thinking in young children.* New York: Holt, Reinhart, & Winston.

Wallis, G. (1926). *The art of thought.* New York: Harcourt, Brace.

Weisberg, R. W. (1999). Creativity and knowledge: A challenge to theories. In R. J. Sternberg (Ed.), *Handbook of creativity* (pp. 226–250). New York: Cambridge University Press.

Weisberg, R. W. (2006). *Creativity: Understanding innovation in problem solving, science, invention, and the arts.* Hoboken, NJ: Wiley.

Winkielman, P., & Knutson, B. (2007). Affective influence on judgments and decisions: Moving towards core mechanisms. *Review of General Psychology, 11,* 179–192.

Winslow, E. K., & Solomon, G. T. (1993). Entrepreneurs: Architects of innovation, paradigm pioneers and change. *Journal of Creative Behavior, 27,* 75–88.

Wittgenstein, L. (2010). *Philosophical investigations.* New York: John Wiley & Sons.

Zeng, L., Proctor, R. W., & Salvendy, G. (2011). Can traditional divergent thinking tests be trusted in measuring and predicting real-world creativity? *Creativity Research Journal, 23,* 24.

Media References

When gaming is good for you: hours of intense play change the adult brain; better multitasking, decision-making and even creativity. R. L. Hotz. http://online.wsj.com/news/articles/SB10001424052970203458604577263273943183932. March 13, 2012.

Video games help with creativity. http://content.usatoday.com/communities/gamehunters/post/2011/11/research-video-games-help-with-creativity/1#.Uu-SRLOA2Uk. November 2, 2011.

Video game playing tied to creativity, research shows. http://www.sciencedaily.com/releases/2011/11/111102125355.htm. November 9, 2011.

Ways video games can actually be good for you. Drew Guarini. http://www.huffingtonpost.com/babblecom/reasons-why-your-kids_b_2664141.html. November 7, 2013.

Video game children are more creative. http://www.telegraph.co.uk/technology/video-games/8868033/Video-gaming-children-more-creative.html. February 3, 2014.

Videogames: A gateway to creativity http://www.miamiherald.com/2013/05/17/3402875/video-games-a-gateway-to-creativity.html. May 17, 2013.

The Impact of Video Game Play on Human (and Orc) Creativity

Nicholas D. Bowman[1], Rachel Kowert[2]
and Christopher J. Ferguson[3]

[1]Communication Studies, West Virginia University, Morgantown, WV, USA
[2]University of Münster, Münster, Germany
[3]Department Chair Psychology, Stetson University, DeLand, FL, USA

In the early 1960s, computing technology had begun to find its way into research laboratories around the world, greatly accelerating the pace of the scientific process in assisting with myriad data processing and analysis procedures. In this rise, while many of these researchers had used computing tools to help in their daily work, few had known the limits of these machines. How much information can they process at one time, and can they handle constant user input? Could this information be displayed graphically in unique and interesting ways, and could the user alter the on-screen display instantaneously? Finally, could the experience be a fun one perhaps that engages the researcher to experiment or even play with the machine itself? These curiosities set into motion the first criteria for "a good computer demonstration" (Graetz, 1981, para. 26) that, through decades of refinement and engagement, became the modern video game.

A visit to the Massachusetts Institutes of Technology during this time would have surely included a stop at the Electrical Engineering Department, running one of these early computers in the Programmed Data Processor-1 (PDP-1)—one of the first commercially available computers with a specific focus on user interface rather than computing cycles (Computer History Museum, n.d.). For budding programmers in MIT's Kluge Room (a word with snarky connotations that describes a set of mismatched parts, often cobbled together for a single function—derived from the German word "Kluge" for "clever"), the PDP-1 represented, according to Graetz (1981), the world's first "toy computer": a mini-computer (compared to then-standard room-sized mainframes) with a native display and an open programming language.

The Kluge Room saw the birth of several different "hacker" computer programs not so much aimed at performing or solving discrete computational problems, but rather to demonstrate the capability of the machines of the time—such as a Bouncing Ball program that displayed (as its namesake suggests) a single pixel "ball" bouncing and careening off the different surfaces of a virtual box, mimicking the physical properties of a real ball. Another game saw onlookers drawing a maze with a light pen, and watching as an animated mouse tried to navigate the maze to find a wedge of cheese (and, for added fun, onlookers could give the mouse a martini to hinder its navigational acumen). A third game was a standard tic-tac-toe variety, which had onlookers playing the classic game against a rudimentary artificial intelligence.

In each of these games—and indeed in the criteria laid out by the original Kluge Room scientists—we see a common element related to play and creativity. Each program was built as a means to an end (demonstration) rather than an end to a means (discrete computation). As such, and as can be deduced by the nature of the nomenclature of the Kluge Room itself, it was a space where play and creativity were encouraged as necessary to push the limits of early computing technology.

The most enduring result of this early activity was the development of *SpaceWar!*, considered by most the first true video game. In the game, two players took control of warring spaceships (the slender Needle and the broad Wedge) locked in space combat around a high-gravity star core located in the center of the screen. Programming of this game required many elements of the earlier playful demonstrations (such as programmable physics logic from Bouncing Ball, and interface design from the mouse maze game) but provided a few novel elements, such as a multifunction joystick that allowed human players to combat each other with their own strategies—learning the affordances of the system as well as the behaviors of the other in order to create and execute effective combat strategies.

To us, the preceding story illustrates the inextricable link between video games and creativity. The earliest known video game was both borne out of and built to encourage creative and playful behavior. Likewise, this chapter provides a discussion of theory and research demonstrating the association between video game play and human creativity. The chapter will begin with a discussion of creativity and a general overview of play to orient the reader with these general concepts, and how they are linked to learning processes. Following this, video games are framed as inherently creative and playful endeavors that are well suited to stimulate the creative process as well as motivate more formal learning. The chapter will conclude by addressing popular dissent around violent video games as entertainment endeavors without redeeming qualities, suggesting that the very unsavory-yet-popular content being critiqued is also quite adept at encouraging creative thought.

CREATIVITY DEFINED

While creativity is an easy concept to understand, it is difficult to define. Numerous definitions have been proposed and many tests and models have been developed that aim to quantify this concept; however, there remains little consensus on how to best explain creativity and the creative power of the brain. One of the reasons for this lack of agreement is because creativity is not a singular concept, but rather represents traits and abilities (i.e., who we are; e.g., "he/she is creative"), processes (i.e., what we do; e.g., "the creative process") and outcomes (i.e., what we produce; e.g., "creative solutions").

Creativity as a product or something that can lead to the production of something is perhaps the most common use of the term. Definitions of this sort include ones that refer to creativity as a "novel combination of old ideas" (Boden, 1996, p. 75), the "process of 'making up' something new and valuable by transforming what is into something better" (Young, 1985, p. 77), or the ability to produce something that is both novel (i.e., original) and appropriate (i.e., useful: Ochse, 1990; Sternberg, 1988). This production of new thoughts, words, or deeds is also thought to be creativity at its most basic level (Fisher, 2004). The innate features of the person who develops the creative product or outcome (e.g., "a creative person") and the processes leading up to these outcomes can also be conceptualized as creativity (e.g., "the creative process"). Similarly, Kaufman (1999) discusses creativity as a multilevel construct that considers the process of being creative, the result of creative thinking, understanding individual differences in creativity as well as studying the times and spaces in which we enact creativity. For example, Gardner (1997) and Russ (1998) define creativity as the ability to solve problems and raise new questions. For them, it is the innate features of the person that are creative and the outcome of that creativity is simply a by-product of the individual's features. Ability-based definitions such as these are reminiscent of the right-brained/left-brained debates, which contend that some people are innately more creative (i.e., right-brained) whilst others are more logical in nature (i.e., left-brained). Conversely, Robinson (2001) argues that it is not the individual nor the outcome that constitutes creativity, but the imaginative *process*. Similarly, Lucas (2001) states that creativity is a *state of mind*.

Due to the multifaceted nature of creativity, it may be more sensible to adopt a working definition that integrates the aspects of "being" (e.g., traits, abilities, and processes) and "doing" (e.g., creating, producing). In other words, rather than of quantifying creativity as a *trait, process, or outcome*, creativity should be considered the assimilation of these factors and the integration of thoughts, ideas, and actions into new directions, solutions, and viewpoints (Young, 1985). A definition such as this provides a better understanding of the concept as well as contributing to a better understanding of its potential impact on individuals, processes, and outcomes.

On the individual level, creativity has been connected with positive psychological development and the achievement of self-actualization, personal fulfillment, and improved mental health (Cropley, 1990; Garfield, Cohen, & Roth, 1969; Rogers, 1961) as well as a range of positive personal characteristics such as flexibility, openness, and courage (Rogers, 1961). More broadly, creativity has been identified as an essential tool for innovation and finding new ways to solve problems (Fisher, 2004; Legrenzi, 2005). Due to its associations with innovation, problem solving, and mental health, there has been a constant interest in understanding the ways in which creativity can be fostered. The role of play has received particular attention in terms of its ability to encourage creativity and promote creative thinking.

PLAY AS A CREATIVE PROCESS

As defined by Huizinga (1949), play is:

> ... a free activity standing quite consciously outside 'ordinary' life as being 'not serious,' but at the same time absorbing the player intensely and utterly. It is an activity connected with no material interest, and no profit can be gained by it. It proceeds within its own proper boundaries of time and space according to fixed rules and in an orderly manner (p. 143).

The core attributes of play described by Huizinga (1949) are integrated within all play forms, from structured activities with explicit rules (e.g., games) to unstructured and spontaneous activities (e.g., playfulness). Playfulness in and of itself has also been discussed as an individual trait (Lieberman, 1977) or as a state of being (Ellis, 1973). To help to better understand the complexity of structured play, Caillois' (1958) identified four play types: Agon, Alea, Mimicry, and Ilinx. Agon refers to the competitive play, as is commonly found in traditional games such as chess or checkers. Alea refers to chance-based games, such as slot machine or lottery play. Mimicry refers to role playing, or assuming the role of a character and progressing through a narrative, and Ilinx refers to play that alters one's perceptions.

In general, the links between play—both structured and unstructured— and creative thinking skills are well documented (e.g., Getzels & Csikszentmihalyi, 1976; Howard-Jones, Taylor, & Sutton, 2002; Lieberman, 1977; Mainemelis & Ronson, 2006; Russ, Robins, & Christiano, 1999; Sternberg, 1988). When establishing the first kindergarten in 1937, Friedrich Froebel developed a set of toys with the explicit goal of helping children learn about numbers, sizes, shapes, and colors (Brosterman, 1997). Montessori (1912) also created a range of materials to promote learning through play. Play has also been associated with a greater disposition towards creativity later in life (Clark, Griffing, & Johnson, 1989; Russ et al., 1999) as well as the stimulation and development of a range of creative processes such as problem finding, framing, and solving, divergent thinking, and practice with alternative solutions (Getzels & Csikszentmihalyi, 1976; Mainemelis & Ronson, 2006; Russ et al., 1999; Sternberg, 1988).

Part of the reason why play is so successful at stimulating creative thinking is because play is a creative process in and of itself. Playful activities allow individuals to approach new and novel situations in unique ways free from external constraints. Play can free one from "means-end" thinking and allow for the adoption of novel and new solutions (Basadur, 1994; Mainemelis & Ronson, 2006; Runco & Sakamoto, 1999). Furthermore, engagement in the activity is intrinsically rewarding, as it offers the spontaneous pleasures of play and playfulness, self-expression, and satisfaction (Fisher, 2004). Through this process, play can foster new, novel associations between ideas, objects, and behaviors (Bruner, 1963). Play stimulates creativity by allowing the exploration and practice of many alternative responses to a particular task without restriction (Getzels & Csikszentmihalyi, 1976; Torrance, 1995).

VIDEO GAMES: TECHNOLOGIES CREATED FOR (CREATIVE) PLAY

While some activities incorporate only a single form of play from Caillois' (1958) taxonomy, video games often incorporate a variety of these elements. For instance, popular video games such as *World of Warcraft (WoW)* and *Call of Duty (CoD)* combine Alea (e.g., through the randomly generated encounters and rewards), Agon (through competition with other players and strategy to navigate the game space), and Mimicry (through the role playing of a character in a fantasy-based world in *WoW* and the adoption of a main character and progressing through the narrative in *CoD*). While these examples highlight the multidimensionality of structured play within video games, video games can also foster unstructured play. For example, *Minecraft*, a highly popular sandbox game (i.e., the player has tools to modify the game space and choose how they want to engage within it), is characterized by its lack of rules and free-form play. In this unstructured space, players are free to engage in almost any way they choose, whether it be through exploring the environment, generating content within the game (e.g., building structures), or interacting with others within the space.

Moreover, video games are unique outlets for play as they provide users a range of playful activities within a single game space. For example, players can explore new lands, solve riddles and puzzles, and cooperate with others to achieve a difficult task, or craft something, all within a relatively short play period. Indeed, Gee (2003) argues that video game play is inherently a learning endeavor, as most video games require the player to familiarize themselves with and eventually master a novel set of associations and rules in any number of novel game environments. This range of playful activities not only contributes to the enjoyment of the medium but also potentially provides a wide range of learning experiences. Furthermore, as "simulated environments," video games are also encouraging players to solve various "real" in-game problems in creative ways, and allow them to do so without real-world consequences (Fisher, 2004; Glynn, 1994). For example, in the popular *SimCity* games, players are tasked with the role of a civil engineer—tasked with building and maintaining successful and thriving cities while carefully balancing economic, environmental and social issues, and threats. However, these consequences are free of real-world penalties, as the player can simply "retry" the challenge. In this sense, video games are unique, as they are able to prove playful spaces that resemble real-world scenarios and situations but yet are distinct from everyday life. On this point, Koster (2003) writes about video game play as a form of inherent edutainment, as progressing through a video game requires the player to constantly learn how to understand and enact any number of abstract activities and associations in a digital space.

Video Games and Flow

While video game play is often thought of as simply a source of fun and entertainment, it is also a vehicle for learning, particularly creative learning, as specified by Koster (2003). Video games are particularly effective sources of creative learning due to the fact that they often induce a state of "flow" (Csikszentmihalyi, 1975, 1990, 1993; Csikszentmihalyi & Csikszentmihalyi, 1988; Moneta & Csikszentmihalyi, 1996, 1999). A "flow experience" refers to a situation of complete absorption or engagement in an activity (Csikszentmihalyi, 1990). As further described by Csikszentmihalyi (1975), when in a flow state:

> ... players [here, not specific to video games] shift into a common mode of experience when they become absorbed in their activity. This mode is characterized by a narrowing of the focus of awareness, so that irrelevant perceptions and thoughts are filtered out; by a loss of self-consciousness, by a responsiveness to clear goals and unambiguous feedback; and by a sense of control over the environment ... it is this common flow experience that people adduce as the main reason for performing the activity (p. 72).

Video games are particularly suited to encourage flow and stimulate learning as they meet the preconditions described by Csikszentmihalyi (1993) that are needed to induce a flow state. As described by Sherry (2004), video games: (1) often provide detailed concrete goals and rules; (2) provide action that can be manually or automatically adjusted to one's capabilities; (3) provide clear feedback (e.g., through scores, achievements, or progress reports, etc.); and (4) provide visual and aural information that helps remove distractions from the task and facilitates the user's concentration. Perhaps most importantly, video games are able to induce flow states when they allow for an optimal balancing of system challenge and player skill (Bowman, 2008; Sherry, 2004) and games that are able to adjust this balance dynamically are often the most successful (Chen, 2007).

When in a state of flow, people experience improved focus on the task, a sense of active control, the merging of action and awareness, a loss of self-awareness, a distortion of the experience of time, and they experience the task as being the only necessary justification for continuing it

(Csikszentmihalyi, 1990). Due to the conglomeration of these qualities, video games are able to induce a state of flow in games ranging from the most casual puzzle games such as *Candy Crush* (in which players learn the role and placement of different colored candy shapes before the system challenges this knowledge with increasingly impossible reaction time pressure and increasingly complex candy obstacles) to more complicated role-playing games like the *Fable* series (in which players learn the basics of navigation and character customization before being challenged by an increasingly complex social and functional hierarchy). These features, combined with video games' accessibility, popularity, and social reinforcement (i.e., players are highly motivated to compete with their peers in video game spaces; see Lucas & Sherry, 2004), contribute to video games being an ideal environment to create and maintain flow experiences (Sherry, 2004) and stimulate learning (Csikszentmihalyi & LeFevre, 1989; Kirriemuir, 2003; Moneta & Csikszentmihalyi, 1996). In fact, games designers such as Chen and Koster and education scholars such as Gee all contend that not only is learning a proxy outcome of video game play (games must be learned in order to be continually played), the lessons learned in video games are not related to uncovering the one solution to a finite problem but, rather, uncovering the multitude of solutions to an infinite number of problems in a given "possibility space" (the term for games coined by famous designer Will Wright of *SimCity* fame). Games designed to encourage flow are games that are constantly challenging the player, who in turn is constantly developing creative ways to overcome those challenges.

Video Games and Authorship

When playing a video game, one is essentially interacting with an unfinished text: developers have written lines of code to represent a digital space populated with its own system of rules and mechanics, narrative, sounds, and digital citizenry. These pieces are carefully crafted so as to be as functional and interesting as possible, yet are given to the player in an inherently incomplete form. Unlike more traditional forms of entertainment media that are created as complete and closed texts (such as books, movies, and television shows), Collins (2013) notes that games are required to be actively used in order to be fully experienced. Moreover, these experiences—as they are subject to the ability and creativity of the gamer—can vary greatly from player to player, or even from one play experience to the next. Indeed, the implicit contract of any interactive environment is that it provides the user control over the form and content of on-screen content (Steuer, 1992), and this interactivity is key to the medium's ability to immerse the player into the game (Tamborini & Bowman, 2010). Bowman and Banks (in press) argued from a Bartheian perspective (re: *Death of the author*; Barthes, 1967) that video games can be considered an example of co-authorship between the designers and the authors, requiring the creative efforts of both in order to be fully realized as finished products.

VIDEO GAMES AS CREATIVE TOOLS: EMPIRICAL RESULTS

To this point, we have demonstrated broadly that video games are tools tailor-made for creativity and play. While not all of the arguments proposed above have been empirically tested, a few studies have found significant associations—both causal and correlational—between increased video game play and a variety of different cognitive and affective faculties associated with creativity. Other work has found that video game players tend to show more positive attitudes towards creative endeavors, as in fact creativity as a novel pursuit in its own right.

Video Games and Cognitive Ability

In early 2010, the US Office of Naval Research (ONR) released the results of an internal study that demonstrated video game players to be as much as 20% "smarter" than nonplayers—at least as reported by mainstream media at the time. More specifically, educational psychologist Ray Perez found that gamers had increased perceptual and cognitive abilities, likely attributed to the manner in which gamers interface with video games. These findings were considered integral to the Department of Defense, as explained by Perez:

> We have to train people to be quick on their feet—agile problem solvers, agile thinkers—to be able to counteract and develop counter tactics to terrorists on the battlefield … It's really about human inventiveness and creativeness and being able to match wits with the enemy. *Freeman (2010, para. 5)*

While the claim that video game play could be more than a mindless leisure activity might have appeared novel at the level of public discourse, it had been an increasingly intense focus of research since at least the mid-1980s. Greenfield (1984) speculated that video games could positively impact our human cognitive capacities, in particular visual capabilities—claims based on correlational data by Griffith, Voloschin, Gibb, and Bailey (1983). Many of Greenfield's speculations were tested with modest empirical support (outlined in Green and Bavelier, 2006), such as the ability for gamers to be more adept at dividing their attention between different tasks (Greenfield, DeWinstanley, Kilpatrick, & Kaye, 1994). Green and

Bavelier (2003) found that playing (at the time) popular video games—such as the sandbox game *Grand Theft Auto 3*, first-person shooters *Half-Life* and *Halo*, and the animated fighting game *Marvel vs. Capcom*—lead to substantial increases in visual attention. Other work using first-person shooters such as *Quake 3* and games from the *Call of Duty* series (Bowman & Boyan, 2008; Bowman, Weber, Tamborini, & Sherry, 2013) has found that cognitive skills associated with eye–hand coordination as well as mental rotation and targeting ability (both moving and fixed) are positive predictors of video game performance and, to a lesser degree, enjoyment.

In terms of broad intelligence—such as those claims made by popular media in response to ORN's 2010 press release—work by van Schie and Wiegman (2006) did find that in a group of Dutch schoolchildren, general intelligence was higher for children who spent an increased amount of their leisure time playing video games. In fact, by the late 1980s, Rabbitt, Banerji, and Szymanski (1989) had found strong and significant correlations between intelligence quotient exam scores and performance at the arcade game *Space Fortress*. Notably, while specific cognitive skills and general intelligence are not per se creativity, both—along with trait personality factors (outside the focus of this chapter)—have been linked to increased creativity (cf. Eysenck, 1995; Guilford, 1968).

Video Games and Creative Ability

While a good deal of research has focused on the association between video games and cognitive skills, recent work has examined the role of video game play in encouraging more positive affect towards creativity and creative thought. As one of the first studies on the topic, Jackson (2012) and Jackson et al. (2012) found in a population of 12-year-olds that those who played more video games as part of their leisure time were significantly more creative than those who did not. Their work found that when given a task to write a story about an elf, there were significant correlations (ranging from 0.40 to 0.59, all at the $p < 0.01$ level of greater) between video game play and the student's creativeness when drawing forms (given an "egg" as a starting point, gamers drew more elaborate shapes than nongamers) and their ability to write a novel story about a fictitious elf character. In addition, these effects held when controlling for race, gender (although boys did play more games than girls, both benefited in creativity gains), other technology usage (such as computers and the internet), general intelligence, and even the content of the game (both violent and nonviolent games increased creativity).

Studies have also found video games to foster positive feelings about the creative process. Ott and Pozzi (2012) gave primary school studies access to a variety of casual puzzle games over a three-year period, and found that as students played more of these games, they demonstrated more curiosity, motivation, and joy related to creativity. Sundar and Hutton (2010) found that heightened arousal levels associated with playing the physical activity game *Dance Dance Revolution* were associated with increased mood and creativity. While one might question whether arousal and mood in their study were induced by game play or physical activity inherent to the game played, other work by Bowman and Tamborini (2012, 2015) has demonstrated that video game play can impact mood—with more demanding games (games that require more control input from the player) resulting in more positive post-game-play mood to a point at which controls are too demanding, resulting in negative mood.

Video Games as Creative Expression

One of the more enduring elements of video games that fosters a creative spirit is the manner in which they allow players to construct identities. Grodal (2000) and Nakamura (2000) similarly argue that a particularly appealing element of video games is their ability to allow users to create and experiment with a variety of different personae. In creating these in-game personae, players have also been known to personify their on-screen character, imbuing them with a sense of agency and personality. In deep interviews with a set of highly engaged *World of Warcraft* players, Banks (2013) found that players actively construct headcanons—or idiosyncratic stories about the gaming experience—that include speculations about how the avatar (the on-screen character) might be affected at the cognitive, behavioral, and emotional level by the relationship between player and avatar. Such an act requires a great deal of thought-projection on the player's behalf into the digital space, as was suggested by subsequent linguistic analyses on these interviews (Banks & Bowman, 2013, 2014).

In a content analysis of in-game behaviors, Wright, Boria, and Breidenbach (2002) found several instances of gamer-created content consider by most to be far beyond a simple act of game play. For example, textual analysis of chat logs from players of the first-person shooter *Counter-Strike* found highly sophisticated usage of contextualized humor and joke-work, from simple naming mechanics (naming oneself "Osama bin laggin" referring to a then-topical news item and referring to lagging—a common issue in online gaming by which a computer network is unable to process data at the same speed as a computer terminal, resulting in a temporarily broken play experience). Perhaps more related to creativity *per se*, their study also found *Counter-Strike* players to be highly adept at using in-game tools to recreate (with great accuracy) real-world simulations of game maps, as well as logos and other elements not native to the original game environment. Related to Wright et al.'s findings (albeit not a research report), in mid-2013 *Time* magazine profiled Jacob Granberry, an artist and fan of the *Game of Thrones* novel-cum-television series, who has overseen a complete digital reconstruction of the land of Westeros in the construction video game *Minecraft*.[1] The land, estimated to be the size of South America in the novels, is built to 1/100 scale in the video game and has had thousands of contributors who apply to assist in the land's construction at http://westeroscraft.com. When working on this construction, gamers usually configure *Minecraft* be played in what is called "Creative Mode" by which players are able to navigate the land freely (by flight, no less) without taking any damage from other players, or needing sustenance in order to survive.

CREATIVITY FROM DIGITAL VIOLENCE?

On first blush, this might seem an odd discussion to have within the larger focus on gaming and creativity. However, given the preponderance of research focused on video games and aggressive outcomes (cf. Anderson & Bushman, 2001; Sherry, 2001) as well as the general popularity and prevalence of the content itself (Smith, Lachlan, & Tamborini, 2003), it seems germane to discuss the impact of such content on players' creativity and playful outcomes.

Labeling Content in Video Games

One of the lingering debates regarding video games involves violent content and whether such content is harmful, particularly for minors. We note upfront that exactly what constitutes a "violent video game" is often vague. For example, in one recent court case in which defense attorneys attempted to blame video games for a mass homicide, one scholar had to acknowledge that definitions of "violent video games" were so broad that even games such as *Pac Man* could be considered "violent video games" (Rushton, 2013). Indeed many older studies of violent video games included games such as *Centipede* and *Zaxxon* (see Ferguson, 2013) as "violent video games" despite that few people consider such games threats to society several decades later. From this, we proceed with the label "violent video games" with considerable caution, noting that this term is so broad and vague that the conceptual space occupied by this term is less meaningful than it may appear.

That having been said, games with violent content certainly tend to be popular sellers. For example, the 2013 release of *Grand Theft Auto V* has set at least seven records for entertainment media sales, including the

---

[1] Footage from the *Time* interview can be found at *Time*'s official YouTube channel: https://www.youtube.com/watch?v=WOZ6RjoNKbw.

generation of $815.7 million within 24h of its worldwide release while selling nearly 12 million individual units (Guenette, 2013). These sales figures are not surprising. Media with violent content have historically been popular, from the epic of *Gilgamesh* through religious texts with violence such as the Judeo-Christian Torah/Bible through Greek and Shakespearian plays, literature and, more recently, movies, television, comic books and, ultimately, video games.[2]

As noted above, exactly what is considered "violent media" or "violent video games" is ill-defined, so much so that a wide variety of art from religious texts such as the Bible of Hindu Ramayana through fairy tales, Disney movies, Looney Tunes cartoons, rock music by bands such as Pink Floyd or Twisted Sister, and basic video games could all be considered "violent media." Indeed, vague definitions of "violent video games" have been used to make frightening claims about violence in even E-rated games (games rated appropriate for all children) despite that most such games would be considered non-offensive by most individuals (Thompson & Haninger, 2001). Regarding the general notion of violence as a construct, recent work by Tamborini, Weber, Bowman, Eden, and Skalski (2013) reported that violence is not only a many-splintered perception variable comprised of audience interpretations of a given act's justification, graphicness and realism, but also that relative perceptions of graphicness (depictions of blood and gore) were the *least* important perception in explaining audiences labeling an act as violent or not. Indeed, such lack of clarity in these terms was one issue that led the US Supreme Court case to strike down attempts to regulate violent video games in the Brown v EMA (2011) case.

Moreover, we posit that assumptions regarding the inherently antisocial and damaging impact of violent video game content is a potentially naïve one. Some studies have implied that video games are easily divided into pools of "violent" and "prosocial" games, with the implication that "violent games are antisocial, and prosocial games appropriate for children" (e.g., Gentile et al., 2009). However, even these studies consistently find that exposure to "violent" and "prosocial" content are highly correlated, suggesting that many games include both violent and prosocial content. Thus we argue it is time to conceptualize games in ways that are more sophisticated and move beyond the content-heavy approach to discussion of "violent video games."

---

[2] This historical popularity of media with violent content has led some scholars to suggest that such media appeal to intrinsic human needs both to confront their own dark side, as well as to confront their fears of death (see J. Kottler's 2011 book, *The Lust For Blood: Why We Are Fascinated by Death, Murder, Horror and Violence* for a protracted discussion on this point). Critiques of media with violent content have also been historical, given that such content bridges debates about morality and freedom of expression.

Moreover, not all audiences who play games with questionable content necessarily view the content as such. In a study on morality and decision making, Joeckel, Bowman, and Dogruel (2012) found that players were more likely to violate tenets of morality such as fairness and harm only when those tenets were not particularly salient to their personal worldview (cf. Haidt & Joseph, 2004). Conversely, when these moral dilemmas were associated with strong moral leanings, violations of those moral tenets were observed less than 20% of the time. Such a finding led the researchers to conclude that video game play is not automatically a question between behaving in a moral or immoral fashion, but also must consider the fact that some in-game decisions are amoral—at least, in the eyes of the player. Similar work by Banks and Bowman (2014) also finds that even in highly immersive and social worlds such as *World of Warcraft*, there is a good deal of variability in how players view their in-game avatar—some regarding the character as a tool used to accomplish nonvalenced (at least, from a moral standpoint) goals.

Objectionable Content and Creativity

Given so much of the debate on video games with violent content has focused on the potential "harm" of such content, relatively little research has focused on the positive aspects of video games with violent content on creativity. Early discussion of the impact of violent games and media on children's creativity mainly was speculative. For instance, Jones (2003) argued that media with violent content serves a developmental purpose for kids both in confronting fears and in fostering creativity. Such early work was non-empirical in nature, however.

More recently, Olson (2010) has drawn on the developmental literature to conclude that interest in video games with violent content is a normal part of development for youth and does not represent a risk factor for negative outcomes. Instead, exploring "edgy" material appears to increase children's ability to process and consider such material, particularly with parental involvement. Indeed, excessive restriction of such content may result in a truncated set of experiences that both decrease children's ability to process negative events in real life, but also decrease the full range of expressive activities. It is important to note that many video games with violent content, including games such as *Doom*, *Bioshock*, *Tom Clancy's Splinter Cell*, and *God of War*, have been enshrined as art by Smithsonian Institute (2012), and there is increasing societal-level appreciation of video games as an art form (cf. Bogost, 2011; Clarke & Mitchell, 2007). Whether censorship/regulation of video games would restrict the creative achievements of youth is a fair question and one yet to be fully explored.

The recent review of video game research by Granic, Lobel, and Engels (2014) provides an excellent backdrop for considering influences on creativity. Granic et al. specifically note that video games with violent content contribute to positive developments in many areas including creativity—findings collaborated by work cited earlier in this chapter (cf. Jackson et al., 2012; Wright et al., 2002). Research by Karla Hamlen has also linked playing video games, including genres with violent content, to creativity. For instance, in one recent paper, Hamlen (2011) found that children who participated in adventure and role-playing games were particularly likely to use their imaginations to put themselves into the story and character motivations. Such games, which would include examples such as *Skyrim* or *Tomb Raider*, may be particularly effective in promoting creativity and imagination in children. Other research by Hamlen (2009) has indicated that video game play, including play in genres with violent content, is associated with increased creativity as indicated by standardized assessment instruments.

FUTURE RESEARCH

At this point, we have defined and explained creativity and play—both at a general level and specific to video games. We have argued that video games are a technology borne of and tailor-made to foster creativity, and we have demonstrated emerging empirical evidence to support these claims. At the same time, we recognize that there has been scant work specifically aimed at studying the impact of video games on fostering creativity in people—with only a handful of studies on the topic since 2010. However, as research into video games begins to broaden in scope beyond a myopic focus on aggressive and antisocial impacts of gaming content to also consider their potential prosocial benefits, future work might consider with much more scientific rigor the impact of these technologies (and their content) on the creative process.

One area of future work might consider giving more careful attention to the more granular associations between different types of video games and creative outcomes. For example, ludic differences that tend to be represented in different video game genres (such as the heavy emphasis on planning and prediction in strategy games or the improvisational nature of game play encouraged by open-ended sandbox games) and these differences are likely related to more specific aspects of creativity (in this case, creative problem solving or expression). In addition, content-specific differences in games—such as games that are more fun and enjoyable compared to games with more somber and meaningful content (cf. Oliver et al., 2013)—might also invoke different emotional and cognitive responses in players, which could relate to various creative outcomes. Related to these points, future work could look to design and test more rigorous case/control designs so that nascent correlational findings (such as those reported by Jackson et al., 2012) can be examined through a causal lens.

Another area of future research might consider the role that video game play has in neuroplasticity—the brain's ability to alter its interconnected structure in response to outside stimuli. While classical thought assumed the brain to be in a comparatively static form from birth, groundbreaking work by Pasual-Leone, Amedi, Fregni, and Merabet (2005) argues that the brain is a dynamic system constantly altered through experience throughout the life-span. Work associating cognitive and video game play has shown these effects to be enduring—for as much as 18 months according to data from the ONR studies, but these studies have not been extended to studying lasting impacts of video game play on creative processes. Already scholars in communication and media psychology have begun to incorporate research involving the neural correlates of game play in terms of the neural synchrony associated with flow states (Weber, Tamborini, Westcott-Baker, & Kantor, 2009), and such work might hold promise for understanding the impact of gaming on the formation and maintenance of neurological networks conducive to creativity.

Yet another area of work might further investigate arguments suggesting simply that more creative individuals are more drawn to video game play in the first place. Sherry, Rosaen, Bowman, and Huh (2006) found that increased cognitive skill scores were more robust predictors of video game preference and enjoyment than social factors (such as self-reported gender) or actual game performance, which can be interpreted to suggest that those with higher cognitive skills (skills related to creativity) are more motivated to play games. Ventura, Shute, and Kim (2012) found that children with higher openness to experience scores, which is a trait often linked with divergent thinking (one facet of creativity; McCrae, 1987) and general creativity (Harris, 2004) across a wide range of domains (Fiest, 1998), were more likely to play a more diverse number of video games. If creative types are playing more video games than noncreative types at very early developmental stages, there is concern that a "Matthew effect" (Walberg & Tsai, 1983) might be observed; that is, individuals already higher in creativity continue to enhance those skills even as those lower in initial creativity begin to play games. Although video games are quite popular in modern culture, not all individuals (in particular, children) play games for a variety of cultural and economic reasons, which could potentially result in creativity skill gaps.

CONCLUSION

As video games occupy a substantially larger role in media and entertainment cultures, social scientists should continue to earnestly and
rightfully study their potential impact on our thoughts, feelings, and
actions. At the same time, there must be a greater recognition that the
impact of this medium can be just as powerful in encouraging the better parts of our humanity as they can the more deleterious parts. In the
1950s, the infamous psychologist Fredric Wertham lambasted the content
of then-popular comic books for their sexual and violent nature, arguing
that their seductive influences on youth culture served as a corrosive social agent contributing directly to juvenile delinquency (Wertham, 1955).
While parents, popular press, and political leaders hailed Wertham as
a public health evangelist for his findings, they all overlooked another
aspect of comic books: their ability to encourage young minds to read
and think creatively about the world around them, such as fans of the
serial Flash Gordon aspiring to careers in space exploration (including
current NASA chief Charles Bolden; cf. Gonzalez, 2012). Indeed later in
life, Wertham spoke at the 1973 New York Comic Art Convention and
expressed regret in that his work resulted in untold numbers of children having their stories—their sources of curiosity into the world and
universe around them, and their autotelic exposure to problem-solving
and alternative perspectives—destroyed by over-zealous public interest
groups (fueled by one steadfast researcher).[3] In this vein, it is our hope
that this chapter presents a case for video games to be a potentially powerful tool which can foster and encourage creative thoughts, feelings, and
actions. While there is still much work to be done (indeed, a paucity of
research exists on this topic), we are hopeful that this chapter might serve
as an orientation to this promising area of future research. After all, the
last group of gamers who sat in a darkened college dorm room engaging
in violent and wanton acts of war ended up establishing the groundwork
for modern computer science and engineering—fields with creativity at
their (star)core.

---

[3] In fact, in 1973 Wertham published a book, *The World of fanzines: A special form of
communication* (Southern Illinois University Press), in which he outlined his theories and
findings on the correlation between comic book fanzines (a special type of comic book
usually written by fans rather than original publishers) and creativity. However, given
allegations about the scientific veracity of his original research as well as public disinterest
in his later work on television and children, Wertham's research was largely ignored.
Indeed, his appearance at the comic convention was viewed at best as dubious.

References

Anderson, C. A., & Bushman, B. J. (2001). Effects of violent video games on aggressive behavior, aggressive cognition, aggressive affect, psychological arousal, and prosocial behavior. A meta-analytic review of the scientific literature. *Psychological Science, 12*, 353–359.

Banks, J. (2013). *Human-technology relationality and self-network organization: Players and avatars in World of Warcraft*. (Unpublished doctoral dissertation). Fort Collins, CO: Colorado State University.

Banks, J., & Bowman, N. D. (2013). Close intimate playthings? Understanding player-avatar relationships as a function of attachment, agency, and intimacy. *Selected Paper of Internet Research, 3*. Retrieved from, https://spir.aoir.org/index.php/spir/article/view/689.

Banks, J., & Bowman, N. D. (2014). Avatars are (sometimes) people too: Linguistic indicators of parasocial and social ties in player-avatar relationships. *New Media & Society*. doi:10.1177/1461444814554898. https://email.ad.stetson.edu/owa/redir.aspx?C=SfwA bShYUUeL3pT7uAU4leHaZ50lWtlI1_H3DvD3jVBh5UHtcrx6eS3KO2bS_Dl3h36ojaoO_ Ks.&URL=http%3a%2f%2fnms.sagepub.com%2fcontent%2fearly%2f2014%2f10%2f16 %2f1461444814554898.abstract" \t "_blank.

Barthes, R. (1967). The death of the author. Aspen, 5–6, item 3.

Basadur, M. (1994). Managing the creative process in organizations. In M. A. Runco (Ed.), *Problem solving, problem finding, and creativity* (pp. 237–268). Norwood, NJ: Ablex.

Boden, M. A. (1996). What is creativity? In M. A. Boden (Ed.), *Dimensions of creativity* (pp. 75–118). Cambridge, MA: MIT Press.

Bogost, I. (2011). *How to do things with videogames*. Minneapolis: University of Minnesota Press.

Bowman, N. D. (2008). A PAT on the back: Media flow theory revis(it)ed. *Rocky Mountain Communication Review, 4*(1), 27–39.

Bowman, N. D., & Banks, J. (in press). Playing the zombie author: Machinima through the lens of Barthes. In K. Kenney (Ed.), *Philosophy for multisensory communication*. New York: Peter Lang.

Bowman, N. D., & Boyan, A. B. (2008). Cognitive skill as a predictor of flow and presence in naturally-mapped video games. In: *Paper presented at the Annual Meeting of the International Communication Association, Montreal*.

Bowman, N. D., & Tamborini, R. (2012). Task demand and mood repair: The intervention potential of computer games. *New Media & Society, 14*(8), 1339–1357. http://dx.doi. org/10.1177/1461444812450426.

Bowman, N. D., & Tamborini, R. (2015). "In the mood to game": Selective exposure and mood management processes in computer game play. *New Media & Society, 17*(3), 375–393. doi:10.1177/1461444813504274 (version 3, original published online in 2013). https:// email.ad.stetson.edu/owa/redir.aspx?C=SfwAbShYUUeL3pT7uAU4leHaZ50lWtlI1_ H3DvD3jVBh5UHtcrx6eS3KO2bS_Dl3h36ojaoO_Ks.&URL=http%3a%2f%2fnms. sagepub.com%2fcontent%2fearly%2f2013%2f09%2f19%2f1461444813504274.abstract %3frss%3d1" \t "_blank.

Bowman, N. D., Weber, R., Tamborini, R., & Sherry, J. L. (2013). Facilitating game play: How others affect performance at and enjoyment of video games. *Media Psychology, 16*(1), 39–64. http://dx.doi.org/10.1080/15213269.2012.742360.

Brosterman, N. (1997). *Inventing kindergarten*. New York: Harry N. Abrams.

Brown v EMA. (2011). Retrieved 7/1/11 from http://www.supremecourt.gov/ opinions/10pdf/08-1448.pdf.

Bruner, J. (1963). *The process of education*. Cambridge, MA: Harvard University Press.

Caillois, R. (1958). *Man, play, and games*. Paris: Gallimard Education.

Chen, J. (2007). Flow in games (and everything else). *Communications of the ACM, 50*(4), 31–34. http://dx.doi.org/10.1145/1232743.1232769.

Clark, P. M., Griffing, P. S., & Johnson, L. G. (1989). Symbolic play and ideational fluency as aspects of the divergent cognitive style in young children. *Early Child Development and Care, 51*, 77–88.

Clarke, A., & Mitchell, G. (2007). *Video games and art*. Bristol, UK: Intellect.

Collins, K. (2013). *Playing with sound: A theory of interacting with sound and music in video games*. Cambridge, MA: MIT Press.

Computer History Museum (n.d.). DEC PDP-1 Collection. Computer History Museum. Retrieved from http://www.computerhistory.org/collections/decpdp-1/.

Cropley, A. J. (1990). Creativity and mental health in everyday life. *Creativity Research Journal*, 3(3), 167–178. http://dx.doi.org/10.1080/10400419009534351.

Csikszentmihalyi, M. (1975). *Beyond boredom and anxiety: Experiencing flow in work and play*. San Francisco, CA: Jossey-Bass.

Csikszentmihalyi, M. (1990). *Flow: The psychology of optimal experience*. New York: Harper Perennial.

Csikszentmihalyi, M. (1993). *The evolving self: A psychology for the third millennium*. New York: Harper Perennial.

Csikszentmihalyi, M., & Csikszentmihalyi, I. S. (1988). *Optimal experience. Psychological studies of flow in consciousness*. Cambridge, UK: Cambridge University Press.

Csikszentmihalyi, M., & LeFevre, J. (1989). Optimal experience in work and leisure. *Journal of Personality and Social Psychology*, 56, 815–822. http://dx.doi.org/10.1037/0022-3514.56.5.815.

Ellis, M. J. (1973). *Why people play*. Englewood Cliffs, NJ: Prentice-Hall.

Eysenck, H. J. (1995). *Genius: The natural history of creativity*. Cambridge, UK: Cambridge University Press.

Ferguson, C. J. (2013). Violent video games and the Supreme Court: Lessons for the scientific community in the wake of Brown v EMA. *American Psychologist*, 68(2), 57–74. http://dx.doi.org/10.1037/a0030597.

Fiest, G. J. (1998). A meta-analysis of personality in scientific and artistic creativity. *Personality and Social Psychology Review*, 2, 290–309.

Fisher, R. (2004). What is creativity? In R. Fisher & M. Williams (Eds.), *Unlocking creativity: Teaching across the curriculum* (pp. 6–20). New York: David Fulton.

Freeman, B. (2010). *Researchers examine video gaming's benefits*. Washington, DC: US Department of Defense. Retrieved from: http://www.defense.gov/news/newsarticle.aspx?id=57695.

Gardner, H. (1997). *Extraordinary minds*. New York: Harper Collins.

Garfield, S. J., Cohen, H. A., & Roth, R. M. (1969). Creativity and mental health. *Journal of Educational Research*, 63(4), 147–149.

Gee, J. (2003). *What video games have to teach us about learning and literacy*. New York: Palgrave Macmillan.

Gentile, D. A., Anderson, C. A., Yukawa, N., Saleem, M., Lim, K. M., Shibuya, A., et al. (2009). The effects of prosocial video games on prosocial behaviors: International evidence from correlational, longitudinal, and experimental studies. *Personality and Social Psychology Bulletin*, 35, 752–763. http://dx.doi.org/10.1177/0146167209333045.

Getzels, S., & Csikszentmihalyi, M. (1976). *The creative vision: A longitudinal study of problem-finding in art*. New York: Wiley.

Glynn, M. A. (1994). Effects of work task cues and play task cues on information processing, judgment, and motivation. *Journal of Applied Psychology*, 79, 34–45.

Gonzalez, R. T. (2012, July 25). How Flash Gordon inspired Charles Bolden to become the head of NASA. io9.com. Retrieved from: http://io9.com/5927753/flash-gordon-science-fairs-and-ron-mcnair-how-charles-bolden-became-the-head-of-nasa.

Graetz, J. M. (1981, August). The origin of Spacewar! Creative Computing Magazine. Archived at http://www.wheels.org/spacewar/creative/SpacewarOrigin.html.

Granic, I., Lobel, A., & Engels, R. (2014). The benefits of playing video games. *American Psychologist*, 69(1), 66–78. http://dx.doi.org/10.1037/a0034857.

Green, C. S., & Bavelier, D. (2003). Action video game modifies visual selective attention. *Nature*, 423, 534–538.

Green, C. S., & Bavelier, D. (2006). The cognitive neuroscience of video games. In P. Messaris & L. Humphreys (Eds.), *Digital media: Transformations in human communication* (pp. 211–224). New York: Peter Lang.

Greenfield, P. M. (1984). *Mind and media: The effects of television, computers and video games.* London: Fontana.

Greenfield, P. M., DeWinstanley, P., Kilpatrick, H., & Kaye, D. (1994). Action video games and informal education: Effects on strategies for dividing visual attention. *Journal of Applied Developmental Psychology, 15,* 105–123.

Griffith, J. L., Voloschin, P., Gibb, G. D., & Bailey, J. R. (1983). Differences in eye-hand motor coordination of video game users and non-users. *Perceptual Motor Skills, 5*(1), 155–158.

Grodal, T. (2000). Video games and the pleasures of control. In D. Zillmann & P. Vorderer (Eds.), *Media entertainment: The psychology of its appeal* (pp. 197–213). Mahwah, NJ: LEA.

Guenette, R. (2013). GTA 5 sets 7 world records on the road to $1 billion. Fool.com. Retrieved from: http://www.fool.com/investing/general/2013/10/16/gta-5-sets-7-world-re-cords-on-the-road-to-1-billio.aspx.

Guilford, J. P. (1968). *Intelligence, creativity, and their eduational implications.* San Diego, CA: Knapp.

Haidt, J., & Joseph, C. (2004). Intuitive ethics: How innately prepared intuitions generate culturally variable virtues. *Daedalus, 133*(4), 55–66. http://dx.doi.org/10.1162/0011526042365555.

Hamlen, K. (2009). Relationships between computer and video game play and creativity among upper elementary school students. *Journal of Educational Computing Research, 40*(1), 1–21. http://dx.doi.org/10.2190/EC.40.1.a.

Hamlen, K. (2011). Children's choices and strategies in video games. *Computers in Human Behavior, 27*(1), 532–539. http://dx.doi.org/10.1016/j/chb.2010.10.001.

Harris, J. A. (2004). Measured intelligence, achievement, openness to experience, and creativity. *Personality and Individual Differences, 36*(4), 913–929.

Howard-Jones, P. A., Taylor, J., & Sutton, L. (2002). The effect of play on the creativity of young children during subsequent activity. *Early Child Development and Care, 172*(4), 323–328. http://dx.doi.org/10.1080/03004430212722.

Huizinga, J. (1949). *Homo Ludens.* London: Routledge & Kegan Paul.

Jackson, L. A. (2012). The upside of videogame playing. *Games for Health Journal, 1*(6), 452–455. http://dx.doi.org/10.1089/g4h.2012.0064.

Jackson, L. A., Witt, E. A., Games, A. I., Fitzgerald, H. E., von Eye, A., & Yong, Y. (2012). Information technology use and creativity: Findings from the Children and Technology Project. *Computers in Human Behavior, 28,* 370–376. http://dx.doi.org/10.1016/j.chb.2011.10.006.

Joeckel, S., Bowman, N. D., & Dogruel, L. (2012). Gut or game: The influence of moral intuitions on decisions in virtual environments. *Media Psychology, 15*(4), 460–485. http://dx.doi.org/10.1080/15213269.2012.727218.

Jones, G. (2003). *Killing monsters: Why children need fantasy, superheroes and make-believe violence.* New York: Basic Books.

Kaufman, J. (1999). *Creativity 101.* New York: Springer.

Kirriemuir, J. (2003). The relevance of video games and gaming consoles to the Higher and Further Education learning experience. Retrieved from www.jisc.ac.uk/uploaded_documents/tsw_02-01.rtf.

Koster, R. (2003). *A theory of fun for game design.* Cambridge, MA: O'Reilly Media.

Legrenzi, P. (2005). *Creativity and innovation.* Bologna: Il Mulino.

Lieberman, J. N. (1977). *Playfulness: Its relationship to imagination and creativity.* New York: Academic Press.

Lucas, B. (2001). Creative teaching, teaching creativity, and creative learning. In A. Craft, B. Jeffrey, & M. Leibling (Eds.), *Creativity in education.* London: Continuum.

Lucas, K., & Sherry, J. (2004). Sex differences in video game play: A communication-based explanation. *Communication Research, 31*(5), 499–523. http://dx.doi.org/10.1177/0093650204267930.

Mainemelis, C., & Ronson, S. (2006). Ideas are born in fields of play: Towards a theory of play and creativity in organizational settings. *Research in Organizational Behavior, 27,* 81–131. http://dx.doi.org/10.1016/S0191-3085(06)27003-5.

McCrae, R. R. (1987). Creativity, divergent thinking, and openness to experience. *Journal of Personality and Social Psychology, 52*(6), 1258–1265.

Moneta, G. B., & Csikszentmihalyi, M. (1996). The effect of perceived challenges and skills on the quality of subjective experience. *Journal of Personality, 64*, 275–310.

Moneta, G. B., & Csikszentmihalyi, M. (1999). Models of concentration in natural environments: A comparative approach based on streams of experiential data. *Social Behaviour and Personality, 27*, 603–638.

Montessori, M. (1912). *The Montessori method.* New York: Frederick Stokes.

Nakamura, L. (2000). Race in/for cyberspace: Identity tourism and racial passing on the internet. Retrieved from http://www.humanities.uci.edu/mposter/syllabi/readings/nakamura.html.

Ochse, R. (1990). *Before the gates of excellence: The determinants of creative genius.* Cambridge, MA: Cambridge University Press.

Oliver, M. B., Bowman, N. D., Woolley, J. K., Rogers, R., Sherrick, B. I., & Chung, M.-Y. (2013). *Video games as meaningful entertainment experiences.* In: Poster presented at the Annual Meeting of the International Communication Association, London, 2013, June.

Olson, C. K. (2010). Children's motivations for video game play in the context of normal development. *Review of General Psychology, 14*(2), 180–187. http://dx.doi.org/10.1037/a0018984.

Ott, M., & Pozzi, F. (2012). Digital games as creativity enablers for children. *Behavior and Information Technology, 31*(10), 1011–1019. http://dx.doi.org/10.1080/0144929x.2010.526148.

Pasual-Leone, A., Amedi, A., Fregni, F., & Merabet, L. B. (2005). The plastic human brain cortex. *Annual Review of Neuroscience, 28*, 377–401. http://dx.doi.org/10.1146/annurev.neuro.27.070203.144216.

Rabbitt, P., Banerji, N., & Szymanski, A. (1989). Space fortress as an IQ test? Predictions of learning and practised performance in a complex interactive video-game. *Acta Psychologica, 71*(1–3), 243–257. http://dx.doi.org/10.1016/0001-6918(89)90011-5.

Robinson, K. (2001). *Out of our minds: Learning to be creative.* Oxford: Capstone.

Rogers, C. (1961). *On becoming a person.* Boston, MA: Houghton Mifflin.

Runco, M. A., & Sakamoto, S. O. (1999). Experimental studies in creativity. In R. J. Sternberg (Ed.), *Handbook of creativity* (pp. 62–92). New York: Cambridge University Press.

Rushton, B. (2013, August 20). Backdooring it: Defense maneuvers around setback. Illinois Times. Retrieved from: http://www.illinoistimes.com/Springfield/article-11440-backdooring-it.html.

Russ, S. W. (1998). Play, creativity, and adaptive functioning: Implications for play interventions. *Journal of Clinical Child Psychology, 27*(4), 469–480.

Russ, S. W., Robins, A. L., & Christiano, B. A. (1999). Pretend play: Longitudinal prediction of creativity and affect in fantasy in children. *Creativity Research Journal, 12*(2), 129–139.

Sherry, J. L. (2001). The effects of violent video games on aggression: A meta-analysis. *Human Communication Research, 27*(3), 409–431. http://dx.doi.org/10.1111/j.1468-2958.2001.tb00787.x.

Sherry, J. L. (2004). Flow and media enjoyment. *Communication Theory, 14*, 328–347. http://dx.doi.org/10.1093/ct/14.4.328.

Sherry, J. L., Rosaen, S., Bowman, N. D., & Huh, S. (2006, June). *Cognitive skill predicts video game ability.* In: Paper presented at the International Communication Association annual convention, Dresden, Germany.

Smith, S. L., Lachlan, K. A., & Tamborini, R. (2003). Popular video games: Quantifying the presentation of violence and its context. *Journal of Broadcasting and Electronic Media, 47*(1), 58–76. http://dx.doi.org/10.1177/1461444805052280.

Smithsonian Institute (2012). The art of video games. Retrieved from: http://www.americanart.si.edu/exhibitions/archive/2012/games/featuredgames/.

Sternberg, R. J. (1988). In R. Sternberg (Ed.), *The nature of creativity: Contemporary psychological perspectives.* Cambridge, MA: Cambridge University Press.

Steuer, J. (1992). Defining virtual reality: Dimensions determining telepresence. *Journal of Communication, 42*(4), 73–93. http://dx.doi.org/10.1111/j.1460-2466.1992.tb00812.x.

Sundar, S. S., & Hutton, E. (2010). Can video games enhance creativity. Effects of emotion generated by Dance Dance Revolution. *Creativity Research Journal, 22*(3), 294–303. http://dx.doi.org/10.1080/10400419.2010.503540.

Tamborini, R., & Bowman, N. D. (2010). Presence in video games. In C. Bracken & P. Skalski (Eds.), *Immersed in media: Telepresence in everyday life* (pp. 87–109). New York: Routledge.

Tamborini, R., Weber, R., Bowman, N. D., Eden, A., & Skalski, P. (2013). "Violence is a many-splintered thing": The importance of realism, justification, and graphicness in understanding perceptions of and preferences for violent films and video games. *Projections: The Journal for Movies and Mind, 7*(1), 100–118. http://dx.doi.org/10.3167/proj.2013.070108.

Thompson, K., & Haninger, K. (2001). Violence in E-rated video games. *Journal of the American Medical Association, 286,* 591–598. http://dx.doi.org/10.1001/jama.286.8.920.

Torrance, E. P. (1995). The nature of creativity as manifest in its testing. In R. J. Sternberg (Ed.), *The nature of creativity.* New York: Cambridge University Press.

van Schie, E. G. M., & Wiegman, O. (2006). Children and videogames: Leisure activities, aggression, social integration, and school performance. *Journal of Applied Social Psychology, 27*(13), 1175–1194. http://dx.doi.org/10.1111/j/1559-1816.1997.tb01800.x.

Ventura, M., Shute, V., & Kim, Y. J. (2012). Video gameplay, personality and academic performance. *Computers & Education, 58*(4), 1260–1266. http://dx.doi.org/10.1016/j.compedu.2011.11.022.

Walberg, H. J., & Tsai, S. L. (1983). Matthew effects in education. *American Educational Research Journal, 20*(3), 359–373.

Weber, R., Tamborini, R., Westcott-Baker, A., & Kantor, B. (2009). Theorizing flow and media enjoyment as cognitive synchronization of attentional and reward networks. *Communication Theory, 19,* 397–422. http://dx.doi.org/10.1111/j.1468-2885.2009.01352.x.

Wertham, F. (1955). *Seduction of the innocent.* London: Museum Press.

Wright, T., Boria, E., & Breidenbach, P. (2002). Creative player actions in FPS online video games. *Game Studies, 2*(2). Retrieved at: http://www.gamestudies.org/0202/wright/.

Young, J. G. (1985). What is creativity? *Journal of Creative Behavior, 19*(2), 77–87.

3

Video Games and Malevolent Creativity: Does One Thing Lead to Another?

David H. Cropley

Defence and Systems Institute (DASI), University of South Australia, Adelaide, SA, Australia

OUTLINE

INTRODUCTION

Do video games foster malevolent creativity? To explore this difficult question, I will speculate that at least three conditions need to be met: (1) that video games, in general, can function as effective learning tools; (2) that video games have the potential to foster broadly antisocial behaviors such as violence and aggression; and (3) that video games have the ability to foster creativity. The first of these may be thought of as a necessary, but not sufficient, condition. If video games, in principle, can foster learning, then we can examine the further questions of *violence* and *creativity*. While there is considerable evidence supporting the former (learning), the question of video games and a relationship to a combination of antisocial behavior and creativity is by no means as clear. As separate constructs, the evidence surrounding video games and antisocial behaviors such as violence, impulsiveness, and aggression is at best inconclusive. The relationship between video games and creativity, by contrast, is not so much inconclusive as lacking. If there is little research on video games and creativity, there is even less on the fusion of intentional harm and novelty generation—malevolent creativity.

In the first part of this chapter, I will begin by outlining the core construct—What is malevolent creativity? I will then examine evidence of video games as training/learning tools. This will be followed by a discussion of evidence of a relationship between video games and antisocial behaviors, in particular violence. After this, I will look at evidence of a relationship between video games and creativity. At this point, I will suggest that the wrong question is being asked. The range and variety of existing video games, violent or otherwise, make investigation of the question "Do video games foster malevolent creativity?" difficult to answer in any conclusive or generalizable sense.

Instead, a more promising approach may be to ask how we would *design* a video game specifically to *foster* malevolent creativity. In the second part of this chapter, I will address this revised question first by examining evidence in support of creativity training in any form. On the strength of research evidence that creativity *is* teachable, I will then propose a set of design criteria that will address what a video game would need to do—what it would look like—if it was to serve the purpose of training for malevolent creativity. The goal of these design criteria is not, of course, to design a game that will engender malevolent creativity, but to assist researchers in understanding what to look for in a game that is to serve as the stimulus for further research in the relationship between video games and (malevolent) creativity. The original question then becomes, in effect, "are any current video games candidates for fostering malevolent creativity?"

PART I—THE EFFECTS OF VIDEO GAMES

MALEVOLENT CREATIVITY

Creativity, both in its everyday sense and in a more formal research context, tends to be presented as a positive and benevolent quality of people, activities, and things (Cropley, Kaufman, White, & Chiera, 2014). Whether examined as a constructive form of self-expression and self-actualization (Richards, 2010), as a tool for generating effective solutions to intractable problems (D. H. Cropley, 2015), or as a vital ingredient of successful organizations (Mumford, Hester, & Robledo, 2012), little research has examined creativity in the context of causing deliberate, intentional harm or damage to others (Cropley, Kaufman, & Cropley, 2008). Where studies have addressed undesirable aspects of creativity, more often than not this occurs in the relatively benign context of a range of *unintended negative* associations—of creative behavior, creative personality, or creative climate (D. H. Cropley & Cropley, 2013; A. J. Cropley and Cropley, 2013; Furnham, Zhang, & Chamorro-Premuzic, 2006; Wolfradt & Pretz, 2001).

While it might seem, therefore, that little attention has been devoted to darker aspects of creativity, there is a thread of research developing along this theme. Clark and James (1999), for example, first argued for the existence of *negative* creativity—this might be exemplified by an employee devising a new way to steal from his or her company. However, in this sense, negative creativity may lack harmful *intent*. A more differentiated concept of creativity, in which intent plays a central role, is that of *malevolent* creativity. This is defined as creativity that is deliberately planned to damage others (Cropley, 2010; Cropley, Kaufman, & Cropley, 2013; Cropley et al., 2008). The relevance and practical importance of the malevolent creativity concept has been validated and further developed through recent work in the area of terrorism by Gill and colleagues (Gill, Horgan, Hunter, & Cushenbery, 2013; Gill, Horgan, & Lovelace, 2011), whereas (A.J. Cropley and Cropley, 2011 and D.H. Cropley and Cropley, 2013) have examined the role of creativity more broadly in relation to crime and criminal behavior.

Most empirical work addressing malevolent creativity looks at negative outcomes or traits associated with creative people. Various studies have shown that creative people are more likely to manipulate test results (Gino & Ariely, 2012); that they are better able to tell more types of creative lies (Walczyk, Runco, Tripp, & Smith, 2008); that they are more adept at using deception during conflict negotiation (De Dreu & Nijstad, 2008); and that creative people demonstrate less integrity (Beaussart, Andrews, & Kaufman, 2013). Other research has indicated that people who show higher levels of malevolent creativity are more likely to be physically aggressive (Lee & Dow, 2011) and to have lower emotional intelligence (Harris, Reiter-Palmon, & Kaufman, 2013).

Another approach to studying malevolent creativity is to find out how potentially negative situational or personal factors may enhance creativity. For example, Mayer and Mussweiler (2011) have found evidence to suggest that when people are primed to be distrustful, creative cognitive ability increased if the person was being creative in private. Riley and Gabora (2012) found that threatening stimuli provoked more creative responses than nonthreatening stimuli. They argue that these types of threats can invoke disequilibrium and creativity can help reduce such cognitive dissonance (Akinola & Mendes, 2008).

Malevolent creativity is a particularly difficult topic to study in the same manner as other possible domains of creativity, given the focus on intentional harm. Thus, studies of malevolent creativity nearly always use hypothetical scenarios (Cropley et al., 2014). Video games, however, provide a context in which intentionally harmful, creative behaviors—malevolent creativity—may be sanctioned, presenting an opportunity to study malevolent creativity in a more authentic context.

VIDEO GAMES: LEARNING AND TRAINING

A logical starting point for the study of video games as a means of fostering malevolent creativity is to ask if video games are capable of fostering *any* sort of behavior, attitude, or skill. Green and Bavelier (2006) approached this question from the point of view of cognitive neuroscience. Turning a traditional lens—the cognitive effects of *less than normal experience*—on its head, they ask, in relation to video games, "… what is the effect of 'more than normal' experience?" (p. 3). Across factors such as *reaction time, visuo-motor coordination, spatial skills,* and *visual attention* they argue that "… in many areas of perception and cognition, video game experience leads gamers to possess perceptual and cognitive skills far beyond those observed in non-gamers" (p. 4). Green and Bavelier go on to report (p. 17) that "Two main areas where the impact of video game training has been examined are in the rehabilitation of individuals with diminished perceptual or cognitive functioning (such as the elderly) and in the training of individuals whose professions required enhanced perceptual capabilities (such as military personnel)."

Reviewing a wide body of literature, spanning a period of more than 20 years, De Aguilera and Mendiz (2003) conclude that video games offer a range of advantages as teaching and learning tools. Griffiths (2002) expands the discussion, noting that the evidence of benefits extends from specific, individual factors such as reaction time and hand-eye coordination, to factors such as self-esteem and self-concept. Indeed, he suggests that video games also support the development of goal-setting and goal-rehearsal, and allow the player to experience novelty, curiosity, and challenge. Mitchell and Savill-Smith (2004) note benefits in relation both to cognitive and social skills (although noting, in parallel, the dangers of excessive use), while Prensky (2005) and Ritterfeld and Weber (2006) both discuss further positives for video games in the context of education and learning.

For the purposes of the present chapter, I will conclude that there is ample evidence to suggest that video games can enhance the development of behaviors, attitudes, and skills.

VIDEO GAMES AND ANTISOCIAL BEHAVIOR

While the earliest popular arcade and home video games of the 1970s—*Pong*, for example—may have given parents, psychologists, and researchers little cause for concern, the pervasiveness, not to mention the growth in realism and violent content of games, has been, for several decades, the subject of much investigation (e.g., Griffiths, 1999; Irwin & Gross, 1995). This concern has been spurred along by notorious cases— the Columbine High School shooting, for example—in which violent video games are thought to have contributed to real-world brutality and bloodshed (Anderson & Dill, 2000). It is easy to understand why this is of concern. If violent video games have a direct, causal relationship with real-world impulsive, aggressive, and violent behavior—if playing such games *causes* people to behave in potentially lethal ways—then some mitigating action is surely warranted. Even if real-world violence is merely correlated to the playing of violent video games then there is still ample cause for concern.

It might seem that the case is clear. Gentile (2011) states that there are "… now dozens of studies of the short-term and long-term effects of violent video games …" (p. 77) and that these support arguments for *causal effects* (e.g., Anderson & Dill, 2000; Anderson, Gentile, & Buckley, 2007; Bushman & Anderson, 2002), *correlational associations* (e.g., Bartholow, Bushman, & Sestir, 2006), and *cumulative effects* from longitudinal studies (e.g., Möller & Krahé, 2009).

Nevertheless, Gentile (2011) has argued for a balance of views on the impact of video games on children and adolescents, highlighting the fact that there remains conflicting evidence. Ferguson (2007), for example, refutes suggestions that violent video games promote aggression, while Wiegman and Schie (1998) suggested an indirect link, with aggressive video games linking only to lower prosocial behavior among boys (as opposed to *increased* antisocial behavior).

Gentile, Swing, Lim, and Khoo (2012) report on less overtly antisocial behaviors. A large ($n = 3034$), longitudinal study confirmed a relationship between time spent playing video games and increased attention problems, reporting also that violent games *may have* an effect on impulsiveness. They did also note a bidirectional causality—children who were more impulsive or had greater attention problems spent more time playing video games, while more time spent playing was linked to increased inattention.

Further studies (e.g., Anderson & Bushman, 2001; Anderson et al., 2004, 2010; Barlett, Harris, & Baldassaro, 2007; Bartholow, Sestir, & Davis, 2005; Bettencourt, Talley, Benjamin, & Valentine, 2006; Bluemke, Friedrich, & Zumbach, 2010; Grossman & DeGaetano, 2009; Kirsh, 2003; Smith, Lachlan, & Tamborini, 2003) all examine aspects of the question of video games and violence, aggression and antisocial behavior. The simple fact that there remains evidence both for *and* against suggests that the strongest conclusion that can be drawn is that there *may be* links between various types of negative behavior and video games.

Kutner and Olson (2008) support this balance of opinions. Though not explicitly ruling out a link between video games and violent behavior, the authors do refute many of the anecdotal links that are frequently cited as evidence. The FBI, for example, concluded that the Columbine High School killers—Harris and Klebold—were *not* influenced by an interest in violent video games, but were depressed and suicidal (Klebold) and sociopathic (Harris). Perhaps most significantly, Kutner and Olson (2008) drew attention to the fact that, "violent juvenile crime in the United States reached a peak in 1993 and has been declining ever since" (p. 8) at the same time that video game popularity has grown sharply.

VIDEO GAMES AND CREATIVITY

According to Kim and Coxon (2013) the small amount of research that examines the impact of video games on creativity presents conflicting evidence. Research by Jackson et al. (2012), for example, suggests that there may be a positive relationship—greater video game playing was associated with higher scores on Torrance Tests of Creativity—while research by Hamlen (2009) claims that there is no relationship between video games and creativity.

Kim and Coxon (2013) went on to make an important point with regard to the potential of video games to foster creativity, whether malevolent or otherwise: "… the deeper the player's knowledge of the program, the less relevant and less productive is creative thinking in playing it" (p. 64). In other words, as a player becomes increasingly familiar with a game, both the ability of the game to surprise the player, and the player's ability to respond to the game in genuinely novel ways, decreases. This seems to present a fundamental limitation with regard to studying possible relationships between video games and creativity.

There may be, however, one element of video games that has the potential to circumvent this decay of novelty. Wright, Boria, and Breidenbach (2002) studied creativity in video games in the context of verbal and textual interactions in multiplayer games—what they called "player talk." They identified within "Creative Game Talk" five categories describing verbal/textual interactions of players in which creativity may be found:

- Names, naming, and identity talk—e.g., the use of unusual or original online names that also flaunt social conventions.
- Joking, irony, and word play—e.g., the use of puns and double-meanings in player-player interactions.
- Map creation, judging, and logo design—e.g., the use of game engines for the development of novel maps or scenarios.
- Changing game rules and technical limits—e.g., finding ways for *dead* players to communicate with *live* team mates, in order to pass on messages about the location of enemies (this is done by the *dead* player requesting a vote for a game map that doesn't exist, the name of which gives a clue to live team mates).
- Popular culture uses and references—e.g., the incorporation of familiar references (Homer Simpson's "D'Oh!") into game talk.

Although the *creativity* of some of the examples given by Wright et al. (2002) might be debated, their discussion does highlight the potential for multiplayer games to introduce novelty, uncertainty, ambiguity, and other factors linked to creativity into game play.

The evidence of a relationship between video games and creativity is therefore unclear. Even where research has claimed a link (Jackson et al., 2012), it is not causal in nature, and may be highly constrained by the design of the games, the primary purpose of which is *not*, in general, the development of qualities such as divergent thinking. Table 1 summarizes the evidence of relationships between video games and the three effects of interest: learning/training, antisocial behavior, and creativity.

While there is compelling evidence to support the use of video games as tools for learning and training, it is unclear if, or to what extent, video games function as tools that facilitate the learning of, or training

TABLE 1   Research Evidence of the Relationship Between Video Games and Different Effects

Video Games and ...	No Evidence	Inconclusive Evidence	Compelling Evidence
Learning/Training			✓
Antisocial Behavior		✓	
Creativity		✓	

in, antisocial behavior, creativity, or indeed the combination of the two, in the form of malevolent creativity. To address the latter issue, it seems that a fundamental limitation of much of the existing research needs to be addressed—namely the fact that most of the research in video games is *ex post facto* in nature. In other words, studies use *existing*, off-the-shelf video games and researchers therefore lack full control over the independent variable(s). In studying video games and violence, for example, the researcher cannot directly manipulate the *amount* or *kind* of violence in a given video game, because that is set by the design of the game. Similarly, to study video games and creativity, researchers must rely on the design of the game, and cannot directly control the amount or kind of novelty, for example, experienced in the game.

At the same time, our concerns as a society are not so much around the question of whether a video game *could be* created that would be highly effective at training individuals for malevolent creativity, but whether or not video games *as they are designed* could, inadvertently, serve this purpose. The fundamental question therefore changes to: What would a video game need to do to—what would it look like—if it was to foster malevolent creativity?

PART II—FOSTERING MALEVOLENT CREATIVITY IN VIDEO GAMES

TRAINING FOR CREATIVITY

A critical premise for the discussion of video games and (malevolent) creativity is the assumption that creativity is *not* a fixed, inborn trait. While some researchers (see Edwards, 2001) still do not believe that creativity, as a psychological characteristic of individual people, can be inculcated where it is not already present, others such as Torrance (1972) were adamant that creativity can be taught. The latter view is also widely supported (e.g., Amabile, 1983). Researchers such as Richards, Kinney, Bennet, and Merzel (1988) and Runco and Richards (1997) showed that in the course of everyday life *ordinary* men and women frequently produce effective novelty in fine arts, the sciences, the humanities, and crafts. Cropley (2001) gave a number of examples of "everyday" creativity, including generation of effective novelty in a women's weekly sewing circle or in a junior soccer team.

These examples imply that many people can produce effectively novel products (i.e., be creative), if the circumstances are right. This is reinforced by the *4Cs model* (Kaufman & Beghetto, 2009). The idea of *mini-c*, *little-c*, and *Pro-c* creativity, as distinct from the *Big-C* creativity of geniuses, suggests that it must be possible for *ordinary* people to generate effective novelty. If creativity is a statistically uncommon trait, but is regularly exhibited by many people, then it must be something that can be learned. Nicholls (1972) went further. He argued that creativity is, in fact, a normally distributed trait like intelligence, and emphasized the importance of creativity in people who have never received public acclaim, and never will.

The Effectiveness of Creativity Training

If creativity is teachable, what can we learn from research that might inform the design of video games as the medium of training? There has been considerable debate over the *effectiveness* of creativity training in the research literature. Doubts have been expressed about whether training actually achieves what it sets out to do, which is to foster creativity (Mansfield, Busse, & Krepelka, 1978). Wallach (1985), for example, argued that the effects of creativity-facilitating programs (in the sense of *structured training activities*, not *software*) are very *narrow* and *specific*, and scarcely generalize to behavior in settings other than those closely resembling the training procedure itself. This would suggest that the best we might hope for is that video games help people to be more creative *in the context of video games*. Treffinger, Sortore, and Cross (1993) concluded that it has *not* been shown that:

- there are clearly definable effects of creativity training on specific cognitive or personal characteristics;
- particular programs foster specific aspects of psychological development;
- people with one particular psychological profile benefit from a specific program, whereas other people need a different one.

This seems to be good news if we are concerned that video games might foster malevolent creativity. Unfortunately, the situation may be far more nuanced, leaving open the door for intentionally harmful creativity.

Whether this is a failure of the training, or a question of *misalignment* of training and desired outcome, is a question that has been touched on by Baer (1996) and explored further in Baer (1998). One possible explanation for these apparent deficiencies is that creativity training has concentrated overwhelmingly, in the past, on the *cognitive* (i.e., *Process*) aspects of creativity, even if factors such as self-concept or positive attitudes to problem solving are sometimes considered. Cropley and Cropley (2000) criticized this narrowness in the conceptualization of creativity inherent in many programs—they called this *fast-food creativity*—and called for an integrative, holistic (or *spinach*) approach. Urban (1997) likewise saw training programs as too narrowly focused. The implication for video game design may be the need for a broader understanding of design criteria—in the same way that creativity is understood to be impacted by cognitive, personal, motivational, and social factors (i.e., 4Ps; e.g., Rhodes, 1961), so too must video game design reflect the contribution of person, process, product, and press to the overall development of creativity.

Despite the concerns just raised, there is, in fact, convincing empirical evidence that creativity training, *properly conceived and implemented*, is effective (Scott, Leritz, & Mumford, 2004a). They identified 70 studies published in or after 1980 in which the effects of creativity training were tested empirically. The studies had to meet strict methodological criteria that eliminated some of the criticisms of earlier research reporting favorable effects of creativity training. The effects of creativity training were tested statistically by calculating *effect strengths* (i.e., the strength of the influence of the independent variable—the creativity training provided). Ma (2006) extended this work, conducting an extensive analysis of creativity training, covering various aspects such as divergent thinking as well as attitudes to creativity, and found a large effect size overall, confirming the findings of previous studies.

There is also considerable evidence of the positive benefits of specific creativity training in school and college curricula. A review by Hunsaker (2005), and specific examples (McGregor, 2001) support the beneficial effects of creativity training in this particular context. DeHaan (2009), for example, studied "specific instructional strategies" to promote creative problem solving in science and engineering, while McFadzean (2002) discussed "paradigm stretching" techniques that may encourage creative ideas. Convincing evidence described by Diamond, Barnett, Thomas, and Munro (2007) showed that specific aspects of mental ability associated with problem solving (cognitive flexibility, working memory, and inhibitory control) were boosted by programs that focused on finding alternative ways to solve a problem.

Debate will no doubt continue regarding what *aspects* of creativity can be taught and trained, *how long* any benefits persist after training, and *who benefits* most from these interventions; however, there seems to be ample evidence that creativity can be fostered and developed through specific activities and with appropriate guidance. This, coupled with the more general potential of video games in learning, paves the way for the use of video games as the training medium for creativity.

The Effect of Creativity Training

Of more direct relevance to the question of video games and creativity is the fact that the strongest effects found by Scott et al. (2004a) were obtained when the criterion was cognitive *processes* (i.e., improvements in people's divergent thinking and problem solving after training). Within the cognitive domain, the single largest effect of creativity training was on *originality* of thinking, although training also enhanced *fluency*, *flexibility*, and *elaboration*. Thus, after training people produced a greater number of surprising ideas—in other words, their capacity to generate novelty improved. The second strongest effect of training was on creative performance (i.e., the creative *products* people generated after training). There were also noteworthy effects on *attitudes* (i.e., *Person*). The effects of creativity training were strong in both children and adults in both educational and non educational organizations, and were found in both gifted and nongifted samples. There were sizable effects for both males and females, but the effects were larger for males, especially with regard to divergent thinking. Thus, it seems that training is able to have a measurable effect on aspects of the *Person*, the *Process*, and the *Product*.

Effectiveness of Different *Kinds* of Training

Evidence is also available that some forms of creativity training work *better than* others—there are differences between training procedures in the *strength* of the effects obtained (Scott et al., 2004a). When cognitive, social, personality, motivational, and combined training procedures— different *kinds* of training—were compared, it was found that the cognitive (i.e., *Process*) approach had by far the largest effect. Scott et al. (2004a) divided *cognitive* training procedures according to the particular process that each procedure emphasized, and found that training in *problem identification* and *idea generation* contributed most to the success of the training.

The best way to foster these processes was to give participants opportunities to analyze novel, ill-defined problems. Mere unfettered expression of unexplored ideas was negatively related to the effectiveness of training. Scott et al. (2004a) also found that highly organized and systematic training, based on realistic examples and involving substantial periods of structured, focused practice (i.e., relevant to a field or domain), was most effective. These factors begin to read like a set of design requirements for a video game, the purpose of which is to develop player creativity.

Finally, training that started by introducing specific relevant concepts and basic principles, then moved to targeted practice aimed at acquiring specific skills, achieved stronger effects than *holistic* training. In connection with the intrinsic vs extrinsic motivation debate, it should be noted that provision of evaluative feedback positively affected improvements in problem solving and relevant performance criteria, but *inhibited* improvement in divergent thinking. The two studies by Scott et al. (2004a) and Scott, Leritz, and Mumford (2004b) are enormously informative with regard to a wide range of factors that influence creativity training. The analysis extends to the effect of different forms of instructional media (lecture, video, etc.), forms of exercise (written, group, etc.) and types of assessment, and has obvious implications for the design of video games as training tools for creativity.

What Abilities Need to Be Trained?

The evidence presented so far tells us that creativity training/education can be designed to deliver specific improvements. The Scott et al. (2004a) data suggest that targeted, specific training is more effective than holistic approaches; however, it seems that this fails to account for some of the more qualitative aspects of fostering creativity. In any discussion of training versus education, we must examine the extent to which we merely wish to develop a skill, in contrast to developing understanding. Is the need in engineering for people who are simply better at generating many ideas, or do we need engineers who also understand when and why the ideas need to be generated?

A bridge between the *quantitative focus* of training and the *qualitative focus* of education is provided by Sternberg (1985), Sternberg and Lubart (1995), and Sternberg and Williams (1996), who describe the link between creative *work* and three *abilities*. Each of these abilities can be developed through training and/or education:

- *Synthetic Ability*: most commonly associated with the concept of *creativity*, synthetic ability is the ability to generate novel, relevant ideas, link disparate concepts, etc.
- *Analytic Ability*: most commonly thought of as an ability to think critically, this ability supports the generation of ideas by evaluating and analyzing their value and potential.
- *Practical Ability*: the ability to implement ideas and move from theory to practice. This ability can be thought of as the transition from creativity to innovation.

Creativity is more than just the ability to generate ideas. It requires a balance of these three abilities, some of which are developed through more quantitative training and some through more qualitative education.

DESIGNING A VIDEO GAME TO FOSTER MALEVOLENT CREATIVITY

Sternberg (2007) noted that "creativity is a habit" (p. 3) and, like any habit, is promoted by three factors. These are: (1) *opportunity* to engage in creativity; (2) *encouragement* when the opportunity is taken up; and (3) *reward* when creative thinking and behavior are exhibited. Building on the potential of video games for learning and the effectiveness of creativity training in a more general sense, we can now turn to a *specific* question—Can video games serve as a means for developing the malevolent creativity habit?

The video game *is* the opportunity, but it must be embedded in a framework that supports the goal of the deliberate development of creativity that is intended to cause harm. *Encouragement* and *reward* are most likely to be found in a game play context that supports multiplayer interaction.

Hypothesis 1: *Interactive, multiplayer* modes form the basis for the development of malevolent creativity in video games.

Although writing about principles for the design of creativity support tools—specifically tools that support *design*—Resnick et al. (2005) touch on design requirements that might be extended to video games as tools for fostering creativity at the next level of specificity. Creativity support tools, they argue, should have:

- a *low threshold*;
- a *high ceiling*;
- *wide walls*.

Hypothesis 2: Video games that provide a *low threshold* (they are easy to start playing, have an intuitive interface and simple controls), a *high ceiling* (they have powerful game engines and support expert use and game play), and that have *wide walls* (they present extensive, diverse game worlds, maps and scenarios, and permit highly varied, uncertain outcomes) will maximize the opportunity for the development of malevolent creativity.

Sternberg (2007) went on to point out "twelve keys for developing the creativity habit …" (p. 8). These are now described in the specific context of design criteria for video games intended to foster (malevolent) creativity:

- Redefine problems—to make *appropriate* choices (whether benevolent or malevolent), we need practice at *making* choices. When those choices do not work out, we need the opportunity to try again. To achieve this we need the opportunity to engage in activities that are open-ended and flexible. Highly constrained, or over-specified, video games therefore will not allow this skill to be developed.
- Question and analyze assumptions—our creativity is facilitated when we are encouraged to ask questions, and not accept problems as they are presented to us. This can be facilitated by a video game that "tolerates" departures from norms. It may also extend to a gaming environment, including multiplayer contexts, that permits, or even encourages, deviation from accepted norms.
- Sell your creative ideas—we need to learn how to persuade others of the value of our ideas. Team-based, collaborative video games engender an environment in which we must become adept at *selling* our ideas to others.
- Encourage idea generation—we need practice at generating ideas, but with constructive criticism. This can be encouraged, as a necessary component of game play.

- The role of knowledge—to be creative in any given domain including, for example, *crime*, requires domain knowledge. Game play that develops specific domain knowledge will facilitate creativity in that domain.
- Identify and surmount obstacles—we need to be presented with challenging tasks so that we build resilience. Video games need to give the player opportunities to fail, and try again. Video games that present the player with problems that are unique and bound by a unique set of constraints build this skill. Game play should *discourage* the reapplication of what worked in another situation, and instead encourage players to focus their energies on finding the new solutions.
- Encourage sensible risk-taking—we need the opportunity to try things, even though they might not work. We benefit from practice at assessing risks and judging their outcomes. Game play that allows risk-taking without *punishment*—whether in the form of in-game penalties or, for example, interaction in a multiplayer environment—will encourage this aspect of creativity. Paradoxically, this may only be possible by establishing some authentic negative outcomes. If the worst that happens in a game is that the player has to start a level again, for example, then the ability to develop risk-taking ability is limited. A game that incorporated the development of sensible risk-taking would need to include some courses of action that had *real* negative consequences. For example, if a poor choice in game play led to the player being locked out of the game for a month, this would attach significant value and authenticity to the process of judging what risks are worth taking.
- Encourage tolerance of ambiguity—by presenting players with *ill-defined* problems. Creative people recognize that ambiguity gives them more space to be creative. This can be as simple as breaking away from a sequential game play paradigm. Multiple possible courses of action, and unpredictable outcomes—game play that is structured around open-ended problems—will foster this aspect of creativity. Even better is game play with *no* defined success criteria, or success criteria *defined by the players* in a multiplayer environment.
- Build creative self-efficacy—allowing players to see that they *can* be creative, so they do not fall into the *I'm not creative* self-fulfilling prophecy. *Requiring* creativity—the generation of effective, novel ideas—as an integral component of game play will allow players to see that they can be creative, and that their creativity is an asset.
- Finding what excites them—games that explore a wider range of subject matter.
- The importance of delaying gratification—game play needs to foster a sense that sometimes you need to work a little longer and harder to get the reward. Pushing players to the full extent of their abilities

is necessary—this might take the form of more adaptive game play that automatically tailors to the ability of the player. This might also include locking players out of easier levels of game play (rather than the reverse). Finally, this might also take the form of much more stringent rewards in game play—making it harder to level up or making those rewards less predictable.

- Provide a favorable environment—in the context of video games, this final point extends across the totality of game design. Games that require only *pseudo*-creativity (blind variation, for example) with no link to effectiveness and outcomes, or games that treat creativity as an occasional add-on, fail to create the right environment. Creativity must be a defining characteristic of video games if they are to foster creativity. Simply expanding a set of options—for example, the number of items that can be combined as weapons in *Dead Rising*— has finite and readily apparent limits.

Hypothesis 3: Video games that implement the principles underpinning Sternberg's 12 Keys will maximize the opportunity for the development of (malevolent) creativity in players.

A key element of the discussion so far is that malevolent creativity is not a different form of creativity, but simply creativity coupled with the intent to cause harm. Thus, what fosters creativity in general also fosters malevolent creativity. The encouragement of malevolent *intent* is therefore developed in parallel with the encouragement of creativity. Gentile (2011) highlights five dimensions which show evidence of effects on players, and which specifically address malevolence in game design:

- the amount of play;
- the content of play;
- the game context;
- the structure of the game;
- the mechanics of the game.

In most cases, however, these effects are complex, interrelated, and often indirect. For example, Anderson et al. (2007) found complex relationships between *amount of game play* and broadly negative outcomes such as poor school grades, verbal aggression, and physical aggression. Perhaps more importantly for present purposes, practice effects known to educational theorists as beneficial for long-term learning (e.g., distributed practice in preference to massed practice; Anderson, 1983) appear to be manifest in video games. Gentile and Gentile (2008), for example, showed a link between video games and increased aggression in particular among game players whose game play was distributed across more regular and frequent intervals.

Hypothesis 4: The development of malevolent creativity will be facilitated by video games that encourage regular, frequent game play.

The *content* of video games seems to be critical. It seems axiomatic that a game involving no violent content is unlikely to foster violent behavior, irrespective of amount of game play. Indeed, there is evidence that prosocial content predicts prosocial behavior (Gentile et al., 2009). Conversely, it might be expected that violent games—those in which violent actions and behaviors are an inherent part of the game—will foster related actions and behaviors among game players.

Hypothesis 5: Video games that provide opportunities to engage in intentionally harmful activities will foster the development of malevolent creativity. This will include opportunities to plan and execute acts of intentional harm, in contrast to engaging in impulsive and unplanned violence.

Gentile (2011) speculates that game *context* may play an important role in determining the effect of the game with respect to violent or aggressive behavior. He suggests that a violent but cooperative game context, for example a team-based *capture the flag* context in a game like *Halo*, might be associated with lower levels of aggressive cognitions, feelings and behaviors, and lower desensitization to violence, compared to an everyone for himself context, even though the general level of violence in the game is the same. There is, however, little if any research on these effects in a video game context.

The game context will play an important role in determining the impact of the video game. The findings of Cropley et al. (2014) suggest, somewhat counter-intuitively, that it is not an overtly illegal game context that maximizes the opportunity for malevolent creativity, but one that is legally and morally *ambiguous*.

Hypothesis 6: Video games that are built around a context that is legally or morally gray, in contrast to games with a clear *good versus bad* context, will be most effective at fostering malevolent creativity.

Gentile's (2011) final two dimensions—the structure and mechanics of the game—address issues of visual interface, realism, and control of the game. It is axiomatic that the more the game looks and feels like the thing, the more effective it will be in developing the targeted skill or behavior. There is no reason to assume that malevolent creativity will be any different.

CONCLUSIONS

While it seems clear that video games have the potential to serve as effective tools for learning and training across a variety of domains, the evidence of links—whether causal or correlational—between video games and antisocial behaviors is far less clear. Similarly, there is scant evidence of a relationship between video games and creativity. Attempting to establish a link between video games and the fusion of antisocial behavior and creativity—i.e., malevolent creativity—is therefore no easier. In the same way that it is easy to fret that violent video games might turn normal children into killers, there is something almost appealing in the idea that a video game might turn a mild-mannered person into a creative, criminal genius. A problem that research studies will face when attempting to address the latter question lies in the fact that we do not really know what such a video game will look like, and how it will play. Is a video game that can foster malevolent creativity simply one that involves violent themes, or one that includes many opportunities for generating novelty, or is it likely to be something more? If malevolent creativity itself is much more than merely generating nasty ideas, then it seems almost axiomatic that video games will need to do more than simply present the player with a wide variety of ways to kill zombies or blow things up. A critical question therefore must be—What are we looking for in a video game that fosters malevolent creativity? To do this, it may be simplest to turn the question on its head and ask how we would design a video expressly for this purpose. With a set of design criteria established, we then have, at our disposal, a set of criteria that allow us to identify suspect games. Among other things, this will help researchers to investigate the question of video games and malevolent creativity by facilitating the selection of games that are likely to cause the effect we are looking for. Likely suspects will be multiplayer games with a realistic interface and intuitive controls, and which present a wide range of diverse and unpredictable outcomes. They will allow players to engage in resourceful, planned, and intentionally harmful activities that are morally and legally ambiguous. By contrast, malevolent creativity seems unlikely to be fostered by games that simply require the player to impulsively blow away zombies or obvious enemies, nor is it likely to be engendered by games that permit only nonconformity and blind variation (pseudo-creativity) or novelty that is purposeless and unrealistic (quasi-creativity). These criteria are likely to rule out many current games, but do not preclude the possibility that one could exist.

References

Akinola, M., & Mendes, W. B. (2008). The dark side of creativity: Biological vulnerability and negative emotions lead to greater artistic creativity. *Personality and Social Psychology Bulletin, 34*, 1677–1686.

Amabile, T. M. (1983). *The social psychology of creativity.* New York: Springer.

Anderson, J. R. (1983). *The architecture of cognition.* Cambridge, MA: Harvard University Press.

Anderson, C. A., & Bushman, B. J. (2001). Effects of violent video games on aggressive behavior, aggressive cognition, aggressive affect, physiological arousal, and prosocial behavior: A meta-analytic review of the scientific literature. *Psychological Science, 12*(5), 353–359.

Anderson, C. A., Carnagey, N. L., Flanagan, M., Benjamin, A. J., Eubanks, J., & Valentine, J. C. (2004). Violent video games: Specific effects of violent content on aggressive thoughts and behavior. *Advances in Experimental Social Psychology, 36*, 200–251.

Anderson, C. A., & Dill, K. E. (2000). Video games and aggressive thoughts, feelings, and behavior in the laboratory and in life. *Journal of Personality and Social Psychology, 78*(4), 772.

Anderson, C. A., Gentile, D. A., & Buckley, K. E. (2007). *Violent video game effects on children and adolescents.* New York: Oxford University Press.

Anderson, C. A., Shibuya, A., Ihori, N., Swing, E. L., Bushman, B. J., Sakamoto, A., et al. (2010). Violent video game effects on aggression, empathy, and prosocial behavior in Eastern and Western countries: A meta-analytic review. *Psychological Bulletin, 136*(2), 151.

Baer, J. M. (1996). The effects of task-specific divergent-thinking training. *Journal of Creative Behavior, 30*(3), 183–187.

Baer, J. M. (1998). The case for domain specificity of creativity. *Creativity Research Journal, 11*(2), 173–177.

Barlett, C. P., Harris, R. J., & Baldassaro, R. (2007). Longer you play, the more hostile you feel: Examination of first person shooter video games and aggression during video game play. *Aggressive Behavior, 33*(6), 486–497.

Bartholow, B. D., Bushman, B. J., & Sestir, M. A. (2006). Chronic violent video game exposure and desensitization to violence: Behavioral and event-related brain potential data. *Journal of Experimental Social Psychology, 42*(4), 532–539.

Bartholow, B. D., Sestir, M. A., & Davis, E. B. (2005). Correlates and consequences of exposure to video game violence: Hostile personality, empathy, and aggressive behavior. *Personality and Social Psychology Bulletin, 31*(11), 1573–1586.

Beaussart, M. L., Andrews, C. J., & Kaufman, J. C. (2013). Creative liars: The relationship between creativity and integrity. *Thinking Skills and Creativity, 9,* 129–134.

Bettencourt, B., Talley, A., Benjamin, A. J., & Valentine, J. (2006). Personality and aggressive behavior under provoking and neutral conditions: A meta-analytic review. *Psychological Bulletin, 132*(5), 751.

Bluemke, M., Friedrich, M., & Zumbach, J. (2010). The influence of violent and nonviolent computer games on implicit measures of aggressiveness. *Aggressive Behavior, 36*(1), 1–13.

Bushman, B. J., & Anderson, C. A. (2002). Violent video games and hostile expectations: A test of the general aggression model. *Personality and Social Psychology Bulletin, 28*(12), 1679–1686.

Clark, K., & James, K. (1999). Justice and positive and negative creativity. *Creativity Research Journal, 12*(4), 311–320.

Cropley, A. J. (2001). *Creativity in education and learning: A guide for teachers and educators.* London, UK: Kogan Page.

Cropley, A. J. (2010). The dark side of creativity. In D. H. Cropley, A. J. Cropley, J. C. Kaufman, & M. A. Runco (Eds.), *The dark side of creativity* (pp. 1–14). New York: Cambridge University Press.

Cropley, D. H. (2015). *Creativity in engineering: Novel solutions to complex problems.* San Diego: Academic Press.

Cropley, D. H., & Cropley, A. J. (2000). Fostering creativity in engineering undergraduates. *High Ability Studies, 11*(2), 207–219.

Cropley, A. J., & Cropley, D. H. (2011). Creativity and lawbreaking. *Creativity Research Journal, 23*(4), 313–320.

Cropley, A. J., & Cropley, D. H. (2013). The dark side of creativity in the classroom: The paradox of classroom teaching. In J. B. Jones, & L. J. Flint (Eds.), *The creative imperative: School librarians and teachers cultivating curiosity together* (pp. 39–52). Santa Barbara, CA: ABC-CLIO.

Cropley, D. H., & Cropley, A. J. (2013). *Creativity and crime: A psychological approach.* Cambridge, UK: Cambridge University Press.

Cropley, D. H., Kaufman, J. C., & Cropley, A. J. (2008). Malevolent creativity: A functional model of creativity in terrorism and crime. *Creativity Research Journal, 20*(2), 105–115.

Cropley, D. H., Kaufman, J. C., & Cropley, A. J. (2013). Understanding malevolent creativity. In K. Thomas, & J. Chan (Eds.), *Handbook of research on creativity* (pp. 185–195). Cheltenham, UK and Northampton, MA, USA: Edward Elgar.

Cropley, D. H., Kaufman, J. C., White, A. E., & Chiera, B. A. (2014). Layperson perceptions of malevolent creativity: The good, the bad, and the ambiguous. *Psychology of Aesthetics, Creativity, and the Arts, 8*(4), 1–20.

De Aguilera, M., & Mendiz, A. (2003). Video games and education (education in the face of a "parallel school"). *Computers in Entertainment, 1*(1), 1.

De Dreu, C. K., & Nijstad, B. A. (2008). Mental set and creative thought in social conflict: Threat rigidity versus motivated focus. *Journal of Personality and Social Psychology, 95*(3), 648–661.

DeHaan, R. L. (2009). Teaching creativity and inventive problem solving in science. *CBE Life Sciences Education, 8*(3), 172–181.

Diamond, A., Barnett, W. S., Thomas, J., & Munro, S. (2007). Preschool program improves cognitive control. *Science, 318,* 1387–1388.

Edwards, S. M. (2001). The technology paradox: Efficiency versus creativity. *Creativity Research Journal, 13*(2), 221–228.

Ferguson, C. J. (2007). The good, the bad and the ugly: A meta-analytic review of positive and negative effects of violent video games. *Psychiatric Quarterly, 78*(4), 309–316.

Furnham, A., Zhang, J., & Chamorro-Premuzic, T. (2006). The relationship between psychometric and self-estimated intelligence, creativity, personality, and academic achievement. *Imagination, Cognition, and Personality, 25,* 119–145.

Gentile, D. A. (2011). The multiple dimensions of video game effects. *Child Development Perspectives, 5*(2), 75–81.

Gentile, D. A., Anderson, C. A., Yukawa, S., Ihori, N., Saleem, M., Ming, L. K., et al. (2009). The effects of prosocial video games on prosocial behaviors: International evidence from correlational, longitudinal, and experimental studies. *Personality and Social Psychology Bulletin, 35,* 752–763.

Gentile, D. A., & Gentile, J. R. (2008). Violent video games as exemplary teachers: A conceptual analysis. *Journal of Youth and Adolescence, 37*(2), 127–141.

Gentile, D. A., Swing, E. L., Lim, C. G., & Khoo, A. (2012). Video game playing, attention problems, and impulsiveness: Evidence of bidirectional causality. *Psychology of Popular Media Culture, 1*(1), 62.

Gill, P., Horgan, J., Hunter, S. T., & Cushenbery, L. (2013). Malevolent creativity in terrorist organizations. *Journal of Creative Behavior, 47,* 125–151.

Gill, P., Horgan, J., & Lovelace, J. (2011). Improvised explosive device: The problem of definition. *Studies in Conflict and Terrorism, 34,* 732–748.

Gino, F., & Ariely, D. (2012). The dark side of creativity: Original thinkers can be more dishonest. *Journal of Personality and Social Psychology, 102*(3), 445–459.

Green, C. S., & Bavelier, D. (2006). The cognitive neuroscience of video games. In P. Messaris & L. Humphreys (Eds.), *Digital media: Transformations in human communication* (pp. 211–223). New York: Peter Lang.

Griffiths, M. (1999). Violent video games and aggression: A review of the literature. *Aggression and Violent Behavior, 4*(2), 203–212.

Griffiths, M. (2002). The educational benefits of videogames. *Education and Health, 20*(3), 47–51.

Grossman, D., & DeGaetano, G. (1999). *Stop teaching our kids to kill: A call to action against TV, movie & video game violence.* New York, NY: Crown Publishers.

Hamlen, K. R. (2009). Relationships between computer and video game play and creativity among upper elementary school students. *Journal of Educational Computing Research, 40*(1), 1–21.

Harris, D. J., Reiter-Palmon, R., & Kaufman, J. C. (2013). The effect of emotional intelligence and task type on malevolent creativity. *Psychology of Aesthetics, Creativity, and the Arts, 7,* 237–244.

Hunsaker, S. L. (2005). Outcomes of creativity training programs. *Gifted Child Quarterly*, *49*(4), 292–299.

Irwin, A. R., & Gross, A. M. (1995). Cognitive tempo, violent video games, and aggressive behavior in young boys. *Journal of Family Violence*, *10*(3), 337–350.

Jackson, L. A., Witt, E. A., Games, A. I., Fitzgerald, H. E., von Eye, A., & Zhao, Y. (2012). Information technology use and creativity: Findings from the Children and Technology Project. *Computers in Human Behavior*, *28*(2), 370–376.

Kaufman, J. C., & Beghetto, R. A. (2009). Beyond big and little: The four c model of creativity. *Review of General Psychology*, *13*, 1–12.

Kim, K. H., & Coxon, S. V. (2013). The creativity crisis, possible causes, and what schools can do. In J. B. Jones, & L. J. Flint (Eds.), *The creative imperative* (pp. 53–68). Santa Barbara, CA: ABC-CLIO.

Kirsh, S. J. (2003). The effects of violent video games on adolescents: The overlooked influence of development. *Aggression and Violent Behavior*, *8*(4), 377–389.

Kutner, L., & Olson, C. (2008). *Grand theft childhood: The surprising truth about violent video games and what parents can do*. New York: Simon & Schuster.

Lee, S., & Dow, G. T. (2011). Malevolent creativity: Does personality influence malicious divergent thinking? *Creativity Research Journal*, *23*, 73–82.

Ma, H. H. (2006). A synthetic analysis of the effectiveness of single components and packages in creativity training programs. *Creativity Research Journal*, *18*(4), 435–446.

Mansfield, R. S., Busse, T. V., & Krepelka, E. J. (1978). The effectiveness of creativity training. *Review of Educational Research*, *48*, 517–536.

Mayer, J., & Mussweiler, T. (2011). Suspicious spirits, flexible minds: When distrust enhances creativity. *Journal of Personality and Social Psychology*, *101*(6), 1262–1277.

McFadzean, E. (2002). Developing and supporting creative problem-solving teams: Part 1—A conceptual model. *Management Decision*, *40*(5), 463–475.

McGregor, G. D. (2001). *Creative thinking instruction for a college study skills program: A case study)*. (Ph.D.) Waco, TX: Baylor University.

Mitchell, A., & Savill-Smith, C. (2004). *The use of computer and video games for learning: A review of the literature*. London: UK Learning and Skills Development Agency.

Möller, I., & Krahé, B. (2009). Exposure to violent video games and aggression in German adolescents: A longitudinal analysis. *Aggressive Behavior*, *35*(1), 75–89.

Mumford, M. D., Hester, K. S., & Robledo, I. C. (2012). Creativity in organizations: Importance and approaches. In M. D. Mumford (Ed.), *Handbook of organizational creativity*. London, UK: Academic Press.

Nicholls, J. (1972). Creativity in the person who will never produce anything original or useful. The concept of creativity as a normally distributed trait. *American Psychologist*, *27*, 717–727.

Prensky, M. (2005). Computer games and learning: Digital game-based learning. *Handbook of Computer Game Studies*, *18*, 97–122.

Resnick, M., Myers, B., Nakakoji, K., Shneiderman, B., Pausch, R., Selker, T., & Eisenberg, M. (2005). *Design principles for tools to support creative thinking*. Carnegie Mellon University.

Rhodes, M. (1961). An analysis of creativity. *Phi Delta Kappan*, *42*(7), 305–310.

Richards, R. (2010). Everyday creativity: Process and way of life—Four key issues. In J. C. Kaufman, & R. J. Sternberg (Eds.), *The Cambridge handbook of creativity* (pp. 189–215). New York: Cambridge University Press.

Richards, R., Kinney, D. K., Bennet, M., & Merzel, A. P. C. (1988). Assessing everyday creativity: Characteristics of the lifetime creativity scales and validation with three large samples. *Journal of Personality and Social Psychology*, *54*, 476–485.

Riley, S., & Gabora, L. (2012). Evidence that threatening situations enhance creativity. In: *Paper presented at the Proceedings of the Annual Meeting of the Cognitive Science Society, Sapporo, Japan*.

Ritterfeld, U., & Weber, R. (2006). Video games for entertainment and education. In P. Vorderer, & J. Bryant (Eds.), *Playing video games. Motives, responses, and consequences* (pp. 399–413). Mahwah, NJ: Lawrence Erlbaum.

Runco, M. A., & Richards, R. (Eds.), (1997). *Eminent creativity, everyday creativity, and health.* Greenwich, CT: Ablex.

Scott, G., Leritz, L. E., & Mumford, M. D. (2004a). The effectiveness of creativity training: A quantitative review. *Creativity Research Journal, 16*(4), 361–388.

Scott, G., Leritz, L. E., & Mumford, M. D. (2004b). Types of creativity training: Approaches and their effectiveness. *Journal of Creative Behavior, 38*(3), 149–179.

Smith, S. L., Lachlan, K., & Tamborini, R. (2003). Popular video games: Quantifying the presentation of violence and its context. *Journal of Broadcasting and Electronic Media, 47*(1), 58–76.

Sternberg, R. J. (1985). *Beyond IQ: A triarchic theory of human intelligence.* New York: Cambridge University Press.

Sternberg, R. J. (2007). Creativity as a habit. In A.-G. Tan (Ed.), *Creativity: A handbook for teachers* (pp. 3–25). Singapore: World Scientific.

Sternberg, R. J., & Lubart, T. I. (1995). *Defying the crowd: Cultivating creativity in a culture of conformity.* New York: Free Press.

Sternberg, R. J., & Williams, W. M. (1996). *How to develop student creativity.* Alexandria, VA: Association for Supervision and Curriculum Development.

Torrance, E. P. (1972). Can we teach children to think creatively? *Journal of Creative Behavior, 6*(2), 114–143.

Treffinger, D. J., Sortore, M. R., & Cross, J. A. (1993). Programs and strategies for nurturing creativity. In K. Heller, F. J. Monks, & A. H. Passow (Eds.), *International handbook for research on giftedness and talent* (pp. 555–567). Oxford, UK: Pergamon.

Urban, K. K. (1997). Modeling creativity: The convergence of divergence or the art of balancing. In J. Chan, R. Li, & J. Spinks (Eds.), *Maximizing potential: Lengthening and strengthening our stride* (pp. 39–50). Hong Kong: University of Hong Kong Social Sciences Research Centre.

Walczyk, J. J., Runco, M. A., Tripp, S. M., & Smith, C. E. (2008). The creativity of lying: Divergent thinking and ideational correlates of the resolution of social dilemmas. *Creativity Research Journal, 20*, 328–342.

Wallach, M. A. (1985). Creativity testing and giftedness. In F. D. Horowitz & M. O'Brien (Eds.), *The gifted and talented: Developmental perspectives* (pp. 99–123). Washington, DC: American Psychological Association.

Wiegman, O., & Schie, E. G. (1998). Video game playing and its relations with aggressive and prosocial behaviour. *British Journal of Social Psychology, 37*(3), 367–378.

Wolfradt, U., & Pretz, J. E. (2001). Individual differences in creativity: Personality, story writing, and hobbies. *European Journal of Personality, 15*(4), 297–310.

Wright, T., Boria, E., & Breidenbach, P. (2002). Creative player actions in FPS online video games. *Game Studies, 2*(2). http://www.gamestudies.org/0202/wright/.

CHAPTER

4

Problem Solving Through "Cheating" in Video Games

Karla R. Hamlen[1] and Fran C. Blumberg[2]

[1]Department of Curriculum and Foundations, Cleveland State University, Cleveland, OH, USA

[2]Division of Psychological & Educational Services, Fordham University, New York, NY, USA

Evidence continues to accumulate indicating that digital games have strong appeal among all ages, and are a context in which many people from diverse populations spend a fair amount of their leisure time. In fact, the video game industry now outperforms both the film and music industries in both the United States (PWC, 2014) and the UK (ERA, 2012). While the stereotype of a typical video game player may be that of a teenage male, the population of gamers is actually becoming more diverse. Close to half (48%) of gamers are now female, and the average age of a gamer is 31 (Entertainment Software Association, 2014). While a significant percentage of gamers are under the age of 18 (29%), the latest Entertainment Software Association (2014) report also demonstrates that adults are spending a great deal of time with gaming as well, now representing 71% of gamers. International findings also attest to the appeal and extensiveness of digital game play worldwide, such as in the UK (see Livingstone & Bober, 2005), in Germany, where 12- to 19-year-olds may spend close an hour per day during the weekdays playing video games (Medienpädagogischer Forschungsverbund Südwest, 2012), and in Australia, where 85% of 5- to 14-year-olds have been reported to play video games or use the computer (Australian Bureau of Statistics, 2012).

According to seminal work by Malone (1981), the appeal of digital game play could be attributed to the sense of challenge, curiosity, and fantasy that game players experienced. These factors remain viable contributors to digital game appeal among current players (Ferguson & Olson, 2013) and may provide the foundation for the creativity that players experience through their game play. For example, the fantastic nature and curiosity inspired by game play may encourage players to craft avatars that may bear little resemblance to their offline selves (see Blascovich & Bailenson, 2011) or to design improbable structures to thwart invasions from supernatural creatures as found in *Minecraft*. In fact, advocates of game play have emphasized the formal and informal educational benefits accrued via opportunities to create and manipulate game content and entities during that play (see Blumberg, Altschuler, Almonte, & Mileaf, 2013; Gee, 2003; Greenfield et al., 1994; Salonius-Pasternak & Gelfond, 2005; Squire, 2006). However, the ability to be creative juxtaposed with the challenge inherent in game play may inspire players to be less cautious than in real life in the moves that they enact (i.e., jumping from a tall cliff) and potentially in the ethics to which they adhere during game play.

We consider the issue of ethics and moral transgressions, as reflected by "cheating," in the context of digital game play in our discussion below. We note from the onset that we do not discount that players' cheating in the course of a game may cause psychological if not actual physical harm to other players within a given game community (see Ribbens, Poels, & Lamotte, 2011). However, we focus our discussion on how breaches in ethical conduct during game play may serve as reflections of players' creativity or perceived opportunities to demonstrate innovation in the mastering of a given game environment. Given the widespread appeal of video game play among diverse ages, our consideration of cheating and its linkages with demonstrations of creativity includes research among both child and adult samples.

WHAT CONSTITUTES CHEATING IN THE CONTEXT OF DIGITAL GAMES?

Cheating is commonly seen as engaging in an act of dishonesty that results in some type of unfair and unpermitted advantage that may or may not harm another. One such act may entail the breaking of rules that are established by society (as in the case of laws whereby one should not steal) or by the community (as in the case of a classroom code of conduct whereby one's comments are recognized by raising one's hand). Clearly, some transgressions or forms of cheating may be seen as more egregious and deserving of punishment than others. For example, stealing may be seen as causing psychological or physical harm which even preschoolers understand as wrong given the consequences that inflicting harm has on others and as deserving of punishment (see Nucci, 2002; Smetana, 2006). However, failing to raise one's hand in class may be seen as less of an infraction as it does not result in physical harm and is not likely to result in psychological harm to others. Furthermore, rules established via a given community, such as a classroom or a group of gamers, may have differential standards for what constitutes a moral breach or act of cheating. Thus, the context in which cheating occurs has ramifications for perceived assessments of its morality.

In the context of digital game play (or potentially any form of game play), cheating may be seen as breaking of rules established within the game or by the game community or as an expected activity given the conventions of game play. In fact, the issue of cheating in the context of game play has emerged as an area of scholarship as reflected in Consalvo's *Cheating: Gaining advantage in videogames* (2007) and Poels' and Malliets' edited volume, *Vice city virtue: Moral issues in digital game play* (2011). Scholars within this burgeoning area, such as Kücklich (2007), contend that understanding of a game requires an appreciation that "… one must play not only by its rules but also with its rules" (p. 355). Research findings support this claim as video game players have been shown to generally develop their own code of ethics that differ according to goals for game play (i.e., winning vs sustained play) and the type of game (simulation vs first-person shooter) (e.g., Hamlen & Gage, 2011). This code usually reflects an unwritten subtext in which players agree that certain behaviors are unfair or unethical. For example, players involved in massively multiplayer online games (MMOGs) inevitably come to some community agreement over what constitutes cheating within that game setting. In such contexts, when a person violates that accepted code of conduct, the response from other members is often some form of collective action to punish the offending member(s) (Consalvo, 2007; Steinkuehler, 2006).

The question remains what constitutes cheating in a digital game. One of the most commonly referred to forms of cheating in single-player games, for example, entails the use of cheat codes. These codes, which may be directly typed in using a keyboard or enacted via button combinations or movement repetitions in the game, are intentionally programmed by a game designer and are generally intended for the designer's own purposes in the play testing of games. Removal of these codes is often not done given the difficulty of doing so and the possibility of introducing new bugs. In fact, in early computer games played on 8-bit computers, players could load a game into the computer memory, access, and reprogram specific parts of the game, and then start the game. This situation allowed for the modification of statements within the program to gain unlimited lives or other perks to help players pass the game; thus, a form of "cheating" through code. Cheat codes, at present, refer to codes that are intentionally placed in the game by the designer and are often left for players who are "in the know" to access additional rewards. Sometimes the rewards facilitate the passing of levels more easily, allowing a player to unlock secret bonuses or levels, or to change the look and/or design of the game (Kuecklich, 2004). In these situations, the use of cheat codes may not necessarily result in unfair advantages.

The term "cheats" is more often used to refer to a variety of hints, tips, and advice for conquering portions of a game, even when unrelated to codes (Kuecklich, 2004). As an example, an online search for help with the game *Candy Crush* will yield many websites offering "cheats" and tips for all levels of the game. Here, there are no secret codes involved, but the tips and advice about how to approach levels are all considered cheats. For example, cheats for a given level of *Candy Crush* might offer counsel about which types of candies to clear first, and which power-ups might be most helpful, similar to asking a friend who has successfully completed the level; there are no codes used.

Other forms of cheating include the review of game guides and walkthroughs that are readily available for consultation through sources such as YouTube. Cheating also has been cited as taking advantage of bugs in a game. For example, in many gaming circles, different methods of solving problems in a game are a source of pride and admiration, particularly when they involve exploiting a mistake within the game programming (Bainbridge & Bainbridge, 2007; Consalvo, 2007). Further modes of cheating include canceling/exiting/escaping in which the player discontinues the game to avoid receiving a low score, using a map that someone else has created to advance through a level, and modifying software to alter the speed at which one proceeds through a game or the moves within levels of the game (Parker, 2007).

Presumably, as the types of games that are available for players become more sophisticated, modes of cheating also will become more innovative. In fact, digital games have been cited as a vehicle for creative expression among child players (see Ott & Pozzi, 2012). Questions remain as to whether the conventions of game play implicitly allow for cheating, or at least forms of it that do not result in physical or psychological harm. Accordingly, excelling in the game environment may require development of novel ways to circumvent formal game rules. Such behavior is clearly a reflection of creativity, as we discuss below.

WHAT CONSTITUTES CREATIVITY?

Creativity is a construct that has been defined, identified, and interpreted in many different ways. However, there is some consensus internationally that creativity is integral to lifelong learning and the development of knowledge for improvement of society (see Ott & Pozzi, 2012). Researchers in the second half of the twentieth century reached some agreement that creativity could be enhanced through one's interaction with the environment rather than simply being an inherent, static quality of the individual (Amabile, 1996; Pyryt, 1999; Torrance, 1962). Thus, contrary to early theories of creativity, these theorists posit that a supportive environment that encourages exploration and influences of culture and participation in activities can foster creativity beyond the level of creativity with which an individual is born. Definitions of creativity now consistently include elements of producing, originality, usefulness (Isenberg & Jalongo, 2006), commitment, sustained engagement (Amabile, 1989; Selby, Shaw, & Houtz, 2005; Torrance, 1967), and interaction between characteristics of the individual and the physical, social, and cultural environment in which they are based (Lewin, 1936). Characteristics of the individual include the motivation to engage in the creative process and qualities such as openness, tolerance for ambiguity, curiosity, self-discipline, and independence of thought (Torrance, 1967). Characteristics of the environment include the necessary materials or circumstances to enact a given product, freedom to explore, and psychological safety (Amabile, 1996).

Early theories of creativity, particularly before the mid-1900s, tended to focus on the individual as a creative being, with creativity serving as an intrinsic characteristic that was out of reach for the average person. In this view, the creativity emanates from within the person whether initiated via divine inspiration, thought processes that differ in the creative individual, unconscious motives of the individual, or the social and cultural interactions that the individual receives from the world around him or her (Starko, 2013). The early views of creativity serve as a foundation for our modern understanding of the creative process. The creative process today, however, is more often viewed in terms of the interaction of intrinsic and extrinsic motivation, convergent and divergent thinking abilities, practice, and need for novel solutions. Thus, creativity can be cultivated within an individual, and can be expressed to varying degrees (Kaufman & Sternberg, 2007; Weisberg, 2006). According to Amabile's Intrinsic Motivation Hypothesis of Creativity, intrinsic motivation is conducive to creativity when an individual may perceive a task as engaging, interesting, or challenging; extrinsic motivation such as that evoked via promise of rewards, praise, or threats of punishment are detrimental to creativity (Amabile, 1983; Amabile & Pillemer, 2012). Video games, which often engage intrinsic motivation such as interest in the game, challenge, or personal entertainment, provide an excellent format for engaging creative thinking, as defined by Amabile.

Creative Problem Solving Through "Cheating"

There have been conflicting findings regarding possible correlations between creativity and ethics. Gino and Ariely (2012) found that, among university students, greater displays of creativity were associated with higher levels of dishonesty in reporting results. In this series of studies, after baseline measurements of creativity were assessed, some participants were primed to engage in creative thinking. Those who were more creative, either at baseline measurements or after priming, were more likely to be dishonest when reporting results in the final stage of the study. There are several possible explanations for this, including the possibility that less concern for rules and ethical standards allows for greater freedom of thought and creativity. The researchers' hypothesis was that greater creativity allows for an individual to more easily justify his or her actions. Another study, however, specifically focusing on doctoral students in science fields, showed opposite results. In this study, creative problem solving was directly related to ethical decision-making (Mumford et al., 2010). This was a correlational study, and does not purport to determine any causal relationships. The argument can be made, however, that doctoral students are a very specific population, and their presence in a doctoral program might play a role in their thinking about ethics or their interest in portraying themselves as ethical decision makers.

While the term creativity may not bring to mind strategies in video game play, finding new and different ways to solve problems and overcome obstacles, both individually and collectively, continues to be an important aspect of many explorations of creative thinking. Video games are one context in which individuals and groups have the opportunity to solve problems in new and different ways. Cheating, depending on the definition, may provide opportunities to extend creative thinking to solve problems in video games in more unique ways.

Creative Cheating Within Video Games

Working Within the Programming—Designed Outcomes

There are many ways to approach an obstacle in a digital game. Some of these approaches work within the game programming, or by playing the game as it was designed and programmed to be played, and these are typically the first approaches a game player will try. Common approaches that work within the game play are trial and error, using tutorials, and exploring all possible areas and actions surrounding a problem. If used in the traditional sense, cheating may be considered any behavior that circumvents the programmed game play and was not intended by the game designer. As we have shown, however, the word cheating has morphed to mean more than this in a video game context, including unique ways to solve problems beyond the traditional trial and error. Some games encourage creative problem solving and reward creativity by including scenarios that can have multiple solutions. In such games, sometimes a nontraditional approach to solving a problem is rewarded, encouraging the more creative players to explore and extend their boundaries in the game. One example of this comes from the game *Fallout 3*. In a quest called "The Replicated Man," the player is directed to either aid a scientist in recovering his escaped android, or the player can instead choose to help the android escape. Either choice offers the player a reward: helping the scientist gains the player technology that permanently improves his or her reflexes, while helping the android allows the player to gain a weapon. The quest is designed such that the player who follows the rules of the game play will eventually have to choose between these two options. By being both clever and duplicitous, however, it is actually possible to get both rewards. To accomplish this, the player must first take the side of the android, who gives the player a gun to kill the scientist. Then the player can betray the android by telling the scientist where the android is hiding instead of using the gun to kill the scientist. Thus, the scientist will give his reward and the player has both rewards. If the player then betrays the scientist and kills him, the android will side with the player and the player can keep both rewards. It is likely that the game designers intended this as a possible scenario, but the quest dialog and options all heavily encourage the player to make a choice, not to play both sides. Thus, this might be a case where players are essentially encouraged to cheat their way into getting extra rewards.

This form of creative problem solving fits closely with Vygotsky's (1978) supposition that role playing (or thinking like the character in the video game) can result in more creative thinking and problem solving. It also aligns with the creative characteristic of risk-taking because, even in the context of a game, risk-taking can produce lower levels of the same types of physical and emotional responses in a player that they would experience when taking risks in real life (Fischer et al., 2009).

Working Within the Programming—Unintended Outcomes

Another way to problem-solve creatively but within the confines of the game programming is to take advantage of ideas or quirks that the game programmers did not consider. An example of this type of creative cheating is shown in the video game *Zoo Tycoon*. In *Zoo Tycoon*, a simulation game, the primary objective is to design and run a successful zoo that makes money. One of the targets toward accomplishing this objective is to keep guests inside the zoo by keeping them happy. A creative cheating method that players have used to keep guests in the zoo is to place large rocks outside the gates so the people do not have an exit. This solution works within the programming of the game, but is not the way the designers intended the game to be played.

Another example of this type of creative "cheating" can be found in the game *Skyrim*, a role-playing game. There is a perk in *Skyrim* called "Necromage" that improves the effectiveness of all your magic against undead, such as mummies and vampires. There is also, within this game, a playing path whereby the player can actually become undead (a vampire). If the player becomes a vampire and also has the Necromage skill, something very surprising happens: All magic that the player applies to himself becomes amplified whereby all enchanted items, potions, and self-directed spells become more powerful, which offers an enormous advantage. It is unclear whether the designers thought of this situation. Technically, there is no error in the programming; the Necromage and Vampire programming does exactly what the game says it does. But the interaction between the two seems sufficiently powerful that it is very possible that the designers did not foresee this trick, in which case some might see this as a form of cheating, or providing an unfair advantage.

Working Outside the Programming

Often, when the in-game approaches to problem solving do not work, a gamer will start working outside of the programmed game play to creatively solve the problem. This can include both working with others to problem-solve collectively, as well as glitching. *Glitching* occurs when there is a programming error in the game, and a player exploits that error to do something they would normally not be able to do in the game. When a player drinks a "Fortify Restoration" potion in *Skyrim*, it is designed to increase Restoration skill only. Due to a programming error, however, it also increases the power of any enchanted item you equip while the portion is active. Gamers who discover this glitch can create overpowered, unstoppable characters that can win the game very easily. This becomes even more of an issue in a competitive multiplayer game. In *Halo*, a first-person multiplayer shooter game, there are known glitches that allow the player to pass through a wall that one should not be able to pass through. Some players exploit these glitches to gain an advantage over their enemy in the game. According to Bainbridge and Bainbridge (2007), the most common response of a gamer when faced with a glitch in the game is to exploit the glitch. Finding glitches and new ways to proceed through the game and overcome obstacles may be considered a source of pride among gamers because they are not easy to find; it is difficult to solve problems in a video game in unique ways because most creative efforts in video games are limited by the game programming. Games are generally released still containing bugs, or problems in the game programming that are not only glitches but can either make tasks more difficult or can sometimes even prevent the player from being able to finish a task in the game. In another form of creative problem solving in digital games, related to these bugs and glitches, some individuals deliberately take on the challenge of locating bugs and glitches in games. They then find ways to overcome the bugs to get the game back on its usual course, since many of these bugs and glitches interrupt the normal game play and keep the player from being able to accomplish goals. Once an individual finds a solution, he or she may then publish it online, which is very useful to others who run into the same problems in the game. This can also be a way to gain notoriety or praise in a video game community.

Hacking

Stepping up to another level beyond taking advantage of simple mistakes in the game programming, hacking involves actually altering the game programming or, when playing MMOGs, altering the information being transmitted to a server to be able to gain advantage in the game. When playing an MMOG, the individual buys a game for their local computer, and the game then connects to a general server. Individuals can figure out how to hack the local copy they are using to make it send false information to the server or get more information from the remote server than they should be able to. For example, in a first-person multiplayer shooter game, there are instances where an individual can hack the local game to give the server information that alters the game design so that the player sees all walls in the game as transparent. This situation enables an individual to find everyone else on the game board, giving them a large advantage over the other players not employing this method. Game designers try to block these methods through anti-piracy programming of local copies of games, but doing so is very difficult to accomplish since there are so many methods for circumventing the game design and the options for doing this are constantly evolving.

Some digital games involve the use of specific and complex button combinations to execute powerful moves in the game. Macros are a form of hack that involve preprogrammed computer software that players can download and program to their mouse, keyboard, or controller so that it will do the complex button combinations for them with one simple button press. Computer and gaming manufacturers actually market lines of keyboards, mice, and controllers that are specifically designed for macros, which presents a problem in online multiplayer games because it changes the level of challenge for players using the macros. For this reason, online multiplayer games are starting to move away from using complex button combinations.

There are also games in which being online for longer periods of time or completing particular actions a certain number of times allows a player's character to level up or allows the player a stronger position in the game. These games often rely on subscriptions or advertising clicks, thus necessitating keeping players online as often as possible. For these types of games, players may choose to cheat by "farming out" their account, which involves paying someone to use their account and perform the action or stay online for long periods of time to give them the perks that come with time and/or repetition of rewarded in-game actions. The individuals who are paid to play others' accounts are often professionals who make their living this way.

To be successful at hacking methods, the hacker who cracks the game code and programs the methods to cheat in a game must demonstrate excellent computer skills, combined with creativity to think of new ways around a system and also, on the side of the game developers, to combat the evolving hacking techniques by revising protections on the game. Using hacks, however, may involve limited creativity, given that they are accessible via simple web searches and downloads. Using the hacks results in advantages that generally reduce the players' requirements for skill and creativity when playing the game.

EVALUATING THE CREATIVITY OF CHEATING METHODS

The two components that comprise creativity in a product, creation, or idea are generally uniqueness and usefulness of the solution or product (Amabile, 1996). Furthermore, the level of creativity associated with cheating or problem solving to overcome an obstacle in a game must be considered in conjunction with the gamer's goals in the game play, the amount of original thinking taking place by the gamer, as well as what the method of game play accomplishes. A gamer who is able to translate goals into in-game actions, but can also find ways to transform the game itself or the system to better accomplish goals reflects what has been seen as creative problem solving in video game play (Ejsing-Duun, Hanghøj, & Karoff, 2013). For example, consider a scenario in which three different gamers independently struggle in *Zoo Tycoon* to keep guests inside the zoo. Then consider the following three responses for their level of creativity:

- Player 1 plays the game as designed and tries various in-game methods such as creating places for the people to eat within the zoo.
- Player 2 searches online and finds the proposed solution of placing rocks outside the gate so guests cannot leave.
- Player 3 thinks of alternatives to the traditionally accepted game play methods and independently decides to place rocks or large objects outside the gate so that guests cannot leave.

Player 1 approached the game through the traditional game play, and engaged in as much creative problem solving as was designed into the game, with limited risks. Players 2 and 3, however, engaged in an activity that might be considered cheating. Both players enacted the same solution. However, the player who thought of the creative solution is displaying more creativity than the player who simply found the idea online and carried it out. This illustrates the point that creativity in video game play must be evaluated not only by the actual solution carried out, but also by the level of unique thinking or ideas, the context, and the relationship between the goal and the solution.

CONNECTIONS BETWEEN CHEATING IN GAME PLAY AND PROBLEM SOLVING IN SCHOOL SETTINGS

Problem-solving styles and work ethic in video game play seem to be similar to, or practice for, real-life problem solving and decision-making. This observation is based on findings demonstrating that, in general, a person who is more likely to give up in a video game when it is difficult is also more likely to give up on a homework assignment when it gets difficult. Similarly, someone who is more likely to ask for help when solving problems in video games is also more likely to ask for help when doing academic work (Blumberg & Altschuler, 2011; Hamlen, 2012). It seems likely, then, that a person who solves problems in unique and creative ways in video games would also be more likely to approach other types of problems, potentially within school, in unique and interesting ways. However, unlike cheating in video games, school is one setting in which some of the creative forms of problem solving that result in unfair advantage are typically not well received. For example, in traditional formal educational settings, teachers generally give assignments and problems with the intent that the child will solve or complete it in particular ways (e.g., reading the text, practicing, using logical reasoning, or asking the teacher for help). When a player practices alternative forms of problem solving through cheating in video games, they might be tempted to forgo these teacher-endorsed problem-solving methods and try something different, such as collaboration, using the internet, or exploring alternative solutions. While this could result in some creative solutions, alternative methods of problem solving may not always be appreciated or accepted in school settings where the focus is often on conforming to particular methods of problem solving and repetitious practice that can be reproduced on assessments (Geist & Hohn, 2009).

Alternate methods of creative problem solving that may be considered cheating or discouraged in academic contexts are often used and encouraged in other real-world settings such as business. It is important for educators to consider what useful problem-solving skills will be in relevant real-world contexts and determine a code of ethics for academic problem solving that mirrors the real-world context. For example, while collaboration, use of the internet, and exploring alternative solutions may be considered getting an unfair advantage (or cheating) in many academic contexts, these same problem-solving methods may be encouraged and useful for solving problems in other areas of life. Instead of considering these methods unethical or forms of cheating, it is suggested that students be involved in determining ethics based on the context and goals of a course, so that they will be better equipped to determine ethical standards that apply to other situations outside of the classroom.

CONCLUSIONS

While cheating has a negative connotation because of its origins, within a video game context, cheating can actually be a form of creative problem solving and thinking outside the box. When evaluating the ethics and creativity of cheating in video games, it is important to consider the goals, the context, and the outcome. The same actions can reflect different ethical standards and different levels of creativity depending on these factors. For students who are engaging in creative problem solving in video games, the rigidness of formal academics may be frustrating because there are limited acceptable methods for solving problems. Instead of considering all alternative problem-solving methods to be allowing an unfair advantage, there may be ways to allow for more freedom while still evaluating creativity and ethics within each context. Educators might want to give students more open-choice activities or to give certain assignments in which any method of problem solving is considered acceptable, which would allow students the opportunity to experience the same type of free problem solving in learning that they experience in entertainment game play. Cheating in video games can offer a venue for creative thinkers to explore, take risks, and experiment without any real-life risk taking place, and problem solving in video games can be practice for problem solving in real life. Using cheating as an easy means of winning or to get out of doing the work can be negative practice for problem solving and work ethic in other contexts, while cheating as a way to try new ideas and approach problems from new directions can be positive practice for thinking creatively in other areas of life.

References

Amabile, T. M. (1983). *The social psychology of creativity*. New York: Springer-Verlag.

Amabile, T. M. (1989). *Growing up creative: Nurturing a lifetime of creativity*. New York: Crown.

Amabile, T. M. (1996). *Creativity in context: Update to the social psychology of creativity*. Boulder, CO: Westview Press.

Amabile, T. M., & Pillemer, J. (2012). Perspectives on the social psychology of creativity. *Journal of Creative Behavior, 46*(1), 3–15.

Australian Bureau of Statistics. (2012). *Children's participation in cultural and leisure activities, April 2012*. Canberra: Australian Bureau of Statistics.

Bainbridge, W. A., & Bainbridge, W. S. (2007). Creative uses of software errors: Glitches and cheats. *Social Science Computer Review, 25*(1), 61–77.

Blascovich, J., & Bailenson, J. (2011). *Infinite reality: The hidden blueprint of our virtual lives*. New York: HarperCollins.

Blumberg, F. C., & Altschuler, E. (2011). From the playroom to the classroom: Children's views of video game play and academic learning. *Child Development Perspectives, 2*, 99–103.

Blumberg, F. C., Altschuler, E. A., Almonte, D. E., & Mileaf, M. I. (2013). The impact of recreational video game play on children and adolescents' cognition. In F. C. Blumberg & S. M. Fisch (Eds.), *New directions for child and adolescent development: Vol. 139* (pp. 41–50). San Francisco, CA: Jossey-Bass.

Consalvo, M. (2007). *Cheating: Gaining advantage in videogames*. Cambridge, MA: MIT Press.

Ejsing-Duun, S., Hanghøj, T., & Karoff, H. S. (2013). Cheating and creativity in pervasive games in learning contexts. In *Proceedings of the 7th European conference on games based learning* (pp. 149–156). Sonning Common, UK: Academic Conferences and Publishing International.

Entertainment Software Association. (2014). *2013 essential facts about the computer and video game industry*. Retrieved August 22, 2014, from: www.theesa.com/facts/pdfs/ESA_EF_2013.pdf.

ERA/Entertainment Retailers Association. (2012). *Games overtakes video as UK's biggest entertainment category in 2011, but video is fighting back*. Retrieved May 17, 2014, from: http://www.eraltd.org/news/era-news/games-overtakes-video-as-uk's-biggest-entertainment-category-in-2011,-but-video-is-fighting-back.aspx.

Ferguson, C., & Olson, C. (2013). Friends, fun, frustration, and fantasy: Child motivations for video game play. *Motivation & Emotion, 37*(1), 154–164.

Fischer, P., Greitemeyer, T., Morton, T., Kastenmüller, A., Postmes, T., Frey, D., et al. (2009). The racing-game effect: Why do video racing games increase risk-taking inclinations? *Personality and Social Psychology Bulletin, 35*(10), 1395–1409.

Gee, J. P. (2003). *What video games have to teach us about learning and literacy*. New York: Palgrave Macmillan.

Geist, E., & Hohn, J. (2009). Encouraging creativity in the face of administrative convenience: How our schools discourage divergent thinking. *Education, 130*(1), 141–150.

Gino, F., & Ariely, D. (2012). The dark side of creativity: Original thinkers can be more dishonest. *Journal of Personality and Social Psychology, 102*, 445–459.

Greenfield, P. M., Camaioni, L., Ercolani, P., Weiss, L., et al. (1994). Cognitive socialization by computer games in two cultures: Inductive discovery or mastery of an iconic code? *Journal of Applied Developmental Psychology, 15*, 59–85.

Hamlen, K. R. (2012). Academic dishonesty and video game play: Is new media use changing conceptions of cheating? *Computers & Education, 59*(4), 1145–1152.

Hamlen, K. R., & Gage, H. E. (2011). Negotiating students' conceptions of 'cheating' in video games and in school. *International Journal of Gaming and Computer-Mediated Simulations, 3*(2), 44–56.

Isenberg, J. P., & Jalongo, M. R. (2006). *Creative thinking and arts-based learning: Preschool through fourth grade* (4th ed.). Upper Saddle River, NJ: Pearson.

Kaufman, J. C., & Sternberg, R. J. (2007). Creativity. *Change, 39*(4), 55–60.

Kücklich, J. (2007). Homo DeLudens. Cheating as a methodological tool in digital games research. *Convergence: The International Journal of Research into New Media Technologies, 13*, 355–367.

Kuecklich, J. (2004). *Other playing—Cheating in computer games. Paper presented at the Other Players conference*. Denmark: Center for Computer Games Research, IT University of Copenhagen.

Lewin, K. (1936). *Principles of typological psychology*. New York: McGraw-Hill.

Livingstone, S., & Bober, M. (2005). *UK children go online*. Swindon, UK: ESRC. Retrieved from: www.lse.ac.uk/collections/children-go-online/UKCGO_Final_report.pdf.

Malone, T. W. (1981). Toward a theory of intrinsically motivating instruction. *Cognitive Science, 5*(4), 333–369.

Medienpädagogischer Forschungsverbund Südwest. (2012). *JIM 2012. Youth, information, (multi-) media: Basic study on media handling 12- to 19-year-olds in Germany*. Retrieved from: http://www.mpfs.de/fileadmin/JIM-pdf12/JIM2012_Endversion.pdf.

Mumford, M. D., Waples, E. P., Antes, A. L., Brown, R. P., Connelly, S., Murphy, S. T., et al. (2010). Creativity and ethics: The relationship of creative and ethical problem-solving. *Creativity Research Journal, 22*(1), 74–89.

Nucci, L. (2002). The development of moral reasoning. In U. Goswami (Ed.), *Blackwell handbook of child cognitive development* (pp. 303–325). Oxford: Blackwell.

Ott, M., & Pozzi, F. (2012). Digital games as creativity enablers for children. *Behaviour & Information Technology, 31*, 1011–1019.

Parker, J. R. (2007). Cheating by video game participants. *Loading, 1*(1).

Poels, K., Malliet, S. (Eds.), (2011). *Vice city virtue. Moral issues in digital game play*. Leuven: Acco.

PWC/Pricewaterhousecoopers. (2014). *Video games*. Retrieved May 17, 2014, from: http://www.pwc.com/gx/en/global-entertainment-media-outlook/segment-insights/video-games.jhtml.

Pyryt, M. C. (1999). Effectiveness of training children's divergent thinking: A meta-analytic review. In A. S. Fishkin, B. Cramond, & P. Olszewski-Kubilius (Eds.), *Investigating creativity in youth: Research and methods* (pp. 351–365). Cresskill, NJ: Hampton.

Ribbens, W., Poels, Y., & Lamotte, G. (2011). Fail with honour or win by cheating? Research into the perceptions and motivations of cheaters in online multiplayer games. In K. Poels, & S. Malliet (Eds.), *Vice city virtue. Moral issues in digital game play*. Leuven: Acco.

Salonius-Pasternak, D. E., & Gelfond, H. S. (2005). The next level of research on electronic play: Potential benefits and contextual influences for children and adolescents. *Human Technology: An Interdisciplinary Journal on Humans in ICT Environments, 1*, 5–22.

Selby, E. C., Shaw, E. J., & Houtz, J. C. (2005). The creative personality. *Gifted Child Quarterly, 49*(4), 300–314.

Smetana, J. G. (2006). Social-cognitive domain theory: Consistencies and variations in children's moral and social judgments. In M. Killen, & J. Smetana (Eds.), *Handbook of moral development* (pp. 119–153). Mahwah, NJ: Lawrence Erlbaum.

Squire, K. (2006). From content to context: Videogames as designed experience. *Educational Researcher, 35*, 19–29.

Starko, A. J. (2013). *Creativity in the classroom: Schools of curious delight* (5th ed.). New York: Routledge.

Steinkuehler, C. (2006). The mangle of play. *Games and Culture, 1*(3), 199–213.

Torrance, E. P. (1962). *Guiding creative talent.* Englewood Cliffs, NJ: Prentice-Hall.

Torrance, E. P. (1967). Nature of creative talents. *Theory Into Practice, 5*(168–173), 201–202.

Vygotsky, L. (1978). *Mind in society: The development of higher psychological processes.* Cambridge, MA: Harvard University Press.

Weisberg, R. W. (2006). *Creativity: Understanding innovation in problem solving, science, invention, and the arts.* New York: Wiley.

CHAPTER

5

Opportunities and Challenges in Assessing and Supporting Creativity in Video Games

Yoon J. Kim and Valerie J. Shute

Instructional Systems and Learning Technologies, Florida State University, Tallahassee, FL, USA

OUTLINE

INTRODUCTION

Creativity as a Twenty-First Century Skill

Young Americans' readiness for the twenty-first century global economy is a growing societal concern (Bybee & Fuchs, 2006; Florida, 2002; Friedman, 2005). Friedman's *The world is flat* (2005) is a well-known example of the literature that describes the world economy's rapid evolution toward completely open, global competition, and the United States' potential loss of global competitiveness as a result. In the same vein, Levy and colleagues (Autor, Levy, & Murnane, 2003; Levy & Murnane, 2004) report that advancements in computer technology are replacing routine cognitive tasks and manual labor, with jobs requiring creative thinking and complex communication skills. Therefore, to gain global competitiveness in the twenty-first century, society must prepare its younger generation with knowledge and skills that are fundamentally different from those in previous centuries. In a survey conducted by the Partnership for 21st Century Skills (2007), the general public expressed similar views: 99% of voters responded that twenty-first century skills such as creativity and collaboration were important for the nation's economic growth, and that school education needs to (and should) support those skills.

Despite the clear need to support twenty-first century skills, business leaders and educators are concerned that young people are inadequately prepared with the requisite skills to succeed in a twenty-first-century economy, even after completing a high-school or college education (Casner-Lotto & Barrington, 2006; Symonds, Schwartz, & Ferguson, 2011). For instance, 431 business leaders were interviewed in an effort to understand employers' views on work-readiness and "twenty-first-century skills" in recent graduates, and they generally agreed that high-school and college graduates lacked both basic and applied skills. A majority (75%) of the business leaders also pointed out that creativity is one of the most important skills (Casner-Lotto & Barrington, 2006).

Creativity generally refers to the ability to produce ideas or solutions that are novel yet appropriate for the problem (Lubart, 1994). Creativity has been of research interest to psychologists for over 50 years, and is now particularly recognized as one of the essential skills needed to succeed in the twenty-first century (e.g., the Partnership for 21st Century Skills, 2007). As Resnick (2007) argues, we are living in a *creative society* where one's success is based on the ability to think and act creatively. However, despite the recognized importance of creativity, current school systems do not adequately prepare younger people to become creative thinkers (Hargreaves, 2003; Sawyer, 2006).

Video Games and Creativity

One medium that has affordances to support creativity in young people is video games. Playing video games is one of the most popular activities for people of all ages in the United States. Fifty-eight percent of all Americans play video games and the average game player's age is 30. And a recent study on media usage in the United States also reported that 67% of youth (ages 8-18) spent an average of 73 min daily playing video games, compared with only 38 min daily reading print materials (Rideout, Foehr, & Roberts, 2010). In 2013 only, Americans spent $21.53 billion on video game-related purchases (Entertainment Software Association, 2014).

How can video games cultivate creativity? Will Wright (2006), a renowned game designer, argues that video games are "dream machines" that have the ability to unleash human imagination. Wright explains that a game is a "possibility space" in which video games start at a well-defined state and end when a specific state is reached. How players reach a specific end is open-ended, and each player can navigate this possibility space by making continuous choices and actions.

Gee (2005) similarly describes how a well-designed game incorporates good learning principles that can support players' creativity. First, players are not mere consumers of the game but producers by making their own actions and choices. At a simple level, what players do and create in the game to progress through levels is a form of production. For example, in the popular "god" game called *Spore*, players create their own species and then the species evolve into more intelligent creatures and civilization. Some games, such as *LittleBigPlanet* or *Portal 2*, have built-in level editor functionality that allows players to modify the games and even create their own levels. Second, good games often encourage players to take risks, explore and try new things, and learn by failing. Failing is not a bad thing in games as it is in traditional education. In fact, failing is one way to get feedback about progress. Learning-by-failing can be found in many games, such as *World of Goo* (see Shute & Kim, 2011), where solving the goo-ball puzzles typically requires multiple trials, per puzzle. Third, video games are "pleasantly frustrating." That is, tasks in a well-designed game are challenging but reside within a range of difficulty levels that gives players a great sense of accomplishment upon completing the task. For example, *Candy Crush Saga* presents levels with gradually increasing difficulties and scaffolds players at earlier levels. When players reach certain proficiency, then the game eventually removes the scaffolding.

Due to those affordances of video games to facilitate creative behaviors and risk-taking, a few researchers investigated possible links between creativity and video games. For example, Hamlen (2009) investigated the relationship between self-reported time spent playing video games per week and performance on the Torrance Tests of Creativity Thinking (TTCT) in fourth and fifth graders. She reported that the number of hours of game play does not significantly predict TTCT performance controlling for gender and grade. In contrast, Jackson and colleagues (Jackson et al., 2012) investigated the relationship between game play time (i.e., participants' response to *how often do you play videogames?*) and creativity using the TTCT, and they reported that playing video games is significantly associated with creativity.

Although investigating correlational relationships between video game play and creativity may be interesting, this line of research does not directly help educators and practitioners to use video games to foster creativity. First, those existing studies (e.g., Hamlen, 2009; Jackson et al., 2012) are based on the assumption that creativity is a "general" construct, and do not consider the possible interplay with or dependence on domains. Second, these studies do not clearly state how creativity is defined in their study (Plucker, Beghetto, & Dow, 2004). Third, how creativity is assessed in these studies is also problematic. That is, many studies view creativity as a unidimensional cognitive ability (e.g., divergent thinking) by using existing creativity tests (e.g., TTCT) that depend heavily on divergent thinking. Finally, these studies did not systematically review *how* specific aspects of creativity can be manifested in video games.

To support creativity using video games in the broader education community, we need to understand the affordances of video games in relation to the multidimensional aspects of creativity. That is, the first question we should ask is: What are some of the cognitive and noncognitive dimensions of creativity that are manifested in video games? In addition, attention needs to be paid to assessment methods that use creative behaviors and products that players create in and outside of video games (Plucker & Makel, 2010). Such behaviors and products are believed to be more valid indicators of creativity than commonly used self-reported measures of creativity (McClelland, 1973; Shute, Ventura, & Kim, 2013).

The purpose of this chapter is twofold. First, we review the current literature on creativity and link the literature with the mechanics and features of popular games that foster players' creative endeavors, both inside (little "g") and outside (big "G") of games (Gee, 2003, 2008). Second, we describe a methodology called stealth assessment as a way to assess creativity in the context of games using examples from *Physics Playground* (Shute & Ventura, 2013).

REVIEW OF THE CREATIVITY AND GAMES LITERATURE

Multiple Dimensions of Creativity

According to Taylor (1988), there are more than 60 definitions of creativity, and there have been countless arguments over the accepted definition of creativity among psychologists (Amabile, 1983). Despite this lack of agreement, there are some common notions of creativity that run through the literature on creativity. First, creativity is generally defined as the ability to produce solutions or ideas that are both novel and effective (Lubart, 1994). Kaufman and Sternberg (2007) similarly have noted that most definitions of creativity consist of three components: novelty, quality, and relevance. That is, creative solutions are novel, of high quality, and appropriate to the given task, or some variant of the task.

Second, the majority of research on creativity (e.g., confluence approaches) suggests that there are multiple variables that need to converge for creativity to manifest (Amabile, 1983, 1996; Csikszentmihalyi, 1988; Sternberg & Lubart, 1992a, 1992b, 1996). For instance, Amabile (1983) emphasized the importance of social and environmental influences on creativity. She noted that creativity is best conceptualized not as a personality trait or a general ability, but instead as a *behavior* resulting from particular collections of personal characteristics, cognitive abilities, and social environments. Similarly, Sternberg and Lubart (1992b) explained that the different approaches to creativity can be viewed as a continuum between "less" contextualized approaches that focus on personal characteristics, and "more" contextualized approaches that include social-cultural variables that influence individuals' creativity. McCrae (1987) stressed that the ability to think creatively in conjunction with an inclination to do so (i.e., disposition) leads to creative productions.

Among these factors that contribute to creativity, Guilford (1956) conceptualized creativity as involving four facets of divergent thinking—*flexibility* (the ability to produce ideas from various categories or classes), *fluency* (the ability to rapidly produce a large number of ideas), *originality* (the ability to produce ideas that are unique, novel, and uncommon), and *elaboration* (the ability to develop the details of an idea and carry it out). Flexibility has been recognized as an essential cognitive skill for creativity (Amabile, 1983) and is defined as the ability to generate a varied pool of ideas by switching among categories and using remote associations (Nijstad, De Dreu, Rietzschel, & Baas, 2010).

Openness to experience, one of the dimensions of the Big-Five factors, refers to a dispositional attribute that is characterized by an awareness of personal feelings and beliefs, receptivity to novel ideas, liberal values, intellectual curiosity, and fantasy (Berzonsky & Sullivan, 1992). Therefore, individuals with higher degrees of openness to experience are described as imaginative, sensitive to esthetics, curious, independent thinkers, and/or amenable to new ideas, experiences, and unconventional views (Costa & McCrae, 1992). A long line of research has supported the strong association between openness to experience and creativity or some aspects of creativity (Costa & McCrae, 1992; McCrae, 1987). For example, McCrae (1987) reported a significant association ($r = 0.4$) between divergent thinking and openness to experience.

Willingness to take risks (i.e., risk propensity) can be defined as the extent to which an individual takes an action knowing there is uncertainty related to the potential pay-off of the action (Dewett, 2007). Risk-taking is associated with openness to change and new ideas (Madjar, Greenberg, & Chen, 2011) and willingness to take risks (and knowing the possibility of failing) has been recognized as an essential trait of eminent scientists and artists throughout history (Csikszentmihalyi, 1997; Sternberg & Lubart, 1996). Sternberg and Lubart (1992b) describe creative individuals as those who "buy low and sell high." That is, creative individuals can come up with undervalued ideas at the moment, because they are very different from widely accepted ideas, but which, in fact, have great potential. Sternberg and Lubart (1992b) further argue that willingness to take risks is a prerequisite for growth and creativity because one needs to go beyond what is commonly accepted, and learn from various failings. Several studies have reported a positive association between willingness to take risks and creativity (Glover, 1977; Glover & Sautter, 1977). For example, Glover and Sautter (1977) reported that willingness to take risks was significantly correlated with flexibility and originality. Willingness to take risks has also been studied in the context of organizational innovations for many years (e.g., Dewett, 2007; Kogan & Wallach, 1964; MacCrimmon & Wehrung, 1990). For example, Madjar et al. (2011) found that willingness to take risks is a significant contributor to individuals' creativity and innovation.

Developmental View of Creativity

In line with the view on the multidimensionality of creativity, the literature on creativity also emphasizes the importance of understanding developmental trajectories of creativity (Feldman, 1999). The developmental view of creativity is especially relevant for the education community as different levels of creativity may provide the basis for supporting students' *learning* of creativity in the classroom (Beghetto & Kaufman, 2007).

Gardner (1993) distinguished everyday creative activities by non experts (i.e., little-c) from groundbreaking creative achievements by eminent scientists and geniuses (i.e., Big-C) in his study of seven renowned individuals, such as Albert Einstein. The recent model developed by Beghetto and Kaufman (Beghetto & Kaufman, 2007; Kaufman & Beghetto, 2009, 2013) further expands this distinction by including mini-c and Pro-C, and proposed four levels of creativity—mini-c, little-c, Pro-C, and Big-C. Mini-c is defined as *"the novel and personally meaningful interpretation of experiences, actions, and events"* (Beghetto & Kaufman, 2007, p. 73). The mini-c idea is based on the dynamic and socio-cultural conception of creativity that everybody has creative potential that begins with an "internalization or appropriation of cultural tools and social interactions" (Moran & John-Steiner, 2003, p. 63). Pro-C, located between little-c and Big-C, represents effortful progression toward Big-C, and people who have expertise in creative domains fall into this category. One of the unique contributions of the Four C Model is that it allows us to think about how we can measure creativity beyond existing creativity assessment techniques.

Sources of Evidence for Creativity in Video Games

The current literature on creativity generally suggests that (a) creativity can be judged by the output of creative processes that is characterized by both novelty and relevance; (b) the creative process represents a confluence of factors including personality traits, attitudes, cognitive abilities, knowledge, and the environment; and (c) creativity is a socio-cultural developmental process that can be assessed at multiple levels. To support and assess people's creativity development in video games, therefore, one needs to consider those three aspects of creativity in relation to different sources of evidence that video games can afford.

As Gee (2003, 2008) convincingly argues, playing video games is a semiotic domain—an area or set of activities where people think, act, and hold particular values in certain ways. Similarly, to become creative in a semiotic domain, one first needs to learn how others behave or what are valued in the domain, and then later need to "buy low, sell high" with their own unique contribution (Sternberg & Lubart, 1992a). Gee further differentiates little "g", a game itself as software, from Big "G", a game and social interaction that takes place outside of the game (e.g., online communities centered on the particular game). We propose that we should consider both sources of evidence (i.e., little "g" and Big "G") and levels of creativity development to support and assess creativity in and outside of video games (Figure 1).

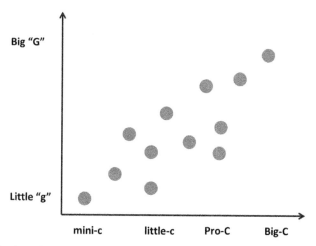

FIGURE 1   Two-dimensional approach to creativity assessment in games.

Each blue dot in Figure 1 represents a unique source of evidence in the continuum of little "g" and Big "G". First, not all games can afford Big "G" as the majority of games remain close to the level of little "g" (e.g., *Candy Crush Saga*). Those games can be considered only for mini-c or little-c in a specific context (e.g., within particular levels). Games that are both at the levels of little "g" and Big "G" can provide a whole range of sources of evidence. For example, *LittleBigPlanet* (LBP) is a puzzle platform game in which the core game mechanic is to navigate the player's character, *Sackboy*, through multiple levels by avoiding hazards (e.g., spikes and fire) and enemies, and earning as many score bubbles and item bubbles as possible without losing the character's life. This game offers three modes of game play: Play, Create, and Share (Rafalow & Salen, 2014). As the game emphasizes user-generated content, players can earn extra items (by popping item bubbles) in the Play mode that they can use later in the Create mode. Therefore, LBP works as a semiotic domain in which players progress from mini-c within the game to little-c or Pro-C outside of the game as they further develop expertise.

Here is an illustration of how LBP can provide evidence for different levels of creativity. When a player initially starts playing the game, she only can manage to unlock levels using rather typical solutions. Later she can come up with very unusual solutions. Such behaviors (as they are still personal interpretations) can be considered as evidence of "mini c" in the little "g." As the player becomes more fluent with the game, she can take screen captures of her creative solutions, and then post them on one of the many online communities related to the game (i.e., little "c" in the Big "G"). Furthermore, after months (or even years) of participating in the online community, she can develop advanced skills to produce creative and elaborate media art pieces around the game, and can become a well-known figure in the LBP community (i.e., Pro-C in the context of Big-G). In their ethnographic study of an LBP online community, for example, Rafalow and Salen (2014) described a user named "Sackdude" in the community who became a well-known figure as he had demonstrated high levels of technical skill and creativity required to create complex and interesting levels that are valued by the members of the LBP community.

Another game that can be considered using this framework is *Portal 2*. *Portal 2* is a popular linear, first-person puzzle-platform video game developed and published by Valve Corporation. Players take a first-person role in the game and explore and interact with the environment. The goal of *Portal 2* is to get to an exit door by using a series of tools. The primary game mechanic in *Portal 2* is the portal gun, which is a device that can create inter-spatial portals between two flat planes. Puzzles must be solved by teleporting the player's character and various objects using the portal gun. To solve the progressively more difficult challenges, players must figure out how to locate, obtain, and then combine various objects effectively to open doors and navigate through the environment to get to the exit door. In addition to resources in the game that can help in the quest, there are also various dangers to avoid—such as turrets (which shoot deadly lasers) and acid pools. All of these game elements can help (or hinder) the player from reaching the exit. As each level has one "correct" way of solving it, players don't have much freedom to be creative within levels. However, as players become more proficient with the game, they can create levels using the Puzzle Creator and further explore an online community called Steam Workshop in which they can share their levels or play other players' levels (i.e., Pro-C in the context of Big-G).

CREATIVITY ASSESSMENT IN *PHYSICS PLAYGROUND*

In the previous section, we reviewed the multidimensional aspects of creativity that can be cultivated inside and outside of video games. We further suggested that creativity should be assessed in the context of video games considering two dimensions: sources of evidence (i.e., little-g and Big-G) and levels of creativity development (i.e., mini-c to Big-C). In the following sections, we describe a methodology called stealth assessment and demonstrate how we designed creativity assessment in a game called *Physics Playground* (PP).

Stealth Assessment

Stealth assessment refers to an approach that weaves assessments directly and invisibly into the fabric of any complex learning environment, particularly digital games (Shute, 2011; Shute, Ventura, Bauer, & Zapata-Rivera, 2009). During game play, players naturally produce rich sequences of actions as the products of continuous interactions with complex tasks. In stealth assessment, evidence needed to assess targeted skills is thus provided by the players' interactions with the game itself (i.e., the processes of play). Inferences on competency states are stored in a dynamic model of the learner (at various grain sizes and at different time points). This contrasts with a typically singular outcome of an activity—the norm in educational environments. Stealth assessment may be used to support learning and maintain flow, defined as a state of optimal experience, where a person is so engaged in the activity at hand that self-consciousness disappears, sense of time is lost, and the person engages in complex, goal-directed activity not for external rewards, but simply for the exhilaration of doing (Csikszentmihalyi, 1997).

New developments in psychometric techniques and cognitive theories have enabled the development of stealth assessment—emphasizing the nature of educational assessment as an evidentiary argument. The core element of stealth assessment is Evidence-Centered Design (ECD) (Mislevy, Almond, & Lukas, 2003; Mislevy, Steinberg, & Almond, 2003). ECD is an assessment design framework that formalizes assessment arguments relative to claims about the learner and the evidence that supports those claims. ECD is flexible enough to reduce constraints of conventional assessment, and allows the use of continuous performances in complex and interactive environments. An overview of the ECD approach is described next.

ECD MODELS

The primary purpose of an assessment is to collect information that will enable the assessor to make inferences about students' competency states—what they know, believe, and can do, and to what degree. Accurate inferences of competency states support instructional decisions that can promote learning. ECD defines a framework that consists of three main models that work in concert.

The ECD framework allows/requires an assessor to: (a) define the claims to be made about students' competencies; (b) establish what constitutes valid evidence of the claim; and (c) determine the nature and form of tasks that will elicit that evidence. These three actions map directly onto the three main models of ECD shown in Figure 2.

A good assessment has to elicit behavior that bears evidence about key competencies, and it must also provide principled interpretations of that evidence in terms that suit the purpose of the assessment. Working out these variables, models, and their interrelationships is a way to answer a series of questions posed by Messick (1994) that get at the very heart of assessment design:

- What collection of knowledge, skills, and other attributes should be assessed?—Competency Model (CM). This can also be phrased as: What do you want to say about the person at the end of the

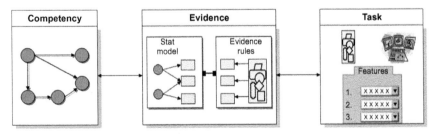

FIGURE 2   Three main models of an evidence-centered assessment design. *Adapted from Mislevy et al. (2003a).*

assessment? Variables in the CM are usually called "nodes" and describe the set of person variables on which inferences are to be based. The term "student model" is used to denote a student-instantiated version of the CM—like a profile or report card, only at a more refined grain size. Values in the student model express the assessor's current belief about a student's level on each variable within the CM.

- What behaviors or performances should reveal those constructs?—Evidence Model (EM). An EM expresses how the student's interactions with, and responses to, a given problem constitute evidence about CM variables. The EM attempts to answer two questions: (a) What behaviors or performances reveal targeted competencies? (b) What's the connection between those behaviors and the CM variable(s)? Basically, an EM lays out the argument about why and how the observations in a given task situation (i.e., student performance data) constitute evidence about CM variables.
- What tasks should elicit those behaviors that comprise the evidence?—Task Model (TM). A TM provides a framework for characterizing and constructing situations with which a student will interact to provide evidence about targeted aspects of knowledge or skill related to competencies. These situations are described in terms of: (a) the presentation format (e.g., directions, stimuli); (b) the specific work or response products (e.g., answers, work samples); and (c) other variables used to describe key features of tasks (e.g., knowledge type, difficulty level). Thus, task specifications establish what the student will be asked to do, what kinds of responses are permitted, what types of formats are available, and other considerations, such as whether the student will be timed, allowed to use tools (e.g., calculators, dictionaries), and so forth. Multiple TMs can be employed in a given assessment. Tasks are the most obvious part of an assessment, and their main purpose is to elicit evidence (which is observable) about competencies (which are unobservable).

In short, the ECD approach provides a framework for developing assessment tasks that are explicitly linked to claims about student competencies via an evidentiary chain (e.g., valid arguments that serve to connect task performance to competency estimates), and are thus valid for their intended purposes.

Stealth Assessment of Creativity in *Physics Playground*

PP is a computer-based game designed to assess and support students' nonverbal understanding of physics principles, commonly referred to as qualitative or conceptual physics. In PP, players draw various objects on the screen using a mouse, and once drawn, these objects become "alive" and interact with other objects. By playing PP, students improve their qualitative understanding of how the physical world operates and how physical objects interact.

PP is characterized by an implicit representation of Newton's three laws of motion, including concepts such as balance, mass, gravity, and conservation of energy and momentum (Shute et al., 2013). These physics principles are operationalized by the use of simple machine-like devices called *agents of force and motion*, including ramps, levers, pendulums, and springboards, to move a green ball to the red balloon on the screen.

Many of the levels in PP can be solved by various solutions, using more than one agent. Thus, PP allows players to be creative and produce interesting mechanical devices that the designers of the game did not expect. Furthermore, players often attempt multiple times to achieve the "awesomest" solution. To assess these creative behaviors in the game, we identified three creativity CM variables—fluency, flexibility, and originality—and identified in-game observables that provide evidence for those variables (i.e., EM variables). Table 1 summarizes the creativity competency and EM variables in PP.

Here is an illustration of how these variables work to assess players' creativity in the context of PP. Figure 3a is how a level called *Attic* looks when the level starts. The most common solution among PP players (and expected by the designers) involved drawing and using a lever to propel the ball to the balloon (shown in Figure 3b). Any trajectory of the ball that deviates from the trajectory shown in Figure 3b can provide evidence for originality as it is very likely to be a rare (thus unique) solution. Only a few players (out of hundreds) created solutions similar to Figure 3c using both a pendulum (to add force to the ball) and a ramp (to guide the ball to the balloon). Such a solution provides positive evidence for both fluency

TABLE 1 Competency and Evidence Model Variables for Creativity Assessment in PP

CM Variables	EM Variables
Fluency	Number of agents used in a problem
	Number of drawn objects per solved problem
	Number of drawn objects per unsolved problem
Flexibility	Number of correct agents attempted in the problem
	Standard deviation among frequencies of agent use [per session] [R]
	Consecutive use of incorrect agent [R]
Originality	Difference between ball trajectory in a solution from the expected trajectory

R indicates negative evidence.

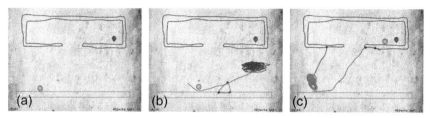

FIGURE 3 The Attic level and two possible solutions.

and originality in PP. That is, while most players used only one agent (e.g., lever), this solution requires two agents, providing evidence for *fluency— Number of agents used in a problem*. Moreover, as the trajectory of the ball in this solution deviates from the common solution, it provides evidence for *originality—Difference between ball trajectory in a solution from the expected trajectory.*

These indicators, as evidence of little-c in the context of little-g, can be identified and scored during game play. For example, in PP, the game engine tracks the trajectories of the player's ball in a successful solution (i.e., the set of X, Y coordinates), and saves them out as a series of vector values in the log file. Those vector values can then be compared to the most common trajectory, and large differences between trajectories are thus evidence for originality.

Establishing these EM variables (i.e., in-game indicators) and scoring rules to decide *when* those indicators provide evidence for creativity can be tricky depending on the nature of a given level or game. Furthermore, as "gaming the system" is not always viewed negatively in the gaming context, differentiating creative solutions from solutions that exploit the features of the game is critical (Kuecklich, 2004). As the very definition of creativity emphasizes both *novelty* and *relevance*, therefore, in-game behaviors that are not appropriate in terms of the rules and mechanics of the game should not be considered as evidence for creativity.

For instance, Figure 4a is a level called *Shark*. As the level starts, the ball lands on top of the blue shark on the left of the screen, and players are expected to create a lever (as shown in Figure 4b) and drop a weight,

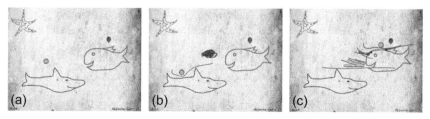

FIGURE 4 The Shark level and two possible solutions.

to move the ball to the balloon. Some of the players, however, figured out that if they quickly draw lines under the ball to stop it from falling on the shark, they can solve this level without using agents of motion (shown in Figure 4c). Although the trajectory of the ball shown in Figure 4c deviates from the one in Figure 4b, such a solution does not provide evidence for *originality* as this solution violates the rules of the game.

The examples above show how we identified evidence for "little-c" in the "little-g" of PP. That is, such assessment uses in-game behaviors specific to the levels of the game. Another source of evidence for creativity that we identified in PP is the levels created by players. We should note that, although using user-created levels for creativity assessment is not completely "stealthy" as it requires holistic scoring by human-raters, it can be considered as assessment of "little-c" or even "Pro-C" in the "Big-G."

To use user-created levels for creativity assessment, we identified features of levels that are aligned with the dimensions of creativity. Table 2 describes relevant creativity dimensions and specific scoring rules used to make holistic judgment about user-created levels.

Based on the scoring rules described in Table 2, the maximum creativity score that a level can receive is 11. Figure 5 includes some of the player-created levels and associated scores based on the scoring rules.

TABLE 2   Scoring Rubrics for Player-Created Levels in *Physics Playground*

Categories	Scoring Rules
Relevance	*Can it be solved?* (This is a screening criterion) • If unsolvable, then don't score other variables → assign 0 • If solvable? → assign 1
Elaboration	*How difficult is it?* (Possible scores: 0, 1, 2, 3, and 4) • Balloon is located above ball • Any agent other than ramp is required • Obstacles to remove/avoid are present • Ball is falling out of the problem space
Originality	*Is it original relative to existing problems?* (Possible scores: 0, 1, and 2) • Almost identical → assign 0 • Has some similarities → assign 1 • Very dissimilar → assign 2
Esthetics	*Is it esthetically pleasing?* (Possible scores: 0, 1, and 2) • Esthetically unappealing with poor visual elements → assign 0 • Plain with completed visual elements → assign 1 • Very pleasant with well-thought-out visual elements → assign 2
Humor	*Is it humorous* (i.e., Does it make you smile?) (Possible scores: 0, 1, and 2) • Not humorous at all → assign 0 • Somewhat humorous → assign 1 • Very humorous → assign 2

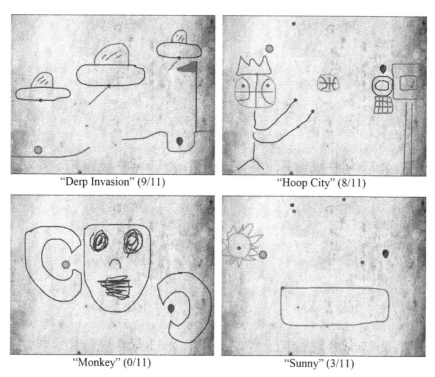

"Derp Invasion" (9/11) "Hoop City" (8/11)

"Monkey" (0/11) "Sunny" (3/11)

FIGURE 5 Examples of player-created levels and associated scores.

"Derp Invasion" is judged to be a fairly creative level as it a medium difficulty level (3/4) that is solvable (1/1), very different from the existing levels (2/2), esthetically pleasing (2/2), and somewhat humorous (1/2). Although "Hoop City" received the same scores for most categories, it scored lower than "Derp Invasion" as it is an easy problem (this can be solved by simply drawing a ramp over the basketball). Although "Monkey" could be a fairly creative level, it scored 0 as it is not solvable (the ball is stuck in the left ear of the monkey, and it is impossible to get it out). "Sunny" scored 0 in the originality category as there is a level called "Sunny" in the game that looks the same as well.

DISCUSSION

Playing video games has become a customary and important part of everyday life for today's youth, and the broader education community has been exploring affordances of video games to support various competencies that are valuable for success in the twenty-first century. In this chapter, we discussed how video games can support creativity development both inside and outside of video games, and described our approach to assess creativity in PP. We based our discussions on the current literature, which views creativity as multidimensional and developmental.

To optimize affordances of video games for creativity development and assessment, there are several challenges that the community of creativity researchers need to address. First, we first need to rethink how we operationalize and validate assessment. As the creativity manifested around a game is considered to be specific to the domain (or the game), the conventional way of validating new assessments is by investigating correlations with existing measures, but that may not be the most reasonable method for creativity assessment in video games. Second, game, instructional, and assessment designers need to further investigate and establish particular design principles that are conducive to cultivating creativity.

Finally, well-designed games are challenging yet highly engaging. Such games often inspire players' imaginations beyond the game, which provides opportunities to support all levels of creativity. Gamers actively seek out interesting and difficult problems, and strive for not just a solution, but the awesomest one. Thus we need to further explore ways to foster players' creativity as an essential aspect of game play, which can lead to creative behaviors in other areas. We additionally propose that games can be used to assess different levels of creativity, and educators and game designers should consider assessment design methods such as stealth assessment and ECD to identify sources of evidence for creativity inside and outside of games.

Acknowledgments

We would like to express our sincere appreciation to the Bill and Melinda Gates Foundation (#OPP1035331) supporting the development of PP and its underlying models (e.g., creativity). We'd also like to thank the PP team at Florida State University—Matt Small, Matthew Ventura, Russell Almond, and Lubin Wang—for infusing their creativity into this project.

References

Amabile, T. M. (1983). The social psychology of creativity: A componential conceptualization. *Journal of Personality and Social Psychology, 45*(2), 357–376. http://dx.doi.org/10.1037/0022-3514.45.2.357.

Amabile, T. M. (1996). *Creativity in context: Update to "The social psychology of creativity"*. Boulder, CO: Westview Press.

Autor, D. H., Levy, F., & Murnane, R. J. (2003). The skill content of recent technological change: An empirical exploration. *Quarterly Journal of Economics, 118*(4), 1279–1333. http://dx.doi.org/10.1162/003355303322552801.

Beghetto, R. A., & Kaufman, J. C. (2007). Toward a broader conception of creativity: A case for "mini-c" creativity. *Psychology of Aesthetics, Creativity, and the Arts, 1*(2), 73–79.

Berzonsky, M. D., & Sullivan, C. (1992). Social-cognitive aspects of identity style. *Journal of Adolescent Research, 7*(2), 140–155. http://dx.doi.org/10.1177/074355489272002.

Bybee, R. W., & Fuchs, B. (2006). Preparing the 21st century workforce: A new reform in science and technology education. *Journal of Research in Science Teaching, 43*(4), 349–352. http://dx.doi.org/10.1002/tea.20147.

Casner-Lotto, J., & Barrington, L. (2006). *Are they really ready to work? Employers' perspectives on the basic knowledge and applied skills of new entrants to the 21st century US workforce.* New York: The Conference Board. Retrieved from: http://www.p21.org/storage/documents/FINAL_REPORT_PDF09-29-06.pdf.

Costa, P. T., Jr., & McCrae, R. R. (1992). Four ways five factors are basic. *Personality and Individual Differences, 13*(6), 653–665.

Csikszentmihalyi, M. (1988). Society, culture, and person: A systems view of creativity. In R. J. Sternberg (Ed.), *The nature of creativity: Contemporary psychological perspectives* (pp. 325–339). New York: Cambridge University Press.

Csikszentmihalyi, M. (1997). *Creativity: Flow and the psychology of discovery and invention.* New York: Harper Perennial.

Dewett, T. (2007). Linking intrinsic motivation, risk taking, and employee creativity in an R&D environment. *R&D Management, 37*(3), 197–208. http://dx.doi.org/10.1111/j.1467-9310.2007.00469.x.

Entertainment Software Association. (2014). *Essential facts about the computer and video game industry.* Retrieved from: http://www.theesa.com/facts/pdfs/ESA_EF_2014.pdf.

Feldman, D. H. (1999). The development of creativity. In R. J. Sternberg (Ed.), *Handbook of creativity* (pp. 169–186). New York: Cambridge University Press.

Florida, R. L. (2002). *The rise of the creative class: and how it's transforming work, leisure, community and everyday life.* Cambridge, MA: Basic Civitas Books.

Friedman, T. L. (2005). *The world is flat: A brief history of the twenty-first century.* New York: Farrar, Straus & Giroux.

Gardner, H. (1993). *Creating minds: An anatomy of creativity seen through the lives of Freud, Einstein, Picasso, Stravinsky, Eliot, Graham, and Gandhi.* New York: Basic Books.

Gee, J. P. (2003). What video games have to teach us about learning and literacy. *Computers in Entertainment (CIE)—Theoretical and Practical Computer Applications in Entertainment, 1*(1), 20–24.

Gee, J. P. (2005). Good video games and good learning. *Phi Kappa Phi Forum, 85*(2), 33–37, citeulike-article-id:3137216.

Gee, J. P. (2008). Learning and games. In K. Salen (Ed.), *The ecology of games: Connecting youth, games, and learning* (pp. 21–40). Cambridge, MA: MIT Press.

Glover, J. A. (1977). Risky shift and creativity. *Social Behavior and Personality: An International Journal, 5*(2), 317–320.

Glover, J. A., & Sautter, F. (1977). Relation of four components of creativity to risk-taking preferences. *Psychological Reports, 41*(1), 227–230.

Guilford, J. P. (1956). The structure of intellect. *Psychological Bulletin, 53*(4), 267–293. http://dx.doi.org/10.1037/h0040755.

Hamlen, K. (2009). Relationships between computer and video game play and creativity among upper elementary school students. *Journal of Educational Computing Research, 40*(1), 1–21. http://dx.doi.org/10.2190/EC.40.1.a.

Hargreaves, A. (2003). *Teaching in the knowledge society: Education in the age of insecurity.* New York: Teachers College Press.

Jackson, L. A., Witt, E. A., Games, A. I., Fitzgerald, H. E., von Eye, A., & Zhao, Y. (2012). Information technology use and creativity: Findings from the children and technology project. *Computers in Human Behavior, 28*(2), 370–376. http://dx.doi.org/10.1016/j.chb.2011.10.006.

Kaufman, J. C., & Beghetto, R. A. (2009). Beyond big and little: The four c model of creativity. *Review of General Psychology, 13*(1), 1–12. http://dx.doi.org/10.1037/a0013688.

Kaufman, J. C., & Beghetto, R. A. (2013). Do people recognize the four Cs? Examining layperson conceptions of creativity. *Psychology of Aesthetics, Creativity, and the Arts, 7*(3), 229–236.

Kaufman, J. C., & Sternberg, R. J. (2007). Resource review: Creativity. *Change, 39*(4), 55–58.

Kogan, N., & Wallach, M. A. (1964). *Risk taking: A study in cognition and personality*. New York: Holt, Rinehart & Winston.

Kuecklich, J. (2004). *Other playings—Cheating in computer games*. In: *The Other Players Conference, Copenhagen, Denmark*. Retrieved from: http://www.computingscience.nl/docs/vakken/vw/literature/03.kuecklich.pdf.

Levy, F., & Murnane, R. J. (2004). *The new division of labor: How computers are creating the next job market*. Princeton, NJ: Princeton University Press.

Lubart, T. I. (1994). Creativity. In R. J. Sternberg (Ed.), *Thinking and problem solving* (pp. 289–332). New York: Academic Press.

Madjar, N., Greenberg, E., & Chen, Z. (2011). Factors for radical creativity, incremental creativity, and routine, noncreative performance. *Journal of Applied Psychology, 96*(4), 730–743. http://dx.doi.org/10.1037/a0022416.

MacCrimmon, K. R., & Wehrung, D. A. (1990). Characteristics of risk taking executives. *Management Science, 36*(4), 422–435.

McClelland, D. C. (1973). Testing for competence rather than for intelligence. *American Psychologist, 28*(1), 1–14.

McCrae, R. R. (1987). Creativity, divergent thinking, and openness to experience. *Journal of Personality and Social Psychology, 52*(6), 1258–1265. http://dx.doi.org/10.1037/0022-3514.52.6.1258.

Messick, S. (1994). The interplay of evidence and consequences in the validation of performance assessments. *Educational Researcher, 23*(2), 13–23. http://dx.doi.org/10.3102/0013189x023002013.

Mislevy, R. J., Almond, R. G., & Lukas, J. F. (2003a). *A brief introduction to evidence-centered design (ETS Research Report RR-03-16)*. Princeton, NJ: Educational Testing Service. Retrieved from: http://www.ets.org/Media/Research/pdf/RR-03-16.pdf.

Mislevy, R. J., Steinberg, L. S., & Almond, R. G. (2003b). Focus article: On the structure of educational assessments. *Measurement: Interdisciplinary Research and Perspectives, 1*(1), 3–62.

Moran, S., & John-Steiner, V. (2003). Creativity in the making: Vygotsky's contemporary contribution to the dialectic of development and creativity. In R. K. Sawyer, V. John-Steiner, S. Moran, R. J. Sternberg, D. H. Feldman, & J. Nakamura (Eds.), *Creativity and development* (pp. 61–90). New York: Oxford University Press.

Nijstad, B. A., De Dreu, C. K., Rietzschel, E. F., & Baas, M. (2010). The dual pathway to creativity model: Creative ideation as a function of flexibility and persistence. *European Review of Social Psychology, 21*(1), 34–77.

Partnership for 21st Century Skills. (2007). *Beyond the three Rs: Voter attitudes toward 21st century skills*. Retrieved from: http://www.p21.org/storage/documents/P21_pollreport_singlepg.pdf.

Plucker, J. A., Beghetto, R. A., & Dow, G. T. (2004). Why isn't creativity more important to educational psychologists? Potentials, pitfalls, and future directions in creativity research. *Educational Psychologist, 39*(2), 83–96. http://dx.doi.org/10.1207/s15326985ep3902_1.

Plucker, J. A., & Makel, M. C. (2010). Assessment of creativity. In J. C. Kaufman & R. J. Sternberg (Eds.), *The Cambridge handbook of creativity* (pp. 48–73). New York: Cambridge University Press.

Rafalow, M. H., & Salen, K. (2014). *Welcome to sackboy planet: Connected learning among LittleBigPlanet 2 players*. Retrieved from: http://dmlhub.net/publications/welcome-sackboy-planet-connected-learning-among-littlebigplanet-2-players.

Resnick, M. (2007). Sowing the seeds for a more creative society. *Learning and Leading with Technology, 35*(4), 18–22.

Rideout, V. J., Foehr, U. G., & Roberts, D. F. (2010). *Generation M2: Media in the lives of 8- to 18-year-olds*. Retrieved from: http://kff.org/other/event/generation-m2-media-in-the-lives-of/.

Sawyer, R. K. (2006). Educating for innovation. *Thinking Skills and Creativity, 1*(1), 41–48. http://dx.doi.org/10.1016/j.tsc.2005.08.001.

Shute, V. J. (2011). Stealth assessment in computer-based games to support learning. In S. Tobias & J. D. Fletcher (Eds.), *Computer games and instruction* (pp. 503–524). Charlotte, NC: Information Age.

Shute, V. J., & Kim, Y. J. (2011). Does playing the World of Goo facilitate learning? In D. Y. Dai (Ed.), *Design research on learning and thinking in educational settings: Enhancing intellectual growth and functioning* (pp. 359–387). New York: Routledge Books.

Shute, V. J., & Ventura, M. (2013). *Measuring and supporting learning in games: Stealth assessment.* Cambridge, MA: MIT Press.

Shute, V. J., Ventura, M., Bauer, M., & Zapata-Rivera, D. (2009). Melding the power of serious games and embedded assessment to monitor and foster learning. In U. Ritterfeld, M. J. Cody, & P. Vorderer (Eds.), *The social science of serious games: Theories and applications* (pp. 295–321). Philadelphia, PA: Routledge/LEA.

Shute, V. J., Ventura, M., & Kim, Y. J. (2013). Assessment and learning of informal physics in Newton's Playground. *Journal of Educational Research, 106*(6), 423–430. http://dx.doi.org/10.1080/00220671.2013.832970.

Sternberg, R. J., & Lubart, T. I. 1992a. Creativity: Its nature and assessment. *School Psychology International, 13*(3), 243–253. http://dx.doi.org/10.1177/0143034392133004.

Sternberg, R. J., & Lubart, T. I. 1992b. Buy low and sell high: An investment approach to creativity. *Current Directions in Psychological Science, 1*(1), 1–5.

Sternberg, R. J., & Lubart, T. I. (1996). Investing in creativity. *American Psychologist, 51*(7), 677–688. http://dx.doi.org/10.1037/0003-066x.51.7.677.

Symonds, W. C., Schwartz, R. B., & Ferguson, R. (2011). *Pathways to prosperity: Meeting the challenge of preparing young Americans for the 21st century.* Cambridge, MA: Harvard Graduate School of Education.

Taylor, C. W. (1988). Various approaches to and definitions of creativity. In R. J. Sternberg (Ed.), *The nature of creativity: Contemporary psychological perspectives* (pp. 99–121). New York: Cambridge University Press.

Wright, W. (2006). Dream machines. *Wired Magazine, 14*(4), 110–112.

6

Content, Collaboration, and Creativity in Virtual Worlds

Thomas B. Ward

Department of Psychology, University of Alabama, Tuscaloosa, AL, USA

In contrast to the bulk of chapters in this volume that focus on computer-based activities that are best described as games, the present chapter is concerned with creativity in virtual settings that are not particularly game-like. Specifically, the chapter examines manifestations of creativity in 3D virtual worlds in which the primary activity is engaging in unscripted social interactions. The term Social Virtual Worlds (SVWs) is used to refer to these types of 3D environments in contrast to Gaming Virtual Worlds (GVWs), which refers to games such as *World of Warcraft* that generally involve clearly defined quests (Jung, 2011). Perhaps the best known of such SVWs is *Second Life*, but many others exist, including *There*, *Kaneva*, *InWorldz*, *IMVU*, and *ActiveWorlds*.

Like many video games that are played on local computers or online, the SVWs considered in this chapter depict richly detailed 3D environments, in which users interact with one another using text chat or voice as modes of communication. However, unlike most video games, a distinguishing feature of SVWs is that users' actions are open-ended such that their form is not constrained by singular goals to be accomplished. The intent of most users is not to kill more of a designated enemy, destroy more objects, pilot a vehicle faster than their competitors, or accumulate more points or power by way of experience and performance in defined competitive activities.

To be sure, it is possible to race vehicles, compete with others in a range of games and accumulate resources in SVWs, but for most users such goals are not especially salient. Instead their goals are myriad and somewhat diffuse, often centering on social interactions with other inhabitants of the virtual world for their own sake. Purveyors of SVWs often emphasize the social nature of those worlds in describing them. For example, the SVW called *There* explicitly states on its quick facts page that it is not a game, but rather a virtual space for social interaction (http://www.prod.there.com/info/whatisthere/quickfacts).

The distinction is not a perfect one in that video games in general and GVWs in particular are not exclusively quest based. They can and do involve a range of social motives and actions. It is also clear that social/cultural communities do emerge from interactions among users of GVWs (see, e.g., Pearce, 2009), and those communities extend beyond online meeting spaces and forums (http://us.battle.net/wow/en/community/) to real-world activities. Examples of the latter include the large network of meetup groups of *World of Warcraft* players (e.g., http://warcraft.meetup.com/) and *Dungeons and Dragons* (e.g., http://dnd.meetup.com/), where like-minded individuals can meet to discuss strategy and find teammates. Conversely, SVWs do allow users to compete with one another in a wide range of games. However, there does seem to be a division into computer-based activities that are relatively more game-like versus relatively more social in nature, and the current focus is on the latter.

As is true with video games in general, there are properties of SVWs that make them ideal settings for examining aspects of creativity (Ward & Sonneborn, 2009). One key feature is that they are broadly accessible. Anyone, anywhere in the world with a computer, and a sufficiently robust internet connection can access these worlds. What this means is that the individuals who populate SVWs are a more diverse sample than typically studied in experimental research on creativity. Any observed trends in virtual worlds, then, can be argued to be at least as broadly indicative of human creative tendencies as those observed in studies conducted with samples of undergraduate research participants.

A second important aspect of SVWs is that the content is typically driven by the concerns of individual users of the world rather than being more determined by the specific quests inherent in GVWs (see, e.g., Jung, 2011). In principle then, creativity might be expected to flourish in SVWs and be limited only by the imaginations of the users. *Second Life*, for example, describes itself as "The largest-ever 3D virtual world created entirely by its users" (http://secondlife.com). Similarly, *InWorldz* describes itself as "a user-created virtual world" (http://inworldz.com). In such worlds, people can modify the avatars they use to represent themselves in multiple ways including dress and body size and type. They can purchase or rent locations and fill them with available content created by other users, including buildings, furnishings, artwork, and landscaping, and they can develop such content on their own. Thus, it is possible to consider the creative tendencies of those who develop or modify content for themselves or to sell to others. In the sections that follow the properties of such content are described along with potential theoretical accounts of why those properties are evident.

A third factor is that SVWs are by their nature interactive. That is, individuals generally do not enter such environments to play solitary games but rather to engage in activities with other people. There are readily available spaces in which people can meet by way of their avatars, thus allowing an examination of creative collaboration and other joint actions by people who are geographically dispersed but virtually together.

Two final aspects of virtual worlds are interestingly opposite of one another. Virtual worlds have been shown to mimic the real world, not only in content (Ward & Sonneborn, 2009), but also in the structuring of basic activities and interactions. It has been shown, for example, that male-female avatar pairs conversing in *Second Life* maintain smaller interpersonal distances and more eye contact than male-male pairs, consistent with some real-world findings (Yee, Bailenson, Urbanek, Chang, & Megert, 2007). In addition, participants assigned taller avatars exert more dominance than those assigned shorter avatars both in virtual interactions and in subsequent real-world interactions (Yee, Bailenson, & Ducheneaut, 2009, Yee, Ellis, & Ducheneaut, 2009). Simply dressing avatars in different garb also affects their interactions in ways consistent with real-world observations. Mirroring the old Western cliché "The good guys wear the white hats," and the finding that in real-world settings individuals wearing black uniforms behave more aggressively than those wearing white uniforms, Pena, Hancock, and Merola (2009) showed that participants assigned black-cloaked avatars developed more aggressive intentions and attitudes than those assigned white-cloaked avatars. Finally, surveys of users indicate that sex role stereotypes are alive and well in SVWs, including the fact that females are more likely to shop and males are more likely to build things (Guadagno, Muscanell, Okdie, Burk, & Ward, 2010).

On the positive side, such commonalities between real and virtual worlds assure us that behavioral tendencies in virtual worlds are similar enough to those in the real world that research on virtual behavior can tell us something about behavior in the broader sense. However, on the negative side, the observed commonalities also carry with them the implication that real-world tendencies may either implicitly or explicitly constrain modes of thought and limit creativity in virtual settings. In virtual worlds, where almost anything is possible, do people nevertheless restrict their thinking based on real-world assumptions and tendencies?

In contrast to the tendency for the created content and interactions in SVWs to mimic the real world, virtual settings also allow objects and actions that are simply impossible in the real world (Ward & Sonneborn, 2009). Among other things, people and objects can be made to hover in space, unsupported by any mechanical devices, avatars can walk through phantom objects, and they can teleport instantaneously from one location to another. Thus, SVWs allow an examination of such impossibilities and their impact on people's tendencies to overcome limitations in their creative thinking.

CONTENT

This section describes some of the content found in SVWs, including the properties of avatars, the specific environments they visit and inhabit, and the objects they build or acquire. It also assesses how the properties of such content can inform us about the nature of virtual creativity.

Avatars, the Self, and mini-c Creativity

Individuals represent themselves in virtual worlds in the form of 3D avatars that are able to move around in and between the various locations in those worlds. Generally, the user chooses an initial avatar from a relatively small set of possibilities. For example, when first setting up an account in *Second Life* and most other virtual worlds, users choose from a small set of male and female avatars the one that they will appear as when they log in for the first time. The set of initial avatars generally vary somewhat in appearance along particular dimensions, such as skin tone, hairstyle, and manner of dress. *Second Life* and some of the other worlds also allow the initial selection of avatars other than ordinary humans, but even those tend to take basically human shapes, such as the a set of "vampires" in *Second Life*. Thus, the process of selecting a starting avatar in most SVWs may influence the majority of users to limit their ways of thinking about themselves to human form, a tendency that is likely reinforced by the overall goal of social interaction. That is, if most participants enter

SVWs with the intent of socializing with other users, it is reasonable to suppose that such goals drive the tendency to stick with avatars of human form, even though other animate and inanimate forms are possible.

Importantly, once users log in to virtual worlds, they are generally able to modify their appearance in one of two ways. The first is to use an edit function to change multiple parameters of the avatar including its size and muscularity, as well as the size, shape, and relative positioning of facial features. Such modifications are easily made, menu-driven, and require little in the way of acquired skills. The second means of modification, which can also be easily used by novice participants, is to purchase shapes and photorealistic skins (the outer covering over shapes) produced by individuals who have developed the requisite skills to generate content of sufficient quality as to be appealing and worth an investment of virtual dollars.

The initial selection and subsequent modification of appearance by individual users bears an important relation to current views about levels of creativity. Specifically, Beghetto and Kaufman (2007; see also Kaufman & Beghetto, 2009) recently expanded on a traditional distinction between little-c and Big-C creativity by introducing the construct of mini-c creativity. Their contention was that the little-c and Big-C distinction did not do justice to the full range of levels of creativity that people exhibit.

As described by Kaufman and Beghetto (2009), the notion of mini-c creativity is related to Runco's suggestions about personal creativity (e.g., Runco, 1996) and Vygotskian notions of cognitive development via play, reflecting the idea that people develop personal understandings of the world around them and the situations in which they find themselves. Such understandings are legitimately viewed as creations, based on an interaction of the structure of the world as given and the knowledge, experiences, and skills of the person experiencing the world. Thus, even young children, and by extension first-time visitors to SVWs, can exhibit a nascent or inchoate form of creativity that does not require a tangible product that qualified others would judge to be creative (i.e., novel and useful). It merely requires the operation of a normal human tendency to create interpretations of experience.

The link between avatar selection/modification and mini-c creativity is that it is reasonable to assume that people's avatar choices reflect their basic personal understandings of their role or intent in coming to a virtual world. Some might wish to project their real-world selves into the virtual world and attempt to make their avatar resemble themselves. Others might wish to present an idealized self that is younger, more attractive, fitter or in some other way different than the way they view themselves in the real world. Still others might to try out aspects of the self that otherwise could not ordinarily be realized, such as representing oneself as someone of the opposite sex or even in nonhuman form, though again the latter tendency might be inhibited by the goal of interacting with other people (see Figures 1–4 for examples of *Second Life* avatars). Thus, examining users' personal understandings of SVWs as manifested in their avatar choices can provide a window on a particular interesting form of mini-c creativity.

There are additional senses in which mini-c creativity manifests itself in SVWs. One is the ways in which people personalize their environments. Residents can purchase or rent land, and can build structures and decorate them inside and out with artwork, furniture, plants, and a wide variety of objects and textures. In effect, they can make a "home" for themselves in the virtual world, and the ways in which they personalize that home can be as much a reflection of their personal creativity as the ways in which they personalize their real-world homes. As with personalizing of avatars, residents can implement the modifications of their environments using their own skills, or they can purchase ready-made objects.

Whereas casual users might exhibit mini-c creativity in their choices of what to buy in order to be consistent with their self-representational goals,

FIGURE 1   Ordinary human male avatar available as starting appearance in *Second Life*.

FIGURE 2   Example of one of many possible animal avatars.

FIGURE 3 Example of a prehistoric animal avatar.

FIGURE 4 A nonhuman avatar, a nightstand.

the producers of that content would be seen as engaging in at least little-c creativity, if not Pro-C creativity. Pro-C is a level Kaufman and Beghetto (2009) added between little-c or everyday creativity and Big-C or eminent creativity in their Four C model of creativity. Both little-c and Pro-C require the generation of products that would be judged by a relevant audience to be novel and useful in some way (see, e.g., Kaufman & Beghetto, 2009). By being willing to spend money on such content, the users who purchase it are providing evidence of such an endorsement, much as bar patrons in the real world might attest to the little-c creativity of a local band by willingly paying a cover charge to go see them.

The little-c versus Pro-C distinction is between creators who can garner an audience and those who can do that successfully enough to make a living at the creative endeavor. Given the relatively low value of the Linden dollar (between 4 and 5 USD per 1000 Lindens) only a small percentage of *Second Life* creators who sell products are able to meet that criterion, but some do. Linden Labs, the company that runs *Second Life*, no longer releases detailed figures on the economy, but data from September 2010 illustrate this point. In that month, there were more than 36,000 users with business profits under $10, and only 191 with profits over $5000 (http://www.gridsurvey.com/economy.php).

A listing of the astonishing array of products that can be purchased is available at https://marketplace.secondlife.com/?lang=en-US. Considering just items in the General category (which excludes adult-oriented products), in October of 2014 there were more than 2.5 million products listed. The listing can be sorted by "best-selling" to reveal both the products and merchants that are most successful in an economic sense. It can also be examined for products in all categories or restricted to items such as apparel, home and garden, and vehicles. Apparel accounts for more than 1.1 million of the listings, and interestingly reveals a pattern consistent with the Guadagno et al. (2010) finding that women shop more than men, with women's clothing items outnumbering men's by nearly 5 to 1.

Beyond financial success, there are many creators in *Second Life* who have produced a great deal of content. Some are featured in a video series known as the Drax Files: World Makers (https://www.youtube.com/playlist?list=PLI0b2jAH3oFvr6J0AhWroB9lmOXRN2xLV). Examples include landscape artist Kriss Lehmann, who creates and sells trees, fences and other landscape features, Jo Yardley, who runs the Berlin 1920s project (an extensive replica of the city from that era), and Barbie Alchemi, founder of Creations for Parkinson's, a site with activities, events and a support group for those with Parkinson's.

It is not completely clear what might constitute Big-C creativity in a virtual setting; however, if extraordinary financial success can be deemed a defining feature, then Ailin Graef (avatar name: Anshe Chung) would meet that criterion (Hof, 2006). According to the report, Graef became the first millionaire in *Second Life* (in US dollars), largely through purchasing, subdividing, and landscaping virtual real estate for rental or resale.

Importantly, the relationship between the mini-c understandings that drive new users' avatar representations and the little-c and Pro-C activities of more skilled content developers highlights a potentially valuable but as yet unexploited feature of the Four C model of creativity. Although it has been useful in characterizing distinct aspects of different levels of creativity, the model also holds the potential for describing the interactions that occur across levels. The economy of *Second Life* and other virtual worlds, conceptualized as mini-c consumers' needs being met by little-c and Pro-C providers, is one such interaction that could be understood via an interactive version of the Four C model.

Content and the Deliberate Imitation of Real-World Structures

SVWs are replete with locations that can be referred to as sims or builds, each of which depicts or represents some distinct building(s) and setting(s). Some of these builds constitute deliberate attempts to duplicate in the virtual world a well-known landmark or structure, and these are re-ferred to as *imitative recreations* (Ward & Sonneborn, 2009). A classic exam-ple is the *Second Life* sim depicting Paris ca. 1900 (Paris, 2014),[1] complete with representations of some of the major buildings as well as the most iconic feature of Paris, the Eiffel Tower. People can visit the sim via their avatars, take a virtual train ride around the city and ascend into the tower, much as they can ascend the real-world version of the tower if they visit the real-world city of Paris. Although no one would mistake the virtual Eiffel Tower in *Second Life* for the real-world structure it is intended to imitate, it is nevertheless a faithful rendition, both in terms of structure and scale. That is, its shape and component architectural parts mirror the real-world tower, and the scale is appropriate in that its size is enormous with respect to the size of typical human-shaped avatars that inhabit *Second Life*. Figure 5 shows a view from a distance of the tower as well as other landmarks of Paris. From the picture, one of the features of *Second Life* sims is evident; they are "islands" surrounded by water.

Another well-known imitative recreation in *Second Life* is the represen-tation of the Alamo (Alamo, 2014). As with the Eiffel Tower, inhabitants can visit this build with their avatars and explore its architecture and artifacts, as well as gaining historical information available from note-cards that are issued when they click on objects in the sim. Similarly, it is a faithful rendition in both structure and scale so that by walking one's avatar through the build one can gain an appreciation of what it might be like to walk through the real Alamo. Other imitative recreations in *Second Life* include the Globe Theatre (Globe Theatre, 2014), in which avatars

FIGURE 5   Shot of virtual Eiffel Tower from a distance.

[1] A conventional method of specifying locations in *Second Life* is by way of a hyperlink that allows users to log in directly to that site or teleport to it if they are already in world. For citation purposes, I treat them as documents and include entries in the References section rather than as whole websites with the address listed in the body of the paper.

can view performances of Shakespeare's plays, and the Blarney Castle (Blarney Castle, 2014), where visiting avatars can virtually observe architecture and kiss the Blarney Stone (see Figures 6 and 7 for pictures of the Alamo and Globe Theatre). Two imitative recreations which are no longer accessible but which were excellent renditions were the Sistine Chapel on the Vassar Campus and a virtual recreation of the Vietnam Veterans' Memorial Wall, where visitors could see the names of those who gave their lives in that war.

What these imitative recreations and others like them have in common is that they are the result of the intentional effort of their creators to develop virtual versions of their corresponding real-world structures. In considering these deliberate imitations, an important question arises: Are these products and the activities that generate them "creative"? My contention is that they are creative in much the same sense that the efforts and products of painters, sculptors, and other visual artists to depict real-world landmarks, people, settings, and objects are creative. The

FIGURE 6   *Second Life* imitative recreation of the Alamo.

FIGURE 7   *Second Life* imitative recreation of the Globe Theatre.

1. CREATIVITY AND VIDEO GAME PLAY

activities involve different sets of technical and esthetic skills, but in each case the intent to depict known objects accurately, whether by means of brush strokes, chiseling and carving or electronic programming, does not render the processes or outcomes uncreative. Indeed, the process of developing these builds clearly involves *intention*, a key ingredient of representation in painting, which would differentiate a work of art from something unintentional, such as a cloud formation, that merely resembled another object (see, e.g., Goldman, 2003).

In addition, the judgment that imitative recreations in SVWs are creative products is supported by the fact that they go beyond mere representation to incorporate novel features neither present nor even possible in the same way in their real-world counterparts. Because it is possible for avatars in *Second Life* to fall great distances, collide with objects and so on, one can leap from the Eiffel Tower without risking one's life as they surely would in leaping from the real-world version. The Alamo, the Globe Theatre, and the Blarney Castle all make use of the hover and focus features available in virtual but not real worlds. Virtual visitors can hover unsupported in any section of the build, including its highest points, and focus their cameras close up on any part of the build without leaving their initial location in the build. Playgoers at the Globe have their cameras automatically adjusted to the center of the stage regardless of where they are seated in the theater so that they have a perfect view of the production, and they can wear a heads up display (HUD) that shows subtitles of the dialog in any of several languages. And like its real-world counterpart, the now-inaccessible Vietnam Veterans' Wall let visitors search for particular names, but unlike the real-world version, the virtual one let visitors teleport immediately to the place on the wall where the searched name is shown.

Imitative recreations in SVWs can certainly be judged in terms of their technical and esthetic qualities, just as attempts at representation in more traditional media can be assessed. Thus, using the dual criteria of novelty and appropriateness for evaluating creative products, the emphasis for imitative recreations needs to be on appropriateness. Do they accurately depict what they are intended to represent? Do visitors come away with a satisfied feeling of having experienced the essence of the real-world entity being depicted? At least for the ones described here, the answer to both questions is emphatically yes.

In contrast to mini-c creativity evident in users' choice and modification of their avatars, and more in line with the little-c or Pro-C development of content for purchase, these imitative recreations would have to be considered as manifestations of at least little-c creativity. Considerable knowledge and skill are required to produce structures of sufficient quality that a "qualified audience" would judge them to be worthwhile products, accomplishing the intended goals of their creators.

An important consequence of these imitative builds is that individual users of SVWs who visit them can acquire at least a simulated experience of visiting these landmarks in real life, even if their life circumstances make it impossible for them to visit the real versions. To the extent that such experiences can be thought of as culturally enriching then, SVWs could play an important supplementary role in increasing users' capacities for creative thought, as it is clear that broad cultural experience can contribute to creative functioning (e.g., Leung, Maddux, Galinsky, & Chiu, 2008). Future research could profitably be directed at the impact of exposure to such cultural content in virtual worlds.

It should be noted that virtual tours of famous landmarks and less familiar structures are commonplace and readily available outside the context of SVWs. Many universities, for instance, have links on their websites to virtual tours of their campuses, real-estate sites are tending to include virtual tours of listed houses, and yes, well-known landmarks, such as the Eiffel Tower, can be seen through virtual visits without visiting an SVW. Thus, in addition to asking the general question about the effects of culturally relevant virtual exposure, it is useful to consider whether or not there is anything special about being represented by one's avatar, a graphical representation of the self, in the environment being toured. It is clear that presence, especially self-presence, is impactful in determining the effect of virtual activities on real-world behavior (e.g., Behm-Morawitz, 2013), but it is yet to be determined whether any benefits of virtual exposure are enhanced by avatar representation in the environment.

Structured Virtual Imagination

There is an enormous amount of content in SVWs that is not specifically intended to mimic well-known landmarks and monuments. This includes but is not limited to buildings, vehicles, furniture, plants, and other objects, all of which are produced by the inhabitants of those environments. The single most striking aspect of those created virtual entities, observable in nearly every sim, is the extent to which they resemble their real-world counterparts. Buildings are structured with four walls and a roof defining their extent, and additional internal walls to partition the space into ordinary rooms, such as living rooms and bathrooms. Cars and motorcycles have four and two wheels respectively, boats have sails, planes have wings, and so on. Chairs have legs, seats and backs, and they rest on the floors of buildings. Although such properties may seem obvious, what is interesting is that they are utterly unnecessary in virtual settings such as *Second Life*. No weather conditions dictate the need for avatars to be protected from the elements by roofs, no wind is available to be caught by sails, and there is no reason why objects would need to be supported by floors, nor is there even any real need for avatars to make use of the sitting afforded by chairs and sofas to rest, as avatars themselves do not tire.

As with imitative recreations, some of this structuring of virtual objects by the properties of real-world objects may be intentional on the part of creators. People may be more comfortable having their avatars in situations that feel familiar rather than alien. Likewise, some of the design of buildings and furniture may reflect the creators' intent to develop spaces that facilitate social interaction. However, some of it likely reflects the operation of the phenomenon of structured imagination (Ward, 1994), in which the form of existing concepts implicitly influences the form of newly created ones.

Structured imagination has typically been studied by having people generate ideas for novel instances of familiar domains, such as imaginary instances of animals, tools, or fruit (e.g., Ward, 1994; Ward, Patterson, Sifonis, Dodds, & Saunders, 2002). The overwhelming tendency is for those imagined creations to closely resemble the most typical instances of the base categories, even when participants are instructed to be as creative as they can (e.g., Ward & Sifonis, 1997), and the structuring appears to be due to the retrieval of highly typical category instances, which are then used as starting points for the novel creations (Ward et al., 2002).

Because structured imagination operates at least partly at an implicit level, it is likely that the same tendency is responsible for some of the mimicking of real-world properties in virtual objects. This tendency can be referred to as *structured virtual imagination*.

Actions as Structured Content

The deliberate recreation of real-world content in SVWs goes beyond the production of virtual objects to include the scripting of animations that cause avatars to execute specific actions, such as couples' dances. Just as inhabitants of *Second Life* can visit sims that accurately represent well-known landmarks, so too can they purchase dance animations that will cause their avatars to execute the moves of specific dances, such as the Samba, Tango, and Waltz, among others. As with imitative recreations, these animation are deliberate imitations of known entities and they are developed by skilled individuals who must be deemed to be operating at least at the little-c level by virtue of the fact that other users are willing to purchase the product. Observing the avatar movements that are guided by these animations reveals that they capture the esthetic pleasingness of real-world versions of those dances.

As with objects, there is also some structuring of less specific actions, such as sitting and lying down, in addition to the intentional mimicking of specific dance moves. Also as with objects, some of the structuring of animations to simulate those actions may be deliberate, but some may be implicit structured virtual imagination. Again, there is no reason in principle why avatars would need to sit or lay down.

Beyond Structure

The emphasis thus far has been on the ways in which the content of SVWs resembles objects and actions in the real world. However, there are striking examples of sims that radically violate real-world constraints. One of these is Inspire Space Park (2014), in which one first lands on what seems to be an enormous flat gray stone platform that hangs in the air surrounded by clouds. In every direction are floating objects, some large, some small. Some of the objects resemble planets or moons and slowly rotate. Some are smaller irregularly shaped rocks. In addition, there are regular chairs as well as blue lounge chairs that hang in the air unsupported. There are also poses unlike the standard ones that cause individuals to sit or recline on surfaces such as chairs. The "orbital sleep" pose put one's avatar in a horizontal position, floating slowly amid the objects in the sim. Likewise, there are meditation poses that cause one's avatar to float in a cross-legged pose rotating in all directions.

Another interesting sim, which unfortunately is no longer accessible in *Second Life*, was Virtual Starry Night, a 3D representation of Van Gogh's famous *Starry Night* painting. Avatars could walk around virtually within the village depicted in the painting. The opportunity to learn about the painting by wandering within a 3D representation of it provides a kind of learning experience unmatched by anything in the real world. A similar role of active participation in simulated experiences that support learning by students is highlighted by Frossard et al. (Chapter 8).

In addition to admiring the creativity inherent in the development of such sims, it is useful to consider the extent to which exposure to them and to other unusual aspects of SVWs might influence the creative behavior of users. Does exposure to the impossible increase creative tendencies?

We know that if people are shown examples of novel items purportedly created by other participants (e.g., imaginary animals that all have four legs, two antennae, and a tail), they tend to incorporate properties of those examples into their own new ideas, even when instructed to avoid doing so (Jansson & Smith, 1991; Marsh, Landau, & Hicks, 1996; Marsh, Ward, & Landau, 1999; Smith, Ward, & Schumacher, 1993). Ordinarily, this conformity effect would be seen as working against creativity. However, it is clear that people will also conform to unusual or incomprehensible properties of examples they are shown, with the consequence that they produce their own versions that have greater creative potential (e.g., Ishibashi & Takeshi, 2007; Landau & Lehr, 2004). Thus, there is reason to believe that exposure to the impossible possibilities of virtual worlds could have a facilitative effect on individuals' creative idea generation.

Collaborative Activities

The discussion thus far has focused largely on the creativity of individual users of SVWs, but the fact that those worlds support user interaction makes them natural candidates for examinations of collaborative forms of creativity, such as creative group problem solving. Larach and Cabra (2010) have recently demonstrated the feasibility of using SVWs (specifically *Second Life*) to facilitate brainstorming. They created a virtual space to be similar to those used in real-world applications of group creative problem solving and developed tools for sharing and tabulating ideas. The study was largely exploratory, but a key finding was that participants and facilitators found the virtual session to be conducive to good group dynamics and teamwork as well as to creative functioning. As the study was exploratory in nature, it did not directly compare SVW group problem solving to other formats, but the results are nevertheless encouraging for the continued investigation of virtual brainstorming.

Taking a somewhat different approach of testing multiple groups of naïve users in different situations, Ward and Roskos (unpublished) gave two- and three-person groups of undergraduate students the task of coming up with as many solutions as they could for how to improve the university. All participants made their suggestions by way of text chat, and there were two main conditions. In one condition participants in the groups were represented as avatars seated around a virtual table together, and in the other they saw the text chat on an otherwise blank screen. Subsequent to performing the main task, participants responded to a short questionnaire concerned with their sense of actually being in the problem-solving environment with the other group members. The question addressed was whether or not the visible avatars would lead to a greater sense of presence and better performance on the brainstorming task. However, at least as measured by some questions, the avatar condition resulted in a lowered sense of presence, and there were no differences in the number of ideas listed by the groups in the two conditions. The exact reasons for the findings are open to conjecture, but the results provide at least a cautionary note that performance will not always be better in enhanced virtual settings.

Yee, Bailenson, and Ducheneaut (2009) have commented on the metaphor of embodiment and concomitant expectations that may underlie at least some of the overwhelming tendency of SVW users to represent themselves as human rather than some other form, and by extension may prevent us from reaping the creative promise of virtual worlds. They point to the strong tendency to produce virtual bodies that mirror our real bodies as a factor that can limit creative thought. They also point to the irony that much of the focus on customization actually puts an emphasis on human form rather than allowing users to escape its constraints. Although it is true that the edit menu allows people to modify their avatars in a huge number of ways, those variations are on the exact manifestation of human form rather than its rejection.

The expectations discussed by Yee, Bailenson, and Ducheneaut (2009) are directly relevant to the promise and pitfalls of group creativity in SVWs. For example, the *expectation of human embodiment* works against the consideration of people adopting other animate forms during brainstorming sessions, thus narrowing the set of ideas that are considered. Would better solutions be thought of if individuals adopted the form of other creatures such as birds, fish, or insects? Moreover, need the avatars be animate at all, and might there be advantages to different members of a brainstorming group being represented as relevant objects, such as flip charts or work tables?

Yee, Bailenson, and Ducheneaut (2009) also introduced the construct of serial embodiment, in which problem solvers can take on different avatar forms throughout a problem-solving session rather than remaining stuck in a single static form. Similarly, Ward and Sonneborn (2009) discussed the possible benefits of users adopting different forms to signify different modes of thought as needed at different points in a problem-solving session, such as representations of DeBono's six thinking hat styles, Sternberg's (1988) mental self-government types, or avatars resembling noted thinkers (e.g., Einstein) to help users identify more strongly with those modes of thought. Although it is an empirical question whether such avatar manipulations would positively influence creative thought, the fact that simple manipulations such as the height and cloak color of avatars can profoundly influence behavior provides at least some encouragement to anticipate such effects.

An additional expectation discussed by Yee, Bailenson, and Ducheneaut (2009) is that of *congruence*, that different avatars have different perspectives that are nevertheless congruent. An extension of this notion is that, much as when people share a problem-solving environment in the real world, it is basically the same environment for all individuals. Though framed differently, the suggestion of breaking that congruence expectation is consistent with Ward and Sonneborn's construct of *individualized collaboration* in virtual environments. The fact that virtual worlds allow individuals to customize their experience of the environment (e.g., set the sun position to midnight versus midday) makes it possible for different group members to experience the situation in distinctly different ways, perhaps more suited to their individual styles and more likely to provoke a broader range of possible solutions to the problem at hand.

CONCLUSIONS

It is clear that SVWs provide unique opportunities to observe creative behavior. These include the manifestation of mini-c creativity in the form of people deciding how to represent themselves in a way consistent with their understandings of their roles and goals in the virtual world. They also include the little-c and Pro-C activities and products of skilled individuals who create various types of virtual content, either with the deliberate intent to mimic real-world objects and actions or as influenced by structured imagination. In addition, there are opportunities to observe the unique role of virtual worlds in supporting group creative problem solving, although the promise has yet to be fully realized. Finally, the role of properties that are unusual or simply impossible in the real world but readily realized in virtual worlds provides fertile ground for assessing the potential facilitative effects of virtual worlds on creative functioning.

References

Alamo (2014). Retrieved October 31, 2014 from: http://maps.secondlife.com/secondlife/UTArlington%20III/159/91/23.

Beghetto, R. A., & Kaufman, J. C. (2007). Toward a broader conception of creativity: The case for "mini-c" creativity. *Psychology of Aesthetics, Creativity, and the Arts, 2*, 73–79.

Behm-Morawitz, E. (2013). Mirrored selves: The influence of self-presence in a virtual world on health, appearance, and well-being. *Computers in Human Behavior, 29*, 119–128.

Blarney Castle (2014). Retrieved October 31, 2014 from: http://maps.secondlife.com/secondlife/Wilde/160/109/34.

Globe Theatre (2014). Retrieved July 11, 2014 from: http://maps.secondlife.com/secondlife/Renaissance%20Island/199/49/27.

Goldman, A. H. (2003). Representation in art. In J. Levinson (Ed.), *The Oxford handbook of aesthetics* (pp. 192–210). Oxford, UK: Oxford University Press.

Guadagno, R. E., Muscanell, N. L., Okdie, B. M., Burk, N. M., & Ward, T. B. (2010). Even in virtual environments women shop and men build: A social role perspective on Second Life. *Computers in Human Behavior, 27*, 304–308.

Hof, R. (2006). Second Life's first millionaire. *Bloomberg Businessweek (The Tech Beat)*. Retrieved from: http://www.businessweek.com/the_thread/techbeat/archives/2006/11/second_lifes_fi.html.

Inspire Space Park (2014). Retrieved July 11, 2014 from: http://maps.secondlife.com/secondlife/Shinda/29/203/1560.

Ishibashi, K. & Takeshi, O. (2007). Exploring the effect of copying incomprehensible exemplars on creative drawings. In *Proceedings of the Cognitive Science Society*. Cognitive Science Society. D. van Knippenberg & M. C. Schippers (2007).

Jansson, D. G., & Smith, S. M. (1991). Design fixation. *Design Studies, 12*, 3–11.

Jung, Y. (2011). Understanding the role of sense of presence and perceived autonomy in users' continued use of social virtual worlds. *Journal of Computer-Mediated Communication, 16*, 492–510.

Kaufman, J. C., & Beghetto, R. A. (2009). Beyond big and little: The four c model of creativity. *Review of General Psychology, 13*, 1–12.

Larach, D. U., & Cabra, J. F. (2010). Creative problem solving in second life: An action research study. *Creativity and Innovation Management, 19,* 167–179.

Landau, J. D., & Lehr, D. P. (2004). Conformity to experimenter-provided examples: Will people use an unusual feature? *Journal of Creative Behavior, 38,* 180–191.

Leung, A.K.-Y., Maddux, W. W., Galinsky, A. D., & Chiu, C.-Y. (2008). Multicultural experience enhances creativity: The when and how. *American Psychologist, 63,* 169–181.

Marsh, R. L., Landau, J. D., & Hicks, J. L. (1996). How examples may (and may not) constrain creativity. *Memory & Cognition, 24,* 669–680.

Marsh, R. L., Ward, T. B., & Landau, J. D. (1999). The inadvertent use of prior knowledge in a generative cognitive task. *Memory & Cognition, 27,* 94–105.

Paris circa 1900 (2014) Retrieved October 31, 2014 from: http://maps.secondlife.com/secondlife/Paris%20Eiffel/26/117/22.

Pearce, C. (2009). *Communities of play: Emergent cultures in multiplayer games and virtual worlds.* Cambridge, MA: MIT Press.

Pena, J., Hancock, J. T., & Merola, N. A. (2009). The priming effect of avatars in virtual settings. *Communication Research, 36,* 838–856.

Runco, M. A. (1996). Personal creativity: Definition and developmental issues. *New Directions for Child Development, 72,* 3–30.

Smith, S. M., Ward, T. B., & Schumacher, J. (1993). Constraining effects of examples in a creative generation task. *Memory & Cognition, 21,* 837–845.

Sternberg, R. J. (1988). Mental self-government: A theory of intellectual styles and their development. *Human Development, 31,* 197–221.

Ward, T. B. (1994). Structured imagination: The role of category structure in exemplar generation. *Cognitive Psychology, 27,* 1–40.

Ward, T. B., Patterson, M. J., Sifonis, C. M., Dodds, R. A., & Saunders, K. N. (2002). The role of graded category structure in imaginative thought. *Memory & Cognition, 30,* 199–216.

Ward, T. B. & Roskos, B. (unpublished manuscript). The effects of being represented as 3D avatars on participants' sense of presence and brainstorming performance.

Ward, T. B., & Sifonis, S. M. (1997). Task demands and generative thinking: What changes and what remains the same? *Journal of Creative Behavior, 31,* 245–259.

Ward, T. B., & Sonneborn, M. S. (2009). Creative expression in virtual environments: Imitation, imagination and individualized collaboration. *Psychology of Aesthetics, Creativity, and the Arts, 3,* 211–221.

Yee, N., Bailenson, J. N., Urbanek, M., Chang, F., & Megert, D. (2007). The unbearable likeness of being digital: The persistence of nonverbal social norms in online virtual environments. *Cyberpsychology & Behavior, 10,* 115–121.

Yee, N., Bailenson, J. N., & Ducheneaut, N. (2009). The Proteus effect: Implications of transformed digital self-representation on online and offline behavior. *Communication Research, 36,* 285–312.

Yee, N., Ellis, J., & Ducheneaut, N. (2009). The tyranny of embodiment. *Artifact, 2,* 1–6.

PART 2

CREATIVITY AND VIDEO GAMES IN EDUCATION

7

Teaching Creativity: Theoretical Models and Applications

Jorge A. Blanco-Herrera, Christopher L. Groves,
Ann M. Lewis and Douglas A. Gentile

Department of Psychology, Iowa State University, Ames, IA, USA

I have not failed 10,000 times. I have not failed once. I have succeeded in proving that those 10,000 ways will not work. When I have eliminated the way that will not work, I will find the way that will work.
—Attributed to Thomas Edison (Furr, 2011)

Although Edison's quote is contrary to intuition, and contrary to the voice of self-criticism, its subversion of the status quo is exciting. It is a voice of enthusiasm, a rejection of dejection, and an affirmation of a future of possibility.

Some modern entrepreneurs also embrace the idea of failure to encourage innovation. The authors of the video-game-centered web show Extra Credits say "Fail faster." They assert that designers can get caught up trying to perfect their ideas before trying them. They state that "The later you fail, the more expensive your failure will be … Your ideas can't be precious" (Portnow, Floyd, & Theus, 2014).

Edison and the Extra Credits hosts are saying the same thing: that you should embrace the testing of your ideas, and not be discouraged when they don't perform as expected. By finding flaws in your attempts, you will find ways to improve them, taking the lessons of a thousand flawed designs to create a better work.

Sometimes, however, our own feedback is flawed. It can be hard to look past our own preconceived expectations and emotional investment, and to give ourselves the honest criticism we need. If we do not have the time, mental resources, or motivation, we may not even identify the need for it. We also may not have access to anyone we can ask to evaluate our ideas. Alone, we may struggle in trying to stretch our creative muscles and practice the ideation/evaluation skills we need for creativity.

With the rise in technology, new tools for testing and feedback have also risen. Video games, an increasingly ubiquitous form of entertainment, are promising tools for practicing the ideation/evaluation cycle. The designing and playing of video games involve guessing, thinking, testing, and repeated opportunities for failure or success.

Video games are excellent teachers (see Gentile, Groves, & Gentile, 2014 for discussion on this topic). Well-made video games are inherently engaging, are widely available, and often offer immediate feedback throughout game play. They also may create a unique state, often called "flow," where practice is most effective (Nakamura & Csikszentmihalyi, 2002).

In this chapter, we will address the idea of considering video games for serious purposes. We address how video games teach, describing a model of learning, and how video games follow learning principles. We describe the idea of flow, and what mechanics of video games lead to this potentially high-learning state. We will cover how the learning model and flow state can foster creativity. Finally, we offer suggestions for how the game and learning principles can be used to foster creativity through games and in the classroom.

NOT YOUR EVERYDAY GAMES

When you're playing simple, fun, and seemingly addictive video games like Candy Crush Saga it's hard to think of video games as anything but entertainment. You might play them on public transport, in line at the bank, or in between business meetings. Nonetheless, many people are turning to video games for serious purposes. With games like *Re-Mission 2* (HopeLab, TRI, Realtime Associates, 2008), children playing a third-person shooter with jetpacks and gooey explosions aren't just having fun. They are playing a game that will help them learn more about and better manage their cancer (Kato, Cole, Bradlyn, & Pollock, 2008). Serious games (games designed for a purpose other than pure entertainment; Micheal & Chen, 2005) have been designed to tackle the challenges faced by our society.

Video game therapies have been designed to help surgery patients distract themselves from the pain of their procedures (Flynn & Lange, 2010). Some clinicians and researchers are treating psychological and physical disorders directly with virtual reality games (Hodges, Anderson, Burdea, Hoffmann, & Rothbaum, 2001). These treatments range from systematic desensitization exposure therapy for those with post-traumatic stress disorder to physical rehabilitation for those with severe physical trauma (Rothbaum, Hodges, Ready, Graap, & Alarcon, 2001; Sveistrup et al., 2003). The military uses video game tools to aid soldiers preparing for combat (Raybourn, Deagle, Mendini, & Heneghan, 2005).

Another well-publicized use of serious video games has come from the University of Washington, where researchers have used video games to crowdsource science. Reshaping and fitting protein molecules together as is needed for AIDS and cancer research is usually a very time-consuming and difficult problem, but researchers have turned it into a puzzle video game, where individuals and teams from around the world play together to find solutions (Eiben et al., 2012). In the game *Fold-it*, players try to reshape protein molecules to produce demonstrations of how these molecules interact in real life. The reshaping process maximizes efficiency and minimizes problems—bonding them, inhibiting certain structures, resizing them, etc. They have had success using the thousands of free work hours from players who enjoyed the game, using the results of this play to discover and publish about the nature of these diseases.

In a similar approach, the People's Lab of MSLGROUP is using video games to spread a social message. They employ a social network game called *Half the Sky* to educate people on the plight of oppressed women trying to establish economic security in Africa. Not only does this game allow people to live virtually through the difficulties suffered by oppressed women, they also use it to connect the gamers to real people that need help. The game is integrated with Facebook and other social media, allowing the players to make donations online. Users can also spread news of the program to their friends through links and "shares." *Half the Sky* has successfully been able to raise awareness for an important social issue, create a free accessible platform from which people can learn, connect with, and donate to those in need, as well as continually spread the creators' message through the world (Makhija, 2013).

These examples illustrate a growing trend of serious games as tools for learning, health, and communication. Video games can be incredibly successful not only in the fields of medical applications, scientific endeavors, and social outreach exemplified above, but also in the field of education because video games themselves are incredibly effective teachers. Even when games are solely designed for entertainment they teach players real-world skills and lessons.

When people play prosocial video games they show more prosocial thoughts and behavior (Gentile et al., 2009; Greitemeyer, Osswald, & Brauer, 2010). When people play violent video games they show significant increased levels of aggression (Anderson, Gentile, & Buckley, 2007; Anderson et al., 2010; Gentile, Lynch, Linder, & Walsh, 2004). When people play action video games, games that require quick reactions to a variety of visual cues, they benefit from faster reaction times and increased performance in a range of visual-spatial cognitive tasks (Achtman, Green, & Bavelier, 2008; Dye, Green, & Bavelier, 2009; Green & Bavelier, 2003). When people play real-time strategy (RTS) video games, which require storing and processing of multiple short- and long-term goals while simultaneously attending to new cues, they show gains in working memory (Basak, Boot, Voss, & Kramer, 2008; Basak, Voss, Erickson, Boot, & Kramer, 2011; Kühn, Gleich, Lorenz, Lindenberger, & Gallinat, 2014). The focused repetition of ideas, expectations, and skills in video games create an exemplary teacher (Gentile & Gentile, 2008).

A MODEL FOR LEARNING PROCESSES IN GAMES

The way people learn in video games can be described using the general learning model (GLM). An overview of this model can be found in Figure 1. The GLM is a model of human learning that incorporates biological, social, and cognitive factors. A single cycle of the GLM serves as a representation of an individual learning episode. The amount of time it takes for one to progress through each stage is intentionally vague. The entire cycle may be completed within seconds, but could take several minutes. This single cycle contains three stages.

The first stage of a GLM cycle begins with two forms of input, including all the qualities of the environment and of the person in a given situation. The person input includes all persistent qualities of the individual that are carried with them into each given moment: genetic predispositions,

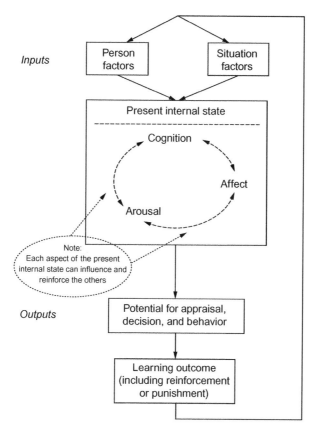

FIGURE 1   Short-term process overview of general learning model. *Gentile et al. (2014).*

stable personality traits, mood, sex, short- and long-term goals, attentional resources, etc. The environment includes all of the qualities of the present situation: all of the characteristics and affordances of the physical environment, as well as other external factors like social influence. These qualities interact to influence the opportunity for learning.

Information in the environment is detected by one's sensory organs. However, perception, or what the mind thinks is being detected, is an interaction between the environment and the person. Perception is a product of detection and learning. The process of perceiving is best considered both a top-down and bottom-up process (Gentile et al., 2014).

Once the situation is perceived, it can influence physiological arousal, affect (feelings or mood), and thinking (cognitions, including both conscious and nonconscious cognitions, such as spreading neural semantic priming). Each of these internal states is related and they can affect each other. For example, if someone is insulted, their arousal increases, they feel anger, and they think that the insult was unjustified. Thinking that it was unjustified—how they did nothing to deserve this, how that person is being completely unfair, how they can't believe anyone would ever do this!—Such thoughts can serve to further increase the feelings of anger and arousal.

Next, the internal states influence decision-making processes in which individuals select a response to the given situational event or context. In this stage, decisions can be made immediately (an impulsive action) or following reappraisal (a thoughtful action). Impulsive actions will usually occur when the individual does not possess the motivation or resources (e.g., time) to reappraise the situation. Impulsive actions will also occur if the individual has received positive feedback from similar responses in the past. This is usually the case with habitual actions like one's morning ritual. People usually don't think too hard about how they are getting ready in the morning, because it has always met their goals in the past and an unexpected failure (a freezing shower or a bad hair day) is unlikely to cause serious problems. However, if the individual thinks the outcome is important, and if the intended action risks an unsatisfying outcome, then reappraisal is more likely. Learning may also occur during this reappraisal process. For example, in completing a math problem, a student may decide to double-check their work—if a changed answer appears more correct (or is reinforced as correct, later, by an authority) the cognitive processes leading to the correction are reinforced. Similarly, if a student makes an impulsive decision, it may be reinforced later (the answer was correct) or punished (the answer was wrong). Impulsive actions that receive regular reinforcement create more deeply engrained habits, and increase the likelihood of similar impulsive actions in future cycles, while impulsive actions that receive regular punishment weaken, and are less likely to be repeated.

Through the processes described here, learning occurs at several stages and is reinforced throughout the cycle. In a simple example, when encountering a person in need, feelings of empathy, and concern may arise, which influence the likelihood of engaging in a helping response. If the helping response is rewarded, the individual may be more likely to identify others in need in the future (a perceptual learning effect), experience empathy and concern for such individuals, and repeat decisions to provide help. This example illustrates that, through repetition, individual learning cycles produce long-term changes in the person which are then carried across situational contexts.

The value of the GLM is in the modeling of learning. Video games have players rapidly and efficiently complete many learning cycles. They are a promising tool for practicing the process of creative production.

GAMES AND FLOW

One of the strengths of video games is that they are naturally inter-active (Squire, 2003). This can help to transport the player into another "world," to have the player craving to play again, and to even lose track of time (this is similar to the research of information processing schol-ars on narrative transportation; i.e. Green & Brock, 2000). One theoretical construct that may help to explain how games can be so captivating is the commonly reported experience of flow. Flow is a state in which one loses track of time, has an extreme focus on the task at hand, finds the task rewarding, and performs optimally (Sherry, 2004). It can be argued that video games can induce this state because they excel at providing players with a task that is immediately rewarding and adapts to their skill level (Csikszentmihalyi, 1990). Understanding flow may be the key to un-derstanding how the engaging power of games may be applied to both creative and general learning.

Flow experiences are reported in a variety of activities. It can happen while playing a sport, performing a piece of music, creating works of art, or simply playing a game with friends (Csikszentmihalyi & Csikzentmihaly, 1991). Some might refer to the state of flow as being "in the zone" while performing a task (Young & Pain, 1999). Flow states can be thought as an extreme form of engagement. Flow states and theories have been de-scribed differently, and although they have been popular, they also have typically been described so vaguely that they were largely impossible to test empirically. Some recent work, however, may provide novel ap-proaches to understanding and measuring it. This section will focus on expanding upon and applying the Weber, Tamborini, Westcott-Baker, and Kantor (2009) conception of flow.

Historically, flow was described phenomenologically in situations where skill and challenge are balanced (Csikszentmihalyi, 1990). People became engaged by the challenge of demonstrating and improving their own skill and are rewarded as they successfully progress and learn (Vygotsky, 1987). Good video games adapt to the player's current skill level, optimizing this cycle of progression and reward. They do this through a variety of methods (Funk, Chan, Brouwer, & Curtiss, 2006). One of the simplest is the use of progressively complicated/harder levels. For example, in *Halo: Combat Evolved*, increasingly difficult game levels will include more enemies, different enemy types, and more combinations of enemy types that require deeper levels of strategy to defeat. The player progresses from fighting basic infantry to land vehicular combat, aerial combat, and storming a fortified position with their choice of vehicles and reinforcements against infantry, elite units, tanks, aerial combat units, and surprises. This forces the player to learn new strategies against the enemy types, to master those strategies, and then learn how to switch between strategies when appropriate.

Balance is crucial. If achieving success becomes too easy, the player progresses with little effort. They feel little reward for accomplishing such a small task again and again, and ultimately become bored (Csikszentmihalyi & Csikzentmihaly, 1991). On the other hand, if achieving success is too difficult, the player sees little chance, if any, to progress and is frustrated. Balancing effort and reward provides the player with an opportunity to gain growth and development from earnest effort. The player is not only explicitly rewarded within the game, but is also intrinsically rewarded with feelings of success and competence.

It is possible that the immediate feedback within games serves to prevent the flow state from being interrupted. The player knows immediately if their current tactic is working. If they are rewarded or punished depending on their performance, they can immediately adapt and continue playing. They can progress at their own pace, and feel greater control over their own progression. Because of this, immediate feedback keeps the player engaged as their actions have direct, observable effects.

Yet, even with immediate feedback, not every action is rewarded, or rewarded equally. A fixed reward schedule (that is, one that happens every single time you do something) is not as motivating as a variable reward schedule (such as slot machines, which reward at random intervals) (e.g., Skinner, 1957; Watson & Skinner, 2001). Many games tend to implement scaled variable and fixed reinforcement alongside the immediate feedback to keep the game as engaging as possible. For example, in *Destiny* (Activision, 2014), players are awarded a certain amount of experience points for defeating enemies. However, every enemy that is defeated has a random chance of dropping an item, and any enemy can drop items of any quality (with more desirable items being rarer). In this game, every enemy defeated gives players a fixed experience point reinforce while also providing a variable "loot" reward system. The "loot" mechanic is remarkably similar to what is seen in slot machines. Defeating enemies is the lever and the game items are the prize. It is common to see players fixate on playing this video game "slot machine" for hours in hopes of hitting a jackpot. This is one of the video game mechanics that likely increases the risk of behavioral addiction to games, such as massive multiplayer online role-playing games (Gentile, 2009).

Immediate feedback with variable reinforcement is not the only tool that video games use to engage flow. At a deeper level, they also use progression and progression feedback for long-term engagement. Skill trees in *World of Warcraft* (Blizzard Entertainment, 2004) allow players to see the growth of their character within a game over time, to measure that growth, and to foresee the rewards that come with this progress. This is also done with progress bars, badges, maps, unlockable content, achievements, quests, and more. The *Call of Duty: Modern Warfare 2* (Activision, 2009) franchise implemented these systems to great success in their multiplayer to give players goals and clear ways to achieve them. A player would see an exciting weapon that could only be used once the player had achieved a certain "level." A progress bar kept track of their leveling progress, badges gave players supplementary goals that granted extra experience, and achievements kept giving them rewards on their path to unlocking their desired gear. These visible markers served to give the player a variety of new goals, to offer a guide to achieving these goals, to show them how much they have accomplished, and to allow them to display their achievements to other players.

These extrinsic reward systems must be used with care and balance. If the game gives the player too much in the way of structure and continuous rewards then the game risks becoming something of a Skinner box simulation (Skinner, 1957). The player simply performs as the game tells them they should, and not much is gained from the experience.

From the perspective of the GLM, the flow experience can be described as the result of the short-term learning processes becoming optimal, fixated on a singular task, and uninterrupted. This can produce more efficient and rapid cycling, maximizing the player's learning potential.

CREATIVITY

Creativity can be thought of as a cyclic process of ideation and evaluation (Lubart, 2001). This approach to creativity is characterized by a period of ideation—coming up with ideas—followed by practical evaluation on the merit of the ideas.

Ideation relies on the process of divergent thinking, which holds four distinct aspects: fluency of ideas, flexibility of categories, elaboration, and originality (Guilford, 1967). Fluency of ideas describes the total number of disparate ideas the creative person can create, flexibility of categories is how many different types of categories those ideas can be organized into, elaboration is how detailed those ideas are, and originality is how uncommon a particular idea is. Ideation in games can take the form of trying different tactics in a strategy game, constructing in-game objects, approaching a group of enemies from a different angle, or just deciding on how to classify winning in the game.

Evaluations should judge both the appropriateness of a solution and whether it can be feasibly implemented. Evaluation stands as a form of convergent thinking, or the ability to derive the most appropriate answer for a well-defined question (Cropley, 2006). Evaluation in games can be immediate and can come from varied sources. Depending on the game, evaluation can come from peers, enemies in the game, or the rules of the game itself. The game can easily tell the player their idea failed by having the player fail, die, or lose immediately. It can also do the same by increasing the difficulty of the game after a failed action. Other players of the game can give feedback as well, either in the game or outside of it. Due to the nature of video games, players often receive feedback or evaluation quickly. This allows players to repeat many ideation and evaluation cycles rapidly.

This rapid cycling is similar to how flow was described. Similar to flow, the game must allow the player to have meaningful choices. If the game does not balance meaningful choices or other game mechanics besides the Skinner box reinforcements, the game can result in detriments to creativity because it does not let the player ideate (Beghetto, 2013). There would be only one right answer, and hence no room for alternative solutions, trial and error, or ideation and evaluation.

The more times someone can cycle through the process of ideation and evaluation, the more chances they have of being successful in a creative pursuit. Additionally, the more practice they have in each step of the process, the more likely they are to succeed in that step (Basadur, Graen, & Green, 1982). As video games and their attendant mechanics have players rapidly and efficiently complete many learning cycles, they are a promising tool for practicing both ideation and evaluation, reinforcing the regular use of these processes in the player. Although theoretically reasonable, very little research exists testing these hypotheses.

GAME ELEMENTS FOR CREATIVITY: APPLIED EXAMPLES

Video games may be a valuable tool for training ideation and evaluation, but game elements can also be applied to traditional learning settings. In a traditional math class, students are given a lecture on a topic, go over some examples, and then are assigned homework to continue practicing on their own. Students are expected to listen to the teacher for the duration of the lecture, to take notes, to understand the examples (or to know when they are confused), to ask appropriate clarifying questions, to participate with expected and nontangential answers, and then to complete the homework correctly as assigned. However, this format may be improved with the adoption of certain game elements. We will use educational examples, such as the partnership between Khan Academy and the Los Altos school district, to exemplify approaches to education that have benefited from the use of game elements. (It is worth noting that in the first year of the Khan Academy and Los Altos school district partnership, the district saw an increase of 73% in the number of students who passed the California Standards Test; Kronholz, 2012.) We will also use examples of video games that use the same elements to illustrate their use in the gaming context. Each section will offer a game element, give examples, and explain its utility in training and improving creativity.

Pace Matching

Pace matching refers to the mirroring of an individual's comprehension level to match that which is demanded by the environment. The interactive nature of video games lends itself to pace matching. The player decides how much and how fast to progress in the game. They can choose to play below, at, or above their own skill level. They have the opportunity to practice their skills again and again until they succeed. They can replay parts of the game they want to improve in, and if the player does not have the necessary skills they need to be successful, they will not progress. Yet, they can always try again until their pace matches that of the game (or they turn down the difficulty so the game pace matches them).

The difficulty settings in *Dance Dance Revolution* (DDR) games (Konami, 1998) are a great example of pace matching. Low difficulties and beginning songs start with relatively few moves at low speeds. The player can choose either to pick more or less difficult songs or change the overall difficulty setting. Increasing overall difficulty gives the player more moves at a faster pace. Different songs let the player not only choose different styles, but also slightly different variations in difficulty.

Some games are more forward in encouraging appropriate pace selection. In the game *Devil May Cry* (Capcom, 2001), the game defaults to normal difficulty. But if the player dies a certain number of times on the same level, the game asks if the player would like to try it on easy mode.

Pace matching in the GLM can be described as a match between environmental demands and the perception and decision-making ability of the person. Pace matching occurs when the person is able to attend to the environmental stimulus, respond accordingly, receive timely feedback, and attend to that feedback. In a game, this means the player understands the demands of the game (DDR says hit the right arrow), the player reacts according to the game demands (player steps on right arrow), the game reads the response and makes the player aware (right arrow icon lights up on the screen), and the player sees the effects of an action (player sees that they received the points for hitting the right arrow). Pace matching may allow users to complete learning cycles of the GLM at a pace that is comfortable for them and makes each cycle more effective. It also can fill the flow requirement of matching difficulty with ability, allowing players, or students, to maintain the flow state longer.

In a standard classroom, even though the top third of students have an average learning rate at least three times faster than those in the bottom third, the teacher introduces the material at one pace (Gentile & Lalley, 2003; Gentile, Voelkl, Mt. Pleasant, & Monaco, 1995). This could force the teacher into a pace that is ineffective for the majority of the class. Without any outside support, like tutors, some children may start seeing the classroom as a negative place, characterized by either boredom or frustration instead of as a place of knowledge and achievement. One way the Khan Academy partnership tackled the problem of pace matching was to "flip" the classroom, making video lectures to be viewed at home, while classroom time is devoted to practice problems that would normally be assigned as homework. This way, the student has control over the pace of the lecture. They can pause it, speed it up, or repeat it as needed. Practicing problems in the classroom allows the teacher to float between students, answering questions and assisting with individual student problem areas as needed (Kronholz, 2012).

An example of a more explicitly creative video game that benefits from pace matching is *Prison Architect*, currently in alpha (Introversion Studios, 2012). The game relies on the ideation of possible designs, and the evaluation of those designs through the continual testing of your security by the prisoners. In a standard game without money cheats, the player starts with a small number of funds and must build a small prison, generally with the lowest security (easiest) prisoners. They may adjust this further by turning continuous intake, or the constant arrival of more prisoners, on or off. As more prisoners arrive, the design must become more elaborate. As you add prisoners of increasing difficulty (medium and maximum security, even the occasional supermax), the player must improve designs to address new and more difficult problems. Yet, if it becomes too hard, the player can either reduce the difficulty of incoming prisoners, turn off continuous intake entirely, or even sell the current prison and enter his or her next scenario with more money; they are thus able to meet the demands of greater difficulty levels. The game allows regular cycling of learning processes, can induce a state of flow through high engagement and challenge adjustment, and creates an ideal environment for ideation followed by rapid, visible evaluation.

Instruction, Practice, Feedback

In video games, players are instructed in skills and given feedback while they practice them. They are told pressing the "A" button is for jumping, they are allowed to press a button, and they see that the character on the screen jumps. They are usually given some sort of object to jump on, across, or over. This immediate application allows the player to understand the usefulness of a skill. The game structure may require jumping for progression through the game or provide other rewards. This basic practice with instruction and immediate feedback allows for rapid and lasting learning. "A" is for jumping, which allows the character to jump, jumping can traverse obstacles, and traversing those obstacles can be rewarded with prizes or progression.

The game *Portal* (Valve Corporation, 2007) is a very popular title that incorporates this instruction, practice, and feedback well. In it, the player is given a tool that will create two portals in solid walls. If the player walks into one, they come out the other. The game explicitly teaches the player how to make these holes, and then offers problems with set goals that test the player's ability to use the mechanic effectively. When the player makes a mistake, death ensues and the player gets to try again. When the player succeeds, they are congratulated and move on to a more difficult problem. The melding of instruction, practice, and feedback allows for rapid cycling through the GLM because it gives players rapid feedback on their actions, lets them adjust accordingly, and provides feedback on those adjustments. It also makes the player an active learner in the game, encouraging engagement and continued attempts.

In a typical math class, the instruction (lecture), the practice (homework), and the feedback (graded work) are separated by days or even weeks. The flipped classroom described above hastens this instruction/practice/feedback cycle. First, the platform in which they watch the video lecture, KhanAcademy.org, links the student directly to practice problems on the material of the lecture. Second, given that the teacher no longer gives a general lecture for everyone, the teacher is free to work individually with students, answer questions, and supply additional problem-solving techniques the student can apply immediately. Third, the problems students are working on are automatically graded so students are immediately aware of deficiencies in their work. The electronic format also provides the teacher with formative data on how each student is performing in each subject and their subtopics, enabling even more focused feedback in the future.

Fold-it (Eiben et al., 2012), the protein-shaping game mentioned earlier, is an excellent example of instruction, structured practice, and immediate feedback. The tutorial begins with simple proteins and explains a single tool that can be used to manipulate it. The player tries the tool, and elements of the protein change or light up to indicate failure or success. The game then continues with instruction for another tool, and another cycle of practice and feedback. Players improve their knowledge base while simultaneously being required to use the acquired skills in novel ways. Ideation and evaluation are the goal, and *Fold-it* combines individual player improvements into a massive pool of possible new approaches to serious disease.

Developing Automaticity

Much like math, video games depend on mastery and automaticity of basic skills learned in early levels to progress successfully in later levels. Video games achieve this by giving the player massed practice of every new skill (that is, a concentrated amount of practice at one sitting) and distributing further practice of that skill throughout the game. Basic skills within games are heavily practiced in early stages (overlearned) and, later, more difficult stages can only be completed if the skills developed earlier in the game have become automatized (a product of overlearning). This automatization frees cognitive resources so that players are able to focus on more novel, difficult demands of the game's level. One can only master the double-jump ledge-grab flip after mastering the basic jump. If you have to analyze the basic jump every time you do it, you may die.

RTS games, like *Warcraft 3* (Blizzard Entertainment, 2004), serve as excellent examples of the role of automaticity in learning. These games require that players collect resources, use those resources to build structures that produce military units, and ultimately create an army used to defeat a computerized opponent. First, players have to learn basic concepts such as how to use the controls and a host of actions that must be executed to win. More basic actions (e.g., using the controls) are automatized first and become foundational for automatizing more complex tasks (e.g., collecting resources). Finally, the game requires that each skill is collectively exercised and challenges the player to use everything they learned to overcome progressively difficult scenarios and foes. Players tend to expand their learning of the game by playing against other humans, which requires higher level strategy and adaptation, all of which is impossible without the ability to automatize and build upon a number of skills—a process that is facilitated by the mechanics of the game.

One popular game that has been used for serious purposes is the RTS game, *Starcraft II: Wings of liberty* (Blizzard Entertainment, 2010). In it, players are subject to extensive practice in managing resources, including dozens, even hundreds, of mobile units. At first, this practice is the focus of play, with minor skirmishes that are mainly used to introduce new units or skills and teach you how to manage them. However, for advanced players, these skills become automatized. Competitive players can achieve such automaticity, and such attendant speed, that they manage their units through 500-600 actions per minute (Lejacq, 2013). Meanwhile, either a game campaign or other players pose challenges that scale in difficulty. A player either advances through increasingly difficult missions, or players compete against players incrementally better than they played before, matched to their skill level. Strategies must adapt to new scenarios and new strategies, and the quality of those strategies is immediately evident in a victory, or flames, death, and defeat. Ideation and evaluation are key, but depend on the automaticity of basic skills to allow higher-level thought.

In the classroom, a student who has overlearned basic arithmetic will find algebra easier than one who is still struggling with each step of the equation. Typical math homework attempts to use massed practice by assigning large problem sets using the same operation. However, they can fall short of distributing the practice throughout the year, instead moving on to new and unrelated operations. They may also fail to sequence the difficulty well, as students vary in how hard or easy they find a skill is to attain—for one student, fractions may be easier than decimals, so fractions should come first. But if decimals come first, the student is frustrated by the material s/he doesn't understand and impaired in learning the material that would otherwise come easily from sequencing that is matched better to his or her current understanding. Further, the delayed feedback associated with the traditional classroom prevents students from identifying both faulty and correct understandings of the material. They may have received an A or they may have received an F, but this result is left unknown for days or even weeks. Perhaps most importantly, traditional classrooms almost never offer correct distributed practice, or regular use of the same skill over time (regular reviews, homework that includes problems from previous modules, etc.). Without this, students may achieve mastery, but cannot develop automaticity.

In contrast, the adaptive programming in the Khan Academy website requires students to answer several problems correctly to progress, allowing students to develop a mastery of the content, but furthermore requires future distributed practice to maintain that mastery and move toward automaticity. Adaptive programming is also a means of pace matching the practice. Those who comprehend the subject well do not receive a series of redundantly easy problems, and those that are struggling get more practice with easier problems until they can achieve mastery. All this is done without adding additional burden to the teacher.

Utility of Failure

True failure does not come from the inability to succeed, but from the inability to try again. Failing in games is natural, which is why save points and repeating missions or puzzles are built into them. Some games, like *Super time force* (Capybara Games, 2014), actually make death a crucial part of the game. In this game, death or failure means respawning with another life like it would in most other games, but the previous life is not erased. All of the actions of the previous life (jumping at point A, shooting at point B) are recorded, and played back with full impact in future attempts. This results in a player being able to plan for failure. They can use a previous life just to pave the way for success in a future one. For example, one character has a shield they can deploy to block incoming fire, another character has a strong far-range shot. The player could choose to spend one life with the shield character to just deploy defensive areas, where in a future life they can use the character with the long shot to shoot from. Failure is no longer a judgment on ability, it becomes an opportunity to learn and learning how to fail to achieve future success becomes a priority.

In contrast, many grading systems and skills assessments in schools do not treat student failures as learning opportunities. They can even discourage students from trying to learn. For example, if a student somehow finds they have a grade of 10% halfway through the semester, there is usually very little they can do to improve their grade to a level they might want. This system gives the student no incentive to keep trying; it promotes surrender and learned helplessness. However, if grading worked similarly to the progression systems within video games, there would be multiple opportunities and multiple paths this student could take and s/he would still receive incentive to keep studying or trying to achieve the desired grade. A grade system like this would involve assignments and assessments that would be taken multiple times over (this has been done in schools when classes adopt a mastery learning approach; Gentile & Lalley, 2003). A system used by Khan Academy shows how this can be done with math problems without necessarily adopting a full mastery learning approach. The work is graded automatically, and the question bank is enormous. If the goal is for the student to learn, it should not matter if they learned it from a lecture or from continuous trial and error in assignments. Second, there should be multiple possible assignments, more than can be possibly done, totaling more points than needed for a desired grade. This gives the student choice and agency in what they practice, and in how they earn their grade. The method also possesses an additional benefit in placing emphasis on the role of effort in learning, rather than attributions for success based on raw ability. Because options for success are always present, students may be less likely to fall prey to learned helplessness (Ames, 1992).

This type of system also encourages divergent thinking. It lets people know that failure is a learning opportunity, and they should try something else. It can let students experiment with new ways of completing assignments, because the goal is eventual mastery of the material instead of the grade (Beghetto, 2013). When failure is not terminal, the student can try again. They can ideate again. This is the basis for the product design principle of rapid prototyping. In rapid prototyping, the idea is to get a working, just barely functional, version of the product created as soon as possible. It is then tested, evaluated, and pushed to its breaking point. The designers learn from how the prototype fails to make an even better prototype, which is again tested, evaluated, and pushed. The designers try to run through this cycle of ideation and evaluation as much as possible, each cycle, each failure leading to a better product.

Sandbox or Free Play

Sandbox mode is a popular game mechanic in which players have no explicit goals and no instructions—they are simply given a set of tools and allowed to play with them how they want and to whatever purpose they want (Olson, 2010). This is a common mode in games that simulate city-building, and has been incorporated not as a mode but as an option in open-world games.

This kind of free play is one of the most basic forms of creative education. Children in kindergarten are given easels and finger-paint without anyone telling them the "right" thing to create. Early music classes may begin with cardboard paper-towel rolls filled with beans and tape on either end, with the children left to shake wildly, beat rhythmically on a hand, or incorporate into roll-shaking dance moves.

Free play can also be achieved in classes outside the arts. An engineering teacher may bring in a box of found parts and tell his class to build something, anything. An English teacher may set time aside for writing, requiring nothing more than pen on paper, leaving topic and form to be defined by the students. Science fairs do this as well—students must play with science, but what they create, and what they test, is up to them.

Games may be able to use free play to foster creativity. For example, *Minecraft* is a game focused around the player's ability to mine resources from their environment and to construct objects and structures. The player ideates and has freedom to construct his or her ideas of protective shelter during the game's day time. During the game's night time, the explosive monsters test the effectiveness of a player's shelter and thereby provide a form of evaluation. If the player survived, they at least know their ideas were good enough, and probably gained some insight into what can be improved. If they didn't, they can restart and try again. The game has players naturally practice a creative ideation/evaluation process in their game play.

CONCLUSION

Edison suggested that ideas are valuable, whether they suit our needs or not. Evaluating ideas leads us to improve our next idea. If we practice divergent thinking, we are better able to engage in useful convergent thinking and develop a useful product.

Video games are and can be used for serious purposes. Models of learning and engagement shed light on the processes needed to learn to proactively exercise creativity. Video games are a powerful tool for learning, because they take advantage of these processes through an accessible and entertaining platform.

We concluded with several examples of video game elements that may be used to foster creativity and learning both through games and through game-like classroom methods. These may stand as exemplars for educators who want to improve creativity in their students. Further game mechanics may be identified and adapted as well, shaping future educational techniques.

Video games are powerful teachers. Yet the spirit of video games, their designers and players, may be the most important part of developing creativity. If we can try 10,000 ways to make a light bulb, making an effort to fail as fast as we can, we may ingrain the habit of creativity, preparing the way for a more creative world, and setting us on a path to a culture of discovery.

References

Activision. (2009). *Call of duty: Modern warfare 2 [video game]*. Santa Monica, CA: Infinity Ward.

Activision. (2014). *Destiny [video game]*. Santa Monica, CA: Bungie.

Achtman, R. L., Green, C. S., & Bavelier, D. (2008). Video games as a tool to train visual skills. *Restorative Neurology and Neuroscience, 26*, 435–446.

Ames, C. (1992). Classrooms: Goals, structures, and student motivation. *Journal of Educational Psychology, 84*(3), 261.

Anderson, C. A., Gentile, D. A., & Buckley, K. E. (2007). *Violent video game effects on children and adolescents: Theory, research, and public policy*. New York: Oxford University Press.

Anderson, C. A., Shibuya, A., Ihori, N., Swing, E. L., Bushman, B. J., Sakamoto, A., et al. (2010). Violent video game effects on aggression, empathy, and prosocial behavior in eastern and western countries: A meta-analytic review. *Psychological Bulletin, 136*(2), 151–157.

Basadur, M., Graen, G. B., & Green, S. G. (1982). Training in creative problem solving: Effects on ideation and problem finding and solving in an industrial research organization. *Organizational Behavior and Human Performance, 30*(1), 41–70.

Beghetto, R. A. (2013). *Killing ideas softly? The promise and perils of creativity in the classroom*. Charlotte, NC: Information Age.

Basak, C., Boot, W. R., Voss, M. W., & Kramer, A. F. (2008). Can training in a real-time strategy video game attenuate cognitive decline in older adults? *Psychology and Aging, 23*(4), 765–777.

Basak, C., Voss, M. W., Erickson, K. I., Boot, W. R., & Kramer, A. F. (2011). Regional differences in brain volume predict the acquisition of skill in a complex real-time strategy videogame. *Brain and Cognition, 76*(3), 407–414.

Blizzard Entertainment. (2004). *World of warcraft [video game]*. Irvine, CA: Blizzard Entertainment.

Blizzard Entertainment. (2010). *Starcraft II: Wings of liberty [video game]*. Irvine, CA: Blizzard Entertainment.

Capcom. (2001). *Devil may cry [video game]*. San Mateo County, CA: Ninja Theory.

Capybara Games. (2014). *Super time force [video game]*. Ontario, Canada: Capybara Games.

Cropley, A. (2006). In praise of convergent thinking. *Creativity Research Journal, 18*(3), 391–404.

Csikszentmihalyi, M. (1990). Literacy and intrinsic motivation. *Daedalus, 119*(2), 115–140.

Csikszentmihalyi, M., & Csikzentmihaly, M. (1991). *Flow: The psychology of optimal experience: Vol. 41*. New York: HarperPerennial.

Dye, M. W., Green, C. S., & Bavelier, D. (2009). Increasing speed of processing with action video games. *Current Directions in Psychological Science, 18*(6), 321–326.

Eiben, C. B., Siegel, J. B., Bale, J. B., Cooper, S., Khatib, F., Shen, B. W., et al. (2012). Increased Diels-Alderase activity through backbone remodeling guided by Foldit players. *Nature Biotechnology, 30*(2), 190–192.

Flynn, S. M., & Lange, B. S. (2010). Games for rehabilitation: The voice of the players. In: *Proceedings of the 8th international conference on disability, virtual reality and associated technologies (ICDVRAT), Chile*. (pp. 194–195). Bloomington, IN: Indiana University.

Funk, J. B., Chan, M., Brouwer, J., & Curtiss, K. (2006). A biopsychosocial analysis of the video game-playing experience of children and adults in the United States. *SIMILE: Studies in Media & Information Literacy Education, 6*(3), 1–15.

Furr, N. (2011). *How failure taught Edison to repeatedly innovate*. Retrieved from: http://www.forbes.com/sites/nathanfurr/2011/06/09/how-failure-taught-edison-to-repeatedly-innovate/.

Gentile, D. A., Lynch, P. J., Linder, J. R., & Walsh, D. A. (2004). The effects of violent video game habits on adolescent hostility, aggressive behaviors, and school performance. *Journal of Adolescence, 27*(1), 5–22.

Gentile, D. A. (2009). Pathological video game use among youth 8 to 18: A national study. *Psychological Science, 20*, 594–602.

Gentile, D. A., Anderson, C. A., Yukawa, S., Ihori, N., Saleem, M., Ming, L. K., et al. (2009). The effects of prosocial video games on prosocial behaviors: International evidence from correlational, longitudinal, and experimental studies. *Personality and Social Psychology Bulletin, 35*, 752–763.

Gentile, D. A., Groves, C. L., & Gentile, J. R. (2014). The general learning model: Unveiling the teaching potential of video games. In F. C. Blumberg (Ed.), *Learning by playing: Video gaming in education* (pp. 121–142). New York, NY: Oxford University Press.

Gentile, J. R., & Lalley, J. (2003). *Standards and mastery learning: Aligning teaching and assessment so all children can learn*. Thousand Oaks, CA: Corwin.

Gentile, J. R., Voelkl, K. E., Mt. Pleasant, J., & Monaco, N. M. (1995). Recall after relearning by fast and slow learners. *Journal of Experimental Education, 63*, 185–197.

Gentile, D. A., & Gentile, J. R. (2008). Violent video games as exemplary teachers: A conceptual analysis. *Journal of Youth and Adolescence, 37*, 127–141.

Green, M. C., & Brock, T. C. (2000). The role of transportation in the persuasiveness of public narratives. *Journal of Personality and Social Psychology, 79*(5), 701–721.

Green, C. S., & Bavelier, D. (2003). Action video game modifies visual selective attention. *Nature, 423*(6939), 534–537.

Greitemeyer, T., Osswald, S., & Brauer, M. (2010). Playing prosocial video games increases empathy and decreases schadenfreude. *Emotion, 10*(6), 796–802.

Guilford, J. P. (1967). Creativity: Yesterday, today and tomorrow. *Journal of Creative Behavior, 1*(1), 3–14.

Hodges, L. F., Anderson, P., Burdea, G. C., Hoffmann, H. G., & Rothbaum, B. O. (2001). Treating psychological and physical disorders with VR. *IEEE Computer Graphics and Applications, 21*(6), 25–33.

HopeLab, TRI, Realtime Associates. (2008). *Re-mission 2 [video game]*. Retrieved from: http://www.re-mission2.org/games/.

Introversion Studios. (2012). *Prison architect (alpha) [video game]*. Surrey, UK: Introversion Studios.

Kato, P. M., Cole, S. W., Bradlyn, A. S., & Pollock, B. H. (2008). A video game improves behavioral outcomes in adolescents and young adults with cancer: A randomized trial. *Pediatrics, 122*(2), e305–e317.

Konami. (1998). *Dance, dance, revolution [video game]*. Tokyo, Japan: Konami.

Kronholz, J. (2012). Can Khan move the bell curve to the right? *Educationnext*. Retrieved from: http://educationnext.org/can-khan-move-the-bell-curve-to-the-right/.

Kühn, S., Gleich, T., Lorenz, R. C., Lindenberger, U., & Gallinat, J. (2014). Playing Super Mario induces structural brain plasticity: Gray matter changes resulting from training with a commercial video game. *Molecular Psychiatry, 19*(2), 265–271.

Lejacq, Y. (2013). *How fast is fast? Some pro gamers make 10 moves per second*. Retrieved from: http://www.nbcnews.com/tech/video-games/how-fast-fast-some-pro-gamers-make-10-moves-second-f8C11422946.

Lubart, T. I. (2001). Models of the creative process: Past, present and future. *Creativity Research Journal, 13*(3-4), 295–308.

Makhija, N. (2013). Half the sky movement: People's insights. *Weekly Citizenship Report, 2*(4), 51–56.

Michael, D. R., & Chen, S. L. (2005). *Serious games: Games that educate, train, and inform*. Muska & Lipman/Premier-Trade, Mason, OH: Course Technology.

Nakamura, J., & Csikszentmihalyi, M. (2002). The concept of flow. In C. R. Snyder, & S. J. Lopezs (Eds.), *Handbook of positive psychology* (pp. 89–105). New York: Oxford University Press.

Olson, C. K. (2010). Children's motivations for video game play in the context of normal development. *Review of General Psychology, 14*(2), 180.

Portnow, J., Floyd, D., & Theus, A. (2014). *Extra credits: Fail faster [video file]*. Retrieved from: https://www.youtube.com/watch?v=rDjrOaoHz9s.

Raybourn, E. M., Deagle, M. E., Mendini, K., & Heneghan, J. (2005). Adaptive thinking & leadership simulation game training for special forces officers. *The interservice/industry training, simulation & education conference (I/ITSEC), no 1: Vol. 2005*. National Training Systems Association, November.

Rothbaum, B. O., Hodges, L. F., Ready, D., Graap, K., & Alarcon, R. D. (2001). Virtual reality exposure therapy for Vietnam veterans with posttraumatic stress disorder. *Journal of Clinical Psychiatry, 62*(8), 617–622.

Sherry, J. L. (2004). Flow and media enjoyment. *Communication Theory, 14*(4), 328–347.

Skinner, B. F. (1957). The experimental analysis of behavior. *American Scientist, 45*, 343–371.

Squire, K. (2003). Video games in education. *International Journal of Intelligent Games & Simulation, 2*(1), 49–62.

Sveistrup, H., McComas, J., Thornton, M., Marshall, S., Finestone, H., McCormick, A., et al. (2003). Experimental studies of virtual reality-delivered compared to conventional exercise programs for rehabilitation. *CyberPsychology & Behavior, 6*(3), 245–249.

Valve Corporation. (2007). *Portal [video game]*. Bellevue, WA: Valve Corporation.

Vygotsky, L. (1987). Zone of proximal development. In M. Cole (Ed.), *Mind in Society: The Development of Higher Psychological Processes* (pp. 52–91). Cambridge, MA: Harvard University Press.

Watson, T. S., & Skinner, C. H. (2001). Functional behavioral assessment: Principles, procedures, and future directions. *School Psychology Review, 30*(2), 156–172.

Weber, R., Tamborini, R., Westcott-Baker, A., & Kantor, B. (2009). Theorizing flow and media enjoyment as cognitive synchronization of attentional and reward networks. *Communication Theory, 19*(4), 397–422.

Young, J. A., & Pain, M. D. (1999). The zone: Evidence of a universal phenomenon for athletes across sports. *Athletic Insight: The Online Journal of Sport Psychology, 1*(3), 21–30.

CHAPTER

8

Teachers Designing Learning Games: Impact on Creativity

*Frédérique Frossard, Anna Trifonova
and Mario Barajas*

Department of Didactics and Educational Organization,
University of Barcelona, Barcelona, Spain

INTRODUCTION

Social, economic, and global changes make it difficult to predict the future of our society, as well as the skills that will be needed for facing it (Beghetto, 2010; Sawyer, 2012). At the same time, the main goal of education is to prepare our children to be successful and competitive citizens (Beghetto & Kaufman, 2014). Creativity is one possible response for addressing this challenge (Beghetto, 2010; Beghetto & Kaufman, 2014). Indeed, creative skills enable students to face the complex nature of life, and creative thinking helps solving nontrivial problems (Dow & Mayer, 2004; Treffinger & Isaksen, 2005; Weisberg, 1998, 2006). Furthermore, creativity has been strongly related to innovation and success (Heunks, 1998). As a result, the idea of nurturing and stimulating students' creativity has gained importance within formal education, and has become a crucial objective to be addressed in the curriculum of many countries across Europe (Beghetto, 2010; Craft, 2005) and around the world (Lin, 2011).

The literature suggests some basic techniques and teacher attitudes for stimulating student creativity. These include questioning students' assumptions, encouraging idea generation, promoting risk-taking and allowing mistakes (Cremin & Barnes, 2010; Ferrari, Cachia, & Punie, 2009; Sternberg & Williams, 1996). Nevertheless, some authors report a lack of concrete guidelines for helping teachers to adopt pedagogical strategies that foster creativity (Lin, 2011). Furthermore, Ferrari et al. (2009) suggest that technologies play a crucial role in learners' lives and should be an integral part of creative school environments. Hence, the need has emerged for teachers to have new models and tools for including creativity in their daily practices.

Digital games, when applied to educational contexts, can promote creative pedagogies in various ways: they have proved to enhance students' intrinsic motivation toward learning (Gee, 2003; Whitton, 2008); they are interactive systems which promote learning-by-doing processes (Aldrich, 2005); they provide meaningful learning experiences by simulating highly interactive scenarios where students face real-world problems (Gee, 2003; Perrotta, Featherstone, Aston, & Houghton, 2013); and they provide risk-free environments in which learners can explore and experiment (Ke, 2009; Perrotta et al., 2013). Nevertheless, there are barriers to the implementation of digital games in formal educational settings, such as the difficulty in reaching a balance between fun and learning, as well as alignment of games with curriculum requirements (Klopfer, Osterweil, & Salen, 2009).

To tackle these obstacles, we have studied and discuss in the present chapter an approach in which teachers create their own learning games (LGs), especially designed to reach specific teaching objectives. For doing so, we proposed and validated the CEGaD model (creative educational game design), which represents the different stages of educational game design by teachers, as well as the influences of the personal and environmental components, from the perspective of creativity. In order to analyze teachers' creativity in the context of game design, we looked at three different dimensions: (a) *process* (the different stages of educational game design); (b) *product* (the LGs created); and (c) *teaching* (the practices at stake during the application of the games).

This innovative approach looks in depth at the potential of game-based learning (GBL) for promoting creative teaching practices. Furthermore, it contributes to a greater comprehension of the phenomenon of creativity as applied in educational contexts. Finally, it provides educational practitioners with concrete examples of creative practices, based on innovative approaches in which teachers design their own educational resources.

The chapter first explores the dominant perspectives, theories, and models of analysis of creativity (Section "Creativity: Dominant Perspectives, Theories, and Models"). Afterwards, it examines the relation between education and creativity, and establishes a list of key characteristics of creative pedagogies (Section "Creativity in Educational Contexts"). The chapter then moves toward the review of GBL as a potential approach to creative teaching (Section "GBL as an Approach to Foster Creative Pedagogies"). Subsequently, it describes a model of analysis of teacher creativity in educational game design (Section "A Model of Analysis of Teacher Creativity in Educational Game Design") and the research approach (Section "Research Approach"), as well as its implementation and validation in real teaching settings (Section "Teachers as Game Designers"). Finally, discussion (Section "Discussion") is followed by the conclusions drawn in Section "Conclusions".

CREATIVITY: DOMINANT PERSPECTIVES, THEORIES, AND MODELS

Creativity has been explored through different paradigms, including pragmatic, psychodynamic, psychometric, cognitive, and evolutionary approaches (Sternberg & Lubart, 1999). In contrast with these linear views, several authors approach this concept as a convergence of multiple dimensions. This allows for a comprehensive exploration of the complexity of creativity, in a holistic manner.

For example, Csikszentmihalyi (1988, 1996) developed a systems approach, in which creativity results from the interplay among three different elements: the *domain* includes a particular set of rules, practices, and evaluation criteria; the *individual* brings a novel variation to the domain, via cognitive processes, personality traits, and motivation; and this variation is evaluated by the *field*, which is composed of various gatekeepers (i.e., experts and scholars who have the responsibility to choose which variations will be reserved in the domain).

In addition, Rhodes (1961) proposes the four Ps model—a multidimensional approach which views creativity as the interactions among four different components, namely *process* (the stages involved in the creation of ideas or outcomes), *person* (the individual characteristics of the creators), *press* (the external environment in which creativity happens), and *product* (the tangible or intangible outcomes of the creative process). Rhodes's categorization has become a standard framework for research on creativity. Indeed, research of these four components is still being conducted (e.g., Runco & Pagnani, 2011).

In order to better understand the concept of creativity and its evolution, the next subsections examine the *process*, *person*, *press*, and *product* components defined in the Rhodes model, reviewing recent published studies on creativity.

The "Process" Dimension

The study of the creative process is described, most of the time, as an iterative sequence of stages (Howard, Culley, & Dekoninck, 2008). The majority of the models consider that the creative process starts with a formulation of the problem, continues with a phase of preparation, and finishes with an evaluation and a refinement of the outcome.

Nevertheless, models vary regarding the process of emergence of ideas. Some authors describe it as sudden and intuitive. For example, Wallas (1926) highlighted an *illumination* stage, in which the individual experiences an insight by creating a new combination or transformation of ideas. Similarly, Csikszentmihalyi (1988, 1996) suggests an *insight* phase. In contrast, other models move toward a more conscious process of idea generation (Howard et al., 2008). For example, Mumford, Mobley, Uhlman, Reiter-Palmon, and Doares (1991) highlight eight processes involved in creative thought: (a) *problem construction* (understanding the situation and providing some structure for interpreting the framework); (b) *information gathering* (collecting information which is relevant to the situation); (c) *concept selection* (organizing ideas into concepts and selecting those which are pertinent to the situation); (d) *conceptual combination* (taking the relevant notions from the concept selection stage and combining them in new and unique ways); (e) *idea generation* (generating new workable ideas deriving from the new reorganization); (f) *idea evaluation* (considering ideas regarding the potential outcomes and resources needed for their implementation); (g) *implementation planning* (considering practical details); and (h) *monitoring* (monitoring the implementation of ideas to collect feedback). In addition, the componential model of Amabile (1983, 1996) describes a sequence of five stages: (a) *problem or task identification* (becoming aware of the task to undertake or the problem to solve); (b) *preparation* (building up or reactivating information which is relevant to the task at hand); (c) *response generation* (generating solutions or response possibilities by searching through available pathways and exploring features of the environment that are relevant to the task); (d) *response validation* (evaluating the response possibilities or solutions); and (e) *outcome* (communicating the outcome, which is evaluated). Besides being widely acknowledged in the field of creativity, Amabile's model understands the creative process according to a multidimensional approach, which considers the influences of the other dimensions (i.e., person, press, and product) of creativity in each stage, in order to make explicit the process of emergence of useful and novel ideas.

The "Person" Dimension

This perspective concentrates on the individual characteristics of the creators, and often consists of identifying personality traits of creative persons through biographical and historiometric approaches (Villalba, 2008). Such approaches lead to identifying creative potential; however, an individual may have creative potential without using it (Runco & Pagnani, 2011).

Multidimensional studies, in contrast, consider individual resources as a single component of creativity, and analyze them through their interaction with other components. Individual components include knowledge, thinking styles, personality (e.g., attributes such as the willingness to overcome obstacles, to take sensible risks, and to tolerate ambiguity), and intellectual abilities (Sternberg & Lubart, 1991, 1995), as well as interest in the domain, concentration, playfulness, discipline, passion, and objectivity (Csikszentmihalyi, 1988, 1996). Furthermore, the importance of the motivational element has been underlined (Csikszentmihalyi, 1988, 1996).

Amabile (1983, 1996) proposes the following categorization of individual components: domain-relevant skills (the individual's knowledge and skills in the particular domain), task motivation (extrinsic and/or intrinsic), and creativity-relevant skills (individuals' personality characteristics, e.g., flexibility and persistent work style).

The "Press" Dimension

This dimension considers the environment in which creativity occurs. The importance of the environment for fostering or hindering creativity is well documented in creativity literature. Most multidimensional theories (Amabile, 1983, 1996; Csikszentmihalyi, 1988, 1996; Sternberg & Lubart, 1991, 1995) view creativity as an interaction between the individual and the outside world.

Environmental factors may be either general or specific (Runco, 2004). General factors include social, cultural, and political factors (Simonton, 1999), such as family upbringing, school experiences, cultural traditions, and the historical milieu (Runco & Pagnani, 2011). In contrast, specific factors refer to interpersonal exchanges or environmental settings. For example, Amabile and Gryskiewicz (1989) highlighted different elements of the workplace environment which can enhance creativity, including freedom, appropriate resources, challenging work, as well as leaders' recognition and support.

Some environmental elements are reported to enhance creativity, including training, expectations, resources, recognition, and reward (Csikszentmihalyi, 1988, 1996). In contrast, other factors could act as inhibitors of creativity, such as time pressure, evaluation, political problems (Amabile & Gryskiewicz, 1989), lack of respect, constraint, lack of autonomy and resources, competition, and unrealistic expectations (Runco, 2004).

The "Product" Dimension

Finally, the product dimension describes the properties of the products, which may be either tangible or intangible results of the creative process (Cropley, 2001). The characteristics of creative outcomes are usually considered to be usefulness and novelty (Amabile, 1983; Howard et al., 2008). Usefulness defines the appropriateness of the product to its context of use. Researchers distinguish between different types of novelty. For example, Craft (2001) introduced a distinction between *Big-C* (outstanding accomplishments of unusual people) and *little-c* (personal) creativity. Kaufman and Beghetto (2009) introduced the Four C Model of Creativity, distinguishing between *mini-c* (interpretive creativity), *little-c* (everyday creativity), *Pro-C* (expert creativity), and *Big-C* (the "legendary" creativity). Furthermore, Moran (2010) introduced *middle-c* creativity, to which the output is considered innovative for an organization or a community.

CREATIVITY IN EDUCATIONAL CONTEXTS

The previous section explored creativity according to various approaches and dimensions. We now concentrate on the study of the phenomenon as applied to the field of education.

Nowadays, governments and businesses recognize the importance of fostering creativity in the field of education. Indeed, students need to be better equipped, so that they can face the increasingly complex nature of life in today's world (Beghetto, 2010).

Nevertheless, creativity is not always valued and promoted in schools (Ferrari et al., 2009). There are claims that the traditional educational system hinders or even kills creativity (e.g., Robinson, 2006). Indeed, creativity requires time, flow, interaction, suspension of judgment, and risk-taking. However, such approaches do not fit with the institutional principles of traditional schools (Ferrari et al., 2009). Formal education is characterized by the transmission of factual bits of information (Beghetto, 2010). Such teaching methodologies tend to look for answers that are known before the question is posed, so students do not need to investigate the issue themselves (Ferrari et al., 2009). As a result, learners act as recipients of knowledge.

In spite of the lack of creative practices in the current education system, teaching seems to be amenable to creativity (Craft, 2001; Lin, 2011). Indeed, recent research considers creativity as a developmental construct and a lifelong process (Craft, 2001; Esquivel, 1995; Lin, 2011). When looking at literature related to creativity in education (e.g., Craft, 2005; Ferrari et al., 2009; NACCCE, 1999), it is possible to highlight three clear characteristics: (a) an inclusive perspective according to which all individuals can be creative; (b) a focus on everyday creativity, which gives importance to students' personal processes; and (c) the belief that creativity can be developed in all school subjects.

In this landscape, teachers are key players for bringing creative practices into the mainstream curriculum (Beghetto, 2010). They should accompany students in the process of knowledge building, by adopting roles of facilitator and fellow collaborator (Sawyer, 2012). Nevertheless, different institutional pressures prevent teachers from adopting creativity-fostering behaviors (Sawyer, 2012). Indeed, teachers have to cover a large amount of material, and prepare students for standardized pedagogical objectives or assessment procedures that do not consider creativity (Cremin & Barnes, 2010).

Therefore, teachers need to find ways to stimulate learners' creativity that relate to the curriculum and to their specific areas of knowledge.

The literature highlights a wide range of practices that can enhance teaching for creativity and/or teaching creatively. However, they often result in long lists of characteristics which sometimes overlap. From recent research (e.g., Cremin & Barnes, 2010; de la Torre, 2006; Ferrari et al., 2009; Sawyer, 2012), we chose the ones that seemed most important, and organized them into different categories. As a result, we obtained a set of key characteristics of creative pedagogical practices (i.e., teaching practices which enhance students' creativity): (a) promoting learner-centered methodologies, which connect to student life and interests, in order to make learning relevant and engaging; (b) allowing for self-learning, by encouraging student ownership, autonomy, and an active role in the production and negotiation of meaning; (c) helping to make connections by creating a bridge between different disciplines, placing knowledge in a wider context, and facilitating the interrelation with previous understandings; (d) boosting exploration and discovery, by tolerating ambiguity, as well as providing a space for experimentation, spontaneity, and negotiation of meaning; (e) providing a safe environment that encourages risk-taking behaviors, by promoting positive, nonjudgmental and comfortable contexts, in which all students are supported, accepted, and can freely interact; (f) adopting flexible evaluation approaches which value student progress, build security, and provide tools for reflection; (g) encouraging collaboration, by facilitating exchanges, solidarity, and cooperative learning methods in which teachers and students share knowledge and information; and (h) relying on different sources, including Information and Communication Technologies (ICT), and often switching between different modes, according to student objectives and needs.

It is now necessary to find methodologies that have the potential to apply these strategies. According to Beghetto (2010), "there is a need for creativity researchers to assist in the development, testing, and implementation of new pedagogical models that simultaneously support the development of creative potential and academic learning" (p. 459). The next section explores GBL as a potential approach to fulfil this need.

GBL AS AN APPROACH TO FOSTER CREATIVE PEDAGOGIES

Digital games appear to promote most of the characteristics of the creative pedagogical practices presented above: they connect to student life, culture, and interests (Gros, 2009; Ulicsak & Williamson, 2011); they allow learners to have an active impact on the game environment, thus giving them a sense of agency (Aldrich, 2005; Gee, 2005); and they encourage risk-taking and exploration (Gee, 2003).

The integration of games into educational contexts can take place in different ways and depths. *Edutainment*, for example, consists of converting some elements of knowledge into a game-like application. In such products, game elements are added to existing educational content. This approach, however, has been reported to have limited potential for fun and engagement (Moreno-Ger, Burgos, Martinez-Ortiz, Sierra, & Fernandez-Manjon, 2008). Another approach consists of repurposing existing commercial games for education, which has the advantage of providing learners with a product that has been explicitly designed for entertainment (Moreno-Ger et al., 2008). However, there are many obstacles to the adoption of this approach in the classroom context, such as the difficulty of aligning games with curriculum requirements, the negative attitudes of some parents and educators toward digital games, as well as technical and logistical issues (Gros, 2007; Klopfer et al., 2009; Ulicsak & Williamson, 2011).

To tackle these obstacles, one solution consists of using games specifically designed for educational purposes, as a way to promote student entertainment and to meet the pedagogical objectives addressed, so as to reach a balance between fun and education (e.g., Moreno-Ger et al., 2008; Whitton, 2010). This strategy allows for the alignment of learning outcomes with gaming outcomes, for specific curricular objectives and student profiles (Whitton, 2010). Furthermore, involving educators in the game design process allows for the achievement of high educational standards (Torrente, Del Blanco, Marchiori, Moreno-Ger, & Fernández-Manjón, 2010).

The game design process is often described in terms of successive stages or phases (Adams & Rollings, 2007; Crawford, 1984; Fullerton, 2008). These stages vary according to different models, but they present several aspects in common: they all include a concept phase which sets the foundations of the game; they mention play-testing activities with the target audience; they often include prototyping activities which consist of testing feasibility; they argue in favor of an iterative process, through which play-testing is performed throughout the entire design process, in order to involve the end-user from the early stages; finally, design documents (storyboards and other game documentation) appear as a common element in all models.

Morales (2012) adapted the phases from the mainly accepted frameworks of the game design process to the particular context of educational game design: informative and analytic phase (defining the pedagogical objectives of the project, the profile of the group of users, and the context of use), establishment of the design hypothesis phase (experimenting and conceptualizing the game ideas, including a description of the main concept of the game, a list of key content which outlines the idea of the game, a general view on the project's characteristics, and a description of the pedagogical aspects of the game), synthesis and representation of the solutions phase (selecting and developing one of the hypotheses considered in the previous phase, including a general vision of the game, the main aspects of technology and audio-visual production, a first approach to production details, and a description of the game world; and at the pedagogical level, integrating the pedagogical objectives and resources of the game), and direction of the production phase (defining design solutions which will guide the production phase, including creative, conceptual, and functional aspects).

A MODEL OF ANALYSIS OF TEACHER CREATIVITY IN EDUCATIONAL GAME DESIGN

As mentioned earlier, we propose an innovative approach in which teachers become game designers, defining the game idea according to the necessities of their students and the specificities of the curriculum, completing the different stages of the game design process, and integrating the created LG within their teaching activities.

In order to investigate teachers' creativity in the design and application of LGs, we followed a multidimensional approach and explored the phenomenon of creativity through the interactions among different aspects: process, person, press, and product.

The process dimension concentrates on the design experience of teachers. To explore it, we applied the componential model of Amabile (1983, 1996) to the context of educational game design, on the basis of the frameworks provided by Adams and Rollings (2007), Fullerton (2008), and Morales (2012). We have modeled the activities of educational game design (i.e., the definition of pedagogical objectives, conceptualization, elaboration, production, and play-testing) with the steps proposed in the model of Amabile (i.e., task identification, preparation, response generation, response validation, and outcome). Moreover, we investigated the influences of the person and press dimensions in these stages.

The product dimension analyzes the LGs created by teachers according to two criteria: (a) usefulness and (b) novelty. Usefulness is the potential to provide entertainment and to meet the planned pedagogical objectives. Novelty is evaluated with respect to little-c (the degree of innovation of the teachers), middle-c (the degree of innovation in the educational community, including student populations and educational centers), and Big-C creativity (the degree of innovation in the LG market).

Finally, the teaching dimension focuses on the processes at stake during the use of the LGs in the classroom, examining both the perspectives of teachers (how they organize educational activities, and their role during the game session) and students (their level of immersion, concentration, autonomy, and social interactions).

As shown in Figure 1, the result of the analysis of each dimension enabled us to define teachers' creativity in the context of design and application of their LGs.

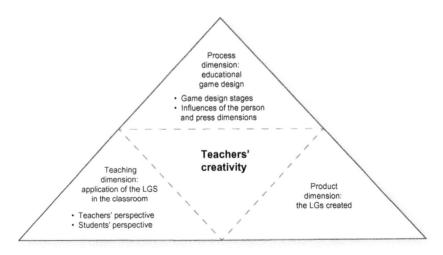

FIGURE 1   Analysis of teachers' creativity in the design and application of LGs.

RESEARCH APPROACH

The study employed a qualitative research design, implementing a multiple case study strategy under a constructivist-interpretive paradigm, in order to describe the complex dynamics of creativity in the context of educational game design. Full details are available in Frossard (2013).

As a first step, an exploratory study was conducted in order to explore teacher attitude, interests, and needs toward GBL and creativity. To do so, two focus groups were organized in May 2010, with 15 teachers from Spanish primary and secondary schools.

On the basis of the focus group results, an approach to educational game design was defined, especially adapted to teachers: the CEGaD model (described in detail in Section "Teachers as Game Designers"). It was introduced to in-service teachers in a training program in February 2011. Twenty-one teachers from seven primary and secondary schools learnt how to use an open-source software for creating adaptable 2D point-and-click adventure games for education.[1] Afterward, an ongoing collaboration process took place during three months (from March to May 2011), in which support was provided to the participating teachers while they were designing their games.

A first cycle of the pilot implementation in classrooms was organized in June 2011, at two sites: one primary and one secondary school in Galicia (a region in the north of Spain). During two classroom sessions, 4 games were tested, involving 5 teachers and 47 students. This implementation served for testing the created games and allowed for collecting a first series of data. A preliminary survey process was carried out in order to refine concepts and test data collection strategies with target users.

A purposeful sampling process was performed, which trimmed down the number of participants to eight teachers. Our final selection included three groups of teachers who collaboratively designed their LGs: two groups from a secondary school and one group from a primary school. These cases are described in detail in the next section.

During a second implementation cycle, conducted in April 2012, at the same sites, the main data collection process was performed. In total, 63 students participated in the GBL sessions with three different games.

The exploration of the different dimensions (i.e., process, product, and teaching) was done using three main instruments for data collection:

- Teacher interviews related to the game design process: These interviews addressed creativity according to the process dimension (i.e., teacher experiences during the different stages of the game design).

[1] We used the eAdventure software for game design http://e-adventure.e-ucm.es/.

- Expert interviews: A second type of interview, involving experts in GBL, looked at product creativity. The final LGs designed by teachers were distributed among seven experts for testing and evaluation. Interviews examined two different criteria, usefulness and novelty.
- Teacher interviews: A third type of interview explored the teaching dimension (i.e., the application of the LGs in the classroom).

In addition, complementary instruments were designed and used for triangulation purposes: a questionnaire and production documents (storyboards and other design materials used by teachers), to explore in depth teacher experience during the design process and student experience during the application of the games in the classroom.

An exploratory analysis of the data enabled us to obtain a general sense of it, reflect how to organize it, and create first ideas and concepts around it. Afterward, data was coded (i.e., text data was divided into different categories of information and labeled in codes). Then, these codes were examined and reduced, in order to narrow data into themes. In order to add additional rigor, themes and subthemes were organized into different layers, from broad themes to more detailed ones, deepening the analysis of each main theme. In addition, the themes were interconnected to highlight their relationships. This resulted in a set of more than 100 categories for the different themes, which were coded for the analysis of the dimensions explored in the study.

The stages of the of the research implementation are resumed in Figure 2.

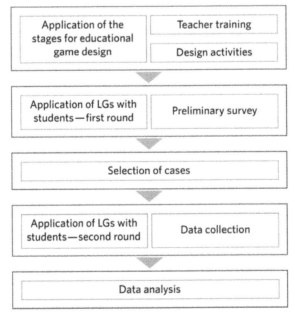

FIGURE 2   Stages of the implementation.

TEACHERS AS GAME DESIGNERS

Our approach was implemented in the context of a multiple case study: Eight Spanish primary and secondary school teachers designed their own LGs, especially tailored to their educational contexts, and applied them with their students.

- *Case 1*: A team of three secondary school teachers designed "Alice's Trip," an adventure game in which the player has to visit different scenes of the city of A Coruña (Galicia) in different historical times. The player interacts with various historical characters and answers the questions they ask. The game aims to familiarize students with the origins of their city. It can be applied in the disciplines of history, geography, Latin, and art history (Figure 3).

  Alice is a Galician teenager who prepares for her school exam. The game starts as she goes walking to the lighthouse Tower of Hercules in her city, A Coruña. There she stops to rest a moment and, like Lewis Carroll's novel's character, she starts dreaming and travels through different time periods of the history of the city. During her trip, Alice meets several characters and interacts with them. She also finds and uses different objects. All conversations and situations relate to local mythology, archeology, legends, traditions, and popular tales.

  Following Whitton's taxonomy of games (2010), the "Alice's Trip" game comprises many elements from the adventure genre—it includes a compelling narrative which uses fantasy elements (i.e., time travel in which a girl gets to meet many characters from the history of Galicia), and the protagonist has to talk with many characters and collect different objects in order to complete her quest. Nevertheless, the question-answer dynamic relates to the puzzle category, which includes quizzes.

- *Case 2*: A team of two teachers of secondary education and vocational training designed the game "Tuning up a Bicycle," which aims to

FIGURE 3 Screenshots from "Alice's Trip" game.

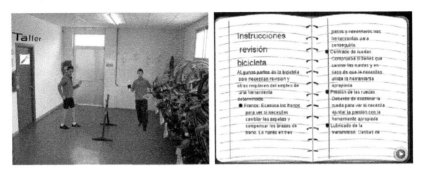

FIGURE 4   Screenshots from "Tuning up a Bicycle" game.

teach the procedures required for revising a bike before using it. The game is directed to students from upper secondary education in intermediate vocational training, in the course on physical activities and sport in natural environments (Figure 4).

The protagonist, a student of the vocational training program "physical and sports activities in natural environments," would like to go on a bicycle tour. To do so, he enters the bicycles workshop of his center. There he meets the repairman, who encourages him to check the different elements of the bicycle and to adjust what is needed in order to go on a safe tour. Following his advice, the student explores the different tools available to him and checks the parts of the bicycle to see which ones need to be fixed and proceeds to the necessary adjustments. According to his actions, the player will receive positive or negative feedback. During the game, the student has the possibility to consult a manual that explains the different steps to tune up a bicycle. The game possesses some characteristics from both the adventure and puzzle genres in Whitton's taxonomy (2010).

- *Case 3*: A team of three elementary teachers designed the game "The Holy Torq," from the adventure type, which aims to introduce students to everyday life in the villages of the Iron Age in Galicia. The game is directed to students from primary education (middle and superior cycles, aged 8–12). It relates to the disciplines of knowledge of the natural, social, and cultural environment, and the Galician language (Figure 5).

In the old Galicia from the pre-Roman times, a young girl called Icía has to find a remedy to save her sick friend Keltoi, who has been hurt as he tried to recover the holy torq that was robbed from King Breogán. To do so, the girl listens to the stories and the instructions of a druid, explores ancient sites (e.g., the dolmen field), and has to recognize and use antique objects (e.g., from pre-Roman times and

FIGURE 5   Screenshots from "The Holy Torq" game.

the Celtic culture). She can also use a book with some additional information to find and use the objects.

Following Whitton's taxonomy of games (2010), "The Holy Torq" is an adventure game—it includes a compelling narrative related to the Celtic culture and the Iron Age. The objective of the game is to solve a quest by undertaking a series of tasks, talking to different characters, and manipulating objects. Hence, the game mainly depends on mental agility.

Process Dimension

The analysis related to the process dimension was used to validate the CEGaD model for creative educational game design, which represents the different design stages followed by the teachers, as well as the influences of the personal and environmental components, from the perspective of creativity (see Figure 6).

The validation of our model has shown that educational game design consists of an iterative process, through which teachers engage in a game design task, define pedagogical objectives and develop new skills, in order to be able to conceptualize, plan, and produce a related LG. Through various iterations, they evaluate the different game elements until reaching a final outcome which they can apply in their teaching contexts. On this basis, teachers eventually take their project further, or undertake new ones.

The study highlighted the importance of the influences of the intra-individual and environmental elements in the stages of the design process. Indeed, game design requires teachers to apply and develop a wide range of domain-relevant skills (expertise in the domain, innovative methodologies, and ICT skills), creativity-relevant skills (openness to experience, persistent work style, and flexibility), while experiencing both intrinsic and extrinsic motivation.

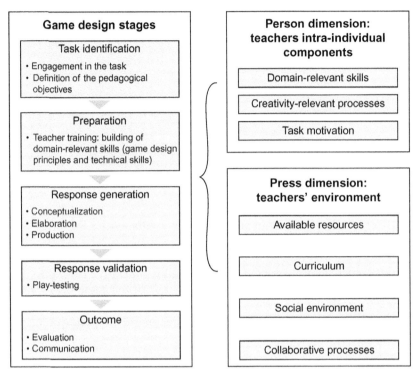

FIGURE 6   The CEGaD model.

Furthermore, game design was strongly influenced by the concrete environment in which teachers worked. They had to adapt the design process to the time available to them, and to take advantage of the spatial and material resources available in their center. The affordances of the digital environment determined the design process. Indeed, teachers had to adapt their ideas to its functionalities. In addition, the game design activities (elaboration of content, production of resources, and evaluation of the LGs) often depended on actors in the educational community outside the group of designers (i.e., the educational center, colleagues, students, and external institutions), as teachers received their support and took their perspectives into account. Furthermore, teachers working in teams experienced rich collaboration processes, in which the dynamics of co-construction occurred, as teachers served as resources for each other, exploiting their different profiles toward common goals. They worked in a flexible, spontaneous manner, thus developing trusting relationships and sustainable collaborations. Teachers worked with the resources available to them and dealt with digital constraints.

Teacher creativity, in the process of game design, is situated at the heart of a complex ecological system that includes interrelated elements, i.e., the intra-individual resources (domain-relevant skills, creativity-relevant processes, and task motivation), the educational community (students, colleagues, and the educational center), the curriculum, the local environment, and the digital environment. Consequently, a multidimensional approach of creativity is fundamental to the study of educational game design.

Product Dimension

The games created by teachers were found to have the potential to provide entertainment and to meet the pedagogical objectives initially addressed. They generally presented clear and constant dynamics, but were lacking in sufficient variety and dynamism to promote adequate student engagement. Moreover, while players did become immersed in the environments of the games, their engagement was low compared to the high quality of audio-visual resources and interactions of the commercial games. This gap limited their potential for entertainment. As for pedagogical aspects, the LGs presented appropriate pedagogical goals, contents, and documentation.

Although the literature highlights the difficulty of aligning games with curriculum requirements (Gros, 2007; Ulicsak & Williamson, 2011), teachers were able to obtain resources which perfectly matched their curriculum objectives. In some cases, the LGs matched several areas of the curriculum, so teachers could adapt the use of the games to their contexts. Nevertheless, the pedagogical objectives supported by the games were sometimes considered by the experts to be superficial, and the contents to lack dynamism. The LGs were well integrated with original complementary learning activities, thus enabling their potential and for the teacher to evaluate students' knowledge. Finally, regarding usability aspects, students could easily learn how to play the games' functionalities. Nevertheless, experts highlighted some problems, which they recommended fixing in order to increase the gaming experience, such as the lack of help functions, or the presence of options that do not lead to any action.

It is worth reporting that teachers were aware of the weak aspects highlighted above. Nevertheless, the context of the design process (time resources, technical skills, and characteristics of the game editor) did not enable them to elaborate a more dynamic design, to deepen educational contents, or to fix the usability problems. Hence, product creativity appeared to be hindered by environmental constraints and teachers' lack of technical skills.

Results showed that teacher creativity, in the context of educational game design, is more related to little-c and middle-c. Indeed, the games created by teachers appeared to be innovative and useful regarding the resources they normally use and create (little-c creativity). Furthermore, the LGs constituted innovative teaching resources for students and for the educational centers (middle-c creativity). In contrast, the games did not compete with the games and learning resources available on the market (Big-C creativity).

Teaching Dimension

Results showed that teachers could successfully integrate their LGs into their educational plan. They organized relevant complementary activities around their games, which enabled them to enhance the pedagogical objectives addressed, as well as ensure the correct assessment of student knowledge. Furthermore, these complementary activities appeared to offer students different perspectives on the elements of knowledge presented in the games, thus helping them to make connections.

For example, for the LG "Alice's Trip," teachers first planned a class through which students would review the different topics of the game (e.g., the history of Galicia and classics of literature). Then, students were able to see videos related to the game topics and visit a museum. Afterwards, they played the game in a classroom session. Finally, teachers planned a debate in which students talked about the questions raised in the game, and a visit to one of the historical sites presented in the game. Students were evaluated on the basis of a report made at the end of the game.

The LG "Tuning up the Bicycle" was used as a concluding activity, after students had been introduced to the concepts taught in a theoretical session, and had applied these concepts through a hands-on session with a bicycle. Hence, the game served as a tool that would enable students to review contents, as well as to self-evaluate. Finally, there was discussion among the students and the teacher. For evaluation there was an exam after the game session.

For "The Holy Torq," teachers planned a lecture in which students were introduced to the topics of the game, the history of Galicia. Afterward, students played the game individually in a classroom session. Finally, there was a debate in which students talked about the topics raised in the game (Figure 7).

Generally, teaching with games moved teachers from the role of instructor to one of observer of the students' learning behaviors. Nevertheless, they maintained an active and dynamic attitude, by monitoring students, offering their constant support, and encouraging students toward successful playing of the games. This compromise between an observing and monitoring stance appeared to promote students' self-learning, and to promote a trusting environment in which students felt free and relaxed. In spite of the limitations of the LGs, learning with games proved to enhance students' enjoyment.

FIGURE 7   Images from the classroom tests of "Tuning up the Bicycle" (left) and "The Holy Torq" (right).

Finally, the study revealed the potential of the research approach to overcome some of the obstacles to the integration of GBL in formal learning contexts, as mentioned by several authors (Klopfer et al., 2009; Ulicsak & Williamson, 2011). Although the literature argues that educators often find it difficult to integrate the playing of games into the time structure of the school day, the results of the study showed that meaningful planning of the GBL activities, embedding the game with the other activities, allowed for a useful integration of the LGs with the classroom activities. Although the authors highlighted technical and logistical issues as a barrier to the successful integration of GBL practices in the classroom, the affordances of the chosen game engine, as well as the quality of the equipment available in the centers, allowed for a perfect unwinding of the GBL activities.

DISCUSSION—THE DESIGN AND APPLICATION OF LGs BY TEACHERS: POTENTIAL TO ENHANCE CREATIVE PEDAGOGIES

The proposed approach (i.e., the design and application of LGs by teachers) enabled teachers to apply most of the characteristics of creative pedagogies previously mentioned:

- Promoting learner-centered methodologies: Game design constituted, for teachers, an opportunity to focus on their students. Indeed, they decided to design LGs in order to connect to their students' interests, create a resource that would be innovative and engaging to them, and get closer to their culture and daily life.
- Allowing for self-learning: Teachers' role in the classroom changed from their usual teaching practices. They moved from an active, central role of organizer, who constantly leads students and gives

them instructions, toward an observer stance and moderating role, analyzing students' behaviors, helping them to gain autonomy and to self-manage their actions. As a result, students became protagonists of the classroom and of their learning processes, by freely interacting with the game elements without requiring their teachers' input.

- Helping to make connections: By providing blended learning opportunities (the game sessions, lessons, and complementary learning activities outside of the classroom), teachers helped students to learn from different perspectives. Hence, while playing the games, students could apply knowledge previously built in the context of different activities. As a result, they could confront different sources of information, critically evaluate them, and develop a multiple and flexible perspective toward one topic. Consequently, teachers were able, through the LGs, to contextualize knowledge in relation to other subjects and to the world outside the classroom.

- Boosting exploration and discovery: The LGs allowed for exploration and immersion in fictional environments. If some games offer the possibility to experiment and interact with the majority of elements and objects included in their structures, some others were not considered to be sufficiently open to promote exploration and discovery.

- Promoting engagement: The LGs designed by teachers present several elements that promote student motivation and enjoyment. First, the proposed topics and narratives were positively valued, as they included elements of interest for the targeted students. In addition, audio-visual elements proved to enhance immersion and engagement. Nevertheless, the dynamics of some of the games were considered, in some cases, too linear and repetitive.

- Providing a safe and trusting environment that encourages risk-taking behaviors: The game sessions were characterized by a relaxed and pleasant classroom environment. Students acted freely, and teachers encouraged them to complete the games. Trusting relationships among students and teachers were observed. Students appeared to be more relaxed than during a common lecture, as they could make mistakes, learn from their errors, and explore new possibilities, without feeling pressured or evaluated by their teachers.

- Adopting flexible evaluation approaches: The study showed that teachers effectively assessed students' knowledge through different types of evaluation strategies (activities comprised inside or outside the game, objective tests, and flexible methodologies).

- Encouraging collaboration: Given the affordances of the game editor, teachers designed individual games. Hence, it is not possible to assume that the GBL activities enhanced collaborative learning. Indeed, students did not jointly solve any pedagogical objectives. GBL scenarios could have included more collaborative

aspects, through activities around the game, or by playing the game on a digital whiteboard.
- Relying on different sources, including ICT: In the game design context, teachers had the opportunity to create ICT-based teaching resources that included different types of media.

Furthermore, we can highlight additional key characteristics of creative pedagogies that have not been mentioned in the literature, but emerged from the results of the study:

- Designing resources especially for students: The research provided teachers with the opportunity to design their own educational resources, especially tailored to their particular contexts and to the specific profile of their students.
- Integrating elements from the students' environment in teaching practices: In the game design context, teachers had the opportunity to use various elements from their students' environment and culture. This enabled students to locate and contextualize knowledge in familiar surroundings, which lead to meaningful learning experiences and outcomes.
- Collaborating with stakeholders from the educational community: The study highlighted the importance of including, in their teaching practices, different actors from the educational community, such as the educational center, students, colleagues, and the local cultural institutions (including museums and city councils, colleagues, and the students themselves). This inclusive approach allows for the consideration of different perspectives, which facilitates the localization of knowledge in a broader context, and its connection with other disciplines and with the outside world.
- Teaching as an inquiry process: In order to create a complete and valid game in terms of content, some teachers proceeded to in-depth inquiry on the topic addressed in their LGs, by searching for information in the museums of the city, on the internet, and asking different actors in their community. This process appeared to be particularly rewarding. Indeed, it is important that teachers continuously investigate in their discipline, in order to re-evaluate and update their knowledge, and to validate their professional expertise.

CONCLUSIONS

We have implemented and validated an innovative approach through which teachers designed and implemented their own LGs in the classroom. Furthermore, we tested the potential of this approach for promoting creative pedagogies.

Educational game design allowed teachers to develop professional creativity from the points of view of little-c and middle-c, providing the opportunity to engage students in their teaching practices, collaborating with different actors of the educational community, questioning their teaching habits, re-evaluating their expertise, rethinking their way of teaching, and implementing student-centered teaching strategies.

This approach opened teachers to innovative and student-centered methodologies. It allowed them to become familiar with GBL. A further step would consist of involving teachers in a second implementation phase in which they would be able to figure out the best way of using digital games in their teaching practices. They would be able, according to their specific educational contexts, to select the adequate way of creating their LGs (e.g., by involving their students or by choosing a different editor), design a relevant product (e.g., selecting the right game genre, and creating engaging game dynamics), and develop creative activities during the game sessions (e.g., integrating collaborative activities).

Future lines of action may include the organization of game design activities on a larger scale (involving collaboration between different schools and a large number of teachers), collaboration between teachers and students in joint projects, and the design of new game genres and technologies. These new studies would respond to problems related to the creativity of the students (i.e., the acquisition and consolidation of creative skills in the processes of learning with games), which are fundamental in the changing information society.

References

Adams, E., & Rollings, A. (2007). *Game design and development. Fundamentals of game design*. River, NJ: Pearson Education.

Aldrich, C. (2005). *Learning by doing: A comprehensive guide to simulations, computer games, and pedagogy in e-learning and other educational experiences*. San Francisco, CA: Wiley, Pfeiffer.

Amabile, T. (1983). The social psychology of creativity: A componential conceptualization. *Journal of Personality and Social Psychology, 45*(2), 357–376. http://dx.doi.org/10.1037/0022-3514.45.2.357.

Amabile, T. (1996). *Creativity in context*. Boulder, CO: Westview.

Amabile, T., & Gryskiewicz, N. (1989). The creative environment scales: The work environment inventory. *Creativity Research Journal, 2*(4), 231–254. http://dx.doi.org/10.1080/10400418909534321.

Beghetto, R. A. (2010). Creativity in the classroom. In J. C. Kaufman, & R. J. Sternberg (Eds.), *The Cambridge handbook of creativity* (pp. 447–463). Cambridge, UK: Cambridge University Press.

Beghetto, R. A., & Kaufman, J. C. (2014). Classroom contexts for creativity. *High ability studies*. http://static.squarespace.com/static/52d6f16be4b0770a479dfb9c/t/5335cb44e-4b04a3a90fca0ab/1396034372625/ClassroomContexts(Beghetto&Kaufman,2014).pdf (last accessed on 30/04/2014).

Craft, A. (2001). Little c creativity. In A. Craft, R. Jeffrey, & M. Leibling (Eds.), *Creativity in education* (pp. 45–61). London and New York: Continuum.

Craft, A. (2005). *Creativity in schools: Tensions and dilemmas*. London, UK: Routledge.

Crawford, C. (1984). *The art of computer game design*. Berkeley, CA: McGraw-Hill.

Cremin, T., & Barnes, J. (2010). Creativity in the curriculum. In J. Arthur & T. Cremin (Eds.), *Learning to teach in the primary school* (2nd ed., pp. 357–373). Abingdon, UK: Routledge.

Cropley, A. J. (2001). *Creativity in education and learning: A guide for teachers and educators*. London, UK: Kogan Page/Psychology Press.

Csikszentmihalyi, M. (1988). The domain of creativity. In R. J. Sternberg (Ed.), *The nature of creativity* (pp. 325–339). New York: Cambridge University Press.

Csikszentmihalyi, M. (1996). *Creativity: Flow and the psychology of discovery and invention*. New York: Harper Perennial.

de la Torre, S. (2006). Creatividad en la educación primaria (Coord.). In S. De la Torre, & V. Violant, (Eds.), *Comprender y evaluar la creatividad: 1*. (pp. 253–266). Archidona, Spain: Aljibe.

Dow, G. T., & Mayer, R. E. (2004). Teaching students to solve insight problems: Evidence for domain specificity in creativity training. *Creativity Research Journal, 16*(4), 389–398.

Esquivel, G. (1995). Teacher behaviors that foster creativity. *Educational Psychology Review, 7*(2), 185–202. http://dx.doi.org/10.1007/BF02212493.

Ferrari, A., Cachia, R., & Punie, Y. (2009). Innovation and creativity in education and training in the EU member states: Fostering creative learning and supporting innovative teaching. JRC Technical Note, 52374. Luxembourg: Office for Official Publications of the European Communities, European Commission.

Frossard, F. (2013). Fostering teachers' creativity through the creation of GBL scenarios (doctoral dissertation). Barcelona, Spain: Universitat de Barcelona, http://diposit. ub.edu/dspace/bitstream/2445/50460/1/FROSSARD_THESIS.pdf (last accessed on 30/04/2014).

Fullerton, T. (2008). *Game design workshop: A playcentric approach to creating innovative games* (2nd ed.). San Francisco, CA: Morgan Kauffman.

Gee, J. P. (2003). What video games have to teach us about learning and literacy. *Computers in Entertainment, 1*(1), 20.

Gee, J. P. (2005). Good video games and good learning. *Phi Kappa Phi Forum, 85*(2), 33. The Honor Society of Phi Kappa Phi. Retrieved from: http://www.jamespaulgee.com/sites/default/files/pub/GoodVideoGamesLearning.pdf (last accessed on 30/04/2014).

Gros, B. (2007). Digital games in education. The design of games-based learning environments. *Journal of Research on Technology in Education, 40*(1), 23–38.

Gros, B. (2009). Certezas e interrogantes acerca del uso de los videojuegos para el aprendizaje. *Comunicación, 7*(1), 251–264.

Heunks, F. J. (1998). Innovation, creativity and success. *Small Business Economics, 10*(3), 263–272. http://link.springer.com/article/10.1023%2FA%3A1007968217565 (last accessed on 30/04/2014).

Howard, T. J., Culley, S. J., & Dekoninck, E. (2008). Describing the creative design process by the integration of engineering design and cognitive. *Design Studies, 29*(2), 160–180, http://dx.doi.org/10.1016/j.destud.2008.01.001.

Kaufman, J. C., & Beghetto, R. A. (2009). Beyond big and little: The four C model of creativity. *Review of General Psychology, 13*, 1–12.

Ke, F. (2009). A qualitative meta-analysis of computer games as learning tools. In R. E. Furdig (Ed.), *Handbook of research on effective electronic gaming in education* (pp. 1–32). New York: IGI Global.

Klopfer, E., Osterweil, S., & Salen, K. (2009). *Moving learning games forward: Obstacles, opportunities, and openness*. An MIT Education Arcade Paper, Cambridge, MA: Education Arcade.

Lin, Y. S. (2011). Fostering creativity through education: Conceptual framework of creative pedagogy. *Creative Education, 2*(3), 149–155. http://dx.doi.org/10.4236/ce.2011.23021.

Morales, J. (2012). Acerca del diseño de videojuegos educativos (doctoral dissertation). Barcelona, Spain: Universitat de Barcelona.

Moran, S. (2010). Creativity in school. In K. Littleton, C. Woods, & J. K. Staarman (Eds.), *International handbook of psychology in education* (pp. 319–359). Bingley, UK: Group Publishing.

Moreno-Ger, P., Burgos, D., Martinez-Ortiz, I., Sierra, J., & Fernandez-Manjon, B. (2008). Educational game design for online education. *Computers in Human Behavior, 24*(6), 2530–2540. http://dx.doi.org/10.1016/j.chb.2008.03.012.

Mumford, M. D., Mobley, M. I., Uhlman, C. E., Reiter-Palmon, R., & Doares, L. M. (1991). Process analytic models of creative capacities. *Creativity Research Journal, 4*, 91–122. http://dx.doi.org/10.1080/10400419109534380.

NACCCE. (1999). *All our futures: Creativity, culture and education.* London, UK: Department for Education and Employment.

Perrotta, C., Featherstone, G., Aston, H., & Houghton, E. (2013). *Game-based learning: Latest evidence and future directions.* Slough, UK: NFER.

Rhodes, M. (1961). An analysis of creativity. *Phi Delta Kappan, 42*, 305–310.

Robinson, K. (2006). Do schools kill creativity? [video file], February 27. Retrieved from: http://www.ted.com/talks/lang/eng/ken_robinson_says_schools_kill_creativity.html (last accessed on 30/04/2014).

Runco, M. A. (2004). Creativity. *Annual Review of Psychology, 55*, 657–687. http://dx.doi.org/10.1146/annurev.psych.55.090902.141502.

Runco, M. A., & Pagnani, A. R. (2011). Psychological research on creativity. In J. Sefton-Green, P. Thomson, K. Jones, & L. Bresler (Eds.), *The Routledge international handbook of creative learning* (pp. 63–71). London, UK: Routledge.

Sawyer, R. K. (2012). *Explaining creativity: The science of human innovation* (2nd ed.). New York: Oxford University Press.

Simonton, D. K. (1999). *Origins of genius: Darwinian perspectives on creativity.* New York: Oxford University Press.

Sternberg, R. J., & Lubart, T. I. (1991). An investment theory of creativity and its development. *Human Development, 34*(1), 1–31. http://dx.doi.org/10.1159/000277029.

Sternberg, R. J., & Lubart, T. I. (1995). *Defying the crowd: Cultivating creativity in a culture of conformity.* New York: Free Press.

Sternberg, R. J., & Lubart, T. I. (1999). *Handbook of creativity.* Cambridge, UK: Cambridge University Press.

Sternberg, R. J., & Williams, W. M. (1996). *How to develop student creativity.* Alexandria, VA: Association for Supervision & Curriculum Development, ISBN: 0-87120-265-4.

Torrente, J., Del Blanco, A., Marchiori, E. J., Moreno-Ger, P., & Fernández-Manjón, B. (2010). <eAdventure>: Introducing educational games in the learning process. In *Proceedings of the education engineering (EDUCON) conference (e-Madrid special edition), Madrid.* (pp. 1121–1126).

Treffinger, D. J., & Isaksen, S. G. (2005). Creative problem solving: The history, development, and implications for gifted education and talent development. *Gifted Child Quarterly, 49*(4), 342–353. https://www.cpsb.com/research/articles/creative-problem-solving/Creative-Problem-Solving-Gifted-Education.pdf (last accessed on 30/04/2014).

Ulicsak, M., & Williamson, B. (2011). *Computer games and learning: A handbook.* London, UK: Futurelab.

Villalba, E. (2008). On creativity. Towards an understanding of creativity and its measures. In JRC Scientific and Technical Reports, EUR 23561. Luxembourg: Office for Official Publications of the European Communities.

Wallas, G. (1926). *The art of thought.* London, UK: Jonathan Cape.

Weisberg, R. W. (1998). Problem solving and creativity. In R. J. Sternberg (Ed.), *The nature of creativity: Contemporary psychological perspectives* (pp. 148–176). New York: Cambridge University Press. ISBN: 978-0521338929.

Weisberg, R. W. (2006). *Creativity: Understanding innovation in problem solving, science, invention, and the arts.* Hoboken, NJ: John Wiley, ISBN: 978-0-471-73999-9.

Whitton, N. (2008). Motivation and computer game based learning. In *Proceedings of ICT: Providing choices for learners and learning.* Singapore: Ascilite, pp. 1063–1067.

Whitton, N. (2010). *Learning with digital games: A practical guide to engaging students in higher education.* New York: Abingdon/Routledge. Retrieved from: http://dmitrov.edu.ru/~ps/files/Learning_with_Digital_Games.-0415997747_0415997755_0203872983.pdf (last accessed on 30/04/2014).

Cognitive Brain Training, Video Games, and Creativity

Oshin Vartanian[1] and Erin L. Beatty[2]

[1]Department of Psychology, University of Toronto
Scarborough, Toronto, ON, Canada
[2]Defence Research and Development Canada, Toronto Research Centre,
Toronto, ON, Canada

The last few years have witnessed an upsurge of research within the fields of psychology and cognitive neuroscience on cognitive brain training. Of course, interest in the effects of training on performance and brain function is not new in either field. What has changed, however, is the accumulation of evidence in support of the malleability of certain abilities and capacities that were hitherto considered primarily fixed. Chief amongst those is working memory (WM), defined as "a multicomponent system for active maintenance of information in the face of ongoing processing and/or distraction" (Conway et al., 2005, p. 770). As this definition makes clear, the need for WM capacity and/or skills is ubiquitous in most instantiations of higher-order cognition such as reasoning, planning, creativity, and judgment and decision making, amongst others (Baddeley, 2003). Earlier conceptualizations perceived WM to be a largely fixed capacity, exemplified by Miller's (1956) "magical number seven" or Cowan's four

(2001) (for review see Ma, Husain, & Bays, 2014). Contrary to those views, there is now a large body of evidence to show that repeated training on tasks that draw on WM can lead to gains in WM capacity and/or skills. This finding has opened the door to using WM training to improve target tasks that draw on WM, both in the lab as well as in applied settings (e.g., schools).

Another ability that until recently was perceived to be primarily a fixed property in individuals is fluid intelligence. Unlike crystallized intelligence that represents the storehouse of knowledge in one's mind, fluid intelligence is defined as the ability to adapt to new situations, and is characterized by increased abstraction and complexity in thinking (Cattell, 1963). Contrary to traditional views, there is now some evidence to suggest that repeated training on a demanding WM task can boost fluid intelligence in adults and children alike (Jaeggi, Buschkuehl, Jonides, & Perrig, 2008; Jaeggi, Buschkuehl, Jonides, & Shah, 2011). Because psychometric intelligence is known to predict performance in a variety of professional and educational domains (Neisser et al., 1996), these findings raise the intriguing possibility that gains in fluid intelligence can enhance performance in domains that draw on fluid intelligence. However, importantly, evidence in support of WM training for enhancing general cognitive function has been inconsistent. For example, a meta-analysis of studies found no effect of WM training on fluid intelligence (Melby-Lervåg & Hulme, 2013). In contrast, a more recent meta-analysis that focused on the family of n-back tasks exclusively showed that training leads to a small but positive effect on fluid intelligence (Au et al., 2015). The set of n-back tasks requires participants to decide, on a trial-by-trial basis, whether a stimulus presented in the current trial matches a target stimulus presented a specific number of trials earlier in the sequence. The letter n denotes the specific number of trials that separate the current trial from the target trial. Despite ongoing controversies about the utility of WM training to improve aspects of general cognitive function including fluid intelligence (Harrison et al., 2013), generally speaking the intellectual landscape reflects a stronger belief in the experience-dependent malleability of core cognitive abilities and capacities than was the case even a decade ago.

In addition to the aforementioned behavioral data in support of the malleability of WM and possibly also fluid intelligence, neuroscientists have also gained traction in understanding training-related neuroplasticity in the brain (for reviews, see Buschkuehl, Jaeggi, & Jonides, 2012; Klingberg, 2010). Specifically, it is now known that WM training affects brain activation in the fronto-parietal network that underlies WM (e.g., Olesen, Westerberg, & Klingberg, 2004). However, WM training has been shown to lead to increases as well as decreases in brain activation in this network, the reasons for which are topics of intense study. For example, in his review of studies, Klingberg (2010) noted a consistent pattern such that short periods of WM training (<3h) had been shown to result in decreased brain activity in this network, whereas long periods of WM training had been shown to result in a mixture of increased and decreased brain activity. Klingberg suggested that one reason for this could be that decreases in activation occur as a result of strategy learning, priming during encoding, and time-on-task effects. In turn, during longer WM training these reductions would be co-occurring with increases in capacity correlated with activity in the intraparietal cortex, middle and superior frontal gyri, and the caudate nucleus. In other words, duration of training may be an important moderator of the relation between WM training and brain activation. Klingberg's interpretation of the pattern of increases and decreases in brain activity as a function of training also suggests that it is only longer training regimens that have the potential to result in gains in WM capacity and/or skills.

A similar inconsistency exists in the evidential base relating brain activity to variations in psychometric measures of intelligence. Specifically, whereas studies that have investigated this relation have by and large converged on consistently observing activations in the frontal and parietal lobes, the *direction* of this relation has varied across studies. On the one hand, many studies have reported an inverse relation between fluid intelligence and metabolic rate in the fronto-parietal network using a variety of cognitive tasks that tap fluid intelligence (Deary, Penke, & Johnson, 2010; Jung & Haier, 2007; Neubauer, Fink, & Schrausser, 2002; Neubauer, Grabner, Fink, & Neuper, 2005; see also Van der Heuvel, Stam, Kahn, & Hulshoff Poll, 2009). This inverse relation has been interpreted as a sign of neural efficiency. Interestingly, a recent review of the literature concluded that this inverse relation is most likely to be observed in the frontal cortex (Neubauer & Fink, 2009). In contrast, there is also evidence showing a positive correlation between neural activity and fluid intelligence (Gray, Chabris, & Braver, 2003; Lee et al., 2006; Luders, Narr, Thompson, & Toga, 2009). Two conclusions can be drawn from this literature, although with varying degrees of confidence. First, by now it is likely safe to infer that WM training will improve WM capacity and/or skills, such that "there is no going back to the notion that working memory capacity is fixed" (Klingberg, 2012, p. 195). Second, and more tenuously, there is evidence to suggest that, at least under some conditions, WM training can lead to increases in fluid intelligence (Au et al., 2015). The accompanying brain data have enabled us to build better models of where these training-related changes occur in the brain, although how these changes are instantiated in the brain are not fully understood (see Buschkuehl et al., 2012).

COGNITIVE TRAINING AND CREATIVITY

Most researchers and practitioners contributing to the literature on cognitive brain training are likely less interested in improving WM capacity per se, but rather more interested in observing training-related transfer to target tasks and outcome measures of interest. Transfer involves the extent to which gains on the trained task transfer to improvements in tasks one did not train on. For example, educators might be interested in whether gains in WM capacity as a function of WM training might transfer to improved scholastic performance on subjects that draw on WM, such as reasoning in history (e.g., Ariës, Groot, & van den Brink, 2015). Similarly, educators might care about the extent to which training-related gains in WM capacity might reduce Attention-Deficit/Hyperactivity Disorder (ADHD) symptoms in sufferers, and improve school performance (see Chacko et al., 2014; Gathercole, 2014; van Dongen-Boomsma, Vollebregt, Buitelaar, & Slaats-Willemse, 2014).

It appears that transfer is strongly influenced by the goodness-of-fit between the specific capacity and/or ability targeted by the training task and the requirements of the target task. For example, we recently examined the effectiveness of a short regimen of training on the n-back task on performance on the delayed matching-to-sample (dMTS) task (Beatty et al., 2014). The n-back is a WM task that necessitates the maintenance and dynamic updating of a rehearsal set (Kane, Conway, Miura, & Colflesh, 2007). In turn, the dMTS is a WM task that necessitates the encoding, retention, and retrieval of stimulus representations in sequential order. We reasoned that training on n-back would benefit performance on dMTS because one of the functions that they both share is updating in WM. Indeed, we found that participants who trained on the n-back performed better on dMTS than a control group that trained on a choice reaction time (RT) task.

However, to enable us to detect the specific phase within dMTS (i.e., encoding, retention, or retrieval) that would distinguish those who trained on the n-back compared to the control condition, dMTS was administered in the functional magnetic resonance imaging (fMRI) scanner. The results demonstrated greater activation in the n-back than the active control group in the retention phase in the left inferior frontal gyrus (IFG). None of the contrasts involving the encoding or retrieval phase revealed any significant difference between the two groups. In other words, the difference in brain activation between the n-back and the active control groups was limited to the retention phase of dMTS. The neural difference localized exclusively in the left IFG has been shown to be involved in the retention phase of delayed nonmatching-to-sample task (de Zubicaray, McMahon, Wilson, & Muthiah, 2001), consistent with the involvement of the ventrolateral regions of the left prefrontal cortex (PFC) in delay-period maintenance in visual WM tasks (Ranganath, Cohen, Dam, & D'Esposito,

2004). Our results suggest that the effects of WM training on transfer-related brain function are likely to be observed in regions that underlie the specific capacity enhanced during training, and subsequently recruited by the untrained task.

The same conclusion can be drawn from the study conducted by Dahlin, Stigsdotter Neely, Larsson, Bäckman, and Nyberg (2008). They demonstrated transfer to a 3-back test of WM after 5 weeks of training on a specific aspect of WM—updating. Importantly, using fMRI, they were also able to determine that the transfer effect was based on a joint training-related increase in brain activation in the trained and target tasks in the striatum. Importantly, no transfer was observed to a task that did not involve updating, and did not engage the striatum. These results suggest that to obtain transfer, it is necessary to train specific aspects of WM (e.g., updating) that are functionally shared by trained and target tasks. Similarly, on a structural level, likelihood of transfer is increased to the extent that training-related changes in brain function occur in the same region that is recruited in relation to the trained process (e.g., updating) in both tasks.

Vartanian et al. (2013) conducted the first study to determine whether a regimen of WM training would be associated with better performance on a test of divergent thinking—the Alternate Uses Task (AUT). Performance on the AUT involves the generation of uses in response to prompts consisting of common objects (e.g., brick). In standard behavioral studies responses are typically scored on four indices: fluency (i.e., number of uses), originality (i.e., statistical infrequency of the uses), flexibility (i.e., number of categories the uses can be placed into), and elaboration (i.e., the level of detail associated with the uses). Because in our study the AUT was administered inside the fMRI scanner, we only collected fluency data by instructing our participants to press a button on an MRI-compatible keypad corresponding to the number of uses they were able to generate in response to each prompt. We did not ask them to vocalize their responses in order to minimize head movement during scanning. Importantly, fluency accounts for the majority of the variance in divergent thinking tasks (Plucker & Renzulli, 1999).

Theoretically, there are at least two reasons to think that WM training could lead to improvement in performance on the AUT. First, divergent thinking draws on WM capacity, evidenced by its loading on executive functions. For example, Gilhooly, Fiortou, Anthony, and Wynn (2007) demonstrated that it is only the later rather than the earlier responses generated in divergent thinking tasks that are truly creative (see also Beaty & Silvia, 2012). This is because whereas earlier uses primarily involve retrieval from long-term memory, later responses involve disassembly and reassembly of object components that draw on executive functions. To the extent that WM capacity is increased, this latter process will likely benefit. Second, we also know that there is a strong positive relation between fluid intelligence and divergent thinking (Nusbaum & Silvia, 2011). To the extent that WM training is capable of boosting fluid intelligence, there might be beneficial effects on divergent thinking. Thus, divergent thinking could benefit from WM training via direct (i.e., WM capacity) and indirect (i.e., fluid IQ) routes.

Vartanian et al. (2013) tested three hypotheses: First, we hypothesized that there would be a positive relation between WM training fluid intelligence. Second, we hypothesized that there would be a positive relation between WM training and performance on the AUT. Third, we hypothesized that there would be a relation between WM training and brain activation in regions of the PFC associated previously with divergent thinking tasks, specifically the dorsolateral (DLPFC) and ventrolateral PFC (VLPFC). Specifically, previous studies had shown that the DLPFC and VLPFC both contribute to divergent thinking performance, but in different ways. Goel and Vartanian (2005) showed that activation in the DLPFC is correlated with the number of solutions generated in Match Problems (i.e., Matchstick Problems; Guilford, 1967), possibly due to increased WM demands to maintain multiple solutions "on-line," conflict resolution, or progress monitoring. In turn, the VLPFC was activated only on those problems that required a lateral transformation (i.e., set shifting; Goel, 1995). These are problems that require movement from one state in a problem space to a horizontally displaced state rather than a more detailed version of the same state (i.e., vertically displaced state). Lateral transformations are necessary for problem solution when the constraints that define the structure or mental representation of the problem must be reduced. Such transformations typically occur when participants generate truly novel solutions to problems.

Two of our three predictions were confirmed. First, our results demonstrated that, compared to our active control condition, WM training led to greater gains in fluid intelligence. Second, compared to our active control condition, WM training was associated with lower brain activation in the DLPFC and VLPFC. We interpreted this finding to mean that WM training is associated with greater neural efficiency in the PFC in the context of divergent thinking. However, our data did not show that WM training was associated with greater fluency in the AUT. Interestingly, a mediation test demonstrated that gains in fluid intelligence mediated the link between WM training and activation in the VLPFC. In other words, WM training was associated with lower activation in the VLPFC during divergent thinking to the extent that it managed to increase fluid intelligence. This finding was informative in highlighting at least one possible mechanism that might underlie the effect of WM training on brain activation during divergent thinking.

There could be three key reasons why we were unable to find an association between WM training and divergent thinking performance. First,

WM training interventions that are particularly effective in boosting WM capacity and/or skill share the feature that they are *adaptive*, meaning that task difficulty is adjusted automatically in relation to improved performance. Although in our study performance on the n-back task improved across sessions, the task itself was not adaptive. Second, we investigated the effect of a short regimen of WM training, consisting of three sessions administered within one week. Practice durations and frequencies in previous studies involving WM training have varied greatly, ranging from one 20- or 30-min session to 20 h spread over 10 weeks (Buschkuehl et al., 2012, Table 1; Klingberg, 2010, Table 2; see also Morrison & Chein, 2011). In contrast, studies involving WM training to improve fluid intelligence have typically employed short training sessions (i.e., $\approx 17\text{-}25$ min) administered with high frequency (8-20 sessions) (Jaeggi et al., 2008, 2011). Our decision to focus on a short and concentrated regimen of WM training was motivated by our desire to assess the feasibility of WM training as an intervention strategy in applied professional and educational settings where the implementation of lengthy training regimens might be impractical. For example, in many educational and vocational settings it would not be feasible to administer 20 training sessions, therefore making it useful to know whether a short regimen is associated with performance benefits. Of course, short training regimens run the risk of not generating sufficient gains in capacity, which could hamper successful transfer. Third, our key dependent variable was fluency. It is conceivable that other indices, in particular originality, draw more heavily on WM capacity and fluid intelligence, and might have been more sensitive measures for assessing the impact of WM training on divergent thinking. These shortcomings could be addressed in future studies.

IMPACT OF VIDEO GAMES ON INFORMATION PROCESSING

A major thrust of research in recent years has been devoted to quantifying the effect of video games on various aspects of information processing. From our perspective, an important starting premise for interpreting findings in this area is that one would expect video games to improve creativity to the extent that they boost specific capacities and/or abilities that are important contributors to creativity in various domains. Here, a brief discussion of domains is in order. Historically, one of the most important debates in the creativity literature has been about whether creativity is a domain-specific or domain-general ability (Baer, 1998; Kaufman & Baer, 2005). Studies of historically eminent creative people have shown that very few individuals show creative accomplishments in diverse domains (e.g., Gray, 1966). More often than not, creativity is seen in only one domain. This suggests a degree of task specificity in the requirements for creativity. For example, few would doubt that creativity in music and writing likely draws on dissociable abilities. Of course, this is not to say that there is no universally necessary cognitive process or ability for creativity. For example, a case can be made about the role of WM in the exhibition of creativity in all domains. In this sense, before one can determine whether video games can improve creativity one must start with a task analysis that isolates the specific capacities and/or abilities trained by the video game in question, and the specific cognitive requirements of the target domain under consideration. Only then can one be in a position to judge the goodness-of-fit between trained and required capacities and/or abilities.

Interestingly, and perhaps not surprisingly, recent meta-analyses of neuroimaging data have demonstrated that the neural bases of creativity are largely domain specific. For example, Vartanian (2012) demonstrated a clear dissociation between the neural correlates of metaphor and analogy, as did Gonen-Yaacovi et al. (2013) for creativity involving verbal and nonverbal tasks. In this sense, it is clear that there is no unitary module for creativity. Rather, as is the case with most other higher-order mental activities such as reasoning and planning (Goel, 2002, 2007), the brain bases of creativity appear to be based on a distributed network, built upon component neural systems that are reconfigured dynamically in relation to task demands. This organization closely reflects Simon's (1962, 2005) conception of the architecture of higher-order cognition as hierarchical, an important feature of which is that they tend to be "nearly decomposable." From an evolutionary perspective such an organization makes sense, because it is more efficient for the brain to reconstitute component systems to serve multiple complex activities than it would be to create separate systems anew for each complex activity.

What are the specific capacities and/or abilities that are known to be improved by various types of video games? Because this literature is too large to review in its entirety within the confines of this chapter, we will focus instead on a comprehensive recent meta-analysis that quantified the corpus of quasi-experimental and experimental studies of video games, and assessed their effects on various aspects of cognitive function (Powers, Brooks, Aldrich, Palladino, & Alfieri, 2013).[1] There are advantages and disadvantages of focusing on a single meta-analysis for assessing the utility of video games for improving creativity. On the negative side, doing so does not allow us to delve into the details of specific studies. On the positive side, meta-analytic approaches facilitate "seeing the 'landscape' of a research domain, keeping statistical significance in perspective, minimizing wasted data, becoming intimate with the data summarized, [and]

---

[1] For the record, there was also an earlier meta-analysis of the effects of video games on performance, but it included only seven published studies (Ferguson, 2007).

asking focused research questions" (Rosenthal & DiMatteo, 2001, p. 59). Given the exploratory nature of our inquiry, we reasoned that focusing on Powers et al.'s (2013) meta-analysis was a good place to start.

Powers et al.'s (2013) meta-analysis had several strong suits. Here we focus on three features that are most relevant for our purposes. First, they divided their studies into five broad information-processing domains: auditory processing, executive functions, motor skills, spatial skills, and visual processing. This is very useful for thinking about how creativity in various domains that map onto each of these categories might benefit from video gaming. Second, they distinguished between studies that were quasi-experimental in design and had sampled already practiced game players from studies that were experimental, in which participants were randomly assigned to game training or control conditions. As they duly noted, "establishing the causality of video-game experience on information-processing skills crucially depends on experimental designs in which randomly assigned participants are trained on a specific game and the outcomes are monitored relative to appropriate controls" (p. 1057). For this reason, we will focus exclusively on the results that involved experimental designs. Third, they distinguished between different types of games: action/violent, mimetic, nonaction, or puzzle. Action/violent games involved shooter games. Mimetic games involved games in which the player mimics the action on the screen. Nonaction games involved educational, sports, and simulation games. Finally, puzzle games comprised *Tetris* and its variations.[2] The distinction involving game type is important because people might carry preconceived notions about which variety might be particularly useful for improving specific capacities and/or abilities relevant to creativity.

First, let's review the results as a function of information-processing domain. Effect sizes were reported in Cohen's d. They were large for motor skills ($d = 0.76$), small for auditory processing ($d = 0.45$), spatial imagery ($d = 0.43$), visual processing ($d = 0.36$), and negligible for executive functions ($d = 0.16$). The reported effect sizes were significantly greater than 0 in all cases except auditory processing, which was based on only two comparisons from a single study. Regarding executive functions, the authors conducted more detailed analyses by investigating its subcategories. The results demonstrated negligible effect sizes for executive-function battery ($d = 0.14$), dual/multitasking ($d = 0.17$), intelligence ($d = 0.06$), task switching ($d = 0.06$), WM/short-term memory ($d = 0.12$), and a small effect size for inhibition ($d = 0.39$). In addition, aside from inhibition, none of the reported effect sizes was significantly greater than 0. These results suggest that whereas there is reason to believe that video games will lead to

---

[2] For quasi-experimental studies they also included a nonspecific game type, but here the focus will only be on experimental studies.

enhancements in motor skills, auditory processing, spatial imagery, and visual processing, the same cannot be said about executive functions.

Next, we focus on the results involving different types of games. The authors reported a large effect size for mimetic games ($d = 0.95$), medium effect size for nonaction games ($d = 0.52$), small effect sizes for action/violent ($d = 0.22$) and puzzle games ($d = 0.30$). The reported effect sizes were significantly greater than 0 in all cases. Unfortunately, the extent to which effects within each of these game types were moderated by information-processing domains was not reported. Overall, these results suggest that engagement in video games across the board can lead to enhancement in information processing, although the effect sizes can vary greatly as a function of the specific type of game one is engaged in.

Based on this meta-analysis, what can we conclude about the potential utility of video games for improving creativity? It would appear that creativity in domains that draw from motor skills stand to possibly gain the most from video game training. Less so would domains that draw on auditory processing, spatial imagery, and visual processing. Finally, the prospect of observing improvements in creative performance via enhancement of executive functions due to video games does not appear promising. However, note that whereas one can associate motor skills, auditory processing, spatial imagery, and visual processing with different domains of creative performance (e.g., motor skills with drawing, spatial imagery with architectural design, etc.), executive functions appear more domain general in the sense that one can imagine their positive contribution across domains. In this sense, the results here suggest that video games appear more promising in improving domain-specific rather than domain-general capacities and/or abilities in relation to creativity. To achieve this, one can carefully isolate those interventions (i.e., video games) that have shown greater promise in enhancing the specific capacities and/or abilities within each category.

CONCLUSIONS

In conceptualizing their meta-analysis, Powers et al. (2013) were keenly aware that when it comes to video games, as is the case in cognitive brain training, the key issue involves transfer (of skills):

> Whether video-game training transfers broadly in order to enhance cognitive skills is a question that is fiercely debated, with some researchers making broad claims that "what video games teach is the capacity to quickly learn to perform new tasks—a capability that has been dubbed 'learning to learn'" (Bavelier et al., 2012, p. 392). In contrast, other researchers have found limited evidence of transfer to untrained tasks (Lee et al., 2012), which suggests that the improvements in information processing associated with video-game play may be due to targeted training involving specific skills (p. 1056).

Their meta-analysis has shown that certain types of information-processing skills are more likely to benefit from video games than others. In turn, this information has implications for considerations of transfer. Specifically, given that by and large executive functions do not appear to benefit from video games, it is unlikely that engagement in video games will confer any benefit (i.e., transfer) to untrained tasks via gains in executive functions. In contrast, there does seem to be evidence to suggest that motor skills, auditory processing, spatial imagery, and visual processing are enhanced by video games. This raises the prospect of investigating the utility of video games for improving creativity in domains that draw specifically from those capacities and/or abilities.

In support of this view, Powers et al. (2013) noted that within each category of games, the benefit of any given game is tied closely to its specific cognitive demands. For example, although one speaks of puzzle games, the actual cognitive ability being trained is more precisely (visual) spatial imagery. This suggests that to optimize the prospects of transfer, the cognitive demands of the specific game under consideration must be isolated, which can in fact vary greatly among games within the same category. This can facilitate assessment of the goodness-of-fit involving the trained capacity and the cognitive demands of the outcome measure of interest—in this case creativity.

References

Ariës, R. J., Groot, W., & van den Brink, H. M. (2015). Improving reasoning skills in secondary history education by working memory. *British Educational Research Journal, 41*, 210–228.

Au, J., Sheehan, E., Tsai, N., Duncan, G. J., Buschkuehl, M., & Jaeggi, S. M. (2015). Improving fluid intelligence with training on working memory: A meta-analysis. *Psychonomic Bulletin & Review, 22*, 366–377.

Baddeley, A. (2003). Working memory: Looking back and looking forward. *Nature Reviews Neuroscience, 4*, 829–839.

Baer, J. (1998). The case for domain specificity in creativity. *Creativity Research Journal, 11*, 173–177.

Bavelier, D., Green, C. S., Pouget, A., & Schrater, P. (2012). Brain plasticity through the life span: Learning to learn and action video games. *Annual Review of Neuroscience, 35*, 391–416.

Beatty, E. L., Jobidon, M.-E., Bouak, F., Nakashima, A., Smith, I., Lam, Q., et al. (2014). Working memory training: Examining transfer from one task (*n*-back) to another (delayed matching-to-sample). In *The Annual Meeting of the Association for Psychological Science, San Francisco, CA, May 2014.*

Beaty, R. E., & Silvia, P. J. (2012). Why do ideas get more creative across time? An executive interpretation of the serial order effect in divergent thinking tasks. *Psychology of Aesthetics, Creativity, and the Arts, 6*, 309–319.

Buschkuehl, M., Jaeggi, S. M., & Jonides, J. (2012). Neuronal effects following working memory training. *Developmental Cognitive Neuroscience, 2(Suppl. 1)*, S167–S179.

Cattell, R. B. (1963). Theory of fluid and crystallized intelligence: A critical experiment. *Journal of Educational Psychology, 54*, 1–22.

Chacko, A., Bedard, A. C., Marks, D. J., Feirsen, N., Uderman, J. Z., Chimiklis, A., et al. (2014). A randomized clinical trial of Cogmed Working Memory Training in school-age children with ADHD: A replication in a diverse sample using a control condition. *Journal of Child Psychology and Psychiatry, 55*, 247–255.

Conway, A. R. A., Kane, M. J., Bunting, M. F., Hambrick, D. Z., Wilhelm, O., & Engle, R. W. (2005). Working memory span tasks: A methodological review and user's guide. *Psychonomic Bulletin & Review, 12*, 769–786.

Cowan, N. (2001). The magical number 4 in short-term memory: A reconsideration of mental storage capacity. *Behavioral and Brain Sciences, 24*, 87–114.

Dahlin, E., Stigsdotter Neely, A., Larsson, A., Bäckman, L., & Nyberg, L. (2008). Transfer of learning after updating training mediated by the striatum. *Science, 320*, 1510–1512.

de Zubicaray, G. I., McMahon, K. L., Wilson, S. J., & Muthiah, S. (2001). Brain activity during the encoding, retention and retrieval of stimulus representations. *Learning and Memory, 8*, 243–251.

Deary, I. J., Penke, L., & Johnson, W. (2010). The neuroscience of human intelligence differences. *Nature Reviews Neuroscience, 11*, 201–211.

Ferguson, C. J. (2007). The good, the bad and the ugly: A meta-analytic review of positive and negative effects of violent video games. *Psychiatric Quarterly, 78*, 309–316.

Gathercole, S. E. (2014). Commentary: Working memory training and ADHD—where does its potential lie? Reflections on Checko et al. (2014). *Journal of Child Psychology and Psychiatry, 55*, 256–257.

Gilhooly, K. J., Fiortou, E., Anthony, S. H., & Wynn, V. (2007). Divergent thinking: Strategies and executive involvement in generating novel uses for familiar objects. *British Journal of Psychology, 98*, 611–625.

Goel, V. (1995). *Sketches of thought*. Cambridge, MA: MIT Press.

Goel, V. (2002). Cognitive and neural basis of planning. In L. Nadel (Ed.), In *Encyclopedia of cognitive science, vol. 3* (pp. 697–703). New York: Macmillan.

Goel, V. (2007). Anatomy of deductive reasoning. *Trends in Cognitive Sciences, 11*, 435–441.

Goel, V., & Vartanian, O. (2005). Dissociating the roles of right ventral lateral and dorsal lateral prefrontal cortex in generation and maintenance of hypotheses in set-shift problems. *Cerebral Cortex, 15*, 1170–1177.

Gonen-Yaacovi, G., de Souza, L. C., Levy, R., Urbanski, M., Josse, G., & Volle, E. (2013). Rostral and caudal prefrontal contribution to creativity: A meta-analysis of functional imaging data. *Frontiers in Human Neuroscience, 7*, Article 465.

Gray, C. E. (1966). A measurement of creativity in Western civilization. *American Anthropologist, 68*, 1384–1417.

Gray, J. R., Chabris, C. F., & Braver, T. S. (2003). Neural mechanisms of general fluid intelligence. *Nature Neuroscience, 6*, 316–322.

Guilford, J. P. (1967). *The nature of human intelligence*. New York: McGraw-Hill.

Harrison, T. L., Shipstead, Z., Hicks, K. L., Hambrick, D. Z., Redick, T. S., & Engle, R. W. (2013). Working memory training may increase working memory capacity but not fluid intelligence. *Psychological Science, 24*, 2409–2419.

Jaeggi, S. M., Buschkuehl, M., Jonides, J., & Perrig, W. (2008). Improving fluid intelligence with training on working memory. *Proceedings of the National Academy of Sciences USA, 105*, 6829–6833.

Jaeggi, S. M., Buschkuehl, M., Jonides, J., & Shah, P. (2011). Short- and long-term benefits of cognitive training. *Proceedings of the National Academy of Sciences USA, 108*, 10081–10086.

Jung, R. E., & Haier, R. J. (2007). A Parieto-Frontal Integration Theory (P-FIT) of intelligence: Converging neuroimaging evidence. *Behavioural and Brain Sciences, 30*, 135–187.

Kane, M. J., Conway, A. R. A., Miura, T. K., & Colflesh, G. J. H. (2007). Working memory, attention control, and the N-back task: A cautionary tale of construct validity. *Journal of Experimental Psychology: Learning, Memory, and Cognition, 33*, 615–622.

Kaufman, J. C. & Baer, J. (Eds.). (2005). *Creativity across domains: Faces of the muse*. Mahwah, NJ: Lawrence Erlbaum Associates.

Klingberg, T. (2010). Training and plasticity of working memory. *Trends in Cognitive Sciences, 14*, 317–324.

Klingberg, T. (2012). Is working memory capacity fixed? *Journal of Applied Research in Memory and Cognition, 1*, 194–196.

Lee, K. H., Choi, Y. Y., Gray, J. R., Cho, S. H., Chae, J.-H., Lee, S., et al. (2006). Neural correlates of superior intelligence: Stronger recruitment of posterior parietal cortex. *NeuroImage, 29*, 578–586.

Lee, H., Boot, W. R., Basak, C., Voss, M. V., Prakash, R. S., Neider, M., et al. (2012). Performance gains from directed training do not transfer to untrained tasks. *Acta Psychologica, 139*, 146–158.

Luders, E., Narr, K. L., Thompson, P. M., & Toga, A. W. (2009). Neuroanatomical correlates of intelligence. *Intelligence, 37*, 156–163.

Ma, W. J., Husain, M., & Bays, P. M. (2014). Changing concepts of working memory. *Nature Neuroscience, 7*, 347–356.

Melby-Lervåg, M., & Hulme, C. (2013). Is working memory training effective? A meta-analytic review. *Developmental Psychology, 49*, 270–291.

Miller, G. A. (1956). The magical number seven, plus or minus two: Some limits on our capacity for processing information. *Psychological Review, 63*, 81–97.

Morrison, A., & Chein, J. (2011). Does working memory training work? The promise and challenges of enhancing cognition by training working memory. *Psychonomic Bulletin & Review, 18*, 46–60.

Neisser, U., Boodoo, G., Bouchard, T. J., Boykin, A. W., Brody, N., Ceci, S. J., et al. (1996). Intelligence: Knowns and unknowns. *American Psychologist, 51*, 77–101.

Neubauer, A. C., & Fink, A. (2009). Intelligence and neural efficiency. *Neuroscience and Biobehavioral Reviews, 33*, 1004–1023.

Neubauer, A. C., Fink, A., & Schrausser, D. G. (2002). Intelligence and neural efficiency: The influence of task content and sex on the brain-IQ relationship. *Intelligence, 30*, 515–536.

Neubauer, A. C., Grabner, R. H., Fink, A., & Neuper, C. (2005). Intelligence and neural efficiency: Further evidence of the influence of task content and sex on the brain-IQ relationship. *Cognitive Brain Research, 25*, 217–225.

Nusbaum, E. C., & Silvia, P. J. (2011). Are intelligence and creativity really so different?: Fluid intelligence, executive processes, and strategy use in divergent thinking. *Intelligence, 39*, 36–45.

Olesen, P., Westerberg, H., & Klingberg, T. (2004). Increased prefrontal and parietal brain activity after training of working memory. *Nature Neuroscience, 7*, 75–79.

Plucker, J. A., & Renzulli, J. S. (1999). Psychometric approaches to the study of human creativity. In R. J. Sternberg (Ed.), *Handbook of creativity* (pp. 35–61). New York: Cambridge University Press.

Powers, K. L., Brooks, P. J., Aldrich, N. J., Palladino, M. A., & Alfieri, L. (2013). Effects of video-game play on information processing: A meta-analytic investigation. *Psychonomic Bulletin & Review, 20*, 1055–1079.

Ranganath, C., Cohen, M. X., Dam, C., & D'Esposito, M. (2004). Inferior temporal, prefrontal, and hippocampal contributions to visual working memory maintenance and associative memory retrieval. *Journal of Neuroscience, 24*, 3917–3925.

Rosenthal, R., & DiMatteo, M. R. (2001). Meta-analysis: Recent developments in quantitative methods for literature reviews. *Annual Review of Psychology, 52*, 59–82.

Simon, H. A. (1962). The architecture of complexity. *Proceedings of the American Philosophical Society, 106*, 467–482.

Simon, H. A. (2005). The structure of complexity in an evolving world: The role of near decomposability. In W. Callebaut & D. Rasskin-Gutman (Eds.), *Modularity*. Cambridge, MA: MIT Press, (pp. ix–xiii).

Van der Heuvel, M. P., Stam, C. J., Kahn, R. S., & Hulshoff Poll, H. C. (2009). Efficiency of functional brain networks and intellectual performance. *Journal of Neuroscience, 29*, 7619–7624.

van Dongen-Boomsma, M., Vollebregt, M. A., Buitelaar, J. K., & Slaats-Willemse, D. (2014). Working memory training in young children with ADHD: A randomized placebo-control study. *Journal of Child Psychology and Psychiatry, 55*, 886–896.

2. CREATIVITY AND VIDEO GAMES IN EDUCATION

Vartanian, O. (2012). Dissociable neural systems for analogy and metaphor: Implications for the neuroscience of creativity. *British Journal of Psychology, 103*, 302–316.

Vartanian, O., Jobidon, M.-E., Bouak, F., Nakashima, A., Smith, I., Lam, Q., et al. (2013). Working memory training is associated with lower prefrontal cortex activation in a divergent thinking task. *Neuroscience, 236*, 186–194.

10

Game Narrative, Interactive Fiction, and Storytelling: Creating a "Time for Telling" in the Classroom

Michael F. Young, Stephen T. Slota, Roger Travis and Beomkyu Choi

Educational Psychology, University of Connecticut, Storrs, CT, USA

OUTLINE

Stories are central to—perhaps even definitional of—human existence, learning, and culture. In Sartre's (1938) words, "a man is always a teller of stories. He lives surrounded by his own stories and those of other people. He sees everything that happens to him in terms of these stories, and he tries to live his life as if he were recounting it." Bruner (2004) likewise reasoned that humans evolved to understand their lives in terms of narrative structure, suggesting that "… a life as led is inseparable from a life as told—or more bluntly a life is not 'how it was' but how it was interpreted and reinterpreted, told and retold" (p. 708). In light of our research in the field of game-based learning, we, too, believe that stories are a core determinant of human learning, and that narrative is the mechanism through which humans construct reality and make sense of the world around them, including the games they play. However, research on the role of narrative in games and in classroom learning is far from conclusive, and we feel that narrative's relevance to education as a whole may not yet be well understood. This has fueled our interest in game-based narratives and how they can support the implementation of instruction and curriculum. In this chapter, we describe narrative through the framework of situated cognition and posit how, viewed this way, narrative might coordinate the learning of groups and create a "time for telling," thus serving as a powerful tool for classroom teaching that addresses goals for curriculum coverage while developing and nurturing teacher and student creativity.

VIDEO GAME NARRATIVES AS INTERACTIVE FICTION

It may seem odd to focus on the relevance of narrative in a book principally written to address the relationship between video games and creativity—after all, "backstory" has been repeatedly labeled a marginal, even irrelevant, contributor with respect to "good" game design despite being a variable of central interest in games research (see Dickey, 2006; Echeverria, Barrios, Nussbaum, Amestica, & Leclerc, 2012; Lim, 2008; Malone & Lepper, 1987; Wouters, van Nimwegen, van Oostendorp, & van der Spek, 2013). However, we believe that video games are built from precisely the same storytelling mechanisms exemplified in ancient bardic tales, Broadway shows, and modern television and movies. Like more traditional forms of narrative, video games are nonstatic, instead presented in context, emergent, on-the-fly, and interactively with the dynamic context established by multiple simultaneous players. Even given a fixed narrative context like the lore that defines *World of Warcraft*'s Azeroth by Blizzard, most video games, particularly massively multiple player games, cannot be played by two players in the same way nor played the same way twice by any single player. Like the ancient bards, each retelling of the story accommodates those listening and incorporates unique elements into each unique version. Because of their inherent overlap, the dynamic interaction of narrative, games, and learning is critical to our understanding of creativity and how we can use games to encourage risk taking, group and individual problem solving, and creative decision making.

To begin unpacking these and other issues, we first want to emphasize how the specific beginning-middle-end structure of anecdotes, legends, lore, and other narrative forms plays an important part in education and culture. Its use in storytelling—and gaming—to disseminate information is not new. In fact, the beginning-middle-end story grammar embedded in oral tradition was essential for our ancestors to communicate morals, values, hazards, reliable food sources, medicines, and social norms until they established a means to preserve their shared knowledge in writing roughly five millennia ago (Woods, Emberling, & Teeter, 2010). In the Darwinian sense, effective narrative was adaptive for our species, and we were selected to learn via narrative. It may have begun with nomadic humans' use of stories to teach the night sky's value for recognizing seasonal weather patterns, optimizing harvest times, and following the migration of caribou and bison, then continued serving as an integral element of adaptation and survival through environmental disaster, resource competition, and more. In *The Republic*, Plato used a story as the primary catalyst for deconstructing and exploring culture, a practice still relevant more than 2000 years later. Shakespeare similarly relied on it to drive interest in philosophical, religious, and political discussion, and contemporary media outlets like MSNBC and Fox News now use it to compel or deter public interest in particular political and social conversations.

What is particularly interesting about the importance of oral and written narratives is that despite the invention of written language, Gutenberg's printing press, and the Enlightenment, illiteracy remained fairly common until the early twentieth century, when the Industrial Revolution necessitated reading, writing, and the development of a free public education system. Surely it should not have taken so long for narrative to be considered an instrumental part of "being human" given that it has served as a cornerstone of our ongoing survival. Nonetheless, there has been a dearth of research aimed at uncovering the psychological and instructional value of narrative that we are still faced—thousands of years after oral storytelling tradition began—with two very complex questions:

1. What are the specific affordances of storytelling and narrative structure for learning?
2. How does the creation and telling of stories induce and nurture creativity?

If the answers to the above were better understood, it might be clearer whether narrative value was a matter of production, reception, or some combination of the two. A situated perspective would dictate that both stories and games occur as dialogical social performances in which two or more individuals contribute to the phenomenon, "telling." It is through narrative that we share knowledge, encourage investigation, and promote creative acts. Visualizing the connection between story "giver" and "recipient" is a bit simpler with video games given that players physically control the way a given story unfolds, but it is interesting to note here that the same basic process is true of any narrative (e.g., art, literature, television, and film). Importantly, this also implies that there are various levels of narrative in any situation through which a story "giver" and "recipient" co-act to construct novel uses for existing tools within a story system (e.g., characters, environments, play mechanics, and in-game lore).

THE VARIOUS LEVELS OF NARRATIVE IN GAMING

If we were to catalog video games based on player-game-narrative interaction, it might make sense to create three groups: (1) games with narratives pre-grounded in transmedia storytelling across movies, books, television shows, comics, other video games, and/or action figures (e.g., *Star Wars: Knights of the Old Republic* by Bioware, *Marvel Heroes 2015* by Gazillion, *Lord of the Rings Online* by Warner Bros. Entertainment); (2) games that have an elaborate history built within the game narrative but are not necessarily an extension of existing transmedia storytelling (e.g., *BioShock* by 2K Games, Bioware's *Neverwinter Nights*, *World of Warcraft*); and (3) games with a straightforward narrative that simply serves to justify play (e.g., *Angry Birds* by Rovio Entertainment, *Cut the Rope* by Zeptolab, *Plants vs. Zombies* by PopCap Games, *Two Dots* by Playdots). Despite its appeal for the sake of simplicity, though, this approach would omit a range of possible narrative affordances not encompassed within the game developer framework. As noted by Young, Slota, and Lai (2012), unexpected emergent player goals frequently lead to unique player-constructed narratives:

> *Grand Theft Auto IV* [by Rockstar Games] ... prompts the player/protagonist to follow a narrative progression through a fictitious parallel of New York City. Though the player can easily follow a given path through the game's story trajectory, the interactions he or she has with the designed content will inevitably differ each time a single mission is played, varying in terms of civilian and property destruction, routes taken to halt a runaway enemy, vehicles chosen for use each time, and more. Additionally, the game's prescribed ruleset offers affordances for play that can deviate wildly from the game's original goal: If the player seeks to intentionally attack police officers instead of fulfilling mission objectives, he or she may exhibit goal-seeking and related cognitive processing that is largely antithetical to the designer's intent. The same could be said for an avid *Halo* [by 343 Industries] player who spends time creating a vehicle catapult using a well-positioned pile of dead bodies or a *World of Warcraft* (WoW) player who aims to find the farthest possible distance to fall from the game's sky ceiling to its lowest level of terrain ... In each of these cases, emergent game-player interactions contain valuable information about the ways players learn from, adapt to, and modify the games they play. There is simply no reason to believe

that players will automatically adopt the goals of the game designers or play using a consistent and identifiable set of cognitive processes (pp. 297-298).

Like a school curriculum, video games have set parameters by design—and for good reason—but even the most streamlined, linear games allow players to manipulate the prescribed narrative in ways that designers cannot and do not anticipate. A game that tells the story of a hero's quest to rescue his betrothed, for instance, might encourage players to share the given story when discussing play experiences with friends—something we will refer to as Video Game Narrative: Level 1, the narrative-as-designed. This can be done directly, as with contemporary social media games and apps that ask players if they would like to share their progress or discuss in-game lore via social media websites (e.g., *FarmVille* by Zynga, *Candy Crush Saga* by King), or indirectly, as with games built to unfold like choose-your-own-adventure stories (e.g., *Fallout*, *Mass Effect* by Bethesda, Telltale Games' *The Walking Dead* and *Game of Thrones*). The problem is that Video Game Narrative: Level 1 is easily altered if the player finds greater value in reshaping the story based on his own goals and intentions. Returning to the *Grand Theft Auto* example cited above, a 5-year-old could pick up the controller and play such that the narrative-as-designed is rendered entirely irrelevant. After all, she might be more interested in enacting the story of playing "house" or "racecars." Similarly, a player could intentionally sabotage his team in *League of Legends* by Riot Games or modify the programming code in *Elder Scrolls V: Skyrim* by Bethesda to transform enemies into Thomas the Tank Engine because it makes for a "better" story. This implies that "telling" as a phenomenon is not just the player-designer interaction but also the intersection of designer intention, player intention, peripheral social interaction, and environmental affordances. Ultimately, the player's individualized experience of the game narrative and the story being told by the designer leads to a different form of player-generated narrative that might best be characterized as Video Game Narrative: Level 2.

Unlike the first two Levels, Video Game Narrative: Level 3 is couched in social collaboration that occurs outside the immediate realm of play. This includes affinity groups that emerge as a result of game play, consisting of metagame sources such as fanclubs, magazines, or websites that alter both the narrative-as-designed (Video Game Narrative: Level 1) and the player-generated narrative (Video Game Narrative: Level 2). The purpose of these affinity groups can range from sharing cheats, hints, and guides to the co-creation or management of fan fiction, game mods, and pirate torrents, all of which encourage discussion about topics like ideal group composition, the most efficient path for completing a series of in-game quests, or the canonical importance of a particular mission. In practice, the narrative outcome of a particular affinity group might include *World of Warcraft* guild members meeting over dinner to discuss the drama unfolding on their guild web forums or the author of a game blog getting into an online argument with his readers about his biases. Neither conversation is directly related to a particular game, but both have the potential to alter future play and dramatically shape the narrative players choose to share during and post play (e.g., a player who avoids a game he otherwise might have enjoyed after reading the negative opinion of an influential critic's review).

Yet, even with this differentiation of narrative levels within video games, scholarly work concerning the relationship between gaming and storytelling tends to devolve into a convoluted rabbit hole of blurred terminology and problems of subjectivity. Whether or not individual games are "good" or "bad," for example, is a common red herring that distracts from the more valuable question: How do particular players playing particular games under particular environmental constraints craft particular narratives that emerge from play (and can possibly help them learn particular school content)? We believe that answering this question relies on a more sophisticated approach to gaming and narrative that draws on contemporary learning theory of situated cognition and considers the rich contexts in which play and storytelling merge with real-world application: *practomime*.

Practomime

To circumvent the potential distractors of video games research outlined above, Travis (2010) suggested that narrative and games are two kinds of the same thing—performances driven by player-game-context interaction. Practomime, as he called it, does not distinguish between individuals participating in a group presentation, acting in a musical, or playing a video game. Instead, any agent-environment interaction that results in a particular behavioral demonstration is comparable to all other agent-environment interactions that result in particular behavioral demonstrations. Put another way, video games, musicals, and group presentations are collectively seen as instances of playful performance rather than a series of mostly unrelated human activities.

This perspective has especially critical implications for formal education given that successful performance is rooted in the alignment of real-world application and the behaviors required of the performer. If task and learning objectives are organized in a 1:1 ratio, the performative narrative can serve as a vehicle for content delivery—Video Game Narrative: Level 1 (e.g., the "story" of covalent bonding) and Video Game Narrative: Level 2 (e.g., the player's takeaway from his play experience) are inherently aligned and can be used to powerfully shape social collaboration in Video Game Narrative: Level 3 (e.g., affinity groups that deconstruct, evaluate, and critique play). This presents players with a richly authentic context and improves the likelihood that they will recognize skills and environmental affordances useful to them both in and outside of play (i.e., transfer).

THE VARIOUS LEVELS OF NARRATIVE IN GAMING

To clarify, practomimetic coursework relies upon familiar game mechanics (e.g., role playing, gear collection, boss fights) to scaffold players toward target learning objectives and perspectives favorable for telling a story about their learning. This takes advantage of narrative in two distinct ways: first, the learner performs as an "operative" on a mission to save the world by fulfilling course learning objectives, and second, the learner performs as a character (e.g., scientist, mathematician, historian, and ancient Roman) on a mission to save the game world, also by fulfilling course learning objectives (see Slota, Ballestrini, & Pearsall, 2013). Not only do players participate as avatars with particular worldviews, but they are led to step back from the game to "tell" about that performance in the form of self-evaluation—an intersection of Video Game Narrative: Levels 1 and 2. This dual-performance tiering encourages metagame activities like the discussion of game mechanics and successful strategies for dealing with particular problems (i.e., Video Game Narrative: Level 3), which then feed back into course reflection and, ultimately, academic achievement.

Teachers, too, are active participants in practomimetic learning environments, and their performances extend beyond those of a traditional instructor. They act as Mission Control agents who organize the operatives' mission and role play as all of the nonplayer characters present within the game world. This allows them to shape the learning environment in real time and emphasize the skills and knowledge considered most important for real-world application. Teachers using practomime also guide metagame activities and learner interactions that promote a granular evaluation process referred to as continuous, embedded, formative assessment. Much in the same way as action in a digital game can be saved and analyzed based on current or previous game-states, continuous, embedded, formative assessment allows instructors to store, review, and apply data and pass it on to colleagues who will teach those same students in the future. This creates a smoother, gradated assessment process that simultaneously permits both pinpointed and longitudinal appraisal and feedback.

Practomimetic learning exemplifies the way narrative can be used to develop, support, and explore creativity and problem solving. It offers the flexibility to customize pedagogy and mechanics without being bogged down by unhelpful conversations about individual genres, tools, or games. It enables educators to construct narrative learning environments that serve as sandboxes-on-rails (i.e., settings through which students engage in open inquiry but are continually guided back to the governing learning objective by a more knowledgeable other). Most importantly, it is not burdened by traditional classroom rules and parameters that tend to limit creativity—it encourages thinking "outside the box" and relies on student composition of individualized stories that guide whole-group learning. In sum, practomimetic activities set the stage for "telling" and are a richly authentic platform for creative educational discussion that bridges the gap between academic and real-world learning. Given additional research and attention, we believe practomime may be the storytelling torch needed to reignite the fading embers of creative thinking and problem solving in formal K-12 education.

STORYTELLING, COGNITION, AND LEARNING

Traditional information processing psychologists might describe the creation of a story as the mental achievement of a disembodied mind, a cognitive act of abstract thinking subsequently conveyed to others as fully formed thoughts are simply spoken or written down. But as our starting assumption, we posit that creating a story is a moment-to-moment interaction of the author and text that unfolds as situated action. Similarly, reading or hearing a story is a negotiation between the author and the recipient that is influenced by the recipient's experiences as situated learning. As noted throughout this chapter, it makes little sense to assume that stories are solely created or interpreted in the head of the storyteller—individual experiences naturally vary from situation to situation depending on context, perception, and emergent intentionality. On-the-fly user-content-environment interactions lead to the detection of new and different affordances offered by objects, characters, and settings, in turn presenting an unbounded array of evolving user goals. This can include, for example, a video game player intentionally seeking to break games through hacking, modding, or performing other actions that open alternative avenues to approach the content-as-designed. At the heart of it, agency and intentionality define the way we interact with game narratives, and the personalized narratives we build as a function of our specific choices and interpretations are those that we tend to share with others—not necessarily the experiences we are expected to have.

This is where purely cognitive descriptions of narrative and creativity tend to fall short. For example, in *The Narrative Construction of Reality*, Bruner (1991) described 10 defining characteristics of narrative that outlined how and why he believed narratives to be so relevant across human history (e.g., Diachronicity, Particularity, Referentiality, etc.). Yet, nowhere in Bruner's description is attention given to the highly situated, socially constructed, and contextually emergent nature of narrative. Instead, Bruner's characteristics assume that all of storytelling and understanding is confined to what happens in isolation in the reader's and writer's heads. Extended to video gaming or classroom storytelling, Bruner's conception of narrative implies that only the storyteller is capable of making narrative valuable, neglecting externalities like context, social interaction, and meta-environments (e.g., online forums, hint guides, modding communities, and fan fiction websites). But in an age of synchronous co-writing where stories can be co-authored by groups (e.g., GoogleDocs), descriptions of the pedagogical affordances of narratives and their value for nurturing creativity have to account for spontaneity, randomness, and nonlinearity. This is a two-way street where the writer's intention and the recipient's interpretation merge into the phenomenon that constitutes "telling." If researchers only address one of the two approaches rather than focusing on the multilevel nature of narrative, we can never develop a full explanation for how and why narrative works instructionally.

Take, for example, the particular arrangement of words in the statement "The old man fell and broke his hip." On its surface, the phrase asserts that two individual events have occurred. However, many readers, drawing from their own experiences, assume a specific time sequence and causality, thereby concluding that the fall broke the old man's hip. In contrast—for an elderly man with osteoporosis—the hip fracture could have preceded and caused the fall. If we alter the statement to say "He broke his hip and fell," we recognize the occurrence of the same two events, but the word choice in the telling of this story may indicate to some readers an opposite time sequence and causality. This suggests that the interaction between the writer and reader includes non-explicit rules through which narrative structure serves as the keystone to understanding. Schank (Riesbeck & Schank, 1989; Schank, 1991; Schank & Abelson, 1977; Schank & Cleary, 1995) emphasized something similar when explaining his version of schemata (i.e., scripts) that he believes organize memory. According to his description, people create and use cognitive scripts to anticipate events and recall them based on story frameworks, planning actions around scenarios we have prospectively played out in anticipation of them happening in the future, making narrative the primary way we understand and interact with the world (Schank & Berman, 2006). This is like mentally "playing through" possible conversations while taking a shower or going for a run. However, if such stories are not grounded in the ontological descent of constraints of the natural universe (i.e., perception and action in the lived-in world), they can only be taken as the ravings of two separate, dissociated minds. Alternatively, if emphasis is placed on the shared point of interaction between writer and reader, we can isolate and identify the unspoken social constructs that govern how and why particular stories, sequences of events, and contexts make sense.

Burke (1945) indirectly addressed several unspoken points of interaction between writer and reader in his pentad of story elements. In order for a writer's narrative to make sense, he argued, five elements must be recognizable to the recipient:

1. Agent (who)
2. Act (what)
3. Scene (when and where)
4. Agency (how)
5. Motive (why).

Regardless of whether the writer refers to these elements directly or obliquely, they are rendered meaningless if the recipient is unable to discern how they contribute to the story—for instance, when a young child attempts to play and comprehend Irrational Games *BioShock*. There is an inextricable link between narrative and context that reinforces the highly situated, social relationship formed between producer and end user. Even if the producer has written something with a specific instructional goal in mind, as with TapToLearn's *Math Vs Zombies*, the end user's prior experiences will inherently inform—or confound—the author's intended interpretation. For example, in *Math Vs Zombies*, a student might have a goal to see how close she could let the zombie get before transforming it, thwarting the designer's goal to enhance math response speed. Similarly, a particular player with particular life experiences playing Wreden's *The Stanley Parable* might interpret it as a drama or psychological thriller rather than a satire of traditional first-person shooters. In short, understanding the value of narrative for learning and sustaining teacher and learner creativity requires an analysis made using situated cognition. Understanding the multilevel nature of narratives and acknowledging the co-constructed dialectic among writer, reader, and social groups provides a context for understanding how narratives may invoke and nurture the creativity of all those involved.

A SITUATED VIEW OF CREATIVITY

Most creativity researchers describe two components of creativity: novelty and task appropriateness (Guilford, 1950; Kaufman & Beghetto, 2009). Drawing on these foundational ideas, there are many theoretical models that suggest how we might describe the creativity of teachers and students in the classroom. One such approach, the Four-C Model (Beghetto & Kaufman, 2007; Kaufman & Beghetto, 2013; Kaufman & Plucker, 2009), makes a helpful distinction by proposing several levels on which teachers and students might be viewed as creative and along which they might be seen to develop their abilities to act creatively.

The first level, "mini-c" creativity, is personal, subjective, and often developmentally precedes the other levels. It consists of individual insights that arise from direct experiences. Teachers who implement a new pedagogical approach for the first time may experience mini-c, a personal feeling that something is new, different, and creative to them. Likewise, students may feel creative when they discover a new word, use a new computer app, or stick their hands into damp clay for the first time. However, as with television reruns missed on original airing, the concept is only new to the individual, not the general population. With feedback and growth, personal experience of creative acts can lead to the next level, "little-c," or everyday creativity acknowledged by others (e.g., peers and administrators). Teachers can experience this when their fellow teachers ask them for advice or come to visit their classrooms to see a lesson they have heard good things about. Students can experience this when their peers watch and copy things they have done. Nearly every person can be creative in this way, but it is just the starting point toward achieving acclaim within a given field. That type of professional honor, known as "Pro-c," can take 10 or more years of dedicated effort extended across repeated trials accompanied by guidance and practice. Yet, even with intense devotion, only an extremely small number eventually reach the pinnacle of "Big-C," or genius creativity, judged in an historical context and based on world-renown associated with life work (e.g., innovations deemed worthy of a Nobel, Pulitzer, or other global acclaim).

While this description might come across as a single, linear spectrum, so-called "creative achievements" do not actually manifest as individual, static entities or in a strictly linear way—especially not with respect to Big-C creative products like those of Newton, Da Vinci, Picasso, Mozart, or Einstein. Even if a teacher could be said to "create" materials for use with her students, the "creation" of worksheets is not something we would likely often define as even a mini-c creative act. However, a history teacher who incorporates *Elder Scrolls V: Skyrim* into a class activity as a foundation for discussing feudalism might be deemed little-c "creative" by her peers. From the situated perspective (e.g., Brown, Collins, & Duguid, 1989; Greeno, 1989, 1997; Greeno & van de Sande, 2007; Lave & Wenger, 1991; Young, 2004), this means creativity arises from an interaction among individuals and objects in the world. It would be incorrect to identify someone as a "creative person" as though creativity were an object carried in a backpack or the sole possession of an individual. Rather, we would say this creative act is emergent in context such that the interaction of that teacher and her environment on a particular occasion together produced creativity. All Four Cs represent this kind of dynamic interplay rooted in individual intentions and the affordances of the particular environment, vitally drawing attention away from purely cognitive acts and placing equal emphasis on agents (e.g., student and teacher) and contexts.

Because the Four Cs represent the interplay of agent and context, we can assume that creative ideas arise from some existing material, whether content, concept, or overarching framework. Harkening back to our introduction to narrative, stories have always been grounded in environmental interactions and aimed at focusing the attention of listeners on particular pieces of useful information key to survival or personal happiness. They are socially assembled and devised to meet the needs of those who tell them and those they hope to influence. At a minimum, this implies that creativity—like narrative itself—is not a product but a continuing and ever-evolving process, something situated cognition might explain as the novel detection of invariants that were present for others to see but, on this occasion, viewed by a particular person with unique goals, were detected and then acted upon. The history teacher who uses portions of *Elder Scrolls V: Skyrim* as a foundation for discussing feudalism is driven by her particular life-world and the experiences she perceives across space-time (Barab & Roth, 2006), so she may recognize unconventional affordances of readily accessible materials and be able to bring together content in a novel little-c or Pro-c way. While it is unlikely that she will attain Big-C creativity, she might be compared to a Picasso or Einstein insofar as their creativity emerged in context and respective of their life-worlds, influenced by perceptions and actions within their given fields of study.

The preceding scenario exemplifies how individuals with little formal teaching experience can become excellent teachers when placed in fertile settings or, conversely, those with advanced teacher preparation and training can become dreadful, uncreative teachers in spite of fertile settings. If a particular individual's life-world and experiences includes academic training but limited exposure to multiple contexts, it is unlikely she will be able to perceive a broad range of affordances in the classroom that might otherwise be used to solve unique, emergent problems. A new teacher with limited teaching experience but widely varied social interactions, on the other hand, might be more likely to detect and act upon classroom affordances to resolve complex behavior management or other instructional issues. In the real world, Big-C individuals like Steve Jobs and Bill Gates were highly successful due to the particular skill sets they developed as a result of having a broad range of nonclassroom experiences in widely varying contexts even though they never finished their post-secondary degrees. This counterintuitive dichotomy implies that fully understanding creativity requires consideration of both properties of the individual (e.g., goals and focus of attention) as well as properties of the environment (i.e., those that invite creative action).

Teaching with games—particularly those that feature elaborate narratives—requires risk-taking on the part of teachers and students. The process includes differentiating instruction and producing a taken-as-shared "time for telling" for the prescribed curriculum. Our research team, for instance, employs narratives in which game and story objectives are built with 1:1 alignment under prescribed curricular objectives (e.g., Common Core State Standards, National Educational Technology Standards) so we can customize storytelling in the context of particular instructional needs (e.g., Slota, 2014; Slota et al., 2013). This enables us to develop optimal generator sets for enhancing creative thinking. No single experience can guarantee the broad recognition of invariant structures across domain that often are a part of creative acts, but increased exposure to a variety of contexts has the potential to provide richly situated experiences and improve the probability of creative outcomes. We believe this approach can expand teacher capacity to perceive and respond with effective, creative, in-the-moment actions that improve overall instruction.

THE SITUATED NATURE OF NARRATIVE AND EDUCATION

Whether education through narrative occurs informally (e.g., reading a novel for pleasure) or formally (e.g., attending a college English class), the two situations are similar with the primary difference being the goals and intentions of the reader and the intentions of the content producer (or teacher). Novelists may have a goal to teach with their writings or they may have a goal to simply tell a story that will amuse or entertain. It is certainly hard to determine the motives of great writers like Shakespeare, but it may be fair to say their primary intention was not formal instruction, at least not under the contemporary interpretation of the word. Still, readers may learn much from these narratives, including history, morals, and cultural norms. Perhaps we can consider this the exemplar of creative teaching: conveying new learning goals to students with amusement or entertainment. Further more, perhaps when such creative teaching interactions occur, they nurture and inspire creative acts on the part of the readers such that reader responses and subsequent actions become more creative as a result of interaction with the narrative. It is these two possibilities—creative teaching with narrative and enhanced creativity of students inspired by narrative—that most intrigue us as educational researchers.

The situated nature of creativity and narrative poses an interesting question: If narrative's effect is entirely dependent on the interaction among writer, environment, and reader, how might various forms of narrative—such as ancient bardic tales, Shakespearean plays, and video games—nurture and develop valued human abilities like creativity? Do we have reason to believe creativity is anything more than an innate ability that can be refined through education? Certainly the Four-C Model suggests a way that creativity might be nurtured, inspired, and even taught. Yet, a full answer, we think, relies on understanding how the intentions of content producers and end users coincide.

Consider the *intentional spring* (see Shaw, Kadar, Sim, & Repperger, 1992). In this thought experiment, a "teacher" who knows the goals for a particular task "transfers" those known objectives to a naïve learner through repeated trials where she gradually releases control to the learner.

Importantly, the teacher teaches solely through co-action that runs counter to the direct instruction approach, a mathematically described model of apprenticeship that is repeatedly highlighted in the situated cognition literature (Brown et al., 1989; Greeno, 1998; Hutchins, 1996; Lave & Wenger, 1991). With this in mind, we would initially posit that narrative can induce creativity by helping readers adopt new goals for action, changing their intentionality by proposing new possibilities for action in the real world based on events that unfold in the narrative. Interactive narrative (e.g., digital games) might further this effect by encouraging "readers" to perform actions within the story that run parallel to opportunities for action in the real world.

How Risk-Taking and Creativity Occur in Teaching

In the early 1990s, the Cognition and Technology Group at Vanderbilt (CTGV) (1990, 1993, 1994) implemented a research program called *The Adventures of Jasper Woodbury* that used narrative instruction to teach mathematics to middle schoolers, strategically crafting stories from everyday life through which middle-school math students could provide various solutions to the kinds of problems that emerge when we go grocery shopping, travel, hold school fundraisers, or schedule the day. They concluded that narrative structure (e.g., beginning-middle-ending story grammar) could enable students to utilize their everyday knowledge in the context of the middle-school math curriculum, including distance-rate-time problems, area and volume computation, compound decimals (i.e., strange combinations of decimals and fractions like those found on gas station signs displaying prices such as 3.98\frac{9}{10}$), and methods for wisely retrieving information external resources (e.g., using the timeline of the story to access a video database).

Such "anchored instruction" stories enabled nontraditional students to contribute to mathematical discussions by using their everyday knowledge and aiding in a collaborative problem-solving process. This deviated from concurrent math computer games like *Number Munchers*, *Math Blaster*, and *Super Solvers* by emphasizing the value of narrative as engaging students' everyday cognition and tapping into fundamental ways through which humans detect and recall information in meaningful ways. However, this approach was also viewed as nontraditional teaching that required risk-taking and creativity on the part of participating teachers. Teachers who were accustomed to telling students what they needed to know prior to challenging them with complex problems at the end of a unit were instead forced to do something quite different: immersing students in an ill-defined problem to be experienced as initially intractable without full understanding of the mathematics involved, then using the problem as a "time for telling" about numbers, ratios, and rates. This helped shape a shared experience among students that warranted learning more about the math or science content identified in the school curriculum. It also required teachers to creatively respond to multiple groups simultaneously working on the anchor problem in multiple ways, drawing from the raw materials of student problem solving rather than from a prepared script.

CTGV's research ultimately showed that it was possible to make 17-step math problems transferable from the classroom to the real world by wrapping them in narrative that drew upon everyday knowledge, nurtured creative thinking, and encouraged risk-taking in the context of problem solving. Here, the takeaway was that narrative carried much of the pedagogical heavy lifting, and simple narratives like those present in *Math Vs Zombies* and *Math Blaster* by JumpStart Games were insufficiently elaborate to trigger school-to-real-world transfer. Moreover, this suggested that no single narrative could provide the ideal context for all learners. In the case of the *Jasper* series, designers were forced to strategically design pairs of 15-min stories to highlight the invariance of mathematical concepts across situations. Our work on practomimetic learning has extended this understanding to show that elaborate narratives can be co-constructed by players and teachers much in the spirit of role playing and games like *Dungeons & Dragons* by Wizards of the Coast. Appreciating how games of this type engage students and teachers in highly situated actions in the classroom requires parallel appreciation of teaching as a skilled craft enacted on-the-fly in a dynamic context or, in short, teaching as situated cognition.

For example, we understand teaching as an intentional act done by dedicated individuals working toward personal goals at various levels and on various space-time scales. A college student might select a career in the teaching profession to satisfy a number of intentions ranging from, at the basest level, the acquisition of necessary resources to sustain life (i.e., a living wage) to, at the more abstract level, deriving joy from helping mold the minds of future citizens, promoting the evolution of social norms, or something as superficial as "having summers off." These goals are intimately integrated with each teacher's respective life-world and are wholly influential on the affordances she is able to act on in the classroom environment. When she goes to work each day, she has a specific set of effectivities (i.e., skills and abilities used to affect the world) associated with her physical attributes (e.g., hands, legs, musculature and musical talent) and her experiences to date, and she is able to act on environmental elements she detects that arise on-the-fly as students come to class and her day unfolds. Because situations continuously change, the affordances of the classroom detected by a teacher also continuously change. This situated description of teaching does not rely on a teacher's analyzing and computing in her head to understand student behavior (e.g., cognitive analysis, representations and mental computation) but rather takes as given that her experience of the classroom is direct, driven by her larger goals and her moment-to-moment intentions. The teacher sees and reacts to the class directly as the lesson unfolds. In short: the world is not in her head, her head is in the world of the classroom (Kirshner & Whitson, 1998).

Imagine a situation where an otherwise high-performing student has fallen asleep in class. Once this situation is detected by the teacher, she establishes two distinct but related goals: first, to wake the student and, second, to determine the cause of the student's fatigue. If this event is early in the semester, she may also adopt a goal to make this a lesson for all students in the class and establish norms and expectations for class participation throughout the rest of the marking period. All of these micro-scale goals feed back into her long-term intentions to be a successful teacher, make a sustainable income, and fulfill biological functions (e.g., survival) across the space-time of her career. In a situated analysis of teaching, this dynamic emergence of new goals establishes a goal space within which the teacher can act toward achievement of the goal, and this goal space controls the teacher's behavior as she perceives and acts on a moment-to-moment basis. The establishment of this goal space also sets the boundary constraints on possible creative actions that she can take. There is an ontological descent of possibilities ranging from: (1) logically possible actions, to (2) physically possible actions, to (3) the constraints of the natural world, to (4) constraints of the world as it exists that day, and finally to (5) constraints of the current classroom as it exists at the moment. Within this ontological descent, the boundaries of the teacher's creativity are set, establishing a situated view of the teacher's creativity.

Creative action on this newly adopted set of goals requires the teacher to detect the affordances of various objects in the classroom. Because she is able to move about the classroom through the rows of desks, she may detect the affordance of walking down the aisle to nudge the student surreptitiously. The classroom is full of books with the affordance of making a loud bang when dropped. The classroom is equipped with a door that creaks and makes a nice bang when slammed shut. The classroom can project audio and video from her laptop computer that stores the audio file of an airhorn being sounded. There is a small plastic recycling can that could be filled with water from a drinking fountain. Detection of the affordances of these objects provides the teacher with options for acting to wake her sleeping pupil. But which option will further progress toward the largest number of her goals simultaneously?

Viewed through the lens of situated cognition, the teacher's behavior will most likely be determined by which action maximally achieves progress toward her current goals across the several goal spaces she has created in the moment. Continuing the story of our sleeping student, let us imagine that the teacher fills the recycling bin at the water fountain and gently slides it under the sleeping student's dangling hand, dipping his fingers into the lukewarm water. This action establishes in the sleeping student a biological imperative that wakes him with a strong urge to immediately seek the teacher's attention and request a hall pass. Viewed as a creative act, this action on the part of our teacher serves to return the sleeping student's attention back to class and the observing students' attention to information that will serve them well in the future. It may also serve as an opportunity for the teacher to pull the student aside and inquire about issues surrounding the fatigue in a more private hallway setting. We might also conclude that the teacher acted creatively by opting for this action over a gentle nudge or loud book drop, both of which might have awakened the student but failed to prompt class attention or presented the opportunity to speak privately with the student about the issue.

It is here that we find significant overlap between the goals and creative opportunities of teachers and game designers. Individuals from both groups have particular goals to shift others' attention to particular elements of a particular learning environment, and those individuals have particular tools at their disposal to make guidance possible within a particular context. One of their shared tools is narrative, our biologically engrained mechanism for emphasizing important bits of information, dictating contextual organization, and making content relevant to the lived-in world. But what is the intersection of games, narrative, and learning? We believe the answer lies in how we define narrative within the game context and leverage that definition toward the alignment of game and learning objectives.

COMBINING NARRATIVE, GAMES, AND CREATIVITY

There are several ways we believe game narratives can be harnessed for the purposes of promoting creativity in the classroom environment. Practomimetic courses, for instance, can induce teachers to adopt creativity as a student learning outcome for teaching and induce students to respond creatively to curricular material. Similarly, they can induce students to adopt goals associated with the curriculum without having a personal, immediate real-world need for the material. This is what we refer to as "creating a time for telling."

In developing innovative means of engaging students, explaining content, and assessing ability, classroom teachers tend to tell stories and produce games, experiments, and outdoor activities that powerfully shape students' life-worlds (Barab & Roth, 2006), thereby providing motivation (in the form of inducing students to adopt new goals) for continued learning. Elementary teacher creativity often takes the form of storytelling or enhancing oral reading with multimedia such as character voices and sound effects. Secondary teacher creativity, by contrast, frequently includes anchoring instruction in rich narratives taken from historical or real-world cases and projects that provide a contemporary context (e.g., period-piece films, primary source documents like letters home from soldiers, project- or case-based learning). Though information presentation through direct instruction can be seen as uninteresting, stories of real-world applications, cases of unexpected problems, and even fictional accounts of situations that enable students to practice, synthesize, and apply what they are study- ing can make classrooms more engaging and effective.

The nurturing and development of creativity in the classroom involves inducing teachers and students to adopt goals related to creativity and shifting their perception to encourage novel perspectives on issues and problems. Narrative has affordances for doing both these things: educating intention (i.e., goals) and attention (i.e., recognizing multiple perspectives).

However, K-12 classrooms have grown increasingly informational and test based rather than imaginative and playful (e.g., Fleer & Peers, 2012), perpetuating the application of direct instruction and suffocation of alternative pedagogical methods like anchored instruction and practo- mime. Here, we present a series of considerations that might be useful for nurturing creativity through narrative among three distinct groups: (1) teachers; (2) individual students; and (3) social circles.

Writing and Telling

Telling a story, particularly in the bardic tradition of adapting the narra- tive to the context of the listeners, is a creative act—one that many teachers enact daily. Adapting characters to an audience, as well as reading the audience while telling the story, require keen perception and divergent thinking to weave entertainment into a pre-structured story framework. The story writer/teller—or, in our case, the teacher—must flexibly cus- tomize a storyline to dynamic story responses while keep specific course objectives in mind. This illustrates one particular affordance of using nar- rative in the classroom: engaging the creativity of the teacher. This could include tapping the narrative from *Portal* by Valve Corp. to encourage general problem-solving skill development as part of an undergraduate general education requirement (Abbott, 2010), *World of Warcraft* to en- courage exolingual co-questing situations for the fostering of secondary language development and intercultural competence (Zheng et al., 2012), and *Lord of the Rings Online* to scaffold comparisons of contemporary and ancient Greek storytelling tradition (Maton, 2012; Travis, 2010). The out- comes of applications like these indicate that game-based storytelling in the classroom may give teachers the freedom to adopt creative pedagogy and creatively differentiate instruction in ways that might otherwise be unachievable, accommodating a wide variety of disabilities, multicultural backgrounds, and divergent student interests.

Reading, Listening, and Playing

Students who participate in practomimetic courses become creative in ways atypical of many classroom interactions (Slota, 2014; Slota et al., 2013). Reading, listening, and playing avatar-based video games leave some things to the recipient's imagination. This aspect of narrative, which relies on the recipient's ability to imagine situations and create missing elements, can certainly become a creative exercise. Drawing on the Four-C description of creativity, many stories enable the recipient to experience things from a novel perspective, giving them opportunities to engage in mini-c activities (e.g., Young, Slota, & Lai, 2012). In addition, when stories are discussed, as in Video Game Narrative: Levels 2 and 3, there is opportunity for others to appreciate a novel interpretation of a story and thus engage little-c creativity. In this respect, the use of narrative in the classroom also presents the affordance of creating opportunities for recipients to produce and reflect on their creativity.

Co-Writing and Social Reading

The least well-described aspect of story production concerns situations where multiple authors sequentially and iteratively co-write a narrative as a back-and-forth or simultaneous interaction among two or more authors. Given the minimal research on this type of interaction, it seems unusual that so many recent technologies appear designed to support exactly this style of co-writing as either text (e.g., GoogleDocs) or elaborate digital constructions (e.g., *Skywind* mod development for *The Elder Scrolls V: Skyrim*). This trend in technology-enhanced story creation is exemplified in role-playing games like *Dungeons & Dragons* and interactive fiction environments including artificial intelligence tools for interactive storytelling (e.g., Aylett, Louchart, & Weallans, 2011; Roth et al., 2012). The same is true of online multiplayer video games through which narrative emerges at least partially as a result of social interaction (e.g., *Dark Souls* by From Software, *Monster Hunter* by Capcom). *Marvel Heroes 2015* is exemplary here given that its extension of existing narrative (e.g., comic books, movies) into a new medium (i.e., online gaming) is co-written as an interaction of the gamespace-as-designed and user interactions within that space (e.g., collaborating to stop Dr. Doom vs. attempting to inhibit group progress). The story never exists in a single author's mind—it is driven by multiple individuals with a variety of experiences, perceptions, and intentions ranging from writers and artists to game designers and comic book fans.

When teachers and students co-write stories, especially those directly tied to curricular goals as with practomime, the unpredictable outcome and iterative structure may support creativity on the part of teachers and students in ways not traditionally seen in classrooms. In these instances, creativity starts with little-c since the act of story writing embodies a shared, social act. What remains to be understood psychologically and abstracted for principled instructional design are the specific affordances that optimally connect interactive storytelling with precise delivery mechanisms and coverage of curriculum. However, it seems clear that the trend toward collaborative writing can only further our interests in utilizing narrative—particularly game narrative—to support classroom creativity.

MAKING NARRATIVE WORK

Even when narratives are well written and engaging in themselves, they may only "work" instructionally for students who have goals associated with the narrative (e.g., becoming a "Loremaster" in *World of Warcraft*). Players with other goals may ignore or be distracted by the narratives (see Slota, 2014; Young, Slota, & Lai, 2012). This may explain the mixed or absent empirical results of narrative effects in learning through video games. Such meta-analytic research tends to sum across many contexts, many teaching strategies, and many instances of learner's goals. As a result, we argue that as a minimum starting point, it is essential to align class objectives with narrative/game play objectives to maximize the probability students will adopt goals for which the narrative has value.

Using the description of the Four-C model of creativity described above, classrooms may be able to support the development of Pro-c expertise by nurturing mini-c and little-c creativity through narrative-based classroom activities. Men and women tend to behave differently in online environments (Guadagno, Muscanell, Okdie, Burk, & Ward, 2011) and, as with Ward and Sonneborn's (2009) description of creativity in *Second Life*, we see the potential for various levels of creativity expression growing from little-c use of customization when using classroom narratives to mini-c during co-writing of narrative, thus contributing ultimately to development of Pro-C creativity.

The relationship between life-worlds, experience sets, and situated creativity invites the opportunity for instructional designers to develop optimal generator sets for enhancing creative thinking (as defined above). While no single narrative experience can guarantee the development of creativity, increased exposure to a variety of contexts has the potential to invite creative acts on the part of both teachers and students, and improve the probability of developing creative potentials. Further exploration is needed to establish this hypothesis, but existing meta-reviews of game-based learning literature (e.g., Wouters et al., 2013; Young et al., 2012) suggest that a situated approach may produce additional intervention ideas for expanding teacher capacity to perceive and respond with effective, creative, in-the-moment actions.

CONCLUSION

Drawing from an historical perspective, we posit that stories are central to human existence, learning, and culture, but exactly how narrative intertwines with our lived-in world remains a controversial topic for scholarly work. We also believe that video game narratives are built from precisely the same storytelling mechanisms exemplified in ancient bardic tales, Broadway shows, and modern film, and, like more traditional forms of narrative, games are nonstatic, presented in context, on-the-fly, and are a dialogic interaction between "giver" and "recipient."

This chapter raised two key questions: First, what are the specific affordances of storytelling and narrative structure for learning, and second, how does the creation and telling of stories induce and nurture creativity? A situated view tells us that narrative must be understood as a two-way dialectic where the writer's intention and the recipient's interpretation merge into the phenomenon that constitutes "telling." We have argued that teaching with games—particularly those that feature elaborate narratives—requires risk-taking on the part of teachers and students. The process enables differentiating instruction and can create a taken-as-shared "time for telling" in the classroom.

To lay a foundation for future educational game development, we highlighted CTGV research that showed the power of narrative to engage students' everyday cognition and tap into fundamental ways through which humans perceive and act on information and derive meaning from real and realistic fictional life experiences. We described Three Levels of Video Game Narrative and how the concept of practomime, by unifying our pedagogical use of games and stories, can serve as an alternative framework from which to view the instructional affordances of narrative.

We believe that, under the right circumstances, the use of narrative can induce teachers and students to be creative, and, in particular, the co-writing nature of storytelling in an interactive, dialogic approach may be especially fruitful for invoking the social nature of creative acts ranging from mini-C to little-C. Our situated cognition approach is a very different framework from the "gamification" approach of implementing simplified behavioral approaches to learning as games in the classroom (Kapp, 2012). The development of better and more effective stories may significantly strengthen the field of game-based learning in a way that will move us toward a deeper understanding of how specific types of games interact with instructional settings to yield desired learning outcomes. Like Super Mario, we must act promptly but with enough caution to ensure we do not dismiss the right castle in favor of another that merely hosts hostile turtles and mushroom people. That, we believe, is the only path to saving our shared game-based learning princess and, of course, living happily ever after.

References

Abbott, M. (2010). *Portal on the booklist*. Brainy Gamer. Retrieved on May 11, 2013, from: http://www.brainygamer.com/the_brainy_gamer/2010/08/portal-booklist.html.

Aylett, R., Louchart, S., & Weallans, A. (2011). Research in interactive drama environments, role-playing, and story-telling. In M. Si, D. Thue, E. André, J. Lester, J. Tanenbaum, & V. Zammitto (Eds.), *4th International conference on interactive digital storytelling (ICIDS 2011) proceedings*. Berlin, Germany: Springer.

Barab, S. A., & Roth, W. M. (2006). Intentionally-bound systems and curricular-based ecosystems: An ecological perspective on knowing. *Educational Researcher, 35*(5), 3–13.

Beghetto, R. A., & Kaufman, J. C. (2007). Toward a broader conception of creativity: A case for "mini-c" creativity. *Psychology of Aesthetics, Creativity, and the Arts, 1*(2), 73–79.

Brown, J. S., Collins, A., & Duguid, P. (1989). Situated cognition and the culture of learning. *Educational Researcher, 18*(1), 32–42.

Bruner, J. (1991). The narrative construction of reality. *Critical Inquiry, 18*(1), 1–21.

Bruner, J. (2004). Life as narrative. *Social Research, 71*(3), 691–710.

Burke, K. (1945). *A grammar of motives*. Berkeley: University of California Press.

Cognition and Technology Group at Vanderbilt. (1990). Anchored instruction and its relationship to situated cognition. *Educational Research, 19*(6), 2–10.

Cognition and Technology Group at Vanderbilt. (1993). Anchored instruction and situated cognition revisited. *Educational Technology, 33*(3), 52–70, March Issue.

Cognition and Technology Group at Vanderbilt. (1994). From visual word problems to learning communities: Changing conceptions of cognitive research. In K. McGilly (Ed.), *Classroom lessons: Integrating cognitive theory and classroom practice*. Cambridge, MA: MIT Press.

Dickey, M. D. (2006). Game design narrative for learning: Appropriating adventure game design narrative devices and techniques for the design of interactive learning environments. *Educational Technology Research and Development, 54*, 245–263. http://dx.doi.org/10.1007/s11423-006-8806-y.

Echeverria, A., Barrios, E., Nussbaum, M., Amestica, M., & Leclerc, S. (2012). The atomic intrinsic integration approach: A structured methodology for the design of games for the conceptual understanding of physics. *Computers & Education, 59*, 806–816. http://dx.doi.org/10.1016/j.compedu.2012.03.025.

Fleer, M., & Peers, C. (2012). Beyond cognitivisation: Creating collectively constructed imaginary situations for supporting learning and development. *Australian Educational Researcher, 39*(4), 413–430. http://dx.doi.org/10.1007/sl13384-012-0073-9.

Greeno, J. G. (1989). A perspective on thinking. *American Psychologist, 44*(2), 134–141. http://dx.doi.org/10.1037/0003-066X.44.2.134.

Greeno, J. G. (1997). On claims that answer the wrong question. *Educational Research, 26*(1), 5–17. http://dx.doi.org/10.3102/0013189X026001005.

Greeno, J. G. (1998). The situativity of knowing, learning, and research. *American Psychologist, 53*(1), 5–26.

Greeno, J. G., & van de Sande, C. (2007). Perspectival understanding of conceptions and conceptual growth in interaction. *Educational Psychologist, 42*(1), 9–23. http://dx.doi.org/10.1080/00461520709336915.

Guadagno, R. E., Muscanell, N. L., Okdie, B. M., Burk, N. M., & Ward, T. B. (2011). Even in virtual environments women shop and men build: A social role perspective on Second Life. *Computers in Human Behavior, 27*, 304–308.

Guilford, J. P. (1950). Creativity. *American Psychologist, 5*, 444–454.

Hutchins, E. (1996). *Cognition in the wild*. Boston, MA: MIT Press.

Irrational Games. (2007). *BioShock*. Boston, MA: 2K Games. Retrieved from, http://www.2kgames.com/bioshock/.

Kapp, K. M. (2012). *The gamification of learning and instruction: Game-based methods and strategies for training and education*. San Francisco, CA: Pfieffer.

Kaufman, J. C., & Beghetto, R. A. (2009). Beyond big and little: The Four C model of creativity. *Review of General Psychology, 13*, 1–12.

Kaufman, J. C., & Beghetto, R. A. (2013). Do people recognize the four C's? Examining layperson's conceptions of creativity. *Psychology of Aesthetics, Creativity, and the Arts, 7*(3), 229–236.

Kaufman, J. C., Kaufman, S. B., & Plucker, J. A. (2009). Contemporary theories of intelligence. In D. Reisberg (Ed.), *The Oxford handbook of cognitive psychology* (pp. 811–822). New York: Oxford University Press.

Kirshner, D., & Whitson, J. A. (1998). Obstacles to understanding cognition as situated. *Educational Researcher, 27*(8), 22–28.

Lave, J., & Wenger, E. (1991). *Situated learning: Legitimate peripheral participation.* New York: Cambridge University Press.

Lim, C. (2008). Global citizenship education, school curriculum and games: Learning Mathematics, English and Science as a global citizen. *Computers & Education, 51*, 1073–1093. http://dx.doi.org/10.1016/j.compedu.2007.10.005.

Malone, T. W., & Lepper, M. R. (1987). Making learning fun: A taxonomy of intrinsic motivations for learning. In R. E. Snow & M. J. Farr (Eds.), *Cognitive and affective process analyses: Vol. 3. Aptitude, learning, and instruction* (pp. 223–253). Hillsdale, NJ: Lawrence Erlbaum.

Maton, N. (2012). *Game-based learning–starring Homer.* MindShift. Retrieved on May 11, 2013, from: http://blogs.kqed.org/mindshift/2012/03/game-based-learning-without-video-games/.

Riesbeck, C. K., & Schank, R. C. (1989). *Inside case-based reasoning.* Hillsdale, NJ: LEA.

Roth, C., Vermeulen, I., Vorderer, P., Klimmt, C., Pizzi, D., Lugrin, J.-L., et al. (2012). Playing in and out of character: User role differences in the experiences of interactive storytelling. *Cyberpsychology, Behavior and Social Networking, 15*(11), 630–633.

Sartre, J.-P. (1938). *La nausée.* Paris, France: Éditions Gallimard.

Schank, R. C. (1991). *Tell me a story: Narrative and intelligence.* Evanston, IL: Northwestern University Press.

Schank, R. C., & Abelson, R. (1977). *Scripts, plans, goals, and understanding.* Hillsdale, NJ: LEA.

Schank, R. C., & Berman, T. (2006). Living stories: Designing story-based educational experiences. *Narrative Inquiry, 16*(1), 220–228.

Schank, R. C., & Cleary, C. (1995). *Engines for education.* Hillsdale, NJ: LEA.

Shaw, R. E., Kadar, E., Sim, M., & Repperger, D. W. (1992). The intentional spring: A strategy for modeling systems that learn to perform intentional acts. *Journal of Motor Behavior, 24*(1), 3–28.

Slota, S. T., Ballestrini, K., & Pearsall, M. (2013). Learning through Operation LAPIS: A game-based approach to the Latin classroom. *The language educator.* American Council on the Teaching of Foreign Languages. Retrieved from, http://www.practomime.com/pdf/tle_art.pdf.

Slota, S. T. (2014). *Project TECHNOLOGIA: A game-based approach to understanding situated intentionality* (doctoral dissertation). Retrieved on May 5, 2015, from: http://digitalcommons.uconn.edu/dissertations/638/.

TapToLearn. (2013). *Math Vs Zombies.* San Francisco, CA: TapToLearn. Retrieved from, http://www.taptolearn.com/MathVsZombies.html.

Travis, R. (2010). *A note on the word "practomime." Living Epic.* Accessed April 22, 2014, http://livingepic.blogspot.com/2010/01/note-on-word-practomime.html.

Ward, T. B., & Sonneborn, M. S. (2009). Creative expression in virtual worlds: Imitation, imagination and individualized collaboration. *Psychology of Aesthetics, Creativity, and the Arts, 3*(4), 211–221.

Woods, C., Emberling, G., & Teeter, E. (Eds.), (2010). *Visible language: Inventions of writing in the Middle East and beyond.* Chicago, IL: Oriental Institute of the University of Chicago.

Wouters, P., van Nimwegen, C., van Oostendorp, H., & van der Spek, E. D. (2013). A meta-analysis of the cognitive and motivational effects of serious games. *Journal of Educational Psychology, 105*(2), 249–265. http://dx.doi.org/10.1037/a0031311.

Wreden, D. (2011). *The Stanley parable*. Retrieved from, http://www.stanleyparable.com/.

Young, M. F. (2004). An ecological psychology of instructional design: Learning and thinking by perceiving-acting systems. In D. H. Jonassen (Ed.), *Handbook of research for educational communications and technology*. (2nd ed.), Mahwah, NJ: Erlbaum.

Young, M., Slota, S. T., Cutter, A., Jalette, G., Mullin, G., Lai, B., et al. (2012). Our princess is in another castle: A review of trends in serious gaming for education. *Review of Educational Research, 82*(1), 61–89. http://dx.doi.org/10.3102/0034654312436980.

Young, M. F., Slota, S. T., & Lai, B. (2012). Comments on Tobias and Fletcher, 2012. *Review of Educational Research, 82*(3), 296–299. http://dx.doi.org/10.3102/0034654312456606.

Zheng, D., Newgarden, K., & Young, M. F. (2012). Coaction in killing and caring: Multimodal analysis of language learning in World of Warcraft play. *ReCALL Journal Special Issue on Games, 24*(3), 339–360.

PART 3

CREATIVITY AND VIDEO GAME DEVELOPMENT

11

Creating Code Creatively: Automated Discovery of Game Mechanics Through Code Generation

Michael Cook

Department of Computing, Imperial College, London, UK

OUTLINE

Computational Creativity	227
ANGELINA	229
Mechanic Miner—Generating Game Mechanics	234
Mined Gems	241
Conclusions	243
References	244

In her book *Rise of the Videogame Zinesters* (Anthropy, 2012), game designer and critic Anna Anthropy offers up a definition of games. She says:

> *A game isn't defined by being fun just as comics aren't defined by being funny. A game is defined as an experience created by rules.* (**Anthropy**, 2012, p. 48)

Definitions can be troublesome, but Anna's is appealing because it leaves a lot out. It's a flexible definition. It doesn't promise too much nor does it exclude too many things from being called games. But above all else, it gets at something fundamental about games—they revolve around

Video Games and Creativity
http://dx.doi.org/10.1016/B978-0-12-801462-2.00011-4

225

systems of rules. This chapter will look at the creative challenge of designing these rules, and how software might one day help us understand, or even replicate, the creative nature of game mechanic design.

In the context of games, creativity brings to mind the awe-inspiring architecture and world design in games like *Dark Souls* (From Software, 2011); the compelling art direction in games like *Journey* (thatgamecompany, 2012); the inventive and powerful sound design and musical composition in games like *Machinarium* (Amanita Design, 2009) and *Botanicula* (Amanita Design, 2012); or the sweeping narratives that bind together great role-playing games (RPGs) like *Dragon Age* (Bioware, 2009). What Anna's definition reminds us is that the systems and rules that make up a game's foundation are perhaps the most important part of delivering on a game's creative goals. If you want to create an *experience* for the player, then you need rules that help form that experience.

The games industry as a community seems to agree, too. Every year there are newly released games praised for their game mechanics in awards ceremonies like the Independent Games Festival's *Nuovo* award. Game jams like the *Experimental Gameplay Project* (Gray, Gabler, Shodhan, & Kucic, 2005) encourage their entrants to explore new ways of interaction and prototype unusual mechanics in a short space of time. Game developers who can invent and balance new systems for us to play with are highly valued, and their creativity is respected just as much as that of composers, artists, and writers.

Game mechanics are more than a source of fun and challenge—they're powerful communicators of meaning, as well. In *By Your Side* (Hazelden, 2011) the player controls a husband and a wife simultaneously with a single input. The game's mechanics tell the player something about the relationship between the two main characters (the player primarily controls the male character, and later on in the game the female character stops mimicking player input and instead does the opposite). Here, the game's mechanics are more than just a reason to solve puzzles—they help carry a narrative and tell part of the story themselves (for more on conveying narratives through games, see Chapter 4 from Hamlen et al.).

This chapter will examine games from the perspective of rules and system design—their *mechanics*—and use this perspective to explore how software can solve creative problems on its own, or help human game developers solve creative problems in new ways. What does it mean for software to be creative? Why are game mechanics an interesting creative challenge to set software? How on earth can developers begin to get software to create, to test, and to evaluate game mechanics? This chapter will try and answer some of these questions in the following pages, and hopefully shed some light on interesting approaches to solve the rest.

Before beginning to look at how software can create game mechanics, though, first it is important to consider how software can create anything at all. What does it mean for a piece of software to act creatively?

COMPUTATIONAL CREATIVITY

Computational Creativity is a rapidly growing subfield of artificial intelligence that concerns itself with whether software can augment creativity in humans, or even act creatively on its own. In a paper summarizing the current state of the field, Colton and Wiggins (2012) describe the area as follows:

> The philosophy, science and engineering of computational systems which, by taking on particular responsibilities, exhibit behaviours that unbiased observers would deem to be creative.

There's lots going on in this definition. It talks about "responsibilities"—being trusted to perform actions in the place of a human performing them. It also talks about *exhibiting* behaviors—being seen to be creative by other people (or other software). Both creators and consumers of modern video games will probably be familiar with the idea of software taking on certain responsibilities in game development. Procedural content generation—a name given to the process of creating game assets automatically through software—is now a common concept in the modern games industry. It can be seen at the forefront of many games, such as *Borderlands'* gun generation (Gearbox Software, 2009) or the procedural landscapes of *Minecraft* (Mojang, 2011). At the same time, it is subtly applied behind the scenes of many other games, in the form of generative middleware such as *SpeedTree* (Meredith, 2004), which is used by major film and game developers to procedurally fill spaces with plants and trees.

That definition of Computational Creativity asks for more than just arbitrary responsibility, however. It asks that the software acts in such a way that *others* might call it creative. This is asking an altogether bigger question than whether software can produce things. Few would claim that *SpeedTree* is being creative when it produces another fir tree on demand from a catalog of templates. What does it take for software to be accepted as a creative agent in a complex process such as game design?

It can mean many things to many different people. Colton, Cook, Hepworth, and Pease (2014) point out that the very *idea* of creativity is "essentially contested" by society, meaning that one of the strengths of the concept is that there is no agreement on what it means. Creativity is also an especially hard concept to tackle with the mindset of an artificial intelligence researcher, too. Eigenfeldt, Burnett, and Pasquier (2012) point out that work in the field of AI is often "evaluated by comparison to some optimal solution" but when it comes to evaluating work in Computational Creativity, "such notions of optimality are not defined" (Eigenfeldt & Pasquier, 2012, p. 144). There is no optimal painting of a bowl of fruit, just as there is no optimal video game about Italian plumbers (of course, Super Mario Bros. 3 (Nintendo, 1988) does come close).

Despite this, some things help increase the *perception* of a piece of software as being creative. Giving software the ability to reflect and evaluate its own performance is a common theme in computational creativity. The ANGELINA software that will feature later in this chapter can write simple commentaries describing how it produces things, for example. Building software which is capable of discussing its own work and justifying its decisions helps reinforce the notion that this software is acting independently and with intentionality and motivation. Another important and recurring concept when discussing creative systems is novelty and surprise. Ritchie (2007), for example, suggests many criteria for evaluating the creativity of a piece of software, but a crucial one is whether the system is capable of producing output which is *novel*. What proportion of the system's output is novel and surprising? And what proportion of novel output is of a good enough quality to actually use?

Just as the IGF and the Experimental Gameplay Project value novel game mechanics produced by humans, Computational Creativity values novelty in the output of software. But in both cases, novelty alone isn't good enough—Ritchie (2007) also asks us to consider what proportion of the software's output is of good quality. In Computational Creativity the ratio of quality items to worthless ones is often referred to as the *curation coefficient*, defined as the percentage of a software's output that is of good enough quality to release and show people. As the creator of a system, do you find yourself throwing away a tenth of the system's output? Half? Nine-tenths? The hope is to reduce this number as much as possible, to show that your system can independently improve and curate its own output.

When it comes to traditional procedural content generation, the curation coefficient is normally very high. When a game developer chooses to include a procedural generator in their game, they normally implement it in such a way that it produces reliably good content, to avoid the game becoming unplayable, boring, or unpredictably difficult. *Spelunky* (Mossmouth Games, 2011) includes a level generator which builds levels out of hand-designed chunks. It lays chunks down carefully in a path from start to finish, and then tweaks them so that they appear slightly randomized without affecting the routes through them to the exit. This means that *Spelunky* can generate tens of thousands of levels without worrying that the level it produces might be broken in some way—the hand-designed chunks are guaranteed to be playable.

Ritchie's criteria evaluate many different things in a creative system, but the tradeoff between novelty and quality is perhaps the most interesting for this chapter. *Spelunky*'s level generator is consistently high quality, but offers little novelty and variation. *Minecraft*'s world generator, on the other hand, offers a breathtaking variety of landscapes because it has fewer constraints and operates on a far larger scale. This grander scale, however, also makes things harder to control. As a result, *Minecraft* sometimes generates landscapes that are incredibly flat and boring, or generates bizarre floating cliff formations that instantly stick out as unrealistic. If *Minecraft*'s output were to be curated by someone, they would probably find themselves throwing away some of its work from time to time, at least.

If software that can explore new ideas and invent novel game mechanics is to be built, it will need to be given the freedom to explore a large state space without restriction, just as *Minecraft*'s world generator tries to do. The challenge is to find a good way of doing this while still being able to tell good ideas from bad ones. Humans have a very good way of doing this: they develop a sense of *taste* and they evaluate their own output accordingly. When game developers play-test their own games, they decide if the game *feels* right, if they consider it to be fun, interesting or meaningful. But getting software to do the same thing is extremely hard, because opinions—like Eigenfeldt and Pasquier's description of creativity earlier on—don't have clean, optimal solutions for software to search for. How can software be developed to get around this problem of separating the good from the bad, while still coming up with novel ideas? Let's examine some systems which attempt to do just that, and consider the challenges they encountered.

ANGELINA

This chapter began by declaring game mechanics to be fundamental to making meaningful, interesting, and enjoyable games. This makes them a huge part of the creative challenge undertaken when designing a game. The chapter then turned to Computational Creativity—Can software take on the same creative challenges that humans do, and how should their success at this be assessed? Different metrics for evaluating creativity were considered, particularly focusing on novelty and surprise, and how the freedom of a system can affect how well it performs in these areas. Video game design seems like a perfect setting to test out Computational Creativity theories and build systems to tackle difficult creative challenges. There has been a wave of interest in this idea recently, with researchers building both tools that augment human creativity and software that acts independently as a creator in the video games domain. One such project is a game design system called ANGELINA.

ANGELINA is an ongoing research effort to investigate some of the issues that arise when trying to build software to act both autonomously and creatively. The aim of the project is to build a piece of software that can act as an autonomous video game designer capable of designing interesting, novel, and meaningful games in their entirety. This means appreciating the creative challenges inherent in every aspect of game development, from visual design and art direction through to the programming of game mechanics.

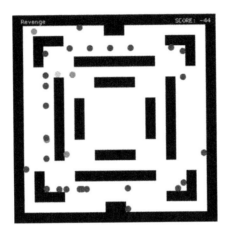

To motivate the system that will be described later in this chapter, it will help to examine how ANGELINA generates its own game mechanics at two different stages in its development. The first version of ANGELINA to consider generated simple two-dimensional arcade games such as the one shown in the image above (Cook and Colton, 2011). The rules are template based, and driven by collisions between entities in the game. The basic template looks like this:

<Object1, Object2 -> Effect1, Effect2, ScoreChange>

This reads as follows: when an object of type Object1 collides with an object of type Object2, apply Effect1 to Object1, Effect2 to Object2, and add ScoreChange to the overall score. Here's a concrete example rule from one of ANGELINA's games:

<Player, Red -> Nothing, Kill, +5>

This rule describes a collect-the-things mechanic—when the player touches a red object, nothing happens to the player, the red object dies, and the player gains some score. To generate one of these rules, the system selects objects from the types that exist in the game, and the effects are sourced from a list of hand-designed effects that encapsulate small game concepts like death or teleportation.

There are interesting combinations that can be built up here through multiple rules that affect different elements of a game. For example, the above rule might be paired with another rule that causes blue objects to destroy red ones as well:

<Blue, Red -> Nothing, Kill, -1>

This combines with the rule above to provide a chase between the player and any blue objects to collect the red objects first. ANGELINA evaluated these rulesets by playing the games itself and applying basic criteria like what the average score was. Using score to measure effectiveness all ties in with the notion of measuring *usefulness*, which is a recurring theme with respect to creativity. It's also a feature that software is particularly well suited to evaluate, because there are fewer ambiguities and subjective notions. Something is either useful or it isn't—this chapter will return to this idea later on.

There are weaknesses with this template-based approach to generating rules, however, especially from the perspective of Computational Creativity. A lot of game design knowledge is being embedded in the system in the form of the hand-designed rule effects. Ideas like teleportation and death are provided to ANGELINA *precisely because* they are expected to yield interesting rules—in a sense, the system is being led.

The system is also being artificially constrained to only consider mechanics driven by two objects colliding on screen. Collision is a common component of game mechanics, particularly in the simple arcade game space this version of ANGELINA was exploring. However, the decision to restrict ANGELINA's search space to a collision-based template also helps restrict it to a space which is likely to yield good mechanics. In fact, if you consider the possible rules that can emerge from the rule template that is defined above, there are few—if any—rules that are objectively bad. It is possible for ANGELINA to produce a game in which the only way to gain score is to die, for instance, but even in this case ANGELINA has managed to use a similar rule such that dying is the game's "end state" and the objective is simply to find a way to gain one point.

Clearly, the system has weaknesses—it's too overconstrained to offer much in the way of surprise, and it inherits a lot of design ideas from a human game developer. Now let's look at a later version of ANGELINA and examine how some of those constraints were relaxed, and what effect they had on the system's ability to design games.

3. CREATIVITY AND VIDEO GAME DEVELOPMENT

Later versions of ANGELINA generated simple platformer-style games in which the player had to collect powerups to reach new parts of the level, similar to the item and exploration mechanics of Metroidvania games (Cook, Colton, & Gow, 2012). The aim of this version of the software was not to allow experimentation in terms of the kinds of mechanics available—instead, the game used a set of powerup types that ANGELINA could place throughout the levels. These powerups included lowering gravity, unlocking doors of certain types, and increasing the player's jump height. Rather than making decisions about the *kind* of mechanic being employed, this version of ANGELINA investigated how a system might be able to precisely set game variables to achieve certain effects.

A powerup was defined as a collectible which applied some change to a game variable. Here's a code snippet from an example powerup that makes the player jump higher:

```
player.jumpHeight = 200;
```

There are two components here: the variable to be changed, and the value assigned to it. When ANGELINA places a powerup in the game level, it chooses a variable from a hand-selected list of variables which are likely to have an interesting impact on the game, and then chooses a value to set the variable to. The value is selected by ANGELINA without any heuristics or predefined settings—it might even choose to lower the player's jump height at first. In order to find good values for the powerups to take, ANGELINA repeatedly plays candidate game designs as part of an evolutionary process, changing powerup values to find ones which work.

The freedom to precisely set variable values in this way, in contrast to the very broad grammar-based templates of the arcade game rules, means that ANGELINA can design powerups which suit the current level design in extremely specific ways. Here's a complete level map of a game designed by ANGELINA for the *New Scientist* magazine:

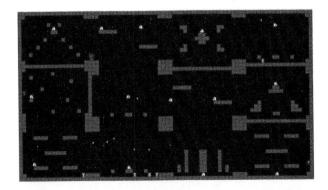

The player begins on the bottom right of the map, and must find a way to reach the computer console at the top left of the map to complete the level. There are two powerups in this level—one on the bottom right, and one on the far left side of the map slightly further up. Initially the player can only reach one of these—the jump height powerup on the right-hand side of the map. This increases the player's ability to move around the map, allowing them to reach the second powerup by jumping up to higher platforms. The difficult aspect of designing such a level is making sure that the second powerup is actually necessary. Can the player skip the second powerup and use the jump boost from the first powerup to complete the level?

To see how ANGELINA stops this from happening, let's take a closer look at one particular part of the level:

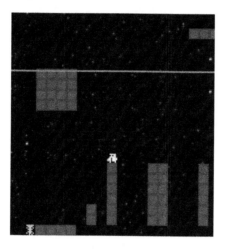

In the image above, the player is standing on the highest point on the bottom section of the level. The first powerup increases the player's jump height by 184 pixels. The red line indicates the maximum jump height after collecting the first powerup. This means that the player isn't able to get up onto the next floor of the level. However, by walking to the far left, they can use their new jump height to reach the second powerup, and return to this point with an increased jump height. This precise value-setting enforces a sense of progression on the player, and allows ANGELINA to design both levels and powerups simultaneously—both the level and the powerup work together to make sure the player can't get to later parts of the level too early, also known as *sequence breaking*. This wouldn't be possible if ANGELINA had been given a fixed set of values it could change the variable to: 100, 200, or 300 pixels, for example. This is possible because it can fine-tune the settings of its powerups and discover interesting interactions like the one illustrated in the figures above.

This system still sorely lacks novelty and surprise—the nature of the powerups are still extremely static and the variables that they modify are all chosen by hand before ANGELINA gets involved—but it shows the value of allowing generative systems to set values in code directly. This work directly inspired the development of the system you'll be introduced to next, and with it one can see a bigger step forward in system freedom.

MECHANIC MINER—GENERATING GAME MECHANICS

There are other examples of projects which attempt to generate mechanics for games besides ANGELINA, like Adam Smith's *Variations Forever* (Smith & Mateas, 2010), but ANGELINA highlights some common problems—systems which are constrained to promising areas of the search space, mitigating the risk of generating bad mechanics but also reducing the opportunity for new ideas; systems which are given a lot of design knowledge beforehand by human game developers, weakening the claim that they are working independently. There is another approach to examine, however—a tool called Mechanic Miner which aims to generate game mechanics in a very different way, by directly inspecting, modifying, and executing game code, rather than using intermediate representations.

For the purposes of this chapter, consider a highly simplified kind of game mechanic. Mechanic Miner will aim to find one-button game verbs that make a small change to something in the game, similar to the powerups mentioned earlier in reference to ANGELINA's platformers, such as lowered gravity or jump boosts. A *verb* is a special kind of game mechanic that a player has direct control over, like jumping in *Super Mario* or firing a bullet in *Space Invaders*. The mechanics we'll be generating will look a bit like this:

```
if(Keyboard.pressed(BUTTON_X)){
        if(toggled)
                someObject.someVariable += someValue;
        else
                someObject.someVariable -= someValue;
        toggled = !toggled;
}
```

Activating the mechanic once toggles the mechanic on, and activating it a second time toggles it off again. This might not perfectly reverse the process, depending on the variable changed.

Mechanic Miner generates simple game mechanics using a programming technique called *reflection*. Reflection is the ability of a programming language to inspect itself and make modifications to a computer program while it is running. This means a program can look at its own code as it executes, such as the example below. This code gets a list of all the different methods (self-contained bits of code) defined in a particular part of the program:

List ms = someObject.getClass().getMethods();

In addition, bits of code can be written using reflection, which dynamically creates code or changes the state of the program. The following Java code segment takes one of the methods found in the list above and tells the program to execute it:

Method m = ms.get(0);

m.invoke();

Mechanic Miner uses reflection to look into a game's code and find things to change when the player presses a button. The mechanics the system aims to generate have two parts: a variable to change, called a *field*, and a value to put in that field. Using reflection Mechanic Miner can write software which scans a computer program and finds methods to call and fields to change, and also write reflective code which makes changes to these fields and methods when the program is running. By combining these two things, Mechanic Miner can build simple one-button game mechanics like the *Super Mario* jump or the *Space Invaders* blaster described earlier.

The field Mechanic Miner wants to change can be found in a program just like retrieving lists of methods in the earlier reflection examples:

List fs = someObject.getClass().getFields();

A Field object can have its value set using reflection too:

Field f = someClass.getField("someVariable");

f.setValue(someObject, someValue);

The bit of code above finds a variable in the game called *someVariable* and then puts a new value in that variable. For example, it might find the player's *health* variable and put the value 100 in it. This would be a bit of code that acted just like a health pack.

In order to generate a random mechanic, Mechanic Miner searches through all the variables and objects in a given game, and identifies fields which contain simple kinds of data like numbers and true/false values (in programming these are called *primitive* types—int, float, or boolean). It's good to limit the system to simple kinds of data here simply because Mechanic Miner should ideally be able to suggest values for the fields, and doing this for more complicated kinds of data like text is much harder (though not outside the realms of possibility, and an exciting area for future work).

Once Mechanic Miner has identified a particular field, it can then select an operator and generate a value for changing the variable in some way. If the field is a number, it can use any arithmetic operator like addition or multiplication, while other types (such as true/false boolean values) may have more limited operators. Mechanic Miner also has some sensible upper and lower limits on the values it can try to supply to the operator. Keeping this range large helps free the system up to change the game in interesting ways; at the same time, it need to recognize that this is already a large state space, and the system needs some constraints to keep it focused.

At this point Mechanic Miner is a system that can generate lots of simple "mechanics" which change a value in the game engine when a button is pressed. Such a system is, however, fairly useless. As one might expect, many of these randomly selected fields are not helpful at all, and in the wrong circumstances can even be damaging. Consider the following examples of one-line mechanics generated by the random generation phase of Mechanic Miner:

```
//Immediately kills the player
//by setting their health to be less than zero
player.health = -10;
//Causes the game engine to crash!
FlxG.worldDivisions = 207;
//Causes the player to become invisible
//by making their on-screen sprite too tiny to draw
player.height = 0;
```

The problem is that while the system has the capacity to be novel, it can't evaluate its own output. It can't tell the difference between an exciting, interesting game mechanic, and a button that makes the game crash. Mechanic Miner needs to be given a way of evaluating and assessing the worth of a mechanic. Detecting the worst cases is simple—things like heap overflows can be detected by simulating the game and immediately throwing away mechanics which cause the game to crash. But what about this mechanic:

```
//Moves the player up by one pixel
player.y -= 1;
```

This isn't a very good mechanic, but it also doesn't cause any obvious catastrophes either. There needs to be a better way of evaluating than simply "does it crash the game?"

When game developers want to test their new mechanics, they play-test prototypical ideas on a sample game level. Mechanic Miner does exactly the same, using a special game level designed by hand. It looks like this:

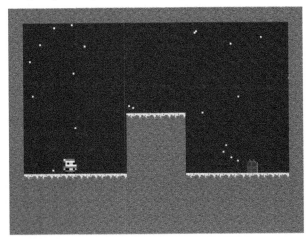

The objective in this level is to guide Santa from his starting point to the present on the right-hand side of the screen. Why this particular level, though? The purpose of the level isn't immediately clear. What criteria is Mechanic Miner using to evaluate its mechanics? Game developers might look for whether a mechanic is fun, whether it interacts with other parts of the game in interesting ways, and whether it conveys something that relates to the meaning of their game. Understanding concepts like fun or meaning are vital in the long term for research into automated game design and procedural content generation. Mechanic Miner uses the level shown above for a much simpler reason, and a much simpler metric: to assess whether a mechanic is *useful*.

Utility may not be the most exotic of properties for a mechanic to have, but people come across it frequently in video games. Puzzle games give players the power to solve the problems they're presented with, action adventures provide abilities that can be used to overcome combat or exploration challenges. Great mechanics are fun to use, but even a bad mechanic usually has some kind of function. Why is utility easier for a system like Mechanic Miner to test for? To see why, let's take another look at the sample level above.

The objective here is for Santa to reach the Christmas present in each level. Santa can only jump a couple of tiles high, so the level displayed in the screenshot isn't actually solvable. Santa can run and jump but he can't get over the wall in the middle of the level. You might be able to tell this just by looking at the screenshot, but Mechanic Miner can also deduce this too, by simulating game play and exhaustively trying out combinations of keypresses to see which parts of the level the player can reach.

"Exhaustively" really does mean exhaustively here. Mechanic Miner has a built-in solver—a special computer program that tries to find solutions to complex problems through careful trial and error. When writing a solver for a game like the simple platformer environment Mechanic Miner works in, you might expect to employ some intelligent search techniques to find optimal paths through the level, like the infamous *Infinite Mario* demo by Togelius (2009). In such cases, heuristics help the solvers find their way from the start to the finish, guiding the search towards known tactics and methods for playing the game. These solvers, however, are being applied to games where the mechanics and systems are known in advance. In the case of Mechanic Miner and its associated game engine, there is a desire to invent *new* mechanics for the game. Not just mechanics that aren't already in this game, but potentially a mechanic that has never been in *any* game ever seen before. It's not possible to rely on an ordinary search guided by rules and intuitions, because there simply aren't any rules or intuitions to give about something you've never seen before.

Instead, what's needed is to build a more flexible kind of solver. A solver that might be extremely inefficient, but is thorough enough that it can work with any mechanic, even ones that it has never encountered before. Although it might sound like an extreme approach, steps can be taken to make "exhaustive search" a little less exhausting. Let's take a look at how the search process in Mechanic Miner works. Below is a pseudo-code outline of the search procedure:

```
while(statelist.hasNext()):
        nextState = statelist.next()
        for(move in moveSet):
                game.loadState(nextState)
                game.applyMove(move)
                if(isLegalState(game) and isNewState(game)):
                        statelist.add(game)
                if(isTerminalState(game)):
                        return game.trace()
```

Let's step through this algorithm line by line. Mechanic Miner maintains a list of *game states* that are yet to be explored by the search algorithm. A game state is a representation of the game at a certain point in time. For efficiency's sake, this does not encapsulate the entire game. Instead, data that needs to be stored in a game state is explicitly defined in the system by the designer. In Mechanic Miner's case it needs only store information about the player, but for more complex games it might need to record enemy data, moving platforms or physics objects, logical states like locked doors or completed objectives. Anything that might be affected by the game—or by the generated code—needs to be stored.

Initially, the list of states only contains the starting configuration of the game. As long as there are still states remaining, the algorithm will keep running—running out of states simply means the level was unsolvable. For each state in the list of unexpanded states, the game will try every valid move in a previously defined *move set*. A move set is defined as a list of button combinations which are valid in the game. This is slightly different from simply pressing every button individually, since this allows combinations of buttons such as pressing jump while moving. However, it is a smaller list than every permutation of button presses—pressing left and right simultaneously can never lead to meaningful progress in the game that Mechanic Miner is considering. Domain-specific heuristics like this help narrow down the search space. Most importantly, the move set will include moves which use the new mechanic, which is assigned to a fixed button on the keyboard or gamepad.

For every valid move set in this list, the currently running game loads the game state being considered. It then applies the selected move set to the game state. To do this, Mechanic Miner simulates holding down all buttons in the move set, and then lets the game run. While the game is running in this way, Mechanic Miner will periodically take snapshots of the game state at intervals. This interval will determine how accurate, and how slow, the execution of Mechanic Miner is. More frequent snapshots will offer a higher-resolution search of the game space, but generating more of these game states will cause the search space to expand rapidly.

When a snapshot is taken, Mechanic Miner will consider whether the snapshot's state of the game is *old* or *new*. There are two conditions to be met that make a game state *old*. Another state must already have been seen before which is identical to the current snapshot within some preset resolution. For Mechanic Miner this means comparing all the game state data like the player's position, velocity or acceleration and seeing if they are less than a certain delta from each previous state. If any states are found that are similar, the second condition is checked. The second condition is that the move history of the current snapshot must be subsumed by this older state. In other words, if it was possible to reach this game state with a subset of the moves that were already made, then the snapshot is not considered new. Otherwise, it gets added to the state list for consideration.

So if the player moves left, then right, then left again, it will eventually reach places that it reached before simply by moving left. If it notices that the game is in the same state it was previously, and it got there by using fewer buttons, it won't bother adding a new game state to the list.

Additionally, Mechanic Miner may also check if a state is *legal*. Mechanic Miner checks that no exceptions have been thrown, for example, to catch cases where mechanics are generated that crash the underlying game engine. This would also be a place to add checks for mechanics which enable the player to leave the level boundaries, or other undesired effects.

Mechanic Miner will keep taking snapshots and simulating the current move's button presses until no progress is being made. This is assessed by comparing snapshots against other snapshots taken for this move set. If the system reaches a snapshot that has already been taken for this move set, it assumes that the move set is no longer changing things in the game (perhaps the player is running into a wall, or stuck in a loop of jumping) and Mechanic Miner stops considering this move. It then moves on to simulate other move sets in the list until no more are left, and then continues onto the next state in the state list.

If, when simulating a move, the player reaches the objective—in our case, they overlap with the exit object represented by the wrapped Christmas present—the state is considered to be successful, and the move history of the current state is recorded as a solution to the level. At this point, Mechanic Miner can exit, or it can continue searching for other solutions.

The algorithm can be seen in action by considering the following game mechanic, generated by the system:

player.acceleration.y *= -1;

Below you can see an annotated version of the testing level, showing the four stages of using this mechanic to solve it.

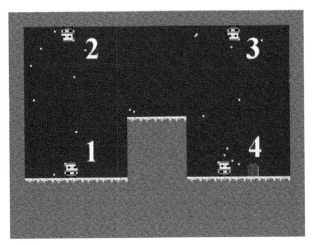

1 shows the starting point of the level, with Santa standing on the left-hand side of the wall in the middle of the level. This is the initial state that Mechanic Miner begins with. Its move set includes things like running left or right, which end with Santa running into walls and making no progress. Santa can also jump, which also inevitably ends in reaching a wall or simply jumping in place. This takes a while to exhaustively search, however, because there are many different combinations and directions to run and jump in, which Mechanic Miner has to explore.

Eventually, Mechanic Miner will try apply a move which includes pressing the button for the mechanic defined above. In the game engine used to build the system, Adam Saltsman's *Flixel*, the acceleration vector is used to simulate gravity acting on an object. By setting the value to be positive in the y direction, an object is gradually pulled downwards. The mechanic being simulated here multiplies the player's acceleration by a negative number, effectively flipping its gravity from down to up, and vice versa. 2 shows the position of the player after applying the mechanic once.

Once in this position, the system can now expand the state to explore new areas of the level. Moving right and left while gravity is pulling the player upwards allows Santa to walk on the ceiling of the level, eventually reaching the position shown by point 3.

Applying the mechanic to the player again flips gravity back to its original direction, pulling the player downwards to point 4. At this point the level is complete, as the player has reached the exit.

As stated earlier, by reaching the exit in this level Mechanic Miner can identify the mechanic as something that provides *utility* to the player, and does not crash the game. It enabled the player to get over a very specific type of obstacle—in this case, a physical obstruction blocking normal movement—and reach an objective.

MINED GEMS

What is a system like Mechanic Miner capable of discovering? This chapter began by arguing that by giving a generative system more freedom in its search space the end result would be a system that was stronger in a creative sense, more capable of surprise and novelty. This chapter has already given an example of a mechanic discovered by the system—a gravity inverting mechanic similar to that used in games like Terry Cavanagh's *VVVVVV* (Cavanagh, 2009). This mechanic was an expected discovery by the system, however—Ritchie calls this the *inspiring set*, a list of examples that were anticipated when the system was being designed. What did the system find that was new?

Some of the generated mechanics highlight the issue with using utility alone as a game mechanic. Consider the following mechanic:

player.jumpHeight += 200;

The above mechanic, and ones with similar effects, were commonly found by the software. While this technically fulfills the utility criteria and helps the player solve the level, it isn't a very interesting result because it primarily extends an already existing mechanic (that of jumping). As Nijman (2013) states, "you must give the player a reason not to press a button." In the case of extending the player's jump height, there's simply no reason not to have it enabled at all times. A technically functional mechanic, but not an interesting one.

Let's look at a more interesting example. This mechanic was generated by the system and met with skepticism initially, as it wasn't clear what its function was:

player.elasticity += 1;

The elasticity is a little-used property of objects in the *Flixel* game engine that affects how they react to collisions. The higher the elasticity of an object, the more it bounces in response to being collided with. The mechanic above allows the player to slowly gain height by repeatedly bouncing in place. This eventually allows them to bounce over the obstruction in the testing level and reach the exit. The elasticity discovery is notable because the designers of Mechanic Miner had not encountered this property before despite using the *Flixel* engine for over two years at the time of building the system. This is a good example of how the system was able to look beyond the gaps in the knowledge of its programmer, and find new concepts that would not have otherwise been uncovered.

The final example to show from Mechanic Miner offers perhaps the most compelling argument for how code generation can lead to surprise, novelty, and maybe even a step towards greater creativity. The following mechanic was generated by the system:

    player.x += 70;

This mechanic was labeled "teleportation." It's an everyday mechanic in most games, and not especially innovative or creative on the face of it—instead, it's the way the mechanic is applied by the system that makes it so interesting. Let's reconsider the illustration of the testing level again.

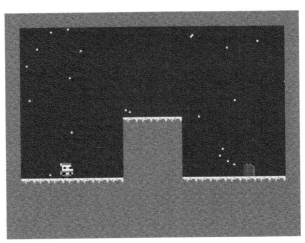

The teleportation distance isn't far enough to simply teleport past the wall as you might expect. Teleporting for that distance leaves Santa stuck in the wall blocks, unable to move. So it's not clear on first look that this mechanic is useful *at all*. Mechanic Miner claims that the mechanic solves this level, though. What's going on?

To understand how this mechanic works, let's look at another piece of code—not written by software though, but by Mechanic Miner's designers. This is the code written into the base game to control what happens when the player tries to jump:

    if(isTouching(FlxObject.FLOOR)){
    velocity.y = -jumpPower;
    }

When the player presses the jump button, the game checks if the player is touching the floor. If they are, the game adds a value to their velocity, pushing them up in the air. The floor check is to ensure that the player can't jump while in the air—this is the only check the game makes.

Remember that Mechanic Miner's simulator doesn't use any particular heuristic to guide its search through the game level. It tries to use everything at its disposal to reach the exit. By doing this, Mechanic Miner discovered the following exploit: jumping and teleporting while in the air can leave Santa stuck in the side of a wall. In most games, this might be considered a glitch, or a bug, and might even leave the player stranded. But there's a bug in the human-written code shown above. If the player is stuck in a wall, they can still jump, because they're touching the floor. Mechanic Miner uses this to jump out of the wall, and then teleport back inside the wall higher up. Using this trick repeatedly—jump out of the wall, teleport back inside—it discovers it can climb up any wall height. It uses this technique to climb over the wall in the testing level and reach the exit.

This last example is interesting not because the mechanic discovered by the system is immediately compelling or exciting, but because the exhaustive nature of the testing process combines with the freedom of the reflective mechanic designer to reveal emergent properties of these mechanics. Ultimately, the mechanic discovered by the system is not really teleportation—it's wall climbing. The emergent nature of this discovery is an exciting indicator of a future in which systems like Mechanic Miner are free to modify and test their own codebases and creatively experiment with what results.

CONCLUSIONS

Games are "experiences created by rules" according to the quote from Anna Anthropy with which this chapter began. One can find where creativity resides in the game design process in many places, but in terms of what makes games unique it is the systems and rules which form a game's foundation that are most important. Software already helps out in so many aspects of game production, from QA and testing through to generating random content—but can software be trusted to take on creative responsibility in the design of games, in crucial areas like the design of game mechanics?

This chapter explored ways in which that might be made possible. It discussed basic approaches to procedural generation, and how they are lacking in areas that are important when it comes to evaluating creativity—properties such as eliciting surprise and being able to contribute novel output. It showed the progress of a system called ANGELINA, and how its early attempts to generate mechanics were stymied by an overreliance on hand-designed content and helpful restrictions. In the end, though, this chapter showed how increased freedom and careful evaluation techniques can lead a less stable system to make great discoveries—it described Mechanic Miner, a system which was given complete freedom to change any aspect of a game's codebase in the search for game mechanics, but avoided producing broken output by evaluating its output through play-testing. This approach of directly manipulating code freed the system up to surprise its creators, and discover emergent properties in the codebase of the game it was modifying.

There are many exciting problems immediately adjacent to the work described in this chapter. Can Mechanic Miner be expanded so that it can write longer pieces of its own program code, with complex effects on different parts of the game? This would allow the system to develop more intricate game mechanics that are rooted more deeply in the game's systems, rather than identifying simple game variables to modify directly. Could a system like Mechanic Miner propose new types of game object on the fly and then develop mechanics pertaining to these objects? Currently, the system is only capable of modifying the game's systems as they already exist. A system that could generate new types of object could invent new game systems, and as a result would have a much wider range of possible outputs.

Perhaps the most interesting questions posed by systems like Mechanic Miner, though, relate not to the cold truths of "game feel" and puzzle solving, but the role of mechanics in conveying meaning that this chapter began by discussing. The techniques described in this chapter are extremely disconnected from the semantics of the mechanics produced—What does it mean for Santa to be able to invert gravity? Why do players connect Super Mario's consumption of mushrooms with an increase in power? Giving systems like Mechanic Miner an understanding of the real world, so that it can develop mechanics which relate to real-world concepts and convey interesting ideas, might be the biggest challenge of all. The reward for building such a system would be a generative system unlike any other in video games—a system that demonstrates creative strength in both the technical design of game systems, and the artistic decision making of building meaning into games. The route to building such a system, as with the construction of Mechanic Miner, will surely come through greater freedom, and fewer restrictions—an approach best served through direct interaction with code.

References

Amanita Design. (2009). *Machinarium*. Daedalic Entertainment.
Amanita Design. (2012). *Botanicula*. Daedalic Entertainment.
Anthropy, A. (2012). *Rise of the videogame zinesters: How freaks, normals, amateurs, artists, dreamers, dropouts, queers, housewives, and people like you are taking back an art form*. New York: Seven Stories Press.
Bioware. (2009). *Dragon age*. Electronic Arts.
Cavanagh, T. (2009). *VVVVVV*. Distractionware.
Colton, S., Cook, M., Hepworth, R., & Pease, A. (2014). On acid drops and teardrops: Observer issues in computational creativity. In *50th Convention on artificial intelligence and simulation of behaviour*.

Colton, S., & Wiggins, G. (2012). *Computational creativity: The final frontier?* In *20th European conference on artificial intelligence.*

Cook, M., & Colton, S. (2011). Multi-faceted evolution of simple arcade games. In *Computational intelligence and games.*

Cook, M., Colton, S., & Gow, J. (2012). Initial results from co-operative co-evolution for automated platformer design. *Applications of Evolutionary Computation Lecture Notes in Computer Science, 7248,* 194–203.

Eigenfeldt, A., Burnett, A., & Pasquier, P. (2012). Evaluating musical metacreation in a live performance context. In *3rd International conference on computational creativity.*

From Software. (2011). *Dark souls.* Namco Bandai Games.

Gearbox Software. (2009). *Borderlands.* 2K Games.

Gray, K., Gabler, K., Shodhan, S., & Kucic, M. (2005). *How to prototype a game in under 7 days.* Gamasutra.

Hazelden, A. (2011). *By your side.* Ludum Dare Entry.

Meredith, K. (2004). *Middleware postmortem: IDV Inc's SpeedTreeRT.* Gamasutra.

Mojang. (2011). *Minecraft. Mojang.*

Mossmouth Games. (2011). *Spelunky.* Mossmouth Games.

Nijman, J. W. (2013). The art of screenshake. Talk at INDIGO game classes *2013.*

Nintendo. (1988). *Super Mario Bros. 3.* Nintendo.

Ritchie, G. (2007). Some empirical criteria for attributing creativity to a computer program. *Mind and Machines, 17*(1), 67–99.

Smith, A., & Mateas, M. (2010). Variations forever: Flexibly generating rulesets from a sculptable design space of mini-games. In *2nd Conference on computational intelligence in games.*

Togelius, J., Karakovskiy, S., & Baumgarten, R. (2009). The 2009 Mario AI competition. In *IEEE congress on evolutionary computation.*

thatgamecompany. (2012). *Journey.* Sony Computer Entertainment.

12

Patented Creativity: Reflecting on Video Game Patents

Casey O'Donnell

Department of Media and Information, Michigan State University,
East Lansing, MI, USA

OUTLINE

INTRODUCTION

Battles over patents are nothing new to technology-focused organizations and relatively common in the video game industry as well (Clapes, 1993). While patents are not equivalent to creativity, patents can be viewed as a metric by which to measure if an idea is "creative" enough to be worth protecting. Furthermore, by exploring what is *not* patented, you can examine what ideas are considered more or less valuable in a community. In the context of the video game industry and game development, patents serve a productive lens through which to understand creativity. In this entry, I look at a handful of patents surrounding digital and nondigital games as a means for better understanding what has historically counted as creativity in game development. Specifically, I examine video game technology-related patents, game mechanic patents, and nondigital game mechanic patents.

In this essay, I use patents, which are one means by which to protect intellectual property, as a stand-in for creativity. In particular, I am using it as a kind of metric for "big C" or "eminent creativity." As even the editors of this volume explore, there are numerous elements of creativity that fall outside what is patented or patentable (Kaufman and Beghetto, 2009), which I acknowledge. However, it does offer insight into what is valued at an organizational level in terms of creatively produced intellectual property. One of the difficult aspects of creativity is to identify it in a broad system like the video game industry, and patents serve for the sake of this chapter as a kind of creativity proxy. The fact that so much creativity is left on the cutting room floor in this process is precisely one reason why I feel taking this approach is interesting. So much of everyday creativity falls outside these lines, and yet the broader political-economy the video game industry is situated in demands a particular emphasis on the "big C."

By examining the developments—i.e. controllers, console designs, and game mechanics—viewed as worthy of protection via patents, an interesting dynamic can be observed in the video game industry. While developers of nondigital games more frequently patent game mechanics, mechanics within video games are very rarely patented. A classic example is the series of patents that surround the board game *Monopoly*. At the same time, the technologies that surround and scaffold video games are frequently subject to a variety of intellectual property rights protections. Two such examples are the visual design of a game console or the functionality of the hardware making up the device. This difference between digital and nondigital games is interesting and worth further exploration.

In this essay, I argue that while the video game industry has largely benefited from a rather lackadaisical approach to game mechanic protection, there is little reason to presume that this will remain the case. The impetus behind not patenting game mechanics is more of historical legacy rather than any set of institutional or professional logics. Much like other technology sectors that arose from the early days of the computer software industry in the United States, early video game development companies focused on hardware design and development. It wasn't until significantly later that game mechanic patents became more commonplace.

TECHNOLOGY

Most frequently, video game-related patents cover the technologies associated with video game distribution. They range from the obvious to the arcane. In some cases, without specific references from documentation accompanying a game technology, it would be difficult to identify these documents as having anything to do with video games. The patent battleground has become increasingly heated over the years. Numerous litigations over access and the right to produce and distribute games have found patent law to be their battleground.

Given that "design" is one of the major factors associated with creativity in video game development, it might even make sense that the video game industry has largely inverted the broader norm that most patents are "utility" patents. "Design" patents stand on even footing (or even dominate) the holdings of video game companies intellectual property, or "IP," portfolios. Nearly every aspect of a video game console makes its way into one or more design patents; even elements of a game console that may never make its way to the consumer market. Controllers, cartridges, consoles, networking devices, peripherals, and numerous other items make their way into design patents and in some cases there may be associated utility patents as well.

Design patents, outside of the context of video games, are less common than utility patents. However, in the context of games, the numbers are quite similar. Design patents cover the appearance of a particular object. They are meant to protect a particular visual esthetic. Utility patents, on the other hand, are meant to cover some sort of useful device, process, mechanic, or method. For example, it would be impossible to patent a chair; however, a design patent could be applied for covering a particularly unique chair design.

Most commonly, amongst video game patents, design patents cover the appearance of game consoles or controllers. The readily identifiable characteristics of game consoles are part of the technology's branding and as such are closely protected. Design patents are the most readily identifiable video game patents. Even as early as the Atari VCS, as can be seen in Figure 1, the visual form of game consoles has been protected and viewed as an important element of the creative work of the game industry.

Most consoles carry with them a series of associated design patents. These same images may also be present in associated utility patents, but the assumption that these devices are specifically esthetically designed to

FIGURE 1   The Atari VCS in patent. *Hardy and Thompson (1977).*

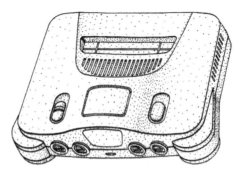

FIGURE 2   The Nintendo 64 (N64) in patent. *Ashida (1995).*

differentiate themselves is clear. The distinctive curves of the Nintendo 64, as can be seen in Figure 2, which separated it clearly from its much more angular competitors in the Playstation and Sega Saturn, were viewed as a strategic differentiator of the device.

Console enthusiasts can even find variants on possible peripherals or other devices that never made it to market throughout a console game system's lifespan. Roads not taken are ubiquitous in the realm of video game patents. Of course, these design patents are actually the least interesting in terms of providing insight into what counts as innovative or creative design. The fact that the majority of utility patents associated with video games focus largely on mechanisms for controlling copy protection and production control is important to note. As one delves into these patents it becomes clear that this is part of a large set of technological and legal machinations that underlie the console game industry.

Video game controllers have been the focus of some of the most contentious patents associated with video games, which may not be all that surprising since the video game's ability to respond to the user and provide an intuitive and robust interface are a critical element of game design and development. Also, video game consoles have fought to not rely on more complex forms of user interaction, such as the keyboard and mouse. Joysticks and various forms of controllers with an array of buttons, nobs, triggers, and other elements have attempted to simplify and clarify the way users interact with the devices. Thus, when exploring what counts as creativity for interacting with the user, custom controllers have dominated. This is also the ground upon which the majority of patent battles have been waged.

While most game players now take the "Directional Pad" or "D-Pad" as quite common, the ability for a directional input device to provide a variety of signals to an underlying game system, as opposed to a single direction, was an innovation. Not particularly identifiable, given the profile of the image, the four-way cross of the now ubiquitous D-Pad (Figure 3) can be traced back to early patent filings by Nintendo.

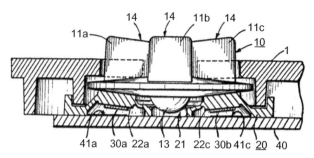

FIGURE 3 The iconic "D-Pad" in patent. *Shirai (1985).*

Controller patents often have a significant number of utility patents also associated with them because of the kind of complexity associated with implementing these systems. These documents detail the underlying implementations as a means of protecting those innovations as competitors move to imitate them in future wars over the marketplace. As such, these documents serve to both protect internally developed IP, but also to spell out for competitors that other means were found to implement similar desired input mechanisms.

As such, as can be seen in Figure 4, this means that increasing amounts of detail are provided. Callouts indicate the variety of elements being discussed and coordinated in the design and creation of input devices. This is often where the distinction between "design" patents and utility patents begins to collapse. Controllers offer a variety of mechanisms between which the user and the underlying game systems can interact. For many years, the controller was the heart of creativity for game companies, combined with the ever-increasing computational devices that they are attached to. The Nintendo Wii serves as an excellent example of how creativity around user input featured over mild increases in the computational capacity of a video game console.

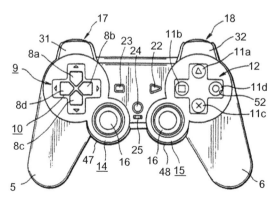

FIGURE 4 The Playstation 1 controller in patent. *Goto and Ogata (1998).*

3. CREATIVITY AND VIDEO GAME DEVELOPMENT

Controls, or buttons, are just one element of this interaction. Increasingly the devices not only receive data, but also transmit game-based data to the player. One of the more intensely litigated was the notion of "force feedback," or variable vibrating systems within controllers. These subsystems within systems create an army of patents that accompany input devices. Force-feedback and more "analog" systems, such as buttons that provide a degree of pressure sensitivity, become increasingly commonplace.

One of the better-known cases of patent litigation amongst game console manufacturers was first fought outside the court, between the companies Immersion and Microsoft, who had recently released force-feedback mechanisms in their Xbox console controller. Microsoft settled the case out of court. Sony, on the other hand, when sued by Immersion, chose to fight the case. Immersion argued that the "Dual-Shock" controller used by both the Playstation (PS1) and Playstation 2 (PS2) violated their force-feedback patents.

Nintendo was notably absent from this litigation battle, for a variety of reasons. Their force-feedback patents were filed roughly at the same time as Immersion's. However, there was not only a difference in how vibrations were being generated, but also in the relationship between those mechanisms and the underlying software of the game system. In Sony's patents, they had failed to establish a connection or "system of exploiting" the vibrations with the content contained within a game (Figure 5).

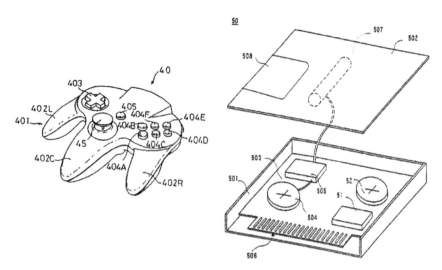

FIGURE 5 The force-feedback system of the Nintendo 64's "Rumble Pack," in patent. *Nishiumi, Koshima, and Nonaka (2001).*

Nintendo, on the other hand, had included these elements in their patent application. Ultimately, Sony's defense failed and Immersion was awarded damages:

> In brief, Immersion prevailed at trial on certain of its claims that Sony's Playstation consoles and Dualshock controllers, in conjunction with 44 accused games, infringed US Patent Nos. 6,275,213 and 6,424,333, owned by Immersion. The jury found that the asserted claims of Immersion's patents were not invalid due to anticipation, obviousness, or inadequate written description. The jury awarded Immersion 82 million dollars as a reasonable royalty for Sony's infringement. The Court later found in favor of Immersion on Sony's inequitable conduct defense and denied Sony's motions for judgment as a matter of law. Sony has appealed the judgment against it. *Sony Computer Entertainment Corporation, 2007*

In this example, more information is known, because the case went to trial. More often than not, cases are settled out of court. What is most interesting, however, is the independently developed technologies that do not trigger litigation. Nintendo, in particular, patents numerous technologies and rarely seems to pursue legal action when similar technologies come later. Nintendo seems to use patents as a means for IP protection, rather than as an offensive mechanism for making money (as Immersion did).

An example of this can be found in relation to the "3D Joystick" found in the controller of the Nintendo 64 (N64) game console. In this patent, Nintendo was relating the angle and degree of pressure placed on an analog joystick to the degree and speed of movement of an object in space. Simply imagine the relation between the N64's controller and Mario's movement in Super Mario 64 for illustration. Anyone who as played a 3D game on a modern console using analog joysticks will recognize this patent applies widely to 3D third-person platforming games (Figure 6).

> The system further includes direction-determining circuitry operable to determine a direction that corresponds to an inclination direction of the operating member based on the inclination amount data, and moving object direction-determining circuitry which determines a moving direction of the object in three-dimensional space based upon the direction determined by the direction-determining circuitry and a point of view angle at which the object is being viewed by the operator in three-dimensional space. *Nishiumi, Koshima, Miyamoto, and Nishida (2005)*.

One can only guess as to why Nintendo takes this particular approach to IP protection, but as can be seen in how game developers broadly view patents as they relate to game development, the perspective makes sense.

The final area where significant patent activity takes place relates to content distribution. While clearly most software and games are broadly protected by copyright regulation, it is also interesting to note that frequently those efforts are combined with a variety of patents that also relate to how games are distributed.

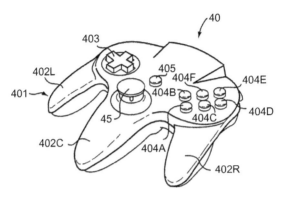

FIGURE 6   The Nintendo 64's 3D joystick in patent. *Nishiumi, Koshima, Miyamoto, and Nishida (2005).*

Both design and utility patents are often combined to make unauthorized reproduction and distribution of game content more difficult. Cartridges are designed specifically to prevent unauthorized games from being played (Figure 7).

Frequently these devices also make use of "cutting edge" technologies that are expensive, which makes it financially unfeasible for many consumers to even consider circumventing these mechanisms. Even when "traditional" technologies are leveraged, like the PS1's use of the "standard CD-ROM" as distribution medium, additional mechanisms are used to ensure the safety of game content. To these ends, though difficult to discern,

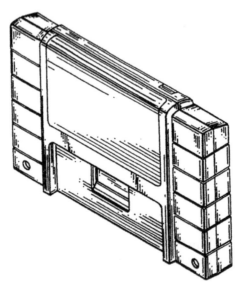

FIGURE 7   The Super Nintendo's cartridge in patent. *Inoue and Ota (1993).*

3. CREATIVITY AND VIDEO GAME DEVELOPMENT

the PS1 made use of encoding a "wobble" on CD-ROM media that would otherwise be difficult to reproduce (Akiyama et al., 2001). These same mechanisms are often used to enforce a wide array of product distribution rules, like region "locking" of devices (1).

Of course, both copy protection and the verification of "authentic" game media is nothing new to the video game industry. However, it is important to note that the content of the games, outside of their ability to interface with and interact with the various technologies, is not the focus of these efforts. Video games themselves and the underlying systems they contain are frequently not the subject of patents. However, there are a handful of notable exceptions, which will now be explored.

GAME MECHANIC PATENTS

Game developers have less frequently pursued patents on game mechanics. While the definition of game mechanic is widely discussed by game scholars (Salen and Zimmerman, 2004; Sicart, 2008), for the sake of this chapter, a game mechanic can be thought of as the system through which a player interacts with a game. Games often have a variety of mechanics. For example, rolling dice in a game of Monopoly is a mechanic that is linked to the movement of the game piece on the board. Most video game mechanic patents are critically linked to underlying technological elements. Put another way, in the majority of cases, even when a game mechanic is patented, it often has close ties to a technological development as well. It is possible that game companies have pursued software patents on abstract technologies, but that same reasoning has largely not been explored as it relates to how games interface with players.

There are, of course, a handful of game mechanic patents in existence. There has also been significant commentary on the part of game developers on how potentially damaging the widespread patenting of game mechanics might be. The most frequently cited example is a game mechanic patent, which amongst other claims was meant to assist players in driving games by offering a constantly updating arrow indicating their next goal. The mechanic was added because rather than keeping players on a single road, they could travel through a relatively open roadway system (Figure 8).

In this patent, virtual arrows, within the world, direct the player where to go. This patent was applied in a variety of arcade games including ones like *Crazy Taxi*. In particular, this component of the patent looked to:

> In the case that the free drive in the town is enabled, the game players might be lost, and it is necessary to indicate to the game players directions to destinations. In this case easily understandable direction indications are necessary.

> ...

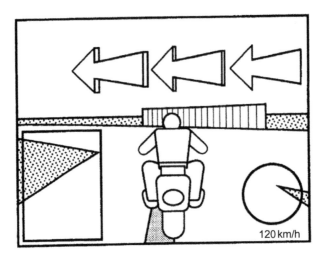

FIGURE 8   Helpful directional arrows for drivers in an open world in patent. *Ando et al. (1998).*

> [D]isplaying arrows which are directed from the direction-indicating positions to the destination being displayed and are not dependent on positional relationships between the direction-indicating positions and the movable object when the movable object comes near to the direction-indicating positions, whereby a moving direction for the movable object to move on is indicated. *Ando et al. (1998).*

The holder of this particular patent, Sega, Inc., actually did pursue legal recourse against several companies that produced driving games that used the in-game direction suggestions, though most of those cases were settled out of court. Yet, many games now use similar game mechanics, despite the fact that this patent is ostensibly still in effect.

Often these examples are used to argue that all game mechanic patents are not just poor work on the part of the patent office, but rather a real risk to the future health of game development (2). There are examples such as "What if DEVELOPER X had patented the first-person shooter?" Of course "DEVELOPER X" would be difficult to identify, though often Id Software, the developers of *Wolfenstein 3D*, will be offered, debatably, as a likely candidate. On the one hand, such a statement is saying we wouldn't have all these first-person shooter games if the mechanic had been patented. However, on the other hand, those same people may likely lament the dominance of the genre of first-person shooters within the broader game industry.

Thus, it is possible that more innovative game mechanics would have come about if developers had been forced to explore new game mechanics, though many would have likely just licensed those patents as part of

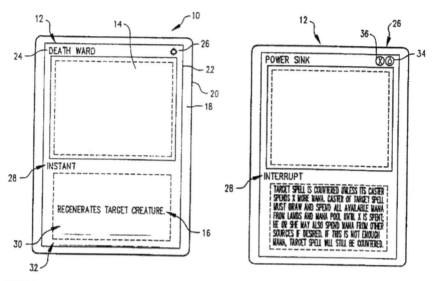

FIGURE 9 *Magic: The Gathering* cards in patent. *Garfield (1997).*

a new-found development process. It is also important to think about the role that prior art would play in this process as well. While mechanics might not be patented, their existence would protect future developers from being penalized from using those approaches.

If you extend the frame of analysis outside digital games, patents are actually much more common. For example, one of the most successful collectable trading card games (CCGs) of the last 20 years, *Magic: The Gathering (M:tG)*, is protected by its own set of patents (Garfield, 1997). These documents were even further refined as the game grew and changed over time (Figure 9).

Despite the fact that *M:tG* was early to the field of collectable trading card games, they demonstrated the power of the market. Of course, this didn't prevent other players from entering the market as well, they simply had to do it differently (Figure 10). Only a few short years later, Nintendo (also a long-time player in the nondigital game realm) had acquired patents related to their collectable trading card game, *Pokémon*.

This contrasts markedly with the broad realm of patents that cover nondigital games. Patents are used to protect a variety of nondigital game mechanics, ranging from card games to board games to tile-based games. The board game Monopoly, in particular, has a long history of patents associated with the game. Thus, while it is possible that game mechanic patents could have a significantly negative effect on video game development, many toy and nondigital game companies have thrived, despite a heavy emphasis on protecting intellectual property via patents.

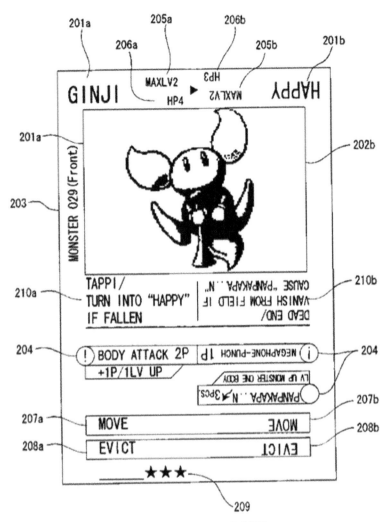

FIGURE 10   *Pokémon* cards in patent. *Sakamoto et al. (2000).*

One cannot patent card games. There is simply too much prior art. Turn-based games have been commonplace for years both in the digital and nondigital realms. Game mechanic patents tend to be highly context specific. They must demonstrate specifically how they are innovative or different and how the underlying systems of a game make use of those innovations. While software patents are often much more vague and use language to make themselves overly vague, game mechanic patents seem to be much more specific. Even within the patent documents of *M:tG*, the link to those historical elements are called out, in order to demonstrate what this new innovation is doing precisely that is worthy of patenting.

> Trading cards are a well-known method of disbursing and collecting information about public figures. A familiar type of trading card is the baseball card that has a photographic depiction of an athlete along with biological and statistical information about the athlete. These baseball cards and other cards dealing with various sports figures are used by sports enthusiasts for gathering information about players and teams. Trading cards have also been developed in other areas, such as the entertainment industry, which depict music performers and television and movie personalities.

> Trading cards are typically exchanged among enthusiasts to obtain cards that are needed to complete a set of related cards to collect cards that are not readily available. *Garfield (1997).*

What made *M:tG* innovative was its marriage of trading cards and playing cards in a new and interesting way. Of course players of the game would be quick to point out that there are numerous game mechanics that also make the game interesting, engaging, and innovative. These are all discussed and described in the patent documents.

Many board game developers actively discuss what are reasonable ways to protect their intellectual property, discussing the range of possible approaches from trademarks and copyrights to patents. Video game developers, and "indie" or independent developers in particular, have been actively critical of patents as a reasonable approach to the protection of their work. However, given the rapid growth of "cloning" in the mobile space, it is possible that developers may view game mechanics differently now than they did previously.

Highlighting the distinction between game mechanic patents and technology patents indexes an important shift within the broader game industry. For the first 30 years of the video game industry, it was technology that drove innovation and counted as creativity. More recently, however, the importance of new technology is still prevalent, but innovation in terms of a game's underlying mechanics has increasingly been cited as critical to its success. Technology was worthy of protection, while game mechanics were important only insofar as they connected with those technologies.

CONCLUSION

While it could be viewed that I am making an argument *for* game mechanic patents, that would be a weak reading of this entry. Rather, I am arguing for viewing game mechanic patents as something distinctly different from software patents. Software patents have by and large been viewed as significantly problematic, if not dangerous, for the software industry. However, while game mechanics are often critically linked to the underlying software of a game, they are different. I have argued elsewhere that video games are not "just" software, they are an assemblage of software, design, and a variety of artistic art assets (O'Donnell, 2012). To view game mechanic patents as interchangeable with any other form of patent does a disservice to the amount of creativity that goes into their creation.

A handful of developers have discussed at length the amount of time and labor that goes into developing even what some might deem relatively "simple" game mechanics. Further, some of the very developers who have been the victims of intellectual property theft or cloning have also been critical of patents as a reasonable approach to protecting intellectual property.

In this entry I use patents as means of exploring what has historically been valued as creativity in the video game industry. Increasingly, technology is only one aspect of that creativity. That isn't to say that game mechanics need to be patented in order to count as valuable intellectual property. Rather, patents tell us what the broader political-economic context of the video game industry has valued and I contrast that with the growing view that innovations and creativity in the development of game mechanics are precisely where the game industry has room for significant growth.

NOTES

(1) I have argued elsewhere that it was the video game industry's success at implementing these kinds of efforts (O'Donnell, 2011) that led other industries to pursue them as well (O'Donnell, 2009). Copyright protection is often simultaneously production protection.

(2) While I might personally agree with this line of argument, it is important to recognize that outside of the context of the video game industry there are many patents related to games and game mechanics that have not hamstrung those industries.

References

Akiyama, Y., Iimura, S., Ogawa, H., Kuroda, K., Suzuki, T., Inoue, A., et al. (2001). *Optical recording and/or reproducing apparatus using wobble signals detected from a groove and pit signals detected from pits on the recording medium to control recording and/or reproducing.* U.S. Patent No. 6430133, Washington, DC: U.S. Patent and Trademark Office.

Ando, T., Tsukamoto, K., Yamaguchi, T., Takasugi, T., Ito, M., & Goi, T. (1998). *Game display method, moving direction indicating method, game apparatus and drive simulating apparatus.* U.S. Patent No. 6200138 B1, Washington, DC: U.S. Patent and Trademark Office.

Ashida, K. (1995). *Game cartridge.* U.S. Patent No. U.S. Patent No. D376795, Washington, DC: U.S. Patent and Trademark Office.

Clapes, A. L. (1993). *Softwars: The legal battles for control of the global software industry.* Westport, CT: Quorum Books.

Garfield, R. C. (1997). Trading Card Game Method of Play. US Patent No. 5,662,332. Washington, DC: US Patent and Trademark Office.

Goto, T. & Ogata, H. (1998). Operating Device for Game Machine. US Patent No. 6231444. Washington, DC: US Patent and Trademark Office.

Hardy, D. A. & Thompson, F. W. (1977). Game Control Console. US Patent No. D251143 S. Washington, DC: US Patent and Trademark Office.

Immersion Corporation & Sony Computer Entertainment. (2007). Immersion Corporation v. Sony Computer Entertainment America, Inc and Sony Computer Entertainment, Inc.

Inoue, Y. & Ota, M. (1993). Cartridge for Video Game Machine. US Patent No. D355414. Washington, DC: US Patent and Trademark Office.

Kaufman, J. C., & Beghetto, R. A. (2009). Beyond big and little: The four C model of creativity. *Review of General Psychology*, 13(1), 1–12.

Nishiumi, S., Koshima, K., Miyamoto, S., & Nishida, Y. (2005). User Controlled Graphics Object Movement Based on a Amount of Joystick Angular Rotation and Point of View Angle. US Patent No. 7102618. Washington, DC: US Patent and Trademark Office.

Nishiumi, S., Koshima, K., & Nonaka, N. (2001). Video Game System Providing Physical Sensation. US Patent No. 6676520. Washington, DC: US Patent and Trademark Office.

O'Donnell, C. (2009). Production protection to copy(right) protection: From the 10NES to DVDs. *IEEE Annals of the History of Computing*, 31(3), 54–63.

O'Donnell, C. (2011). The Nintendo Entertainment System and the 10NES chip: Carving the videogame industry in silicon. *Games and Culture*, 6(1), 83–100.

O'Donnell, C. (2012). This is not a software industry. In P. Zackariasson & T. L. Wilson (Eds.), *The video game industry: Formation, present state and future* (pp. 17–33). New York: Routledge.

Sakamoto, Y., Furuta, N., Imai, K., Suzuki, H., Katayama, M., Kishi, K., et al. (2000). Card Game Toy for Use in a Battle game. US Patent No. 6601851. Washington, DC: US Patent and Trademark Office.

Salen, K., & Zimmerman, E. (2004). *Rules of play: Game design fundamentals*. Cambridge, MA: MIT Press.

Shirai, I. (1985). Multi-directional Switch. US Patent No. 4687200. Washington, DC: US Patent and Trademark Office.

Sicart, M. (2008). Defining game mechanics. *Game Studies*, 8(2).

Tension and Opportunity: Creativity in the Video Gaming Medium

Grant Tavinor

Faculty of Environment, Society and Design, Lincoln University,
Lincoln, New Zealand

THE STRUCTURAL TENSIONS IN VIDEO GAME WORKS

As a significant recent development within the arts, it is natural to consider video games in terms of the philosophical and psychological theories developed to account for traditional art forms and the practices involved in their creation (Tavinor, 2009a, p. 10). While creativity might seem a principally psychological phenomenon, indispensable considerations in the understanding of creativity in an artistic medium are the materials and techniques available to artists. Creativity in game design, as in other creative artistic endeavors, does not generate novelty from whole cloth, but draws on the formal and material potential, and also the constraints and complications, embodied within a historically evolving artistic medium. This chapter explores how the structural tensions and complications within video games provide opportunities for creative development within that medium.

Recent gaming history provides a vivid example of both the creativity of games and of how games manifest such internal tensions. *BioShock Infinite*, the 2013 follow-up to the 2007 first-person shooter *BioShock*, includes a profoundly satisfying story. It is also an immensely creative game. While it is beyond the scope of this essay to explain the game's narrative—especially the surprising and reflexive final scenes that I would not want to spoil for the reader—the end of the game is both dramatically rich and formally satisfying. It is so in a large part because of how it so adeptly engages the structural potential of the interactive video gaming medium, advancing it in creative ways. The game ends on a philosophical note where the potential of the video gaming medium to trace paths through unique narrative space allows for reflection on the free will, perhaps illusory, that exists within both everyday life and game play.

And yet despite the extraordinary success of the narrative of *BioShock Infinite* some gaming critics discovered problems in the presentation of other aspects of the game. In particular, the abundant and graphic violence, attributable to the first-person shooter genre, struck some players and critics as out of keeping with the artistic aspirations so evident elsewhere in the game. The early scenes of *BioShock Infinite* are especially appealing for their beautiful and detailed presentation of the world of Columbia, a city in the clouds that is depicted with a great deal of verve and artistic color. The player's early exploration of the environment hints at the political and social tensions within this world but it is a largely peaceful experience that succeeds in establishing the tone of philosophical mystery and wonder that pervades the game. This tone changes abruptly, however, with an eruption of shocking and graphic violence, and following this a desperate and violent protracted battle in which the player shoots and bludgeons his way through a long series of enemies.

Most players of the game are prepared for this eventuality—violent game play is an essential aspect of the genre within which *BioShock Infinite* exists—but the success of the esthetic aspirations of the initial sequence makes this tonal schism especially prominent, leading one to judge that the shock was precisely the effect intended. How one responds to the sudden interjection of violence in the game will largely owe to personal taste but it is evident that some players were dismayed by the violence. For example, in a widely read critical piece on the game, Chris Plante observed that his wife.

> [...] was excited to play BioShock Infinite, the new first-person shooter from the haloed developers Irrational Games. Her video game experiences are few, mostly the easy-to-play shorts made by *thatgamecompany*. But Infinite and its inescapable

ad campaign piqued her interest. A video game about American exceptionalism, religious zealotry, the limitations of science and poor parenting sounded to her like a great book or film. The first 15 minutes enthralled her, as she took the fantastic voyage into a city in the sky, and then protagonist Booker DeWitt buried a steel claw into a police officer's face, and proceeded to shot grapefruit sized holes into the heads of another dozen human beings. Plante (2013).

For some potential players, then, the sudden violence in the game will be distasteful and is likely to discourage further playing of the game. Some players might even think that yoking such an artistically promising scenario to the violence of the first-person genre is a lost opportunity and counts as a structural flaw inherent within the gaming medium.

My intention here is not to make judgments about the ethical propriety of the violence found within video games—even though I would probably be prepared to defend *BioShock Infinite* from its artistic critics—rather I simply want to identify the structural problem inherent in this example because of its potential to illustrate a feature of the creative processes involved in game design. The formal issue illustrated here is an instance of what has recently come to be known in games studies as "ludonarrative dissonance": that is, an apparent problem of internal coherence within a game that occurs where the structural features generated by game play—principally, the rules and objectives that drive game play—clash or contradict with those due to the narrative aspects of the game (Hocking, 2007). In the example here the dissonance occurs because of an uneasy fit of the extreme violence of *BioShock Infinite* with the artistic and philosophical tone of the game's narrative, but more generally this dissonance owes to the fact that gaming artifacts often betray *mixed artistic and ludic intentions*, and that the requirements of one function of the game artifact may actively subvert an alternative purpose. I will discuss several such cases later in this essay, but no doubt readers will be able to add their own additional examples of the clashing of the formal and representational elements of games. These functional contradictions are not restricted to inconsistencies between the game play and narrative aspects of games as in *BioShock Infinite*, but may also involve aspects of characterization and character development, cinematography, the representation of the space of a game world, the esthetic qualities through which the game world is rendered, and even the basic logical coherence of the fictional world of a game. Hence, ludonarrative dissonance seems to be a species of a more general kind of tension that sometimes exists between the various structural and formal aspects of video games.

It might seem from the forgoing that this issue is specific to game design, or entirely counts as a *difficulty* with the medium of gaming. But neither of these situations is the case, because firstly the existence of such formal tensions is quite common where an artistic work manifests a variety of formal, representational and imaginative artistic intentions, and where the artist hopes to produce an artistically coherent work from disparate elements. Secondly, far from necessarily counting as a fault within a medium, such conflicts often provide opportunities for artistic creativity within that medium. In the following sections, I will explore how such structural tensions provide opportunities for episodes of problem solving, the solutions to which count amongst the genuinely creative achievements in recent gaming.

A couple of brief notes on method will be useful here to situate this chapter within the wider creativity research literature. In their review of theories of creativity, Aaron Kozbelt and colleagues identify a distinction in creativity research between the "scientific" and "metaphorical" orientations (Kozbelt, Beghetto, & Runco, 2010, p. 21). They argue that each may have benefits for thinking about creativity and that both may be required to progress the field. Metaphorical approaches may seek to "provide alternative representations of creative phenomena" where scientific approaches have the "underlying goal of mapping the empirical reality of creative phenomenon" (2010, p. 21). I'm a philosopher of the arts, and I see much of what I do, here and elsewhere, as meeting the former metaphorical brief, particularly through applying to video games the conceptual frameworks that have been developed by philosophers for understanding the arts, and also by connecting video games to enduring problems within the philosophy of the arts. Though I will attempt to connect the issues here to the empirical psychological literature on creativity, much of this chapter will be composed of the criticism and interpretation of games, itself an activity that may have a creative function in video game design in identifying the design problems that sometimes prompt creative episodes.

Kozbelt and colleagues also note that a now familiar claim is that creativity can be assessed under different empirical schemas, sometimes known as the "'four P's of creativity': *process, product, person* (or personality), *place* (or press)" (2010, p. 24, italics in original). These differing schemas are characterized by the focal point they adopt toward creative activities, and each generates characteristically different methods and research questions. All are likely required for a global view of creativity, however. The current chapter focuses on creative products and, to some extent, the processes involved in the design of the products, particularly the design problems that provoke the creative episodes to which the products are responses. Partly, this reflects my orientation as a philosopher of the arts, where the *work* and *medium* are principal points of concern. But this focus also stems from my thesis that materials and medium are an indispensable consideration in the understanding of creativity in video gaming.

THE COMPLEXITY OF CREATIVE PRODUCTS

A signal example of the potential complexity of the mixed artistic and ludic intentions of video games is *Grand Theft Auto V*, a game so overstuffed with content that it defies easy comprehension and critical evaluation. As a representational artifact the game is simply enormous, comprising a three-dimensional fictional world the design of which is the focus of a great deal of originality. The enormity of *Grand Theft Auto V* is attributable not only to its vast fictional landscape, but also to the numerous game play, narrative, and artistic ambitions inherent in the game.

In terms of game play, the player can spend his or her time driving tow trucks, racing cars, walking a dog, mountain biking, fighting gun battles, stealing cars, performing hits and assassinations, conducting robberies and heists, hunting wildlife, flying aircraft, and outrunning cops and other adversaries. Much of this game play is structured into missions, but a significant portion of the game play of *Grand Theft Auto V* is occasioned by the free exploration of the open environment. This open-world fictional environment provides an easy means of combining all of these game play activities, in that the fiction of the game—the player is a protagonist in a game world crammed with opportunities for action—motivates and structures a diverse range of game play activities. As a result, the game is an extraordinarily fun and engaging experience, and like other instances of the open-world genre in which it exists, it gives the natural experience of stepping into a vivid fictional world (Tavinor, 2009a, pp. 61-85).

The complexity of the game is not restricted to this abundant game play content, because the game also presents a complex narrative. *Grand Theft Auto V* tells the story of three criminals whose paths wind around one another, allowing for the exploration of familiar cinematic tropes: Michael is trying to escape his former criminal life while dealing with its demons and ghosts; Frank is tired of his life in the ghetto and of the petty thuggery that he feels is holding him back from bigger things; Trevor is a meth cook who charges erratically and belligerently into insane criminal adventures. These stories are rendered in an optional mission format that may take the player 40 or so hours of gaming to complete; but while the narrative is reflected in the events that constitute game play missions and is experienced by the player through their fictional role as protagonist, significant portions of the narrative are also presented in a cinematic and non-interactive mode in the form of *cut-scenes* (Klevjer, 2014, pp. 301-309). During these cinematic sections of the game, the player's engagement switches to an imaginative and interpretative mode more characteristic of traditional media such as film. Moreover, while the interactive game play activities cohere around the agency of the protagonist, unfolding naturally through the player-directed activities, the narrative portions of *Grand Theft Auto V* are often structured more deliberately by engaging cinematic techniques such as scripted dialog, careful combinations of camera shots, background music, and choreographed action (Klevjer, 2014, p. 306). These factors lend an aspect of obligation to the narrative portions in the game in that the interactive potential of the fiction is temporarily subverted so that a determinate sequence of fictional events necessary to the narrative can be portrayed.

There is a great deal of incidental depictive content in *Grand Theft Auto V* that does not easily fit under either heading of game play or narrative, but which composes much of the flavor and thematic material of the game. For example, the game contains a great deal of sociological and cultural commentary that one can explore and interpret independently of the core game play and narrative. One theme that is explored in multiple ways throughout the game world is that of UFOs, extraterrestrial visitation, and conspiracy culture; much of this content is actually hidden throughout the world, and its presence, at first only rumored, was the subject of a great deal of online speculation. The eventual discovery of UFOs in the game world provided one of the more notable *Easter Eggs* in the game. The *Grand Theft Auto* series of games is famous for this kind of humorous sociological and cultural comment, and the presentation of the material in the game adds a rich interpretative dimension to the game.

Finally, *Grand Theft Auto V* is a profoundly satisfying audio-visual artifact and a great deal of its interest as a game resides in the success of its three-dimensional rendering of a varied and vivid fictional environment. Los Santos is a fictionalized version of the geographical area around Los Angeles, and contains virtual depictions of Downtown LA, Santa Monica, East LA, Hollywood and Beverly Hills, and further afield, the Inland Empire, the Mojave Desert, and the forests of the Central Coast and Big Sur. These areas are often represented with a striking effectiveness because of the artistic techniques now available to game design. Notable is the treatment of variations in light and atmosphere in the game world—including the changes due to a dynamic weather system and time of day—that allow the game to capture much of the characteristic look of the real geographical area, ranging from the opaque smog of the Los Angeles basin, the mist-diffused light of the Redwood forests of the Central Coast, to the clear shimmering heat of the Mojave Desert. Combined with the excellent architecture and environmental design, these artistic assets make *Grand Theft Auto V* a frequently beautiful work of art—driving in the desert at midnight a sudden thunderstorm is surprisingly visceral in its effect, giving an uncanny feeling of being amongst the clattering thunder and heavy drops of rain.

Not unexpectedly given the breadth of creative ambitions within the game, *Grand Theft Auto V* sometimes has difficulty in fitting these diverse depictive and artistic assets together into a coherent whole. First, the very ambition and scope of the game can simply be challenging from a critical perspective. When assessing whether *Grand Theft Auto V* is a successful or good game, one hardly knows where to begin: there is just so much to the game, and it has so many fictive, artistic and ludic features, that its overall success is difficult to gage. Of course, in lots of obvious ways it is a good game: it is often beautiful; the visuals capture a real and uncanny sense of Los Angeles and the American Southwest; it has engaging and exciting game play, interesting characters; and is simply a great deal of fun to explore and play. But the simplistic framing of whether *Grand Theft Auto V* is a "good game" disguises a complexity here in that one is instantly drawn to consider the various artistic and ludic assets for their individual virtues and note that these tend to stand and fall on their own merits. Indeed, the quality of the aspects of the game do vary: some of the narrative, for example, is quite juvenile, and the character Trevor frequently strays into a mere gratuitous caricature of a violent video game protagonist (though perhaps intentionally, as we will find).

These kinds of internal critical variations exist in other artistic media of course, but because of its complex ambitions *Grand Theft Auto V* also courts a range of what seem to be medium-specific tensions, particularly in how it reconciles the game play and narrative fictions presented. These specific tensions were also present in the game's predecessor, 2008's *Grand Theft Auto IV*, where a common critical complaint was that the sympathy encouraged in the narrative for the protagonist Niko Bellic was actually subverted by the violent activities the player-character had to perform during game play. In the narrative of the earlier game Niko's ostensible story is that of a man trying to escape his violent past by moving to America, but in practice Niko falls so easily into violence during the game play portions of the game—and he must do so if the player is to complete the game—that any real reflection on Niko's real character throughout the game should lead to the conclusion that he properly motivates disgust rather than sympathy. The interpretative significance of the game's fiction seems internally contradictory.

This case of ludonarrative dissonance owes to the varied functions of protagonists within video games. In the context of game play a player-character is foremost a functional shell that provides the player with an epistemic and agential game world proxy through which he or she fictionally acts within the world (Tavinor, 2009a, pp. 70-84). This character is experienced and controlled from a first-person imaginative perspective where players frequently consider *their own fictional activities* in the game world (even if, as in *Grand Theft Auto V*, the character is visually represented in the third person so that the proxy's visual perspective does not match with that of the player). In the context of the game play, these fictional activities are mostly generated by the rules and objectives of the game, and because of the themes of criminal violence that compose the game play within the open-world action genre, a significant proportion of the play within the *Grand Theft Auto* series is constituted by violent actions such as thefts, assaults, and murders. Moreover, the player is motivated, in the guise of a player-character protagonist, to perform these actions to meet the objectives of game play. In the context of the narrative of the game, however, a key role of the character—if not its principal role—is to serve the story, providing a target for an interpretive engagement where one is more likely to consider a character in a third-person perspective, querying the character's actions and motivations and judging the character's depicted qualities in the mode one is likely to in appreciating a film or novel. By having the character bear these two functions and their attendant interpretative modes, it is as if *Grand Theft Auto IV* requires the tacit interpretative separation of the game play and narrative fictions. Moreover, the two aspects of the fiction seem to be *quarantined* so that only partial inferences are warranted between game play and narrative episodes: the Niko seen in game play is *not quite* the Niko one experiences in the story sections. However, this implied separation can prove awkward for the reflective player and provides a strong source of ludonarrative dissonance that counts as a critical fault in the game.

The depiction of the protagonist within *Grand Theft Auto V* seems aware of this potential difficulty, and how the game deals with the tension provides one aspect of its genuine creative achievement. In a notable departure from the earlier game, *Grand Theft Auto V* provides the player with three protagonist roles to play, and that the player may freely switch between once they are unlocked by completing story missions. These protagonists engage in characteristically different activities within the missions that compose their narrative arcs. Michael's story is a domestic narrative where he deals with the tensions between his desire to maintain his family and the unwanted interruptions of his former criminal life; as a result, Michael's story motivates game play activities like yoga, dealing with the troubles of his family members, visiting various game world characters for nonviolent or noncriminal reasons, but also ultimately planning robberies and committing crimes. Frank's story, as one of a thug on the rise, involves activities characteristic of a gangster in the hood, including a lot of car theft and fast and reckless driving. Finally, the meth dealer Trevor clearly exists in the world as a conduit for the over-the-top violent and morally offensive action seen elsewhere in the open-world action genre. Indeed, when the player first steps into the role of Trevor after playing the early sections of the game as Michael and Frank, the violence comes as a sudden shock and establishes a very different tone in the game.

The availability of switching perspectives afforded by the multiple protagonists allows for a more consistent and narratively compelling depiction of a wide range of game play activities. Michael can now genuinely motivate the sympathy that was only so awkwardly elicited in the case of

Niko—and especially so given that so much of the disreputable behavior that Michael finds himself committing results from the actions or presence of the other protagonists. Moreover the game is able to convincingly deal with much of the extreme violence required by the criminal-themed game play by having this arise from the psychologically conflicted and explicitly morally worrisome character of Trevor. It is also this context that allows for the proper understanding of the most notorious scene in the game, where the player, in the guise of Trevor, is asked to perform acts of torture, including extracting teeth and electrocuting his victim. By arising out of the role of Trevor, who at times in the game seems like a knowing wink to the gratuitous violence of the genre of open-world action gaming, this game play activity is both coherently placed in the narrative and also allows more thoughtful players some reflection on the role of violence in the game. As a result the violence may not be quite so insidious or immoral as some players and critics initially suspected. It is likely that some players did find Trevor's portions of the game distasteful; but whatever the moral qualms about Trevor's activities, they do not pose the formal problem for the game's narrative that they would if they were combined with the rest of the game play into a single player-character role.

The inclusion of multiple protagonists within *Grand Theft Auto V* also provides opportunities for further creative uses of the medium: in particular, it allows missions to encompass a wider, more varied, and subsequently more interesting range of game play activities, especially where the switching of protagonist roles is encouraged within a single mission; it also lets the narrative of the game switch tone and focus and rove between story threads, allowing for a narrative complexity not possible where there is a single player-character. However, the key message I want to draw here is that a creative achievement in this game owes to the fact that much of the previously tacit and formally awkward quarantine between game play and narrative fictions is purposely embodied and accounted for within the narrative itself through the technique of multiple protagonists, and so what was previously a formal obstacle in the medium provides the occasion for a creative solution that itself opens up additional creative opportunities.

In the above I am actively engaged in the critical assessment both of the problems inherent in games and the creative solutions offered to those problems. Of course it might be asked whether the aspects I have picked out for attention *actually are creative solutions*; the forgoing could be a purely subjective and idiosyncratic characterization and assessment of the game. It might even be questioned whether features identified were even *intended* by the game designers as solutions, and surely one criterion of a creative solution is that it is intended to address an acknowledged problem. Whether the presence of artistic or esthetic features in an artwork are constrained by the actual intentions of the artist is an issue that has a

3. CREATIVITY AND VIDEO GAME DEVELOPMENT

long history in the philosophy of the arts (Beardsley & Wimsatt, 1946). But this also raises a problem familiar within the psychological literature on creativity: How does one identify and measure the creativity of products and people? Theorizing and studying what might seem to be a subjective phenomenon clearly depends on some objective means of identifying the construct. One answer to this problem is the "Consensual Assessment Technique" developed by Theresa Amabile (1982). Under this method "a product or response is creative to the extent that appropriate observers independently agree it is creative" (1982, p. 1001). While this technique is foremost an attempt to solve a technical problem in the design of creativity studies, it also fits easily with the role played by artistic criticism and theorization where the identification of creativity frequently depends on the agreement of "appropriate observers" (in this case critics and game theorists).

ARTISTIC MEDIA, MIXED INTENTIONS, AND CREATIVE PROBLEM SOLVING

A little can be said about the deeper reasons for these apparent structural contradictions within the gaming medium. Most video games are works of fiction, depicting imaginary worlds and experiences for the purpose of player interpretation, engagement, and play (Tavinor, 2014). The content of these fictions is one of the primary focuses of creativity in game design and in recent years video games have presented a vast range of compelling and vivid fictional worlds: Los Santos is a profoundly different world to *BioShock Infinite's* Columbia, but both excel in depicting artistically and interactively rich imaginary situations. And yet as detailed above, the fictions in these games clearly have multiple and mixed uses. From the beginning of gaming one central role for fiction has been to portray the game play algorithm by providing its representational embodiment to the player (Tavinor, 2011). In the early game *Colossal Cave Adventure* (1976), this fiction is text-based, and players discover the content of the fictional world by reading text such as the game's famous opening:

> Somewhere nearby is Colossal Cave, where others have found fortunes in treasure and gold, though it is rumored that some who enter are never seen again. Magic is said to work in the cave.

The *affordances* (Sharp, 2014, pp. 97-98) for action of the player in this game are similarly text-based, in that the player enters simple verb-noun phrases to fictionally perform actions and so make moves in the game.

Recent games have increasingly explored the advances in graphical techniques to render their fictional worlds and affordances, but in these instances the role of the fiction is the same. While the program that ultimately instantiates the contingent functionality of a game—its responsiveness to player input and its interactivity—is composed of a rule-following computational algorithm, the *representational level* at which a player engages with this algorithmic structure in most video games, and certainly all those discussed here, is a set of imagined places, peoples, and activities presented by the gaming artifact (but also partly inferred and elaborated by the imagination of the player in their interpretation of the game's fiction). These fictive aspects constitute the rules, objectives, and affordances of the game, and moreover are key to the identity of a given game in that the ontology and identity of a game is partly determined by its artistic assets, including the fictive content and themes of the game (Tavinor, 2011). Playing *Grand Theft Auto V* essentially involves adopting a role in a fictive game of make-believe, something that ties it—and the video gaming medium in general—very closely to other creative endeavors involving fiction, and allows us to adapt and extend on the theoretical approach developed to explain other artistic media (Walton, 1990).

But while much of the fiction of a given game is designed to serve the game play rules and objectives, the narrative potential of fiction also clearly finds its way into many video games. It is obvious that some game designers like to tell stories, and denying this impulse, or underplaying the significance of the narrative fictions within games, is a hopeless theoretical position. Indeed, this narrative impetus has long been seen in gaming, including the early text-based games referred to earlier, which often included rudimentary narrative content, and developed into the more narratively sophisticated genre of "interactive fiction" epitomized by games such as *Zork* (1977-1979). As gaming has become more impressively visual because of technical and artistic advances, the narratives presented by games have gravitated more and more toward traditional cinematic forms, borrowing widely from the artistic techniques found in the cinematic medium. And so in some recent games one has the impression of almost playing through a movie, and the game employs many of the devices and tropes borrowed from the cinematic arts. *Heavy Rain* (2010) hews very close to cinematic conventions, while engaging much of the interaction of the player through "quick time events" that are cued by, and influence, game world and narrative content. For this reason the philosopher of the arts Berys Gaut includes video games within his theory of the cinematic arts, characterizing them as a case of "interactive cinema" (2010, pp. 12-13).

It is clear from the forgoing discussion that there are formal consequences of the mixed intentions and artistic borrowings now embodied in game design. Another example comes from the consideration of the virtual camera and its use in providing both game play and cinematic perspectives on the fictional worlds of games. During game play the key need for the virtual camera to meet is informational and action-based: even if there is a simultaneous desire to have a given scene be visually impressive, what is most pressing during game play is that the player has enough information to effectively act in the game world. This means that the visual depiction of game play needs to be spatially precise and explicit; consequently much design effort goes into how the virtual camera tracks and displays the action. (This is not to deny that some games intentionally restrict the informational content of their visual presentations, whether through obstacles or lighting effects in the environment or visual techniques such as the "fog of war" commonly found in third-person turn-based or real time strategy games.) But while there are also informational needs in the cinematic narratives that compose much of the narrative content of games, particularly in the form of cut-scenes, because the visual presentation of such scenes is not to be the occasion of player interaction, their spatial presentation need not be as replete or precise in terms of the information provided to the viewer. Indeed, while in some video games one can often have a very determinate idea of the layout of a space— I know my way around Los Santos reasonably well—the geographical layout of non-interactive narrative fictions can remain very indistinct. But as a result, such narrative sequences are free to take on a more purely esthetic and cinematic approach in their depiction of the fiction.

Games have not always successfully balanced these mixed informational and cinematic representational demands. Some earlier third-person action games were frustrating experiences precisely because of the imprecise way the virtual camera was employed. In particular, the attempted cinematic staging of the game world during game play often meant that important parts of the action could become occluded in the environment, making achieving the goals of game play needlessly difficult. In a game like 2000's *Devil May Cry*—a stylish game in part because of its cinematic approach to the virtual camera—the camera's position would sometimes mean that the player saw an opponent only at the very last second. It was often difficult to keep track of an opponent's precise position and control of the player-character could be problematic because of the changing cinematic orientation. Recent games have responded to such problems— which seemed ubiquitous in early 2000s third-person action games—by employing better environment design, allowing for switchable perspectives and manipulable virtual cameras, and, no doubt, by better overall production values and a quality control that has eliminated many such infelicities. But creative solutions to the problem have also been forthcoming, including the use of artificial intelligence to predict the position of the player in respect to the action and to anticipate and enact effective and visually impressive perspectives (Burelli & Yannakakis, 2011).

Again, the theoretical point of interest here is that because of the mixed intentions behind these game fictions and their visual representation to the player—to present a precise and replete spatial world to allow ease of interaction, and to make this world visually impressive by using the cinematic techniques often borrowed from the medium of film—a structural or design problem is entailed. And it is one that often calls for creative solutions that become the substance of subsequent game design. Indeed, what we can see through this example is that design features that were originally solutions to a particular problem often become fixed as *typical* representational techniques of the medium in that various genres of gaming are now defined by their visual perspectives. This is a formal issue seen in the arts generally (Walton, 1970), and which provides another theoretical point of contact between games and the arts. Creative and novel features frequently become standard features with which a genre of game might be associated or defined, even to the extent that the *absence* of such features may count as convention-breaking or even disconcerting for the player. One famous example of this is the exclusion of scripted cut-scenes—a previously conventional mode of depicting narrative content—from the game *Half-Life*, which while it may aid immersion in the game world, arguably causes its own difficulties for the narrative (Tavinor, 2009a, p. 121).

Finally, this creative medium progression can be taken a step further as we find in the original *BioShock*, where a representational technique initially aimed at reconciling a structural problem can itself become a reflexive concern of the game; and in this case providing one of the most creative and discussed episodes in recent gaming. *BioShock* is famous for a particular scene involving the phrase "Would you kindly" where it is made clear that the player-character has been a pawn in someone else's game. Ostensibly this is a narrative device used to undermine the player's sense that they have been the protagonist of the game, but what is also satisfying about the scene is how it makes an artistic virtue of the declarative instructions that are often necessary in the gaming medium. To be able to play games effectively players have a variety of informational needs beyond the immediate visual depiction of the game environment. A key part of game play is learning the rules and affordances of a game, and because these may not be immediately evident in the graphically presented world a game must find some way of making these obvious to players. It is also often necessary for games with complex and large environments that players know where their goals and objectives are in a game world, and again, a game needs to effectively transmit this information to the player. A particularly blunt way of providing such information is by including explicit on-screen linguistic or iconic prompts, but such explicit instructions can seem like awkward impositions on the game world fiction.

In *BioShock* the goals and objectives of the game are partly integrated in to the narrative substance by being delivered over radio by another character in the game world, with whom the player is encouraged to have sympathy, but whom the player learns in a revelatory scene is a gaming equivalent of an untrustworthy narrator. This is a technique also employed by *System Shock 2*, an earlier game also developed by Irrational Games. What is artistically fascinating about this technique, however, is that the manipulation of the game world character intentionally echoes the manipulation of the player by the game medium: both the player and his character have been ordered around the game world for reasons other than their own, even as there has been an overwhelming sense of freedom in the exploration of the fictional world of Rapture. This reflexive layering of narrative and structural concerns deepens the philosophical and artistic achievement of the game in that the intentional foregrounding of the manipulation of the player by the game allows the narrative to comment on the illusory freedom of gaming and on the nature of the political manipulation that *BioShock* has as one of its key thematic concerns (Tavinor, 2009b). Hence again, a structural demand of a gaming medium—in this case the informational needs of the player—becomes the occasion for a creative artistic solution.

Further connections can be made with the creativity literature. Returning to the four Ps of creativity—*process, product, person, place*—we can say a little more about the specific processes involved here. The focus in this chapter has been on the design problems inherent in the gaming medium, particularly those involved in reconciling different functional aspects of a single work, and how these lead to creative opportunities. In the psychological literature the creative process is sometimes characterized as involving multiples stages including an important early "preparation" stage where a difficulty is defined and attempts are made to gather information about the problem (Kozbelt et al., 2010, p. 30). The examples identified above seem easily characterized as involving the stages of "problem finding" and "problem construction" performed by game designers (Kozbelt et al., 2010, p. 31). However, it may be that these functions are also partly divested through wider gaming culture because the feedback from critics and theorists may have an important role in game design by identifying both critical faults and their ideal solutions. The earlier examples here of the identification of "ludonarrative dissonance" by the blogger Clint Hocking, and the frequent criticism of cinematic cameras in action games, and the evident awareness and response to both faults in subsequent game design, are important potential instances of this feedback.

We might also question the kind of creativity at play in the examples under scrutiny here. In the psychological literature a distinction is often made between "esthetic" and "functional" creativity; that is, between creative episodes that aim to produce qualities for esthetic contemplation or pleasure with no further objective beyond these intrinsic features, or to create products that have some functional potential, whether it is in the realm of technology, commerce, or science (Cropley & Cropley, 2010, p. 301).

The examples of creativity discussed here might initially seem to be the products of functional creativity because they aim to resolve design problems that have a functional role in game play. They also pertain to a medium that is strongly commercially driven, involving *products* in a very saleable sense (indeed, products that routinely have an extraordinary commercial success). And yet there is a tradition that sees games, like art, as abstract from ordinary life, having an interest beyond their practical use, or "disinterested" (Huizinga, 1955, p. 9). One important criterion against which the creative solutions detailed above are assessed is their *elegance* in dealing with structural problems such as ludonarrative dissonance, and the creativity of video games is often assessed in such esthetic terms. In fact, functionality and esthetics frequently go hand in hand, and maintaining that there is a clear distinction between the two may owe to a formalist assumption that properly esthetic activity has no functional, practical, or representational end (Bell, 1914; Beardsley, 1981). That games are necessarily unproductive or disinterested is an assumption that has recently been questioned in games studies (Juul, 2005, p. 35). Ultimately, both esthetic and functional creativity are in evidence in games, often combined in the same product.

NARRATIVE AND INTERACTIVITY

Quite a different example of the problem of structural dissonance, and one that further illustrates the contribution of tensions and complications of artistic materials to the potential for creativity within a medium, is provided by the excellent 2013 survival-horror game *The Last of Us*. This example also ultimately allows us to consider another aspect of the creativity involved in video games: that attributable to the player in the act of playing. *The Last of Us* depicts a post-apocalyptic world that has been devastated by an epidemic owing to a mutation of the *Cordyceps* fungus that infects human hosts, producing fungal growths within their increasingly distorted bodies and causing them to become mindless and aggressive monsters. The game tells the story of Joel, a survivor of the initial outbreak 20 years previously, who is tasked with transporting a 14-year-old girl Ellie across the country so that the secret of her strange resistance to the infection can be studied by a group of surviving doctors. The game is a harrowing experience for the player and the action lurches from one desperate situation of survival to another.

Part of the success of *The Last of Us* as a game is how it integrates the game play and narrative content within its fictional world in a way that avoids some of the structural tensions that have been the focus here. In fact we can see two aspects to the potential for dissonance with this game: the demand to balance the violence of the survival-horror genre with the depiction of a sympathetic character who is perpetrating much of the violence; and the integration of interactivity—a virtue of game play—with the narrative of the game, where interactivity is not always such a desirable trait. The means by which *The Last of Us* meets both of these formal challenges seem very creative indeed.

I introduced this essay with an example of the first kind of structural dissonance from the game *BioShock Infinite* where the structural infelicity involved the mixed significance of violence in a game world. As we discovered, while the first-person shooter genre necessitates a great deal of fictionally violent action for the substance of its game play, the clear artistic intentions of the game—the implied sympathy for the protagonist, the beautiful nature of the game world, and the often otherworldly experience of esthetic exploration—sometimes seemed at odds with this game play content. In *The Last of Us*, the solution to this tension is achieved by a deliberate characterization of the nature of the fictional world and the motivations and moral assessment of the people acting within it. A frequent theme of the fiction of the game is the desperate nature of survival in the post-infection world, and how the precarious situation in which the characters find themselves—essentially, the last days of humanity—affects the morality of their actions. The player-character protagonist Joel frequently resorts to brutal action within the narrative, even resorting to torture, but usually these actions are the results of events forced upon him by other people equally willing to resort to brutality. As a result of this context the violent game play entirely fits with desperate nature of the world, and hence squares with the narrative of the game. This strategy was subsequently noted and praised in some of the critical responses to the game: a review on the gaming website Edge, contrasting *The Last of Us* with *Uncharted*—the previous game series produced by the developer Naughty Dog, and from which *The Last of Us* derives many of its game mechanics—argued that "the game tastefully avoids the ludonarrative dissonance that arises from Drake being presented as a friendly treasure hunter while asking players to pile up hundreds of bodies wherever he sets foot. Joel kills because he has to, and there's no winning smile when the shooting stops, just overwhelming relief" (Edge Magazine, 2013).

Moreover, the character of Joel is successful in reconciling the game play and narrative functions because ultimately his nature as a moral agent is conflicted: it is very much the point of the devastating final scenes of this game that the sympathy with which he has drawn from the player is compromised by his final acts of murder and deceit. Joel's desperate violence in his dealing with the infected ultimately spills over into his actions within the story, including a final painful lie to Ellie. And so the abundant and disturbing violence found in the game play also finds a natural and convincing expression in the narrative, partly explaining the notable artistic success of the final scenes of the game.

The second aspect of *The Last of Us* that is worth consideration here concerns the role of the player within this fiction. For the most part here I may have seemed to assume that the creativity inherent in games is only that of game designers, but of increasing interest to games scholars is the creativity and meaning-making activities that players bring to their interactions with games (Sotamaa, 2014, p. 6). Players clearly make a creative contribution during game play, something we can understand by considering games as a kind of "co-creative" art form where the work is only displayed following the engagement of the player (Smuts, 2005). This player agency is an important aspect of the "interactivity" of games (Lopes, 2001). According to Gaut, playing video games counts as a kind of performance akin to that found in the performance arts (Gaut, 2010, p. 153). Partly the performance of a game is carried out by the underlying program or algorithm of the game, and so is "automated," but according to Gaut such automated compliance "leaves available to the user the more interesting part of performance—interpretative performance" (Gaut, 2010, p. 146). Thus in the case of video games (and other interactive artworks) the performance role is typically played by a single individual who is also a member of the *audience* of the work because of his or her interpretative activities. Playing a game involves both making decisions that are necessary to the work being rendered, and also interpreting the work as affected by these decisions. This performative role opens an avenue for player creativity, and the ability of games to sustain creative interpretative performance of players is highly valued. Moreover, as I will argue below, the combination of these two roles—performance and interpretation—in a single individual generates a feedback loop through which the meaning of games can be compounded in interesting ways.

While choice seems a clear virtue within game play, when it comes to narrative, player choice can often have the undesirable effect of dissipating the effect of a narrative. Placing the onus on players to discover or enact the narrative of a game—essentially to be a performer—opens up the possibility that they simply will not do so, whether because they lack interest in the story, become distracted, or fail to perceive or understand the narrative cues built into the game. If the rendering of a game narrative is to be interactive and so involve the interpretative and decision-making activities of the player, this demands a motivated, thoughtful and perhaps even creative player, and these are qualities which cannot always be relied on.

This leads to a further structural tension within the medium of gaming between giving the player enough freedom to find her own way through the narrative content and having the story be sufficiently directed or motivated so that it can unfold as intended by the author. This potential for narrative dissipation is particularly evident in open-world games such as *Grand Theft Auto* and the western-themed game *Red Dead Redemption*. Of course, many game players simply do not care enough to engage with the narrative of such games, choosing instead to merely play in the game world unconcerned with finishing the mission-based campaign. But even motivated players may face challenges, particularly where the vastness of a game world or narrative structure makes the role of producing the narrative a demanding task. To play through the narrative of *Grand Theft Auto IV*, for example, involves obligatory sections of travel through the game world which can become an annoyance, and this may be a reason why most players never finish the campaigns of such games (Phillips, 2009). The abundant divertissements built into such game worlds in the form of side-missions and incidental tasks provide further distractions from the story content.

A conventional way of solving this medium tension between player interactivity and determinate narrative structure is to have the narrative entirely discrete from the game play, being presented in pre-rendered cut-scenes. This separation frequently leads to some very artificial and unsatisfying game experiences. The game *Unreal Tournament 3* (2007) is particularly guilty here, in that the content of game play frequently bears only a vague relationship to the narrative, with game play missions effectively being shoehorned into the narrative structure. Indeed, the cut-scenes often tend to become an interruption or distraction from the substance of the game itself, and this has become a common critical complaint concerning the use of cut-scenes. As noted earlier, it was in response to this issue that *Half-Life* dispensed with third-person narrative cut-scenes altogether.

Another means of resolving the tension is to incorporate the narrative into the first-person rendered game world, but to do so in a very controlled or staged way by building the narrative events into the levels of a game. This method of conveying narrative through obligatory and tightly scripted level is frequently called "on rails" narrative because it has the effect, like the game play for some early third-person action games, of leading the player though a determined path in the fictional world, in this case being a narrative path (Tavinor, 2009a, 2009b, p. 119). For some critics this narrative technique seems like a straitjacket, compromising what they see as the potential freedom inherent in interactive game narrative. However, the strategy also presents creative opportunities. The *Modern Warfare* series of games, where the narrative is conveyed largely through a series of tightly scripted levels, provides a reasonably successful employment of this technique. For example, in the opening scenes of *Modern Warfare 2*, now widely known as "No Russian," the initial level is designed to lead the player though a scripted episode where he or she plays a role in a terrorist atrocity in a Russian airport. This allows the narrative of the game to provide the background and rationale for the events that follow in the story, but to do so in a way that gives the player an aspect of agency within the scene (shooting innocent civilians is not obligatory in the level).

This episode is now morally notorious, but the point of interest here is that the scene advances the narrative of the game directly through the depiction of a level of game play: the function of the massacre in the game can be seen as a motivation for the upcoming action and scene setting for the paranoid "false-flag" military storyline. The player's fictional agency in the scene also allows for interpretative activities that would be unavailable if the scene had been rendered in a non-interactive cut-scene, in that for a thoughtful player it has the potential to prompt the player's own emotional response to their complicity in the slaughter, if he so decides to participate in the atrocity.

The Last of Us engages with the structural tension between narrative and player choice in a similarly interesting way. The narrative of the game culminates in a ruinous final scene where Joel is provoked with a blunt ethical dilemma. Ellie has been prepped for a surgery that may lead to the understanding of her resistance to the disease, but that will ultimately kill her. Joel must choose either to save Ellie, for whom he has a growing fatherly love, or to sacrifice her for the sake of the potential cure. Standing between Joel and Ellie is a doctor—apparently a largely innocent character—armed with a scalpel. One can imagine such an ethical dilemma being depicted in conventional film, of course, but because it is a video game *The Last of Us* is able to do something quite striking in this sequence, employing a strategy that enriches the ending with additional ethical implications. At the moment where Joel's final decision is made the act is forced into the player's hands: the player must perform the actions of killing the doctor to save Ellie. Joel's eventual decision to save Ellie—and to betray both those who gave him his task and the hopes of wider humanity for survival—provides a deeply troubling but dramatically satisfying ending to the game.

The sequence also provides a creative resolution to the problem of interactive narrative because of how the game lines up the formal demands of its game play with the trajectory of the narrative. Killing at least one of the doctors is a precondition both of advancing though the level and of saving Ellie in the story, and so the interactivity of the medium of gaming is exploited to draw the player into the dilemma, potentially implicating the player in the moral substance of the pivotal scene of the game. As the game play forces the player into performing an action to proceed in the level, in the story Joel's character and his care for Ellie force him into performing the actions he does. The tension between depicting game play that is satisfactorily interactive, and a narrative that charts a determinate path, is solved then by introducing a *forced move* into the game, intentionally subverting the interactivity of the game play to make a narrative point. The scene has a kind of *quasi-freedom*: players are responsible for performing the actions that render the scene, but they have no choice given their desires and the means of action available to them. Thus the desire for interactivity in games is balanced with the firm trajectory necessitated by narrative by aligning the lapse of real freedom in the interactive structure of the game with the lack of real freedom in Joel's predicament. Again, the structural features of the game's medium, including their potential complications, make available a fascinating piece of artistry.

CREATIVITY IN THE VIDEO GAMING MEDIUM

Given the inevitability of mixed artistic aims, games designers will likely always struggle with the kind of formal challenges described in this chapter. This seems to be a general fact about the development of artistic and creative media, however. This much we can see from the history of art, where artists working in newly developed media have frequently confronted the issue of how to continue with established artistic forms within the context of a medium with distinctive capacities and limitations. Indeed, the problems inherent in a new artistic medium often lead to the creation of solutions that prove to be enduring achievements of the form. And while we might be tempted to see creativity as a behavioral or psychological phenomenon, and as arising from and most strongly associated with psychological cognates such as inspiration, insight, and genius, it is clear that though owing much to the psychology of artistic intentions and acts, creativity does not entirely reduce to these. Creativity in a medium such as video gaming owes just as much to the formal and material qualities of that medium, to the tensions, constraints, potentials, and problems that creative people are faced with when they engage with a developing tradition of artistic design.

Creativity arises from and through a culture. These wider sociocultural aspects of creativity have not gone unnoticed in creativity studies (Csikszentmihalyi, 1988). It should be noted here that many recent games are iterations on a theme in being either instances of an established game genre or the latest version of an established franchise. Furthermore, almost all recent games are collaboratively authored in being the products of large design teams and studios. The episodes of creativity under discussion here cannot just be thought of as resulting from acts of insight by creative individuals, rather they are almost always the product of teams of such individuals returning to a familiar medium, building on their own and other's previous achievements in the medium. Such collaborative creativity brings with it the consideration of additional sociocultural factors concerning how groups work to produce creative results (Hennessey & Amabile, 2010, p. 580). But it also means that creativity in gaming is very much a matter of the identification of enduring design problems associated with a medium, incremental creative advances in solving these problems, and the production of a resulting material culture of creativity.

In this chapter, I have focused on the products of creativity. However, my conception of the material products of creativity is a rather broader one than that usually seen in the psychological literature because I see the medium—material and historical—with its enduring structural challenges and opportunities as both a prompt for and product of creativity. Much of the psychological literature sees creativity as stemming principally from psychological features, such as personality (Feist, 2010) and affect (Ward & Kolomyts, 2010), or cognitive styles such as divergent thinking (Guilford, 1968), with the products of creativity often playing a merely evidential role in assessing these psychological aspects. This is a natural result of the most robust creativity literature stemming from personal, social, or cognitive psychology rather than disciplines such as sociology or philosophical esthetics, where a focus on culture, and its structures and material products, might be more natural. But if the generative role assigned to the *products* of creativity in this chapter is correct, the creativity of video games also partly derives from the structural potential of the medium itself and to the cultural forces such as commerce and art that sustain the medium as an ongoing focus of creative activities.

References

Amabile, T. (1982). Social psychology of creativity: A consensual assessment technique. *Journal of Personal and Social Psychology, 43,* 997–1013.

Beardsley, M. C. (1981). *Aesthetics: Problems in the philosophy of criticism* (2nd ed.). Indianapolis: Hackett.

Beardsley, M. C., & Wimsatt, W. K. (1976). The intentional fallacy. In D. Newton-De Molina (Ed.), *On literary intention* (pp. 1–13). Edinburgh: Edinburgh University Press.

Bell, C. (1914). *Art.* London: Chatto & Windus.

Burelli, P., & Yannakakis, G. N. (2011). Towards adaptive virtual camera control in computer games. *Smart Graphics, 6815,* 25–36.

Cropley, D., & Cropley, A. (2010). Functional creativity: 'Products' and the generation of effective novelty. In J. C. Kaufman & R. J. Sternberg (Eds.), *The Cambridge handbook of creativity.* Cambridge: Cambridge University Press.

Csikszentmihalyi, M. (1988). Society, culture and person: A systems view of creativity. In R. J. Sternberg (Ed.), *The nature of creativity: Contemporary psychological perspectives.* New York: Cambridge University Press.

Edge Magazine. (2013). *Review of The Last of Us.* Retrieved from August 20, 2013, http://www.edge-online.com/review/the-last-of-us-review/.

Feist, G. J. (2010). The function of personality in creativity: The nature and nurture of the creative personality. In J. C. Kaufman, & R. J. Sternberg (Eds.), *The Cambridge handbook of creativity.* Cambridge: Cambridge University Press.

Gaut, B. (2010). *A philosophy of cinematic art.* Cambridge: Cambridge University Press.

Guilford, J. P. (1968). *Creativity, intelligence, and their educational implications.* San Diego, CA: Knapp/EDITS.

Hennessey, B. A., & Amabile, T. A. (2010). Creativity. *Annual Review of Psychology, 61,* 569–598.

Hocking, C. (2007). *Ludonarrative dissonance in Bioshock.* Click Nothing Blog. Retrieved from June 1, 2014, http://www.clicknothing.typepad.com/click_nothing/2007/10/ludonarrative-d.html.

Huizinga, J. (1955). *Homo Ludens: A study of the play element in culture*. Boston, MA: Beacon Press.

Juul, J. (2005). *Half-real: Video games between real rules and fictional worlds*. Cambridge MA: MIT Press.

Klevjer, R. (2014). Cut-scenes. In J. P. Wolf, & B. Perron (Eds.), *The Routledge companion to video game studies*. New York: Routledge.

Kozbelt, A., Beghetto, R. A., & Runco, M. A. (2010). Theories of creativity. In J. C. Kaufman, & R. J. Sternberg (Eds.), *The Cambridge handbook of creativity*. Cambridge: Cambridge University Press.

Lopes, D. M. (2001). The ontology of interactive art. *Journal of Aesthetic Education, 35*(4), 65–81.

Phillips, B. (2009). *Xbox live gamerscore, completion stats show major trends*. Gamasutra. Retrieved from June 18, 2014, http://www.gamasutra.com/php-bin/news_index.php?story=25818.

Plante, C. (2013). *Opinion: Violence limits Bioshock infinite's audience—My wife included*. Polygon. Retrieved from April 30, 2013, http://www.polygon.com/2013/4/2/4174344/opinion-why-my-wife-wont-play-bioshock-infinite.

Sharp, J. (2014). Dimensionality. In J. P. Wolf & B. Perron (Eds.), *The Routledge companion to video game studies*. New York: Routledge.

Smuts, A. (2005). Are Video Games Art?. *Contemporary Aesthetics, 2*. http://www.contempaesthetics.org/newvolume/pages/article.php?articleID=299

Sotamaa, O. (2014). Artefact. In J. P. Wolf, & B. Perron (Eds.), *The Routledge companion to video game studies*. New York: Routledge.

Tavinor, G. (2009a). *The art of videogames*. Malden, MA: Wiley Blackwell.

Tavinor, G. (2009b). BioShock and the art of rapture. *Philosophy and Literature, 33*(1), 91–106.

Tavinor, G. (2011). Videogames as mass art. *Contemporary Aesthetics, 11*. http://www.contempaesthetics.org/newvolume/pages/article.php?articleID=616

Tavinor, G. (2014). Fiction. In J. P. Wolf, & B. Perron (Eds.), *The Routledge companion to video game studies*. New York: Routledge.

Walton, K. (1970). Categories of art. *Philosophical Review, 79*(3), 334–367.

Walton, K. (1990). *Mimesis as make-believe*. Cambridge, MA: Harvard University Press.

Ward, T. B., & Kolomyts, Y. (2010). Cognition and creativity. In J. C. Kaufman, & R. J. Sternberg (Eds.), *The Cambridge handbook of creativity*. Cambridge: Cambridge University Press.

Creative Interactivity: Customizing and Creating Game Content

Katharina-Marie Behr, Richard Huskey
and René Weber

Department of Communication, University of California Santa Barbara,
Santa Barbara, CA, USA

CREATIVE INTERACTIVITY: CUSTOMIZING AND CREATING GAME CONTENT

Have you ever watched a movie where you rooted for the protagonists, feared for them and cheered with them throughout the story? And, once the movie is over, felt sad because the story is over? Or, did you feel like some characters should have been portrayed differently? That the movie should have had a different ending altogether? Now, imagine what it would take to bring the cast of the movie back together and shoot a sequel, change certain aspects of the movie, or elaborate on a part of the story that you think should have been told in more detail. Clearly, this would require considerable effort and, at least for the average moviegoer, is impossible to do. The same goes for most other forms of entertainment media. For audience members, it is rather difficult to add another chapter to a book, record another album track, or change the appearance of a character in one's favorite TV series.

This is different with video games because of their interactive nature. Unlike traditional media such as television and movies, the interactive features of video games allow users to manipulate both form (e.g., design elements, style, and medium) and content (e.g., the message, the storyline, and the meaning) (Grodal, 2000; Weber, Behr, & De Martino, 2014). Players can—and even have to—interact with a game in order for it to progress and for its story to unfold. But video game interactivity (VGI) is not limited to these aspects of the playing experience. In most games, players can also access game settings and adjust various parameters to match their preferences. This might range from simple manipulations of game settings such as muting or unmuting sound effects to very complex choices like using third-party software to add new features to a game. Thus, players can influence game content by manipulating and combining various game features (Raney, Smith, & Baker, 2006). For instance, a *World of Warcraft* (Blizzard) player who installs the Carbonite add-on (a combination of the game's map, head-up display, sound, chat, and item database) receives guided instructions for how to accomplish various game objectives. This may allow for more efficient play compared to players without Carbonite who must explore the expansive game world in order to accomplish game objectives.

While such instances of customization require relatively little creativity, the interactive nature of games often provides opportunities for greater creative expression. Some games afford players the ability to generate entirely new content (Richards, 2006). For example, players use game technology to develop additional items, levels that relocate games to different environments, or even so-called "total conversions" with different storylines and game types (Postigo, 2003, 2007). *Defense of the Ancients* (DotA) is a famous example where a small group of designers used the level editor provided in *Warcraft III: Reign of Chaos* (Blizzard) to create an entirely different form of game play. Thus, in addition to the game content created by the developers, players co-create (Morris, 2003) their own content.

In this chapter, we turn our attention to the unique nature of VGI and how interactivity allows for creative expression. Specifically, we focus on content creation that takes place beyond core game play, namely customizing game settings and creating new content through modifying games. We argue that both phenomena provide players an opportunity for creative expression. Drawing on Amabile (2012), we understand creativity as "the production of a novel and appropriate response, product, or solution to an open-ended task" (p. 3). A behavior is creative if it is not only new, but appropriate to the task to be completed or to the problem to be solved. Thus, creative responses must be "valuable, correct, feasible, or somehow fitting to a particular goal" (p. 3). Moreover, Amabile (1983) recognizes that creativity is not a categorical construct—behaviors can be more or less creative. At the low end are commonplace solutions to the problems experienced in everyday existence. High levels of creativity are found in works of art, scientific breakthroughs, and other behaviors where an elegant solution is applied to a difficult problem. Thus, degree of creativity arises from both individual and environmental factors.

In the following section, we will briefly frame content creation as an aspect of interactivity. Subsequently, we will describe customization via game settings and content creation via game modifications in more detail. Along the way, we discuss how each relates to player creativity. This chapter concludes with a discussion of research on motivations for and effects of video game entertainment as a result of customization and content creation.

CONTENT CREATION AND INTERACTIVITY

The first definitions of interactivity were related to content access or usage (Richards, 2006), and were best suited for understanding the relationship between medium and experience. For instance, linearly reading text in a book is considerably less interactive than the nonlinear experience of using hyperlinks to navigate a website. However, these early conceptualizations of interactivity in terms of information access ignored the relationship between interactivity and content creation. Modern definitions treat interactivity as "the possibility for users to manipulate the content and form of communication and/or the possibility of information exchange processes between users or between users and a medium" (Weber et al., 2014) This is a wide-ranging definition and it mirrors the various perspectives that have been developed on the subject. For instance, interactivity has been conceptualized rather broadly in order to compare very different media applications such as online weather forecasts vs. e-mail vs. text messaging (e.g., Leiner & Quiring, 2008; Steuer, 1992). Other approaches conceptualize interactivity very specifically for selected media offers like websites and available technological features like hyperlinks (e.g., Liu, 2003; Liu & Shrum, 2002; McMillan & Hwang, 2002; Warnick, Xenos, Endres, & Gastil, 2005; Wu, 1999). Interactivity is usually described from one of the three perspectives (Bucy & Tao, 2007): (1) as an exchange of messages between two or more communicants; (2) as a technological attribute or media feature; or (3) as a user perception.

Importantly, content creation is not a key aspect of these concepts. The first approach treats interactivity as process-related and refers to the communication settings of a mediated environment (e.g., whether the communication process is linear or nonlinear), the kind of participant relationships that are developed, to what extent the roles of sender and receiver are exchangeable, and to what extent messages are reciprocally dependent (Kiousis, 2002; Rafaeli, 1988; Rafaeli & Sudweeks, 1997). These approaches put an emphasis on how messages are *exchanged*, but not on how they are *created*. The second and third approaches appear different but are closely related: Technology-oriented concepts of interactivity focus on media attributes that make "an individual's participation in communication settings possible and efficient" (Lee, Park, & Jin, 2006, p. 261), such as the number of hyperlinks on a website (Warnick et al., 2005), the rate at which user input can be assimilated into the mediated environment, the number of action possibilities, and the ability of a system to map its controls to changes in the mediated environment (Steuer, 1992). The third approach focuses on how users perceive and use the technological features of a medium (e.g., Leiner & Quiring, 2008). Again, content creation is neither of major importance for technology-oriented approaches nor for approaches focusing on user perceptions. While these concepts do account for two-way communication, this is often limited to counting (perceived) options for users to provide feedback, such as feedback forms and "contact me" buttons on websites (Liu & Shrum, 2002; McMillan & Hwang, 2002). Taken together, we can conclude that most interactivity concepts focus on accessing existing content. Unfortunately, these conceptualizations of interactivity overlook options for adjusting or creating new content, features that are usually limited when browsing a website but are common when playing a video game.

Indeed, recent technological advances grant users considerably more agency than simply accessing content; therefore a broader perspective should be applied when conceptualizing VGI. How players interact with a video game is not limited to actually playing the game, even though this is certainly the inner nucleus of VGI and comes to mind first when thinking of interactivity and video games. In their work on adolescents and video games, Raney et al. (2006) noted that a high degree of *modification* (e.g., options to create characters, change backgrounds, and adjust audio effects), and options to *personalize* or *tailor* games to players' specific intentions and interests are interactive features that contribute to the games' appeal. Weber et al. (2014) found that besides game-play-related and technical dimensions of VGI,[1] the nongame-play-related dimension *customization/co-creation*

---

[1] Game-play-related dimensions included *exploration* (i.e., the extent to which players can control narrative, objectives, and pace of a game), the game's *artificial intelligence* (i.e., how the system responds to player actions); and *perceptual persuasiveness* (i.e., the extent to which the game provides a sense of "being there"). Technical interactivity dimensions included *feature-based interactivity* (the ability to adjust technical game features like advanced graphic options, sound, music, dialog, game control layout to meet player expectations) and *controller responsiveness* (the appropriateness and ease of use when interacting with the game's interface).

contributes to interactivity experiences. *Customization/co-creation* is possible when game designers grant players agency over specific details of a game and describes the amount of control players have over content-relevant features, for instance the ability to control the physical appearance, abilities, performance, accessories, and equipment of game characters and to create new game characters, accessories, and equipment. *Minecraft* (Mojang) demonstrates this point nicely. *Minecraft* is classified as a sandbox game, one in which game features are designed to encourage players to generate novel content.

For their VGI scale, Weber et al. (2014) hypothesized that customization and co-creation would be separate dimensions of interactivity where customization occurs when players use game settings to change existing characters and objects in a game and co-creation takes place when players use a game engine, level editor, or similar tools to develop entirely new content for a game. However, it seems that from a player's point of view, there is no strict distinction between customizing a game via game settings compared to developing new content using the game's technological basis. Rather than a dichotomy, customizing games and co-creating content is probably a continuum ranging from simple in-game options to complex modification scenarios. However, the endpoints of this continuum seem to be very far from each other (e.g., using the mute/unmute option in a browser-based game compared to creating a total conversion that equips an existing game with a different game environment, game play, and story). In order to address the unique characteristics of these endpoints on a continuum for content creation in video games, we will look at customizing and creating new content separately in the following sections.

CUSTOMIZING GAME CONTENT

Video games vary considerably in the degrees of freedom they offer players to customize the game according to their preferences. Browser-based casual games like *Bejeweled* (PopCap Games) and *FarmVille* (Zynga) usually offer very few options to adjust game settings (e.g., choosing the level of difficulty from one out of several game modes). Games that are played on personal computers usually offer additional options to adjust the game to the computer's performance (e.g., changing the displayed graphic details), and in most computer and video games users can adjust the game control layout according to their preferences. These mostly technical features ensure that users can avoid frustration caused by delayed feedback from the game or from sounds and music that are experienced as annoying. Players can also adjust these game settings to avoid frustration caused by tasks that are perceived as too difficult or too easy, or that otherwise prevent success in the game.

Adjusting a game to computer performance and individual skills would probably not be considered particularly creative. Using game settings to adjust the sound volume is neither a response to an open-ended task nor a novel response. However, technical game features can be used in creative ways. For example, there is anecdotal evidence that users of first-person shooter (FPS) games like *Counter-Strike* who compete online against other players set the graphic details to the lowest possible level in order to compensate for slow internet connections, even if their computers are perfectly capable of displaying all graphic details. While this is certainly not intended by the game developers, such behavior can still be considered a creative response by the players to a game play situation where speed matters more than graphics. If creativity is conceptualized as a continuum ranging from low to high levels (Amabile, 2012) this response could be positioned near the low-creativity end of the continuum.

Besides technical aspects, many games allow players to adjust parameters that are directly related to the game's narrative and content. This applies first and foremost to character customization. For example, in the 2011 role-playing game *The Elder Scrolls: Skyrim* (Bethesda Softworks), players can customize the character's appearance down to facial features like the breadth and length of the nose or the shape of the eyebrows. They can also choose among several fantasy races for their character that come with different cultures and specific skills. Importantly, these choices affect performance. For instance, players who chose a race with strong magic skills will perform better when using spells and charms; however, this decision also affects how different nonplayer characters will react to the player character and whether they will be friendly and helpful or more reserved.

In other genres such as FPS games, players can customize the equipment a character carries by combining different weapons, ammunition, and protection gear. Such decisions have a considerable impact on content. For instance, in the popular *Call of Duty* series, players can outfit their character differently according to preferred play style. Those who prefer to "camp" (stay in a fixed location and score opportunistic kills by surprising enemies) might select heavy armor, long-range weapons, and equip their character with stealth skills. Alternatively, players who prefer fast-pace and aggressive action often outfit their character with comparatively lighter armor, weapons suited for close quarters combat, and abilities that maximize speed and accuracy. These decisions are known as "loadouts" and they grant players the ability to creatively optimize a character for a preferred play style. Moreover, players regularly share different loadout configurations online, either as a demonstration of creative mastery of the game, or in an effort to gain feedback from other players.

In general, users prefer playing with a customized avatar compared to a predetermined or assigned character. For instance, the ability to customize an avatar is associated with increased self-report feelings of presence as well as elevated skin conductance levels (a measure of arousal) (Bailey, Wise, & Bolls, 2009). The more options players have to customize a character's appearance, abilities, performance, and accessories and equipment, the more interactive they rate a video game (Weber et al., 2014). In fact, a content analysis on game recordings of participants who had played an FPS showed that of their entire playing time, participants spent 14% using the equipment menu to customize the character's appearance and equipment, twice as much time as they spent in combat situations (Weber, Behr, Tamborini, Ritterfeld, & Mathiak, 2009). These results suggest that players not only enjoy the opportunity to customize their character, but also that players use customization features to creatively tune their character based on momentary game demands.

If players have the option to create a main protagonist for a game in (almost) any way they like—How do they choose to design their character? Several studies support the idea that players prefer avatars that are similar to themselves in terms of personality features (Hsu, Kao, & Wu, 2007; Hsu, Lee, & Wu, 2005; Ogletree & Drake, 2007; Trepte & Reinecke, 2010). Playing with a (customized) character that is perceived as similar to oneself is related to increased enjoyment (Hsu et al., 2005; Trepte & Reinecke, 2010).

However, players also account for a game's context when creating an avatar. When asked to create an avatar for game scenarios that require features commonly perceived as masculine, such as physical strength, or feminine, such as "warm" or "affectionate," players seem to apply a mixed strategy (Trepte, Reinecke, & Behr, 2011): Both men and women preferred "male" avatar features when they expected to play games prejudged as "masculine," and "feminine" features for avatars in so-called "female" games. A similar outcome has also been observed for player roles seen as more "masculine" (e.g., warriors and paladins) or "feminine" (e.g., priests and mages) (Ducheneaut, Yee, Nickell, & Moore, 2006). This suggests that in terms of avatar attributes, video game players prefer avatars designed to meet the requirements of the games (and possibly even stereotypical gender roles). Avatar features that are chosen in accordance with the game's demands help facilitate mastery of the game, which in turn increases enjoyment (Grodal, 2000; Klimmt & Hartmann, 2006; Tamborini et al., 2011). Deciding what equipment the player's character should carry is of strategic importance for being successful in the game. Yet when it comes to biological sex, players seem to strive for identification with their avatar—men preferred male avatars and women favored female avatars. In sum, the participants create male or female characters to match their own sex, but equip these characters with personality features based on perceptions of game requirements.

In sum, options to customize a game are an important aspect of VGI. This applies to technical characteristics of a game, but also—and probably more so—to options for customizing the player's character and its equipment. Games which can be customized are rated as more interactive and enjoyable, and users prefer playing with characters they can adjust to meet game requirements and to resemble aspects of themselves. Finally, these opportunities to customize a game to suit individual needs allow players to creatively alter the video game experience.

MODIFYING GAME CONTENT

Within the definition of creativity offered by Amabile (2012), customizing a game and altering individual game characters can be considered the less creative endpoint of content creation in video games. Alternatively, modifying a video game may represent the more creative endpoint. In the following, we will provide a brief introduction to the technical and historical background of this complex phenomenon, and analyze the development of game modifications as a creative activity and regarding its contributing factors to creativity.

Modifying games means that players use the program code of a game, editor, or software development kit designed by game manufacturers (Humphreys, Fitzgerald, Banks, & Suzor, 2005) to change game items, characters, environments, and game rules. Such behavior is quite different from customization. Customizing content uses affordances embedded within a game whereas modifications are technical alterations to the affordances of a game. These modifications of commercialized computer games are also called "mods" (Postigo, 2003, 2007). They are pieces of software, often distributed over the internet for free, for players to download and use mods. Usually, installing mods requires a legal copy of the original, commercialized game installed on the player's computers (Humphreys et al., 2005).

Users first started to modify games at computer labs of universities in 1962 with the game *Spacewar* (Herz, 2002; Laukkanen, 2005). Game enthusiasts modified text-based adventures like *Dungeons & Dragons* or *Star Trek* in the 1970s (Kushner, 2002, 2003), and games like *Castle Wolfenstein* in the 1980s (Au, 2002; Laukkanen, 2005). With the advent of games using 3D graphics in the early 1990s, like *Wolfenstein 3D* and *Doom*, modding became quite popular (Kushner, 2003). *Doom* was published in 1993 and by May of 1994, the first user-generated editors for the creation of new levels could be found on the internet. Soon the game's manufacturer, id Software, permitted the use of modifications so long as they were not commercialized. In an unprecedented move, id Software went so far as to publish parts of the game's program code (Lowood, 2006). The popularity of *Doom* was surpassed by the success of *Quake* (id Software), released in 1996, as well as *Half-Life* (Valve) and *Unreal Tournament* (Epic Games), both being released in 1998. To this day, the development of modifications is still a phenomenon that applies mostly to games played on personal computers. Games that are played on video game consoles such as a PlayStation (Sony), an Xbox (Microsoft), or a Wii (Nintendo) are less accessible in technical terms. Among the more than 6200 modifications hosted by The Mod Data Base (www.moddb.com)—one of the largest communities for modders—less than 100 modifications are for game consoles or mobile phones.

Some mods alter small components of a game whereas others fundamentally change the very nature of a game. For example, the largest unofficial website for *The Sims* games (Maxis/Electronic Arts) currently hosts more than 930,000 modification files for *The Sims 1*, *The Sims 2*, and *The Sims 3*, among them more than 150,000 pieces of clothing and almost 2000 pets (The Sims Resource, 2014). For the role-playing game *The Elder Scrolls: Skyrim*, more than 36,000 unique mods (available on nexusmods.com) change the game character's appearance or equipment, add remodeled cities, new quests, dungeons, or new companions to the game (e.g., Batman and Chuck Norris), or increase the usability of the game interface. Interface modifications are also very popular for massively multiplayer online role-playing games (MMORPGs) like *World of Warcraft* (Blizzard). For instance, the modification *Recount* graphically displays damage and healing. This popular mod was released in 2007 and has been downloaded more than 51 million times from www.curse.com (World of Warcraft Add-ons, 2014). An extreme example for a game modification is the *Star Wars Mod: Galactic Warfare*, a total conversion for the 2007 FPS game *Call of Duty 4: Modern Warfare* (Activision). *Galactic Warfare* was released in 2009. It combines the *Call of Duty* game play with a Star Wars setting and transforms the game into a battle between imperial and rebel forces, using authentic Star Wars locations, characters, and weapons. One of the most popular total conversions is *Counter-Strike*, created in 1999 by two students as a multiplayer version for the single-player FPS game *Half-Life*. *Counter-Strike* was later purchased by the game manufacturer Valve and released as a commercial add-on (Morris, 2003).

It is hard to quantify the proportion of computer game players who engage in modifying games, but it is a niche phenomenon. In a survey among adolescent boys and girls in grades 7 and 8, two in five boys and one in five girls indicated that they liked to "mod" games, but this also included downloading new characters, weapons, clothing, or storylines from the internet (Olson et al., 2007). A study among boys and girls in grades 5–9 showed that 38% of the participants had modified a computer game by developing new levels or scenarios, characters, clothing, items, interfaces, or the use of cheatcodes (Hayes, 2008). Given that it is technically much easier to use a cheatcode than to create a modification, we assume that the relatively high proportion of participants who indicated that they had modified a game is, to a large extent, due to those who had used a cheatcode before. To the best of our knowledge, no newer studies have investigated this topic, but it is most likely that the numbers have dropped since 2007/2008. This may be especially true as computer games have lost market shares to mobile games and apps (Entertainment Software Association, 2014). However, core communities of mod makers are still very active, as the lively discussions on dedicated online forums such as *The Mod Data Base* demonstrate.

If players miss something in a computer game, they are not facing a purely algorithmic task. Players who develop mods must first perceive a problem (e.g., the game does not allow for customizing a character as desired) and then devise a technical solution that resolves the perceived problem. This is a heuristic task with no single, obvious solution. Such open-ended tasks are a prerequisite for creativity (Amabile, 2012), and we argue that developing game modifications can certainly be considered a creative activity (see also Cook, Chapter 11). According to the componential theory of creativity (Amabile, 1996, 2012), creativity is influenced by domain-relevant skills, creativity-relevant processes, task motivation, and by a surrounding environment with factors that might serve as obstacles or stimulants to intrinsic motivation and creativity. To the best of our knowledge, no study has yet investigated creativity-relevant processes such as the ability to use wide, flexible categories for synthesizing information, and the development of game modifications.

Research on game modifications has primarily focused on skills, motivation, and the social environment. Domain-relevant skills like expertise, knowledge, technical skills, and talent are clearly important for developing modifications. Creating a mod requires a wide range of skills from graphic design, physics, mathematics, and computer programming to project management (Laukkanen, 2005; Sotamaa, 2004). As video game technologies increase in power and complexity, so have the skills required for developing modifications (Steinkuehler & Johnson, 2009). While some modifications are developed by individuals or small groups other modification projects are developed by teams, some of which have 25 or more members who specialize in different tasks such as writing code or drawing and animating characters and objects (Postigo, 2007).

People are most creative when they are intrinsically motivated by the interest, enjoyment, satisfaction, and challenge of the work itself, compared to being motivated by extrinsic factors like surveillance, competition, evaluation, or requirements to complete tasks in a predefined way (Amabile, 2012). For most users, developing game modifications is a hobby, but not a job. Most publishers allow modifications of their games only if the results are not commercialized (Kushner, 2003; Sotamaa, 2003). Some modders see their hobby as a chance to promote their skills, to attract the attention of professional game developers, and eventually find a job in the games industry (Behr, 2007; Postigo, 2007; Theodorsen, 2008).

While this seems to be considered a possibility, it is generally viewed as a highly unlikely career path among modders (Behr, 2010).

Instead, typical intrinsic motivations are more important. Qualitative surveys among modders identified eight different motivational dimensions: (1) Playing—improving and personalizing the gaming experience through modding; (2) hacking—acquiring knowledge about computer and games technology; (3) researching gathering information about selected topics of modifications like historical weapons; (4) creative endeavors/artistic work—using modifications as a medium of expressing one's creativity; (5) cooperation—working in teams with others and being a member of a community; (6) facing challenges in the process of modding; (7) receiving appreciation for their work as important motivations for modders; and (8) the experience of fun and entertainment (Behr, 2007; Postigo, 2003, 2007; Sotamaa, 2004; Theodorsen, 2008). In a quantitative online survey among 194 computer game players who had worked on a modification before, engaging in creative activities was the most important motivator (Behr, 2008, 2010): Modders wanted to develop something based on their own ideas and enjoyed the creative activity in and of itself. Modders also worked on their projects because they wanted to improve the original games, because they enjoyed mastering the challenges that came with these projects, and simply because they liked the games and enjoyed spending time adjusting them to their individual preferences. Improving one's computer skills, being a member of a team and receiving positive feedback from the community, and entertainment were less important motivators.

As noted previously, the social environment is an important contributor to creativity. Computer game players who develop and use modifications use online communities as their main communication medium for creative expression (Morris, 2003). They develop and maintain forums, chat services, and websites revolving around their favorite games and modifications. Unlike open-source software communities who often compete with manufacturers of proprietary software (Bonaccorsi & Rossi, 2003; Sen, 2007), game modders and the game industry enjoy a more cooperative relationship. Game manufacturers allow the modification of their games as long as mods can only be used in combination with original copies of the game, are not commercialized, and as long as no copyrights are infringed (Kushner, 2003; Sotamaa, 2003). It has been criticized that game manufacturers exploit the "free labor" (Terranova, 2003, June 20) provided by game players as game developers claim copyrights for all modifications (Baldrica, 2007; Grimes, 2006; Kuecklich, 2005; Postigo, 2003) and use the mod communities as free resources for market research and marketing (Grimes, 2006). But as Sotamaa (2005, p. 10) notes: "first of all mod makers are certainly not entirely vulnerable and secondly one of the reasons why modding remains fascinating for hobbyists is exactly the close co-operation with industry." Taken together, we argue that modifying games is a particularly creative form of VGI.

CONCLUSION

In this chapter, we have considered how two aspects of interactivity, customization and co-creation of game content, allow players to express a wide range of creative outlets in video game environments. These creative activities are not necessarily play behaviors, per se. Instead, they are activities often done in an effort to improve, augment, or otherwise alter the game before actual play occurs.

Customization and co-creation represent just one of the many ways in which video game users might choose to express creative behavior. There are several other ways to examine creative play behaviors that result from interactive game features. For instance, players focused on exploration might use video games as means for developing complex, alternative narratives. Such behavior might take several forms. For instance, in role-playing (e.g., *World of Warcraft*) or sandbox-style games (e.g., *Minecraft*) players might choose to create novel stories in an attempt to express a particular creative vision for their character, the game, or both. Players may even choose to record these narratives in a new form of artistic expression known as machinima (a portmanteau of machine, animation, and cinema) (for a discussion, see Jenkins, 2006).

Broader still, players may combine components of VGI such as controller responsiveness and artificial intelligence to develop individualized play styles. For instance, some FPS players adopt play strategies that are more brash and aggressive whereas others prefer a finesse strategy (e.g., Weber et al., 2009). The point is that VGI affords players considerable opportunity to express their creativity while providing academics a useful framework for investigating creative player behaviors.

References

Amabile, T. M. (1983). *The social psychology of creativity*. New York: Springer.
Amabile, T. M. (1996). *Creativity in context*. Boulder, CO: Westview Press.
Amabile, T. M. (2012). *Componential theory of creativity*. Westview Press.
Au, W. J. (2002). *Triumph of the mod*. Retrieved from March 2, 2006, http://www.salon.com/tech/feature/2002/04/16/modding/.
Bailey, R., Wise, K., & Bolls, P. (2009). How avatar customizability affects children's arousal and subjective presence during junk food-sponsored online video games. *CyberPsycholgy & Behavior*, 12(3), 277–283. http://dx.doi.org/10.1089/cpb.2008.0292.
Baldrica, J. (2007). Mod as heck: Frameworks for examining ownership rights in user-contributed content to videogames, and a more principled evaluation of expressive appropriation in user-modified videogame projects. *Minnesota Journal of Law, Science & Technology*, 8(2), 681–713.
Behr, K.-M. (2007). Creating game content: User-generated computer game modifications. In *The 57th annual conference of the international communication association (ICA), San Francisco, May 24-28, 2007*.

Behr, K.-M. (2008). The development of computer game modifications: Creators of game content explored. In *58th annual conference of the International Communication Association (ICA), Montreal, Kanada, May 22-26, 2008*.

Behr, K.-M. (2010). *Creative interaction with computer games: The development of computer game modifications from an appropriation perspective [Kreativer Umgang mit Computerspielen: Die Entwicklung von Spielmodifikationen aus aneignungstheoretischer Sicht].* Boizenburg: Vwh.

Bonaccorsi, A., & Rossi, C. (2003). Why open source software can succeed. *Research Policy, 32,* 1243–1258.

Bucy, E. P., & Tao, C. C. (2007). The mediated moderation model of interactivity. *Media Psychology, 9,* 647–672.

Ducheneaut, N., Yee, N., Nickell, E., & Moore, R. J. (2006). Building an MMO with mass appeal: A look at gameplay in World of Warcraft. *Games and Culture, 1*(4), 281–317.

Entertainment Software Association. (2014). *Sales, demographic and usage data. Essential facts about the computer and video game industry.* Retrieved from September 8, 2014, http://www.theesa.com/facts/pdfs/esa_ef_2014.pdf.

Grimes, S. M. (2006). Online multiplayer games: A virtual space for intellectual property debates? *New Media & Society, 8*(6), 969–990.

Grodal, T. (2000). Video games and the pleasures of control. In D. Zillmann, & P. Vorderer (Eds.), *Media entertainment* (pp. 197–213). Mahwah, NJ: Erlbaum.

Hayes, E. R. (2008). Game content creation and IT proficiency: An exploratory study. *Computers & Education, 51*(1), 97–108.

Herz, J. (2002). Gaming the system: What higher education can learn from multiplayer online worlds. In *The Internet and the University: Forum 2001: Forum of the future of higher education & EDUCAUSE. (Hrsg.)* (pp. 169–191) Cambridge, MA: Hrsg.

Hsu, S. H., Kao, C.-H., & Wu, M.-C. (2007). Factors influencing player preferences for heroic roles in role-playing games. *CyberPsychology & Behavior, 10*(2), 293–295.

Hsu, S. H., Lee, F. L., & Wu, M.-C. (2005). Designing action games for appealing to buyers. *CyberPsychology & Behavior, 8*(6), 585–591.

Humphreys, S., Fitzgerald, B., Banks, J., & Suzor, N. (2005). Fan-based production for computer games: User-led innovation, the 'drift of value' and intellectual property rights. *Media International Australia: Incorporating Culture and Policy, 114,* 16–29.

Jenkins, H. (2006). *Convergence culture: Where old and new media collide.* New York: New York University Press.

Kiousis, S. (2002). Interactivity: A concept explication. *New Media & Society, 4,* 355–383.

Klimmt, C., & Hartmann, T. (2006). Effectance, self-efficacy, and the motivation to play video games. In P. Vorderer & J. Bryant (Eds.), *Playing video games: Motives, responses, and consequences* (pp. 133–145). Mahwah, NJ: Erlbaum.

Kuecklich, J. (2005). Precarious playbour: Modders and the digital games industry. *Fibreculture Journal, 5.* Retrieved from January 20, 2009, http://www.journal.fibreculture.org/issue5/kucklich.html.

Kushner, D. (2002). The mod squad. *Popular Science, 261*(2), 68–72.

Kushner, D. (2003). *Masters of doom. How two guys created an empire and transformed pop culture.* London: Piatkus.

Laukkanen, T. (2005). *Modding scenes: Introduction to user-created content in computer gaming.* Tampere: University of Tampere Hypermedia Laboratory.

Lee, K. M., Park, N., & Jin, S.-A. (2006). Narrative and interactivity in computer games. In P. Vorderer & J. Bryant (Eds.), *Playing video games: Motives, responses, and consequences* (pp. 259–274). Mahwah, NJ: Erlbaum.

Leiner, D. J., & Quiring, O. (2008). What interactivity means to the user: Essential insights into and a scale for perceived interactivity. *Journal of Computer-Mediated Communication, 14*(1), 127–136.

Liu, Y. (2003). Developing a scale to measure the interactivity of websites. *Journal of Advertising Research, 43*(2), 207–216.

Liu, Y., & Shrum, L. J. (2002). What is interactivity and is it always such a good thing? Implications of definition, person, and situation for the influence of interactivity on advertising effectiveness. *Journal of Advertising, 31*(4), 53–64.

Lowood, H. (2006). A brief biography of computer games. In P. Vorderer & J. Bryant (Eds.), *Playing video games. Motives, responses, and consequences* (pp. 25–41). Mahwah, NJ: Erlbaum.

McMillan, S. J., & Hwang, J.-S. (2002). Measures of perceived interactivity: An exploration of the role of direction of communication, user control, and time in shaping perceptions of interactivity. *Journal of Advertising, 31*(3), 429–442.

Morris, S. (2003). WADs, bots and mods: Multiplayer FPS games as co-creative media. In M. Copier & J. Raessens (Eds.), *Level up: Digital Games Research Conference (CD)*. Utrecht: Faculty of Arts, Utrecht University.

Ogletree, S. M., & Drake, R. (2007). College students' video game participation and perceptions: Gender differences and implications. *Sex Roles, 56,* 537–542.

Olson, C. K., Kutner, L. A., Warner, D. E., Almerigi, J. B., Baer, L., Nicholi, A. M., et al. (2007). Factors correlated with violent video game use by adolescent boys and girls. *Journal of Adolescent Health, 41*(1), 77–83.

Postigo, H. (2003). From Pong to planet Quake: Post-industrial transitions from leisure to work. *Information, Communication & Society, 6*(4), 593–607.

Postigo, H. (2007). Of mods and modders: Chasing down the value of fan-based digital game modifications. *Games and Culture, 2*(4), 300–313.

Rafaeli, S. (1988). Interactivity: From new media to communication. In R. P. Hawkins, J. M. Wiemann, & S. Pingree (Eds.), *Advancing communication science: Merging mass and interpersonal processes* (pp. 110–134). Thousand Oaks, CA: Sage.

Rafaeli, S., & Sudweeks, F. (1997). Networked interactivity. *Journal of Computer-Mediated Communication, 2*(4). Retrieved from July 15, 2010, http://jcmc.indiana.edu/vol2/issue4/rafaeli.sudweeks.html.

Raney, A. A., Smith, J. K., & Baker, K. (2006). Adolescents and the appeal of video games. In P. Vorderer & J. Bryant (Eds.), *Playing video games: Motives, responses, and consequences* (pp. 165–179). Mahwah, NJ: Erlbaum.

Richards, R. (2006). Users, interactivity and generation. *New Media & Society, 8*(4), 531–550.

Sen, R. (2007). A strategic analysis of competition between open source and proprietary software. *Journal of Management Information Systems, 24*(1), 233–257.

Sotamaa, O. (2003). Computer game modding, intermediality and participatory culture. In *The Nordic Network "Innovating Media and Communication Research," Sonderborg, Dänemark, December 1-5, 2003.*

Sotamaa, O. (2004). Playing it my way? Mapping the modder agency. In *Vortrag auf der Internet research conference 5.0, University of Sussex, UK, 19-22 September 2004.*

Sotamaa, O. (2005). "Have fun working with our product!": Critical perspectives on computer game mod competitions. *Proceedings of DiGRA 2005 conference, June 16-20, 2005.* Canada: Vancouver.

Steinkuehler, C., & Johnson, B. Z. (2009). Computational literacy in online games: The social life of mods. *International Journal of Gaming and Computer-Mediated Simulations, 1*(1), 53–65.

Steuer, J. (1992). Defining virtual reality: Dimensions determining telepresence. *Journal of Communication, 42*(4), 73–93.

Tamborini, R., Grizzard, M., Bowman, N. D., Reinecke, L., Lewis, R., & Eden, A. (2011). Media enjoyment as need-satisfaction: The contribution of hedonic and non-hedonic needs. *Journal of Communication, 61,* 1025–1042. http://dx.doi.org/10.1111/j.1460-2466.2011.01593.x.

Terranova, T. (2003). *Free labor: Producing culture for the digital economy.* Retrieved from April 28, 2014, http://www.electronicbookreview.com/thread/technocapitalism/voluntary.

The Sims Resource (2014). Retrieved April 27, 2014, from http://www.thesimsresource.com/.

Theodorsen, J. (2008). *Participatory culture on web 2.0: Exploring the motives for modding video games*. Unpublished Master thesis, Amsterdam, The Netherlands: Amsterdam School of Communication Research, Universiteit van Amsterdam.

Trepte, S., & Reinecke, L. (2010). Avatar creation and video game enjoyment: Effects of life-satisfaction, game competitiveness, and identification with the avatar. *Journal of Media Psychology, 22*, 171–184. http://dx.doi.org/10.1027/1864-1105/a000022.

Trepte, S., Reinecke, L., & Behr, K.-M. (2011). Playing myself or playing to win? Gamers' strategies of avatar creation in terms of gender and sex. In R. E. Ferdig (Ed.), *Discoveries in gaming and computer-mediated simulations: New interdisciplinary applications* (pp. 329–352). Hershey, PA: Information Science Reference.

Warnick, B., Xenos, M., Endres, D., & Gastil, J. (2005). Effects of campaign-to-user and text-based interactivity in political candidate campaign web sites. *Journal of Computer-Mediated Communication, 10*(3), http://dx.doi.org/10.1111/j.1083-6101.2005.tb00253.x.

Weber, R., Behr, K.-M., & De Martino, C. (2014). Measuring interactivity in video games. *Communication Methods and Measures, 5*(3), 181–202.

Weber, R., Behr, K.-M., Tamborini, R., Ritterfeld, U., & Mathiak, K. (2009). What do we really know about First Person Shooter Games: An event-related, high-resolution content analysis. *Journal of Computer-Mediated Communication, 14*(4), 1016–1037.

World of Warcraft Add-ons (2014). Retrieved May 1, 2014, from, http://www.curse.com/addons/wow.

Wu, G. (1999). Perceived interactivity and attitudes toward web sites. In M. S. Roberts (Ed.), *Proceedings of the 1999 conference of the american academy of advertising* (pp. 254–262). Gainesville, FL: American Academy of Advertising.

Index

Note: Page numbers followed by *f* indicate figures and *t* indicate tables.

Printed and bound by CPI Group (UK) Ltd, Croydon, CR0 4YY

08/06/2025

01896873-0004